Madness in the Streets

Madness in the Streets

How Psychiatry and the Law
Abandoned the Mentally Ill

Rael Jean Isaac
Virginia C. Armat

THE FREE PRESS
A Division of Macmillan, Inc.
NEW YORK
Collier Macmillan Canada
TORONTO
Maxwell Macmillan International
NEW YORK   OXFORD   SINGAPORE   SYDNEY

The Free Press
A Division of Macmillan, Inc.
866 Third Avenue, New York, N.Y. 10022

Collier Macmillan Canada, Inc.
1200 Eglinton Avenue East
Suite 200
Don Mills, Ontario M3C 3N1

Printed in the United States of America

printing number

2 3 4 5 6 7 8 9 10

Library of Congress Cataloging-in-Publication Data

Isaac, Rael Jean.
    Madness in the streets: how psychiatry and the law abandoned the mentally ill / Rael Jean Isaac, Virginia C. Armat.
        p.   cm.
    ISBN   0-02-915380-8
    1. Mentally ill—Deinstitutionalization—United States. 2. Ex-mental patients—Mental health services—United States.
3. Community mental health services—United States.   I. Armat, Virginia C.   II. Title.
RC439.5.I78 1990
362.2'08'6942—dc20   90-37735
                                                                           CIP

To Dr. Noble A. Endicott
and
Anna M. Newall

Contents

Acknowledgments

W E would like to thank all those we interviewed for their cooperation: the patients and ex-patients, the family members, the professionals. Above all, we are indebted to Ted Hutchinson, a member of the California Alliance for the Mentally Ill, who provided us with both extensive research materials and invaluable counsel.

We are also grateful for the generous help of Dr. Richard Abrams, Dr. Paul Appelbaum, Dr. Thomas Ballantine, Midge Decter, M. Stanton Evans, Dr. Jeffrey Geller, Dr. Desmond Kelly, Joel Klein, David LeCount, Eugene Methvin, Prof. Benjamin Nelson, Noreen O'Connor, Dr. E. Fuller Torrey, and Dr. Darold Treffert. We would also like to thank Dr. Bertram Brown for permission to consult his papers in the National Library of Medicine.

In Erwin Glikes we had the guidance of an editor of extraordinary gifts. At the outset, his thoughtful comments helped us to shape the book's structure and his criticisms of the first draft resulted in a sharper, tighter, better manuscript.

Finally, we thank those who underwrote the research for this project: the Achelis, the Earhart Foundation, the J.M., and the John M. Olin Foundations. The following staff or board members were especially helpful: David Kennedy at the Earhart Foundation, Christopher Olander at the J.M. Foundation, Mary Caslin at the Achelis Foundation, and Kim Ohnemus and Janice Riddell at the John M. Olin Foundation. Leslie Lenkowsky at the Institute for Educational Affairs coordinated the project and gave unflagging support, as did Tom Skladony, also of the Institute.

Erich Isaac provided unflinching aid and needed criticisms, chapter by chapter, in the spirit of caring and "tough love."

Introduction
The Shame of the Streets

In 1949 journalist Albert Deutsch wrote *The Shame of the States,* an indictment of the appalling conditions in state mental hospitals. Today he would surely indict "the shame of the streets." Many of our modern institutions for the mentally ill exist in the open air: parks, alleys, vacant lots, steam grates on our city pavements.

At St. Mary's of Bethlehem Hospital—Bedlam, as it came to be called—Londoners used to pay to watch the antics of the mad, a custom continued in the early asylums of this country. They would jeer at the fenced-off wretches from a distance, provoking them to ever more crazed behavior. But at least, in those days, the insane escaped physical harm at the hands of their tormentors.

Now a thuggish subculture actually celebrates violence against mentally ill vagrants. Thus, in Santa Cruz, one group of adolescents who preyed upon them sported T-shirts emblazoned with the words "Troll-busters." A psychiatrist aptly describes our policy of discharging helpless human beings to a hostile community as "a return to the Middle Ages, when the mentally ill roamed the streets and little boys threw rocks at them."[1]

Descriptions of the mentally ill in the most degraded conditions of the past apply equally well today.

> The inmates . . . had the appearance of wild animals—beards and hair were matted with straw and infested with lice; their clothes were tattered, their nails grown long like claws, their bodies encrusted with dirt and filth. They presented pictures of complete neglect.[2]

This is a portrait from the depths of that notorious hellhole, the Bicêtre Hospital of Paris, before Philippe Pinel struck the chains from fifty-three male lunatics imprisoned there in 1794. The straw and the chains have an old-fashioned ring; the rags, the filth, the complete neglect are up to the moment. As columnist and former *New York Times* editor A. M.

Rosenthal summarizes: "If your leg is broken, the city will take you away: if your mind is broken, you just lie there forever."[3]

There is one major difference between past and present mistreatment of the mentally ill. *In the past, the morally progressive elements in society deplored existing conditions and sought to institute a humane system of care. Today, those who claim to be morally progressive crusade to prohibit such care.* When New York City's Mayor Edward Koch in 1985 ordered the police, in subfreezing weather, to pick up people lying on the streets and take them to shelter, New York's Civil Liberties Union formed a "freeze patrol." Its goal was not to ensure that people did not freeze, but to hand out leaflets informing them of their *right* to freeze![4] Indeed, under the headline, "Deaths from Cold Soar as Homeless Increase," the *New York Times* reported a National Centers for Disease Control finding that in 1988 the number of deaths by freezing topped a thousand, having more than doubled in ten years.[5] In Washington, D.C., a Veterans Administration surgeon reported an "epidemic" of limb amputations because of frostbite among the homeless.[6]

The very term "homeless," which self-proclaimed advocates have employed to define the problem, is a misguided simplification. It implicitly validates Coalition for the Homeless founder Robert Hayes's claim that there is a three-word solution to the crisis: "Housing, housing, housing."[7] In fact, it obscures precisely what could make the problems of this population manageable—that "the homeless" include people in need for different reasons. The term thus works to prevent those needs from being rationally addressed, much less met.

Moreover, while seemingly innocuous, the term "the homeless" masks a political message: that the problem is an economic one, that responsibility rests with a heartless American government and society which have denied the poor that most basic of human needs—a place to live. Advocate Mitch Snyder, whose fasts before the White House to obtain funding for shelters drew national attention, declared that with Ronald Reagan's "very candidacy, war was declared on the poor."[8] In Snyder's implicitly Marxist analysis:

> The homeless are simply surplus souls in a system firmly rooted in competition and self-interest, in which only the "strongest" (i.e., those who fit most snugly within the confines of a purely arbitrary norm) will survive.[9]

And Robert Hayes has written:

> The crop of wretchedness is fertilized by a federal administration whose policies toward the poor are increasingly characterized by their heart-

lessness, a heartlessness symbolized by human beings living and dying in cardboard boxes.[10]

"Homeless" advocates may actually object when efforts are made to clarify the composition of the homeless so that something can be done to meet their varying needs. Anthropologist Louisa Stark, head of the National Coalition for the Homeless, decried the attention going to alcoholics and the mentally ill on the grounds this detracted attention from the "structural defects" of society.[11] But as former Housing and Urban Development assistant secretary Kenneth Beirne points out, it *is* vital to know the size and nature of the problem.[12]

What then is the size of the "homeless" population, and what proportion are mentally ill? To be sure, the total number is *not* the two to three million routinely used in press reports. That absurdly high figure came from Mitch Snyder, who told a congressional committee in 1980 of 2.2 million Americans without homes, raising the estimate a year later to three million. In 1984, Snyder admitted, the "number is meaningless. We have tried to satisfy your gnawing curiosity for a number because we are Americans with western little minds that have to quantify everything in sight, whether we can or not."[13] Nonetheless, "homeless" advocates—with the backing of most journalists—echo these numbers repeatedly and even have attacked a series of careful attempts to come up with accurate estimates because these invariably produce much lower figures.

A 1984 survey by the U.S. Department of Housing and Urban Development estimated there were between 250,000 and 350,000 without homes in 1983. Snyder promptly declared that officials behind the report reminded him "of nothing so much as a school of piranha, circling, waiting to tear the last ounce of flesh."[14] The report was widely attacked and yet subsequent research indicated it was close to the mark. In 1986 Richard Freeman and Brian Hall of Harvard in a report for the National Bureau of Economic Research concluded that the much maligned HUD figures were "roughly correct." (Their exact estimate for 1983 was 279,000).[15] In 1988 the U.S. General Accounting Office examined twenty-seven studies and found the high-quality research produced a median homeless rate of 13 per 10,000, half that of the lower-quality studies and a very far cry from the over 1% of the population used by Snyder and most of the press.[16]

The University of Massachusetts's Dr. Peter Rossi, who headed the Chicago Homeless Study, the first attempt to apply modern sampling methods to the study of this population, has noted wryly: "In general, empirically credible attempts to estimate the size of the homeless population have produced numbers well below the expectations of the advocacy community."[17] (Because Rossi's Chicago study produced figures less than a tenth of those that Snyder—on what basis it was impossible to say—had advanced for Chicago, it, too, produced an uproar.)

There is evidence to suggest that the population living in streets and shelters has grown in the last few years. Richard Freeman has estimated the number jumped to 400,000 by 1988,[18] and the Urban Institute in 1987, in a study financed by the U.S. Department of Agriculture, came up with 600,000. This was a deliberately high figure, according to one of its authors, Martha Burt, "based on our desire to err on the side—as a government study—of overestimating rather than underestimating."[19] (HUD's experience was still fresh in the minds of Washington bureaucrats.)

Aware of how inflated their own figures were, "homeless advocates" were unhappy that the 1990 U.S. Census undertook to count the homeless population, and were divided about whether to cooperate in the census effort. The *New York Times* of March 4, 1990 reported that Mitch Snyder burned census forms to show his opposition to the count. Others concluded the effect of a boycott on their credibility was too great, and decided to cooperate while simultaneously criticizing whatever figures emerge as too low.

Why has the media resolutely backed Snyder's unsupported and wildly inflated figures? Public opinion analyst S. Robert Lichter posits that the homeless story has become the 1980s counterpart of the 1960s civil rights crusade—another stark moral issue that calls for journalists to awaken the national conscience and spur public action.[20] In this case, many seem prepared to defy all evidence to proclaim that those on the streets are average American families down on their luck,[21] and to multiply by a factor of six or more numbers already serious enough to constitute a crisis. Yet misrepresenting the size and nature of the problem only impedes solutions.

Ineluctably, the majority of "the homeless" need more than housing. Most studies have found that 30–40% suffer from major mental illness—schizophrenia, manic-depressive illness, and clinical depression.[22] In 1982 the National Institute of Mental Health (NIMH) funded ten fact-finding projects in individual cities to identify the extent of mental illness in the shelter and street populations. By 1986 the completed studies found the percentage currently mentally ill to range from a high of 56% in St. Louis to a low of 25% in New York City.[23] A twenty-county study in Ohio found 30% mentally ill, while the studies of Los Angeles and Baltimore came up with 33%.[24] A more comprehensive Baltimore study, using clinicians from Johns Hopkins University Medical School to perform actual diagnoses on homeless individuals, was published in *The Journal of the American Medical Association* in 1989: it found major mental illness in 42% of the men and 48.7% of the women.[25]

While there are fewer women on the street, studies have consistently uncovered far greater incidence of mental illness among them. At Boston's oldest and largest shelter, the Pine Street Inn, fully 90% of the women were considered mentally disabled.[26] Mental illness is also especially high among the "street people," who are not included in a number of "homeless" studies that focus on the easier-to-reach shelter population. The severely ill avoid shelters partly because of paranoia, but also because of the very real violence endemic to many of them.

Even in New York City, with its overall rate of only 25% mentally ill, a study of individuals sleeping on grates, in doorways, and in abandoned buildings determined "that 60 percent exhibit evidence of schizophrenia as manifested by disorganized behavior and chronic delusional thinking."[27] (Estimates of the ratio of those sleeping on streets to those using shelters vary widely from study to study. The 1984 HUD study estimated that nationally there were almost twice as many "homeless" sleeping outside shelters as in them. On the other hand, the 1988 General Accounting Office report found that of nine studies of the "homeless" in specific cities, only one had found more people on the street than in shelters.[28])

Moreover, the proportion of mentally ill even in the shelter population seems to be growing. HUD's 1988 survey of shelters (this time HUD did not attempt to estimate the number on the streets) found shelter managers reporting a sharp increase since 1984 in the incidence of mental illness among those in the shelters. Although every region of the country reported an increase, it was highest in the South, going from 14% to 43%.[29]

In addition to mental illness, both the street and shelter populations have a high rate of substance abuse. The 1989 just-mentioned study in Baltimore found 68% of the men and 31% of the women to be alcoholics, and 22% of the men and 16% of the women drug-addicted. Thirty percent of the mentally ill compounded their problems with substance abuse.[30] To a great extent then, the "chronic homeless," as against those whose situation is temporary, are those too disabled to take advantage of the welfare safety net or the national increase in job openings since 1980.

The mentally ill are the subject of this book, and their plight should properly receive the greatest attention. This is partly because the mentally ill are least able to stay off the street; they are apt to cycle rapidly out of housing if that is the only form of assistance provided. Psychiatrist E. Fuller Torrey has worked with homeless mentally ill women in shelters in Washington, D.C. and is himself the author of a book on the homeless mentally ill, *Nowhere to Go*. Commenting on homeless advocate Mitch Snyder's claim that all the mentally ill need is love and a home, Dr. Torrey told us:

> You can put them in a home and give them love, but they're still schizo-phrenics out of touch with reality. Until they are treated for the disease you can give them all the love and all the homes in the world and you still have a chaotic situation.[31]

The background of one Boston man is by no means atypical. In a four-year period, he had lived in two community residences, a board and care home, a halfway house, three nursing homes, a veterans' home, a hotel, three homeless shelters, and a mental hospital. After a brief stay in each he would say "I can't stand this place any longer. The storms are all around me," and take off.[32]

The mentally ill who lack housing are often unable to cook, maintain minimal personal hygiene, care for housing, or manage money. Another "homeless" man in Boston receives government disability payments that could purchase housing but spends the money instead on radio equipment that he barters in the street. He sleeps in a duct of one of the Boston area's universities.[33] It is a fantasy to believe such people will manage money in a way that will permit them to remain in independent housing.

Above all, the mentally ill on our streets merit primary attention because, apart from children, they are the most vulnerable and helpless of the so-called homeless population, and thus can make the greatest moral claim upon community support. As Dr. Torrey put it:

> In my mind it's clear that the single biggest part of the homeless problem is mental illness. It's also the most visible part of it. The public generally is not worried too much when they pass the wino down in the park. The assumption is that the wino is drinking the wine and addicted to alcohol and has chosen to exercise the addiction. . . . On the other hand, when you go into the same park and see people hallucinating, there is a totally

different reaction. There is not that volitional element to it. . . . A disease like schizophrenia is very unpleasant. No one would ever sign up for it. People realize that. So it is the seriously mentally ill among the homeless that bother people and *should* bother people.[34]

A few statistics tell much of the story. In Buffalo, in the course of 1982, seventy-two discharged psychiatric patients were arrested as they wandered on the grounds of Buffalo State Psychiatric Center and three general hospitals with psychiatric units—most of them charged with trespassing. There are twice as many mentally ill persons on the streets and in shelters as there are in our public mental hospitals.[35] There are as many individuals suffering from serious mental disorder in our jails and prisons as there are in our public mental hospitals.[36] A study followed a sample of 132 patients released from Central Ohio Psychiatric Hospital in the first three months of 1985. Within six months of their release, *over a third* had become homeless. The figures would undoubtedly be worse in other states, for Ohio's mental health system is rated as one of the top ten in the country.[37]

Oddly, the more present policy fails, the more committed decision-makers become to it. In 1986 New York State announced plans to cut the number of psychiatric beds by a third over the next decade, from 20,000 to 13,000.[38] (They had already been cut by 80% in the previous thirty years.) The state moved vigorously to implement the timetable, and by late 1989 had brought the number of beds down to 15,000.[39] At the same time, in New York City's municipal hospitals, mental patients were crammed into hallways and emergency rooms, some handcuffed to wheelchairs for days, waiting for beds occupied by people in turn waiting for one of the scarce beds in state hospitals.

The situation has become so bad that doctors at the psychiatric wards of city hospitals told the *New York Times,* "the mental-health system is heading for a collapse."[40] In California, police are reluctant to take even the most seriously mentally ill on the streets to the hospital. A spokesman for the Sacramento police complained that time to do the paperwork was usually longer than the individual's stay in the hospital![41]

Intent on pushing patients out, public mental hospitals all too often exhibit little interest in where they go. The New York State Office of Mental Health's own survey for 1979–80 found that 23% of mental patients were released to "unknown" living arrangements; one hospital discharged fully 59% of its patients to "unknown" destinations.[42] Merion Kane, an articulate Washington, D.C. resident, reports that her son was twice discharged from St. Elizabeth's Hospital with a trash bag containing his belongings, a token, and the address of a shelter.[43] It remains a common practice for hospitals to release patients directly to shelters.

To replace mental hospitals, we have thus brought back the eighteenth- and nineteenth-century poorhouse, which threw together the mentally retarded, the mentally ill, drug and alcohol abusers, criminals, the physically disabled elderly, mothers with young children, and so on. It was precisely to remove the mentally ill from such settings that Dorothea Lynde Dix in the 1840s embarked on her crusade to build state mental hospitals in restful, bucolic settings. Ironically, as municipalities around the country search desperately for more shelters, they have discovered long-abandoned buildings on state mental hospital grounds. Dr. Torrey writes:

> During the 1960s and '70s, many buildings at Manhattan State Hospital were closed as patients were deinstitutionalized. As the number of homeless individuals in the city climbed rapidly, however, one of these buildings was reopened as a men's shelter. . . . Some of the same mentally ill individuals who once used that building as hospitalized patients now use it as shelter residents. The difference is that now there are no nurses, no doctors, no medication, and no treatment.[44]

It is noteworthy that the authorities at Manhattan Psychiatric Center (as Manhattan State has been renamed) brought suit against the shelter's opening, protesting that proximity of *homeless* people would endanger the hospital's patients.[45]

The contrast—or rather lack of contrast—in treatment of the mentally ill between centuries past and our own is the more remarkable because of the breakthroughs in treatment of mental illness that have occurred in the last fifty years. Until then, while keepers could be kind or cruel, physical treatments had as little efficacy as those used in Bedlam in 1815. Its head at that time, Dr. Thomas Monro, reported to a Parliamentary investigating committee:

> Patients are ordered to be bled about the latter end of May, or the beginning of June, according to the weather, and after they have been bled, they take vomits once a week for a certain number of weeks; after that, we purge the patients.

Dr. Monro said that this had been the practice long before his time, "handed down to me by my father, and I do not know any better practice."[46] Neither did anyone else. In the United States, bizarre remedies were tried, ranging from whirling chairs and whirlpool baths to ovary compressors and extraction of teeth and various organs, believed to be foci of infection of the brain.

In the last fifty years, however, there have been spectacular advances. Various shock therapies were introduced in the 1930s which proved particularly effective in delusional depressions, followed in the 1950s by chlorpromazine (Thorazine) for schizophrenia and, in the 1960s, lithium and anti-depressants. But while there was little objection over the centuries to the useless, even harmful, nostrums to which the mentally ill were subject, our laws now block access to the effective treatments available.

While the mentally ill are a significant percentage of "the homeless," only a small proportion of the almost two million Americans who suffer from major mental illness are on the streets. If the human disaster in our public places has any benefit, it may be finally to focus public attention on mental illness, whose ravages for the most part occur outside public view. There was good reason for the attack on the gigantic, overcrowded, understaffed, overwhelmed mental institutions in the decade immediately following the end of World War II. But after the 1960s, when the role of state mental hospitals as providers of long-term care for the mentally ill dwindled dramatically, the misery of the now often abandoned mentally ill remained concealed from public view, too diffused to attract attention. Indeed, it was so well hidden that in 1986 *Science* reported that a recent CBS–*New York Times* poll found that only 1% of respondents thought mental illness was a major health problem![47] This despite the fact that even now, in the era of radical deinstitutionalization, schizophrenia still accounts for 40% of *all* long-term hospital beds.[48]

Out of the public eye, the largest proportion (40%) of the mentally ill have been cared for by their families, forced into the role of mini-institutions, living in sometimes daily terror of what the untreated person might do to them or to himself. Or the mentally ill have stayed in coffin-like rooms in deteriorated inner-city SROs (single room occupancy hotels). Festering sores while they flourished, their passing is now lamented because they did contain for a while, however dreadfully, the problem of the mentally ill, set adrift without aftercare in an indifferent community.[49] Others went to nursing homes or board and care homes, which at least provided food as well as shelter.

Often, hospital discharges of patients to families are only superficially more appropriate than to shelters. James Howe, formerly president of the National Alliance for the Mentally Ill (an organization of family members with chapters throughout the country) describes being approached by a frail old woman at a meeting in Maryland, distraught because her son had just been discharged into her care.

> You talk about deinstitutionalization. They sent him from Springfield State Hospital [in Maryland] back to this woman who is 92 years old. He's 55. What the hell did they do that for? They're under pressure from the state to push people out. If they can browbeat the parents into taking them, even though they know it isn't a viable situation with a woman that old, it gets them out of their sight.[50]

All over the country families report pressure from hospital staff to resume care of very ill persons in their homes. Often the barely treated patient simply appears without warning at the parents' front door.[51]

Elizabeth Hilton, whose son has been intermittently on the street for the last ten years, co-chairs a network of families with homeless and missing children. She says:

> There's a very important point with people like him [her son], and many of the homeless. ... He responds beautifully to medication, and a great many of the homeless do. ... I really believe a large percentage of the homeless mentally ill can be saved, and I don't give up hope when it looks very very bad and blue.[52]

Hilton's son and others like him are "protected" from the treatment that could save them from a degraded existence by laws passed in the late 1960s and 1970s, which dictate that no care at all be provided unless the person actively seeks treatment, or is clearly "dangerous." Since in mental illness the organ that makes decisions is the same organ that is diseased, the law fosters insanity.

Unable to secure treatment for those they love, families are as much victims as the mentally ill themselves. June Wild (who co-chairs the homeless mentally ill network with Hilton) and her husband feel paralyzed by their inability to help their schizophrenic son.

> What can we do? Johnny won't live under a roof—he lives under the bushes and eats the plants he finds out there. He won't take medication and he's not violent so he never gets picked up by the police and taken to the hospital. Some people think you are not taking care of your loved one. I got asked by the housing policy director of the governor of the state— where's the family? I said I'd love to be able to [take care of my son], but I can't. I have no control. He's eighteen years old.[53]

In Manhattan's Chelsea district Rebecca Smith—once valedictorian of her class at the Hampton Institute in Virginia—froze to death in the cardboard box that had been her "home" for eight months. Her daughter told the *New York Times* that while her sixty-one-year-old mother, long ill with schizophrenia, had refused their help, she was loved, and had "beautiful grandchildren and comes from a wonderful family."[54]

Eighty-year-old Edward Holder, a retired psychologist and former career army officer, described to us how he would don old clothes to look for his sons, both middle-aged and mentally ill, who were living on the streets of Washington, D.C. Holder is bitter: "The authorities say it is their choice and their right to live like stray animals. Why is rapid suicide illegal and gradual suicide a right?"[55]

The reality is even more bizarre than the law suggests. Those seeking treatment in the public sector (i.e., without insurance) find that even if they *request* treatment, they cannot obtain it unless they are considered dangerous, and so, could be committed and treated *without* their consent. We interviewed a mentally ill woman—the ex-wife of a prominent psychiatrist—who had been on the street and denied entry to a series of Philadelphia hospitals. Finally, in desperation, she sliced open her knees in order to rank as "dangerous" enough to be admitted.[56] Even at the Solomon Mental Health Center in Lowell, Massachusetts, rare in its dedication to serving the severely mentally ill, we were told: "Elective hospitalization is not where it's at. The stringent criterion is, 'Is this person committable?' Yes, it is tough to get in."[57] As Robert Hayes points out, "New York City at this point has virtually no more voluntary admissions to [public] psychiatric beds. The only way you get in is if you're brought in kicking and screaming by the police."[58]

Under these circumstances, streets and shelters are increasingly filled with chronic mentally ill young people, particularly males. Many have never received any more treatment than a few days in a general hospital emergency room. They slide into the long downhill course of chronic schizophrenic illness, often exacerbating their condition by taking the "treatments" readily available on the street—drugs and alcohol. In effect, they have been deprived of any chance for recovery for, as was recognized even in the nineteenth century, treatment in the early, acute stages offers the best hope for arresting serious mental illness.

Occasionally, the mentally ill make headlines through random acts of violence: given our legal system's endorsement of "the right to be crazy," the miracle is that these incidents are not more frequent. Juan Gonzalez had warned staff at a Manhattan shelter: "I'm going to kill. God told me so. Jesus wants me to kill." Columbia Presbyterian Hospital, to which the shelter sent him, released Gonzalez within forty-eight hours. Two days later he stabbed nine persons aboard the Staten Island ferry, two of them fatally.[59] Jorge Delgado, who clubbed to death an usher with a brass prayerbook stand after running naked through St. Patrick's Cathedral, had been arrested eleven times and hospitalized seven times.[60]

As we shall see, while such incidents receive enormous publicity, the victims of the mentally ill are much more commonly their own families. An especially terrible incident occurred in November 1987. On his way to Thanksgiving dinner, while his wife, unsuspecting, waited in the car, twenty-six year-old Bartley Dobben burned his two-year-old and thirteen-month-old sons to death by putting them in a transfer ladle at the foundry where he worked. Diagnosed earlier as suffering from paranoid schizophrenia, the young man, his father said, refused to take his medication.[61] Many families live in fear of violence from their mentally ill family member, and in not a few cases, their worst fears are realized.

How did all this happen? The abandoned mentally ill are so ubiquitous, it is hard to remember that the shame of our streets is a recent phenomenon. As Senator Daniel Patrick Moynihan says: "It came upon us all of a sudden. No warning. No explanation."[62] Psychiatrist-essayist Charles Krauthammer laments: "Thirty years ago, if you saw a person lying helpless on the street, you ran to help him. Now you step over him. You know that he is not an accident victim. He lives there."[63] Similarly, it is only during the last two decades that families have been unable to secure any treatment if their severely ill loved ones (who typically deny that there is anything wrong with them) refuse to accept it. A family is often faced with the choice of turning the sick person out into the streets—or becoming prisoner to madness in their own home.

Reluctant to take responsibility for the policies that put the mentally ill on the street, public officials and civil libertarians alike have tried to minimize the role of deinstitutionalization. At the beginning of the 1980s there were such remarkable declarations as that of Dr. Stanley Hoffman, director of research and evaluation for the New York City Regional Office of Mental Health, who said the homeless were "relatively well-educated, relatively well-functioning, well-traveled, middle class dropouts, who have learned to maneuver the system and who move around."[64] As late as 1984, a New York State Department of Social Services report to the governor and legislature insisted that less than 15% of those in shelters had any mental health problems, and only 20% had any substance abuse problem.[65]

As scores of studies made the absurdity of these figures obvious, officials—often echoed by the press[66]—engaged in intellectual sleight-of-hand to "prove" that even if there were large numbers of mentally ill on the streets, the emptying of institutions could not be responsible. They argued that the overwhelming number of long-term patients had been discharged in the 1960s and 1970s. Since massive homelessness was a problem of the 1980s, its cause could not be deinstitutionalization. What this overlooked was the accumulation of helpless people released in successive waves as hospitals emptied. True, many went *initially* to their families, boarding homes, or SROs. They wound up in back alleys and public places as they wandered off, their parents died, and large numbers of SROs—the squalid Band-Aid hiding abandonment of the mentally ill—disappeared in the decade of the 1980s. Moreover, the "uninstitutionalized" population on the street—the chronically mentally ill young people who years ago would have gone to state hospitals—were as much a product of the policy as the long-term patients who had been formally "deinstitutionalized."

Unsurprisingly, the civil libertarian lawyers who have spoken up on behalf of "the homeless" are far from eager to advertise their own immense role in today's tragedy. More than any other single group, they have been responsible for changing our laws governing civil commitment, making it impossible to hospitalize and to treat many of the most severely ill patients. Now, as satirist P. J. O'Rourke puts it, they become the "people advocating programs to solve a problem caused by the programs these people advocated."[67] And so lawyers from New York's Civil Liberties Union, which worked to eliminate involuntary civil commitment, declare loudly that the homeless are ordinary people whose plight derives from such "root causes" as low welfare payments.[68]

As we have seen, they are supported in this position by the advocacy groups who view "the homeless" as victims of an unjust economic and political system; such groups, to obtain public support, also argue these are average people down on their luck. To his credit, "homeless" advocate Robert Hayes has brought a series of suits to force New York State and City to provide appropriate care in the community for mental patients cavalierly dumped out of hospitals. And by 1989 Hayes was admitting that the Coalition had also shied away from discussing addiction for fear the public would lose sympathy. "The bottom line," he now said, "is that we have to tell the truth."[69]

Deinstitutionalization did not "just happen." This book will examine the roots and unfolding of the tragedy that has befallen the mentally ill over the last thirty-odd years. The policies shaping their fate have now affected virtually all Americans, who experience their public places as disordered scenes of what journalist Myron Magnet calls "craziness, drunkenness, dope and danger."[70] Those misguided policies resulted from a convergence of movements, ideas, and academic theories fashionable in the 1960s.

These were primarily movements and ideas on the political left, which used the mentally ill as catspaws in their struggle against middle-class American culture. But amazingly, the political center—and even the political right—failed to comprehend the profoundly radical impact these ideas concerning mental illness would have on the social order—and accepted the programs that devolved from them, indeed, as we shall see, with myopic enthusiasm.

In the 1960s, the New Left challenged a host of American institutions, from marriage to government to universities. State mental hospitals were an easy target: great warehouses of abandoned souls, they were hard to defend. As psychiatrist Paul Appelbaum points out, psychiatry in general was vulnerable because it exerted police power over unwilling patients through the civil commitment process.[71]

But the challenge cut deeper than merely another attack on a particularly vulnerable institution. The counterculture denied the very existence of mental illness, calling it the specious invention of a repressive establishment that 'labeled' social nonconformists "insane." The left defined those stigmatized as mentally ill as simply another oppressed group, like blacks, women, gays, who should have freedom to pursue their alternative lifestyle.

Many commentators have noted the radical egalitarianism of the adversary culture, its hostility to all hierarchies and distinctions. What has escaped notice is the way that denial of mental illness has dissolved the most fundamental distinction of all: that between sanity and madness. For the most radical egalitarian claim of the left was that all realities were equal. Some countercultural intellectuals, including psychiatrist R. D. Laing, went so far as to invert the consensual order. The mad were sane, the sane mad. After all, the mad rejected the unacceptable, irrational reality of a rotten social system, while those called sane conformed to the sick values of the culture.

Theories fashionable in sociology gave spurious academic respectability to the counterculture's denial of the boundary between sanity and insanity. So-called labeling theorists argued that it was the label, or stereotype, rather than the underlying behavior that lay at the root of a variety of social problems. Applied to mental patients, the theory argued that mental patients were just people who behaved a little differently, were stigmatized by labels, and put in institutions whose baleful influence then *caused* them to be unable to function independently.

The dominant political currents and sociological theories of the 1960s proved synergistic: mutually reinforcing one another, they lent conviction and credibility to a lie that triumphed as the basis for public policy. State mental hospitals, in which hundreds of thousands of patients were still warehoused in 1960, cried out for reform. But no sensible reform could follow from the fallacy that the illness those institutions addressed, however inadequately, did not exist.

Those attempting to hold the line against the inroads of the counterculture on a wide range of issues did not understand the importance of this issue. On the contrary, the idea that mental illness did not exist, by a strange irony, moved to the cutting edge of conservative thought. As formulated in the prolific writings of psychiatrist Thomas Szasz, the idea seduced first libertarians, who viewed mental illness as a dangerous entry point for denying man's responsibility for his own actions. And conservatives generally condemned the expansion of the insanity defense in the 1960s, which eventually included such imaginative constructs as diminished capacity from "Twinkie" consumption.[72] (Twinkies were, and are, a popular "junk food" snack.) There was considerable sentiment on the right that insanity was simply another liberal excuse for immoral behavior.

And so, far from mobilizing against the destruction of the institutions and laws that had governed treatment of the mentally ill, the right joined the demolition squad. A bipartisan consensus shaped our present laws governing mental illness. California's Lanterman-Petris-Short Act of 1967 (taking effect in 1969), which inaugurated the wave of state legislation sharply restricting both the grounds for involuntary hospitalization and its length, passed both houses without a single dissenting vote.[73] Although, as we shall see, the legislation was rooted in radical premises about the nature of mental illness, legislators did not look beneath the surface. Conservative Republicans saw a way to save money; liberal Democrats saw a way to expand civil rights. The promise of saving money by doing good was irresistible.

There was no recognition of the implications of what was being done. During the 1970s, in one state after another, legislators (often propelled, to be sure, by court decisions) gave up the community's authority to intervene to care for the mad. Only when an individual posed an *imminent* threat to his own life or that of others could society step in. The left had been working on a variety of fronts to affirm the individual's freedom from standards of behavior imposed by the community. Now madness itself would become another avenue for the expression of legitimate human autonomy. With this one masterstroke the radical left had laid the ground for destruction of the middle-class social order. An enormous insoluble social problem would result. Cities would become ungovernable as they could no longer maintain any standards of behavior in public places.

Today the Bedlam on our streets is upsetting to the average citizen, corrosive of civilized society, and above all cruel and degrading to the mentally ill themselves. As E. Fuller Torrey rightly points out, the "freedom to be insane is an illusory freedom, a cruel hoax perpetrated on those who cannot think clearly by those who will not think clearly."[74] Despite major developments in the medical knowledge of mental illness in the 1970s, the hoax that mental illness does not exist continues to haunt our public policy.

PART I

Anti-Psychiatry: Birth of a Social Delusion

Chapter 1

The Origins of Anti-Psychiatry

In the 1960s a mad idea was born—the notion that there is
no such thing as mental illness. Where this falsehood came from, why it
became widespread, even fashionable, is a fascinating chapter in the
history of social delusions. Unfortunately, that history also offers a
painful illustration of the truism that ideas have consequences—today,
visible and tragic, what essayist-psychiatrist Charles Krauthammer calls
"an army of broken souls foraging and freezing in the streets."[1]

The major mental illnesses (chief among them schizophrenia,
manic-depression, and depression) are diseases of the brain. A series of
scientific breakthroughs beginning in the early 1970s (to be discussed
in Chapter 8) has established this beyond serious question. And in fact,
as psychiatrists Martin Roth and Jerome Kroll point out in *The Reality of
Mental Illness,* prior to Freud the dominant European view regarding
mental illnesses was that they were organic diseases.[2] Most nineteenth-
century superintendents of asylums for the insane in the United States
agreed. Isaac Ray, one of the best known of the early superintendents,
said: "No pathological fact is better established . . . than that deviations
from the healthy structure are generally present in the brains of insane
subjects."[3]

Flirtation with the view that mental illnesses have primarily psychological causes, Roth and Kroll note, is only a brief interlude when
seen in historical context, covering at most the period 1900–1970.
While Freud himself never treated schizophrenics and predicted a
number of times that chemistry would ultimately yield a cure, his

followers ignored his caveat. In their view, family upbringing, especially the "schizophrenogenic mother" (psychoanalyst Frieda Fromm-Reichmann coined this odious term in 1948) produced schizophrenia.

But whatever the theory of cause, there was unanimity that mental illness was an enormous and ever-growing problem. In 1950, the Council of State Governments reported that while the general population had risen 2.6 times between 1880 and 1940, the population of state mental hospitals had risen 12.6 times.[4] It continued to grow until 1955, when it peaked at 559,000. (A hundred years earlier the number of insane in state and county institutions was 8,500.[5]) In those years the proportion of institutionalized mentally ill in relation to United States population had risen a hundredfold!

In 1955, journalist turned mental health lobbyist Mike Gorman published a book whose title summed up the situation—*Every Other Bed.* Half of all hospital beds in the United States were occupied by the mentally ill, and half of those, a quarter of the total, were held by people diagnosed as schizophrenic. New York Senator Daniel Patrick Moynihan reports that in the early 1950s "mental illness was seen as perhaps the most pressing problem New York State faced—bond issue followed bond issue to build institution after institution."[6]

If, in 1955, the numbers were bleak, medically the outlook was more hopeful than ever before. Starting in the 1930s, new treatments appeared that, for the first time, dramatically improved the condition of at least some patients for at least some period of time. Different forms of shock treatment were developed, first using the chemical metrazol, then insulin, and finally electricity to induce convulsive seizures. The celebrated Portuguese neurologist Egas Moniz received the Nobel prize for developing the lobotomy. It is one of only two such awards, to this day, to be awarded for an achievement in psychiatric treatment. (The other went to Julius Wagner von Jauregg for the malarial treatment of syphilis and its accompanying dementia.) Although primitive, and often with damaging effects on personality, these early operations lessened the agitation of patients, allowing many to return to their homes.

Most important was the discovery of the major tranquillizers in the early 1950s. The calming properties of chlorpromazine (initially developed in the search for a better antihistamine) were discovered in France by surgeon Henri Laborit, and in this country reserpine was synthesized by Ciba Pharmaceuticals from the rauwolfia root. These drugs transformed the atmosphere of mental hospitals. The fighting, kicking, head-banging, and cursing vanished. Bedlam was laid to rest.[7] A new spirit of optimism imbued the staff of these hospitals. The drugs also made it possible for substantial numbers of former inmates to function in the community.

Why then, in the 1960s, with mental illness finally beginning to respond to medical treatment in a way that strongly suggested its biological basis, should the bizarre conceit take hold that this ancient, ongoing, and universal scourge did not in fact exist? Why would such an untruth not be summarily dismissed? What would make a significant public leap to embrace it? And how on earth could it become a foundation for public policy? For, as we shall see, the laws passed in the 1970s, and many of the critical judicial decisions of recent decades, derive from this delusion.

A convergence of related theories in several disciplines, including psychiatry and the social sciences, spawned what became known as "anti-psychiatry." The lead was taken by two psychiatrists, Dr. Ronald D. Laing in England and Dr. Thomas Szasz in the United States. But were it not for the rise of the counterculture in the 1960s, the anti-psychiatry movement would certainly have been no more than a curious footnote in the history of psychiatry. To understand why anti-psychiatry resonated so strongly within the counterculture it is necessary to examine the role of consciousness-expanding drugs.

LSD, Schizophrenia, and the Counterculture

Drugs, above all LSD (lysergic acid diethylamide) were central to the development of the counterculture in the 1960s. (LSD was first synthesized in 1938 in Switzerland by Dr. Albert Hofmann while he was investigating the properties of ergot, a rye fungus rich in medicinal alkaloids, for Sandoz Laboratories. He discovered its properties as an hallucinogen in 1943, after he absorbed a small dose through his fingertips). Initially, psychiatrists were excited by LSD because the ingestion of tiny amounts induced in normal patients many of the symptoms of schizophrenia: hallucinations, intense anxiety, paranoia, unusual color perceptions, and feelings of depersonalization—where the boundaries between the self and beyond dissolved. LSD held out the promise that model psychoses could be artificially created and then studied under laboratory conditions.

In a period when Freudian theories blaming the family for schizophrenia reached their peak of popularity within the psychiatric profession, LSD revived interest in theories of biological causation. It now seemed plausible that a metabolic dysfunction might cause psychotic disturbances. Understanding the mechanisms by which LSD produced its effects might point the way to a cure for schizophrenia.

Ironically, the very drug that sparked new investigation into the biology of schizophrenia paved the way for denial of its existence. For LSD soon found enthusiasts outside the psychiatric profession. In 1953 the well-known writer Aldous Huxley took mescaline under the supervision of a young British psychiatrist, Dr. Humphry Osmond, who believed that schizophrenia might be a form of self-intoxication in which the body produced its own hallucinogenic compounds. Huxley described his experiences in *The Doors of Perception,* a book that was to have profound effects on the youth of the next decade. He concluded that the brain screens out all but a fraction of the great "Mind at Large." Huxley wrote:

> To make biological survival possible, Mind at Large has to be funneled through the reducing valve of the brain and nervous system. What comes out at the other end is a measly trickle of the kind of consciousness which will help us to stay alive on the surface of this particular planet.[8]

Certain chemicals could suspend the activity of the screen, affording people a more intense view of reality and the nature of things.

Two years later, in 1955, Huxley took LSD, and in his words experienced "the direct, total awareness, from the inside, so to say, of Love as the primary and fundamental cosmic fact." In a subsequent exchange of letters with Huxley, Dr. Osmond coined the term "psychedelic" (combining the Greek psyche and delos—spirit made manifest) to describe the LSD experience. Huxley proposed "phanerothyme" (meaning "visible smoke"): "To make this trivial world sublime/Take half a Gramme of phanerothyme." Osmond countered with a couplet of his own "To fathom hell or soar angelic/Just take a pinch of psychedelic."[9]

At first, those who took LSD did so under the guidance of psychoanalysts. They were the most privileged members of society: movie stars, writers, wealthy individuals. But the drug rapidly was taken up by the "beat generation" of poets and artists. Because it could give rise to more mystical consciousness and ego-shattering experiences, LSD dovetailed with the beats' rebellion against unthinking conformity, society's emphasis on getting ahead, and material possessions.

Such use of LSD led to controversy within the psychiatric profession. Many psychiatrists who had worked experimentally with LSD considered it dangerous, a drug whose chief effect was to trigger states of intense anxiety. The debate came to a head at an international conference on the use of LSD in therapy in 1959, chaired by the influential psychiatrist Paul Hoch (later New York State's Commissioner of Mental Health). Hoch himself had studied the effects of LSD on psychiatric patients. He insisted that LSD and similar drugs disorganized the psychic integration of the individual. Unlike the major tranquillizers, which calmed patients, LSD made psychiatric patients worse. Hoch declared he had never had a subject who wanted LSD a second time.[10] Osmond, who had been using LSD to treat alcoholics (and who described the LSD experience as one of overwhelming beauty, awe, and wonder), found himself in the minority.

But while LSD's critics might triumph at conferences, they were losing in the field. In 1960 Timothy Leary tried *psilocybin,* or the "magic mushroom," in Mexico. From then on, he would dedicate himself to exploring consciousness-expanding drugs, as a faculty researcher at Harvard, and eventually as their unabashed acolyte. Thus Leary described the experience of the more powerful LSD as "an endless flame that contained everything—sound, touch, cell, seed, sense, soul, sleep, glory, glorifying, God, the hard eye of God. Merged with this pulsing flame it was possible to look and see and participate in the entire cosmic drama."[11] Dismissed from Harvard, Leary began a crusade of altering human consciousness through psychedelic drugs.

By the mid-1960s the psychedelics, chiefly LSD, fueled a rapidly growing counterculture whose epicenter was San Francisco. Legal until 1966, LSD was manufactured by the millions of doses in "factories" owned by entrepreneurs who were also believers in the drug culture. Ken Kesey, author of the wildly successful anti-psychiatric 1962 novel *One Flew Over the Cuckoo's Nest,* first learned of LSD in 1960 through a federally funded research project at a Veteran's Hospital in Menlo Park. The one-time high school wrestling champion, then a graduate student in creative writing at Stanford, took advantage of the high pay offered for volunteers willing to take the psychotomimetic drug—$75 a day. A few weeks later, he had taken a job as night attendant in the psychiatric ward, where an array of psychedelics were available. Kesey reported that once he had taken LSD the men in the psych ward no longer seemed strange to him. "After I took LSD, suddenly I saw it. I saw it all. I listened to them and watched them, and I saw that what they were saying and doing was not so crazy after all."[12] While high on both peyote and LSD, Kesey wrote his novel of the rebel Patrick McMurphy, who sacrifices himself in the effort to liberate the victims on the psych ward from their warden, the psychopathic Nurse Ratched.

With his earnings from the novel Kesey set out to do for the country what McMurphy had done for the robot society of the psych ward: enliven, rejuvenate, and humanize it, in this case, by converting all who would listen to psychedelics. Staging public initiations, "Electric Kool Aid Acid Tests," replete with strange costumes, dancing, videotapes, flashing lights, rock and roll, he would turn on hundreds of people in a single session. Kesey also toured the country by bus with his Merry Pranksters. In their costumes, their bus aglow in hallucinogenic bright colors, the acid-high Pranksters, the media in hot pursuit, spread the message of new ways of seeing and experiencing the world—parodying the famous Dupont slogan—through chemistry.

The Counterculture Celebrates Craziness

It was not surprising that counterculture groups should feel kin- ship with the mentally ill. The hallmark of Pranksters, Diggers, and Yippies was each group's attempt to outdo the other in outrageous behavior. And who were the mentally ill if not folks whose behavior conformists considered outrageous? Were not the mentally ill, then, the unsung pioneers of their own nonconformist, anti-establishment effort?

Moreover, as Todd Gitlin, former head of Students for a Demo- cratic Society (SDS), points out in his 1987 book on the 1960s, the counterculture was intent on escape from rationality. Subordinating feeling to reason had produced, in its view, an impersonal, bureaucratic, deeply unsatisfying society. And who had escaped furthest from ratio- nality, if not the mad? The counterculture was also romantic, yearning for simple people with whom to identify. The American Indians were such models: oppressed, natural, primitive, deeply American, adepts and users of psychedelic substances in religious rituals.[13]

The mentally ill, too, could be seen as a group that had failed to adjust to society's demand for repression of natural feelings. Ken Kesey portrays the men on the ward as victims of an insane conspiracy, "The Combine," that controls the world outside. The ebullient McMurphy tells Harding, one of the patients:

> You ain't crazy that way. I mean—hell, I been surprised how sane you guys all are. As near as I can tell you're not any crazier than the average asshole on the street....[14]

Beat elder statesman Seymour Krim's account of his life as a mental patient, published in 1961, reinforced the view that insanity was merely a label that a sinister power structure imposed on ordinary people.

Twice hospitalized in 1955, Krim was given insulin and then electro-shock treatments. His experience taught him that "*insanity* and *psychosis* can no longer be respected as meaningful definitions—but are used by limited individuals in positions of social power to describe ways of behaving and thinking that are alien, threatening, and *obscure* to them."[15] (In fact, Krim illustrated the strong genetic component in mental illness—his mentally ill older brother Herbert died while undergoing a prefrontal lobotomy.)

Krim introduced the idea, to become increasingly popular in the 1960s, that in an insane society insanity was the true sanity. In Krim's words, echoed and reechoed since by countless others, "*the actual living through of much that used to be called 'insanity' is almost an emotional necessity for every truly feeling, reacting, totally human person in America at this time.*"[16] (Italics added.)

The counterculture reasoned that insofar as the insane experienced reality differently, perhaps they did so more authentically. Those who took LSD felt they experienced a higher reality. If LSD, as psychiatrists said, was a psychotomimetic drug, then schizophrenia might also yield a superior form of perception. The perceptions of the insane were treated as "weird," but reality on psychedelics was "weird," with strange juxtapositions making sense, and logical thought seeming nonsense. It was easy to deduce then that the same ignorant establishment that condemned drugs and drug users had mislabeled as insane those who had simply achieved access to transcendent reality, albeit without the catalyst of psychedelics.

The notion of schizophrenia as voyage-of-discovery—to be expanded by Ronald Laing—originated with Gregory Bateson, a well-known anthropologist, husband of the even better known anthropologist Margaret Mead. Bateson was an early enthusiast for LSD and studies of the drug were conducted at the Mental Research Institute in Palo Alto, where Bateson worked. In his 1961 introduction to *Perceval's Narrative,* the nineteenth-century diary of the mentally ill son of England's Prime Minister Spencer Perceval, Bateson suggested that schizophrenia might be a naturally curative process.

> It would appear that once precipitated into psychosis the patient has a course to run. He is, as it were, embarked upon a voyage of discovery which is only completed by his return to the normal world, to which he comes back with insights different from those of the inhabitants who never embarked on such a voyage. Once begun, a schizophrenic episode would appear to have as definite a course as an initiation ceremony—a death and rebirth. . . . [17]

Political Radicals Discover Mental Illness

For the political radicals of the New Left, championing the rights of the mentally ill was also attractive. There was considerable tension, certainly in the early 1960s, between the counterculture and the New Left. Their affinities were obvious—the rebellion against authority, the disdain for all institutions, the passion for expressive behavior. And the overlap in membership between the two was enormous. Nonetheless, to many in the counterculture the possibility of remaking the world and achieving liberation through political action was an illusion, an absurd irrelevance in the cosmic scheme that drugs opened up to human understanding. Timothy Leary said that there was no difference between Fidel Castro (then the New Left's idol) and Ronald Reagan (then governor of California, and its bête noire), for both were hung up on power politics.[18] Some in the counterculture felt the simple experience of ultimate reality through LSD would produce the millennium—if only enough people, and most especially the world's leaders, could be induced to "turn on."

For political radicals, the mentally ill were useful on several counts. First, they could help score rhetorical points. Thus, New Left father figure Herbert Marcuse in his 1968 book *Negations* declared that established society is insane and those who function normally in it are themselves sick.[19] At a 1967 conference, he described psychiatry as "one of the most effective engines of suppression"; he called upon it to become a "subversive undertaking," preparing the ground for struggle on the political level.[20]

On a more mundane level, the mentally ill were a group to be "liberated" along with blacks, Hispanics, and Third World peoples. The mentally ill were an especially attractive cause because they were imprisoned, not in the invisible institutional complexes of law and custom but in the concrete mortar and brick of the asylum: incarcerated, their every moment regulated, often mistreated. Psychiatry was portrayed not as a healing profession but as capitalism's invention to suppress dissidence (as indeed it has been frequently used in the Soviet Union).

Finally, anti-psychiatry appealed to the New Left because it was anti-science and anti-technology. British social psychologist David Ingleby, himself a strong anti-psychiatric advocate, points out that in its attacks on psychiatry, anti-psychiatry focused on

> traditional sources of legitimation, medicine and science; before the politics of psychiatry could be uncovered, the spurious authority and impartiality it borrowed from medicine and science had to be dis-

pelled. . . . Science had only confused the issue because its fundamental premise, that people were like things and could be studied in the same way as things, was degrading and farfetched.[21]

It was in this matrix that the ideas of Ronald Laing and Thomas Szasz caught fire. Without them, whatever romantic attitudes toward madness the counterculture had, there would have been no anti-psychiatry movement. They gave the authority of psychiatry to anti-psychiatry. They were counterexperts, claiming credentials from an authority and framework they disdained in order to challenge their peers. Moreover, while insanity was a topic that only temporarily absorbed the energies of a Kesey or Krim, as professionals, Laing and Szasz would stay involved for the long haul; Laing, especially, would recruit a cadre of psychiatrically trained followers. Their impact would prove enormous. As Peter Sedgwick, a New Left activist unusual in that he was also an incisive critic of anti-psychiatry, put it:

> Seldom can a vanguard minority of researchers, opposed to the main orthodoxies of a dominant applied science, have achieved in so short a span of years a cultural and even political dominance of their own among progressive circles of the public with a pretension to discrimination in the matter of ideas.[22]

R. D. Laing and *The Divided Self*

Born in Glasgow in 1927 and raised in a strict Scottish Presbyterian household, Ronald David Laing studied medicine at Glasgow University and then served in the British army from 1951 to 1953. There was little in this background to suggest the anti-establishment prophet Laing was to become. Influenced by the emergent social psychiatry movement pioneered by Maxwell Jones during World War II, Laing, in 1953, had set up an experimental "therapeutic community" for twelve of the most disturbed chronic schizophrenic patients on his ward in a Scottish hospital. Within eighteen months all twelve women were out of the hospital; within another year all were back in.

Laing derived from this that a change in the way schizophrenics were treated could change the course of their disease and that the family, with whom the women were able to remain so briefly before relapsing, created the disease. There was nothing revolutionary in these conclusions; the family as the cause of schizophrenia was a convention in psychiatry at the time.

Laing's first book, *The Divided Self,* written in the late 1950s and published in 1960, marked a departure in that while many psychiatrists had sought to explain *why* the individual became ill by looking at the family, Laing treated the behavior itself as intelligible, a "rational strategy" in the face of a terrifying family environment. In *The Politics of Experience,* Laing claims that in "over 100 cases where we studied the actual circumstances it seems to us that *without exception* the experience and behavior that gets labeled schizophrenic is *a special strategy that a person invents in order to live in an unlivable situation.*"[23] (Italics in original.) Strongly influenced by Jean-Paul Sartre, Laing sets out, as he says in the preface to *The Divided Self,* "to make madness, and the process of going mad, comprehensible."[24] His method is to "decode" the apparently senseless communications of the schizophrenic.

Emil Kraepelin, the founding father of modern psychiatry, in a 1903 text, had described the symptoms exhibited by a schizophrenic patient on display before a lecture room of students. As Laing now reinterprets the meaningless (to Kraepelin) outbursts of the patient, they represent "a dialogue between his own parodied version of Kraepelin, and his own defiant rebelling self." For example, the patient says "You don't whore for me?" To Laing, this means the patient "feels that Kraepelin is objecting because he is not prepared to prostitute himself before the whole classroom of students."[25] Laing analyzes the delusions of one of his own hospitalized patients, "Julie," who calls herself "Mrs. Taylor." For Laing this means "I'm tailor made. I'm a tailored maid; I was made, fed, clothed and tailored." Julie also believes she was born "under a black sun. She's the occidental sun." Laing explains that Julie had become an "accidental son" whom her mother "out of hate had turned into a girl." Laing argues that Julie's is "a very cogent point of view."[26] Of course, given the will and enough imagination, virtually any statement can be so "decoded" by the creative psychiatrist.

The New Left Discovers Laing

Initially, *The Divided Self* had little impact. Rejected by seven publishers, it sold a mere 1,600 copies in the first four years.[27] It took off, however, after Laing's alliance with the New Left made him a cult figure. In *Bomb Culture,* one-time activist Jeff Nuttall describes how the collapse of the ban-the-bomb movement in 1962 left English activists stranded until, through Laing, they "discovered" mental illness. Schizophrenics were unable to adjust to society. But, noted Nuttall, "if the patterns of society centered around the H bomb, was it not possible that schizophrenia was a tortured means to a fuller existence . . . to a life more properly human?"[28]

Laing established Kingsley Hall in 1965 in London as a treatment center to give troubled people "an opportunity to live and grow through their madness."[29] It became a countercultural mecca, with close ties to the New Left, the British "underground" movement, and the artistic avant garde. From 1962, Laing's essays and speeches began to appear in such New Left countercultural forums as *Peace News, New Left Review,* and Timothy Leary's *Psychedelic Review.*

By 1965 Laing was prepared to give a broader meaning to *The Divided Self.* In his preface to the Pelican edition, Laing declares the book is a condemnation of the social order, of "one-dimensional men" who repress transcendence, of the statesmen of the world who are more dangerous and estranged from reality than those called insane.[30] And when Laing's essays were published in book form as *The Politics of Experience* in 1967, they had enormous impact.

That same year, Laing helped to organize a Dialectics of Liberation conference and signed a militantly anti-capitalist statement called the May Day Manifesto. By 1970 a commentator on the British New Left could assert that "Ronald Laing must be accounted one of the main contributors to the theoretical and rhetorical armoury of the contemporary left."[31]

When he visited the United States for a whirlwind lecture tour in the early 1970s, Laing found himself a celebrity, confronting huge posters of himself and bumper stickers proclaiming "I'm mad about R. D. Laing." He fielded interview requests not only from the underground press but from *Reader's Digest, Playboy,* and the "Today" show. He reported receiving letters from people who said *The Politics of Experience* had completely changed their lives.[32]

Through interacting with the counterculture, Laing became more radical, which in turn increased the appeal of his ideas. In *The Divided Self,* schizophrenia existed, even if as a "rational strategy." And Laing occasionally wobbled even on the matter of its rationality. He wrote: "The kernel of the schizophrenic's experience of himself must remain incomprehensible to us. As long as we are sane and he is insane, it will remain so."[33] Moreover, he recognized the suffering of the schizophrenic, his "distinctiveness and differentness, his separateness and loneliness and despair."[34] But in *The Politics of Experience,* Laing wrote: "There is no such 'condition' as schizophrenia but the label is a social fact and the social fact a *political event.*"[35] One of the other psychiatrists at Kingsley Hall, Joseph Berke, actually maintained that "we find that a person who is labeled insane is often the sanest member of his or her family."[36]

Schizophrenia as "Hypersanity"

In the mid-1960s Laing began to toy with the idea of schizophrenia as not merely intelligible, but a life-enhancing experience. In the future, he wrote, we might see schizophrenia as one of the forms in which "the light began to break through the cracks in our all-too-closed minds."[37] For, he had now concluded, "madness need not be all breakdown. It may also be breakthrough. It is potentially liberation as well as enslavement and existential death." According to Laing, it is the ostensibly normal man who suffers from "the condition of alienation . . . of being unconscious, of being out of one's mind."[38]

But if normality is "a cruel fiction," then, "what we call madness may be a process of coming terrifyingly awake to those 'normal' contradictions and confusions to which most of us are ordinarily fast asleep." To become genuinely sane, the sane must go mad. Laing declares: "We can no longer assume that such a voyage [schizophrenia] is an illness that has to be treated. . . . Can we not see that *this voyage is not what we need to be cured of, but that it is itself a natural way of healing our own appalling state of alienation called normality?*"[39] (Italics in original.) For Laing, schizophrenia may prove the salvation of society. "Our society may itself have become biologically dysfunctional, and some forms of schizophrenic alienation from the alienation of society may have a sociobiological function that we have not recognized."[40]

Here was a truly novel conception. No psychiatrist had ever claimed psychosis was a higher form of sanity, a mystical apprehension of reality—a "hypersanity." To be sure, under those circumstances the conventional forms of treatment for mental illness, whether medication, electroshock, or even psychotherapy or family therapy, are all counterproductive.

The psychiatrist's chief role is to serve as a "guide" in the healing voyage through madness. Laing seems to have picked up this notion from Bateson, who had likened schizophrenia to an initiation ceremony, and from Huxley, whose trial of mescaline, chronicled in *The Doors of Perception,* grew out of Osmond's interest in the relation between consciousness-altering drugs and schizophrenia. At one point, Huxley experiences terror on the drug and writes that he now knows where madness lies. The schizophrenic, he says, "is like a man permanently under the influence of mescaline, and therefore unable to shut off the experience of a reality which . . . scares him into interpreting its unremitting strangeness, its burning intensity of significance, as the manifestations of human or even cosmic malevolence, calling for the most desperate countermeasures, from murderous violence at one end of the scale to catatonia, or psychological suicide."[41] The answer, Huxley reasons, could be a psychiatrist who acts as guide through the experience, reassuring schizophrenics "by day and even while they are asleep" that "the ultimate Reality remains unshakably itself."[42]

Laing's Appeal

Much of Laing's appeal lay in his use of his psychiatric credentials to define the establishment as insane. The sane were mad, the mad sane, and psychiatrists the craziest of the lot. Sometimes Laing suggests there may be such a thing as mental illness after all. It is something from which psychiatrists suffer and that they project upon their patients.

> [I]f you want a perfect example of schizophrenia, just read a psychiatric text like Bleuler's (1951) textbook on schizophrenia or any of Kraepelin . . . or any number of more recent things, and you will see manifested in the mentality of the psychiatrist the very disease, the very psychopathology, that is projected onto the person who is supposed to be the patient.[43]

The small-scale assaults of psychiatry upon the individual become paradigms for the huge lunacies and systematic violence perpetrated by Western imperialism. It was small wonder college youth were enthusiastic. And while in the 1960s all this seemed hyberbole typical of the times, the New Left's assault on the distinction between sanity and insanity would prove the most far-reaching and radical of its many inversions of assumptions underlying the social order.

Laing attracted a group of psychiatric disciples (some American) to Kingsley Hall, several of whom were far more committed to a crude left-wing politics than their mentor. Joseph Berke, Leon Redler, and David Cooper, who introduced the term anti-psychiatry, participated with Laing in the Congress on Dialectics of Liberation in 1967. Cooper, who organized the Congress, was the most prolific writer, and often sounded more like a Marxist than a psychiatrist: "To act politically means simply regaining what has been stolen from us, starting with our consciousness of our oppression within the capitalist system."[44]

Cooper's anti-establishment rhetoric was too much even for British radical Jeff Nuttall. Nuttall reports telling Cooper his feeling that he should have been in a concentration camp to truly "suffer the century," and receiving the reply: "To suffer society is enough. Society is a concentration camp." Nuttall's comment was "Christ, what a nut."[45] For Cooper, "all delusions are political declarations and all madmen political dissidents."[46]

Although many of Laing's followers retained their radical faith, Laing himself was to prove a disappointment to his admirers on the Left. Ultimately, Laing was far more interested in the countercultural than the political currents of the 1960s. In 1971, he left England to spend six months in a Buddhist monastery in Ceylon, then seven months in India studying Yoga and Zen, followed by a brief stay in Japan.

Delving into mysticism, Laing drew further and further from the concerns of his young left-wing followers. On his return to England, he dove into theories of birth trauma. Arthur Janow had popularized the notion that birth experiences had a profound effect on later life in *The Primal Scream,* published in 1970, followed by *The Anatomy of Mental Illness* a year later. In October 1972, speaking at a Friends meeting house in London, Laing offered the hypothesis that "umbilical shock" at the moment of cord-cutting "can make a profound difference for the rest of one's life, I think."[47] In this phase, Laing postulated that trauma affecting an individual's later development could be traced not only to "clamping and cutting of the cord, immediately inducing umbilical shock," but to the very implantation of the fertilized ovum in the womb of an unwilling mother. As Sedgwick has observed, even his most ardent devotees had trouble following him on these forays into obstetrical technology.[48]

Laing now abandoned some of the extreme positions that had made him a hero in the 1960s. In *Sanity, Madness and the Family* and *The Politics of the Family,* the irrationality of the individual finds its rationality in the context of an irrational family. But in the early 1970s Laing complained that his work had been misinterpreted, that he was not against families. He also dropped his celebration of schizophrenia as a voyage into a mystical inner space. "I would never recommend madness to anybody."[49] The "new" Laing, speaking on subjects like "the evolution of self in Western society" on his rare lecture tours, essentially dropped from sight until his death in 1988, at the age of sixty-one. That Laing distanced himself from his own earlier ideas drew little attention: his enduring legacy was the profoundly erroneous notion that mental illness was some kind of liberation from the falsities of society.

Thomas Szasz: Oracle of Autonomy

Anti-psychiatry's second father is Dr. Thomas Szasz. It is hard to imagine a more unlikely pair than Szasz and Laing. Born in Hungary, educated in the United States, Szasz produced his iconoclastic *The Myth of Mental Illness* just a year after Laing's *The Divided Self;* his manuscript, too, was initially rejected. The resemblance ended there. An unsparing libertarian, Szasz had nothing but contempt for the New Left. He even rejected the term "anti-psychiatry":

> [T]he anti-psychiatrists are all self-declared socialists, communists, or at least anticapitalists and collectivists. As the communists seek to raise the poor above the rich, so the anti-psychiatrists seek to raise the "insane" above the sane.[50]

Szasz would offer a variety of "proofs" that mental illness did not— indeed could not—exist,[51] but in the end his grounds are philosophical, deduced logically from his libertarian views. There is no effort in Szasz, as there is in Laing, to "understand" the perspective of the schizo-phrenic, to undercut the reality of insanity by making the apparently bizarre perceptions of its victims intelligible. There are no mentally ill people in Szasz's world at all.

Yet as Charles Krauthammer has noted, "like the atheist who can't stop talking about God, Szasz cannot stop talking about psychiatry." And talk he does, sounding the same themes repetitively, obsessively, in more than four hundred reviews and articles and twenty books over three decades. The grounds of the argument shift somewhat as time passes. In 1961 theories of family causation were influential in psychia-try; by 1987 an enormous amount of evidence had been assembled that severe mental illness had a biological basis. Szasz's arguments take into account these changes, but his own views have not altered in the least. In 1960, a year before the publication of his *The Myth of Mental Illness,* Szasz wrote: "Mental illness is a myth, whose function is to disguise and thus render more palatable the bitter pill of moral conflicts in human relations."[52] We asked him in 1989 if he still believed mental illness was a myth and he replied: "I believe that like I believe the earth is round."[53]

Whatever Laing's failings, he recognized that there were people in pain (in *The Divided Self* he wrote that "the schizophrenic is desperate, is simply without hope").[54] For Szasz mental illness is purely and simply a test case in human liberty. It is this orientation that has made Szasz such a favorite with the legal profession, which in the 1960s began to arrogate to itself the decision-making power that had belonged to psychiatrists. While Laing is rarely quoted in the precedent-setting briefs and judicial decisions that effected this transfer of power, Szasz is quoted constantly and at length.

Szasz is intent on asserting man's freedom to act and his responsibility for what he does. Szasz declares: "Autonomy is my religion." He writes:

> Why do I place so much emphasis on autonomy? Autonomy is a positive concept. It is freedom to develop one's self—to increase one's knowledge, improve one's skills, and achieve responsibility for one's conduct. And it is freedom to lead one's own life, to choose among alternative courses of action so long as no injury to others results.[55]

Given this definition, Szasz must deny the reality of mental illness. For it is precisely the freedom to make reasoned choices among alternative courses of action, the ability to develop one's self without assistance (treatment, for example), that those suffering from mental disease lack. His own emphasis on autonomy, once he granted the existence of mental illness, would force him to emphasize the need for treatment to restore the capacity of the mentally ill to exercise autonomy in any meaningful sense of that word.[56]

In his book entitled *Schizophrenia,* Szasz treats the disease as an invention of psychiatrists:

> [I]f there is no psychiatry, there can be no schizophrenics. In other words, the identity of an individual as schizophrenic depends on the existence of the social system of (institutional) psychiatry. Hence, if psychiatry is abolished, schizophrenics disappear. . . . There assuredly remain persons who are incompetent, or self-absorbed, or who reject their "real" roles, or who offend others in some other ways. But if there is no psychiatry, none of them can be schizophrenic.[57]

Dr. Fuller Torrey, who was at one time deeply influenced by Szasz, now says of this book:

> His book on schizophrenia is one of the silliest books that you can find. It's absolutely absurd. The fact is that Szasz knows nothing about schizophrenia; has never treated people with it; has a private psychoanalytic practice in Syracuse and doesn't know what he is talking about.[58]

Our own conversation with Szasz supported Torrey's view. Asked what he would do for someone hearing voices and fearful of hurting herself, Szasz said:

Before you come to me you have to make an appointment and I make my own appointments. So when you call on the phone I would ask you, why do you want to see me? I don't want to get involved with someone I can't help.[59]

The 'Word Magic' of Thomas Szasz

Szasz disposes of mental illness by verbal sleight of hand. "Mental illnesses do not exist; indeed they cannot exist, because the mind is not a bodily part or bodily organ."[60]QED, there is no such thing as mental illness. As one of his critics has aptly observed, Szasz seems to think words can create and destroy, a belief in "word magic" that one usually loses at the age of two.[61]

What about a disease of the brain? Szasz waffles here. Sometimes he says yes, that is possible, but then "lesions" would have to exist and pathologists have not found them. Suppose lesions were to be found? Then, says Szasz, such diseases and behaviors would no longer be considered "mental" illnesses and become the property of neurologists rather than psychiatrists.[62] Roth and Kroll, in their trenchant critique of anti-psychiatry, *The Reality of Mental Illness,* point out that 150 years ago there were virtually no diseases for which the lesions or physical causes could be established in life and few were discovered after death. By Szasz's criteria, diseases were then very rare. Nonetheless, they note dryly, " 'non-diseases,' manifest in great mental and physical suffering and causing premature death in childhood or early adulthood, were very common."[63]

Perhaps uncomfortable with his myth today–disease tomorrow position, Szasz at other times employs word games to dismiss the possibility of brain disease as an explanation for strange behavior. Logically, says Szasz, such an explanation is inadmissible.

> [A] *defect* in a person's visual field may be satisfactorily explained by correlating it with certain definite lesions in the nervous system . . . [but] a person's *belief*—whether this be a belief in Christianity, in Communism, or in the idea that his internal organs are "rotting" and that his body is, in fact, already "dead"—cannot be explained by a defect or disease of the nervous system.[64]

Szasz is caught in his own contradictions. On the one hand he says the chief support for the idea of mental illness as a medical disease comes from diseases like neurosyphilis or senile dementia: these mimic the symptoms of mental illness, but correctly speaking are diseases of the brain, not the mind. On the very next page he says that to be analogous to "real" disease, diseases of the brain would have to reveal themselves by neurological signs like impaired gait or vision, not behavioral symptoms like depression or paranoia. Recently, stung by critics who pointed out that a variety of illnesses involved no detectable "lesion," Szasz has said that this does not defeat his argument because he regards such persons "as having bodily diseases without presently demonstrable pathoanatomical or pathophysiological correlates or lesions; in other words they suffer from what I call *putative* diseases."[65] But why then should schizophrenia not rank as a putative disease?

Writing in 1987, after so much evidence had accumulated that schizophrenia and the affective disorders were brain diseases, Szasz enlisted the alleged support of pathologists for his position, citing their "firm disavowal of mental illnesses as real—that is, cellular—diseases." He specifically cites Stanley L. Robbins as senior author "of what is perhaps the most widely used textbook in the field, *Pathologic Basis of Disease* (3rd ed.)." Since Robbins and his co-authors never mention schizophrenia or manic-depressive psychosis, according to Szasz, they "implicitly reject the reality or somatic basis of mental illness." Psychiatrists, Szasz declares, "ought to convince pathologists that schizophrenia is a brain disease before they take it upon themselves to tell the public that it is such a disease."[66]

We checked with Robbins concerning Szasz's interpretation. He replied dryly:

> I cannot agree with Dr. Szasz when he states that the authors of *Pathologic Basis of Disease* "reject the reality or somatic basis of mental illness." Our text is devoted to the morphologic changes induced by disease and therefore does not include many conditions unassociated with morphologic change, for example, the well-known jet-lag induced by the dislocations of circadian rhythm following air travel. Analogously, there are well documented psychiatric disorders which to date have not been related to neurochemical or morphologic abnormalities, although such may be found in the future and at such time will receive treatment in our text.[67]

Reasoning by Analogy

Szasz complains that "using language badly is called 'Schizophrenia,'" but in fact a good part of his own argument against the reality of mental illness consists precisely of "using language badly." When

Szasz is not defining mental illness out of existence, he is extirpating it by analogy. Szasz provides lengthy comparisons between mental illness and institutions or behavior the reader will find morally offensive: slavery, persecution of witches and Jews, the Inquisition. His aim is to contaminate the concept of mental illness through repugnant, if inappropriate, parallels.

Thus, Szasz devotes most of *The Manufacture of Madness* to likening mental illness to witchcraft, glibly announcing in the introduction: "I shall compare the belief in witchcraft and the persecution of witches with the belief in mental illness and the persecution of mental patients."[68] No evidence is offered for the validity of the analogy. The reader is simply told that to believe in the reality of mental illness is tantamount to a belief in witches.

Slavery and the Inquisition are also favorite Szaszian correspondences. Szasz writes: "The practice of 'sane' men incarcerating their 'insane' fellow men in 'mental hospitals' can be compared to that of white men enslaving black men."[69] Psychiatry is "slavery disguised as therapy." As to the Inquisition, Szasz says: "Institutional psychiatry is a continuation of the Inquisition. All that has really changed is the vocabulary and the social style."[70] The religious sanctions "of confinement in a dungeon or burning at the stake" have been replaced "with the psychiatric sanctions of confinement in a hospital or torture called treatment."[71]

For those still unconvinced, Szasz throws in the persecution of the Jews. "The rhetoric of rejection couched in the vocabulary of race (stigmatization as a Jew)" equals that "couched in the vocabulary of medicine (stigmatization as mentally ill.")[72] *In short, the reader is bullied into rejecting the reality of mental illness.* His instinctive rejection of slavery, the Inquisition, burning witches, and Nazi treatment of Jews is transferred, through Szasz's "analysis by analogy" to the evil institution of Psychiatry.

But for all his emphasis on the alleged brutality of psychiatry, it is Szasz's ideology that is truly inhumane. In a 1975 speech in California he declared that he did not give psychotropic drugs and did not promise patients he could make them better: "They can go home and blow their brains out."[73] In Szasz's world, the fit survive, and others have the "right" to go to the wall. He maintains that they *should* do so, because we must recognize "the brutal facts of the human destiny: namely, that not everyone can 'make it' in life; that those who cannot are not sick."[74]

Szasz Versus the Family

If Szasz's libertarianism made him an unlikely guru for the left, aspects of his thought appealed to the counterculture. Without romanticizing the mentally ill, Szasz defined them as an oppressed group and mental illness as akin to a capitalist conspiracy. "Powerful interests," he said in 1967, demanded that an ever greater number of the superfluous people in industrial nations be treated as mentally disabled so that they would become consumers of services.[75]

Moreover, in a sense, Szasz was even more anti-institution and anti-authority than Laing and his disciples.[76] In *Law, Liberty and Psychiatry* he asks: "Which should we prefer, *the integrity of the family or the autonomy of the individual?*" (Italics in original.) Szasz opts for the latter, but he recognizes the challenge his views pose to "our traditional ideas about the duties and rights of family members."[77] Szasz rightly observes that mental illness is above all a problem for families because, unlike other institutions (e.g., the university, the employer), they cannot dismiss the individual who fails to fulfill his assigned role. Families, says Szasz, have three options: they can beg the family member to alter his behavior; they can sever the relationship; they can enlist psychiatric help and secure involuntary commitment for their recalcitrant relative.[78]

In fact, Szasz's first option is (to use his favorite word) simply a myth. A mentally ill person cannot alter his behavior on command or entreaty, for he is a prisoner of his aberrant mental processes. That leaves the family only two choices: to withdraw from the family member or seek treatment for him, which he may resist. "Unlike legal separation or divorce," says Szasz, "commitment achieves a separation of family members on ostensibly medical grounds." For society, "it ensures the maintenance of family relationships, loyalties, and responsibilities as positive moral values."[79] (As we shall see in Part V, now that Szasz's views have had a revolutionary impact on our legal system, as he predicted, families have come under enormous strain. Some do "withdraw," even flee from their mentally ill relative, whom they may physically fear. More often, the family remains involved and struggles to obtain some kind of treatment, often forced to assume a para-institutional role.)

In addition, there is a radical relativism at the core of Szasz's writing that has appealed to the left. Denying mental disability, Szasz was impelled to accept the validity of all perceptions of reality. Szasz defends the paranoid schizophrenic: he has "reasons" for his beliefs, even if they are offensive to anyone "obsessed with rationality."[80] He attacks psychiatry for creating "officially forbidden" definitions of reality. The woman who says she is the Virgin Mary, the man who says he is Jesus Christ, for Szasz, are merely examples of "human conflicts."[81]

Szasz's Following

A loner by temperament and offering no alternative treatment program, Szasz did not attract the kind of following Laing enjoyed at Kingsley Hall. Young radicals were enthusiastic about his work, but misunderstood or ignored the libertarian root of his anti-psychiatric polemics. Szasz did not become the campus cult figure that Laing was. Certainly, he was no player to the gallery. One former student at the University of Michigan recalls how he went to applaud a lecture by Szasz in company with a large student audience of fellow New Left sympathizers, only to find themselves roundly denounced by Szasz from the platform.

Nonetheless, Szasz did become the center of a small circle at Syracuse, where he is professor at the Upstate Medical Center of the State University of New York. One of those in the circle whose books reflect his influence is Ronald Leifer, a psychoanalyst and sociologist, whose 1969 book *In the Name of Mental Health* proclaimed that the supposedly strange behavior of the mentally ill merely required deeper inquiry. "Such an inquiry will usually reveal that this person is pursuing conventional goals in an extraordinary fashion or using ordinary means for unusual goals."

The so-called mentally ill individual, for Leifer, is not distinguished by "his hidden 'pathological' mental processes. He is set off by the fact that social and psychiatric authorities wish to stigmatize, deface and control his conduct."[82] Another colleague, Ernest Becker, an anthropologist and Pulitzer Prize-winning author, acknowledged the debt his *Revolution in Psychiatry* owed to Szasz. The book, published in 1964, dismissed the medical model as "reductionist" and set out to reconstruct psychiatry as a "broad, human science."[83] (Medicine, in this view, is presumably "inhuman.")

It is noteworthy that the startling discovery by the Szaszian coterie at Upstate Medical Center that mental illness did not exist seems to have had no effect on the treatment administered to actual patients. Psychiatrist Peter Breggin, who has become Szasz's chief disciple, abandoned a residency at Harvard to work under him in the early 1960s. He describes the environment at Syracuse as "by far the most intellectually stimulating I'd ever experienced." Yet, in the hospital, Breggin reports: "They did everything. They did shock. They did drugs. They did psychoanalysis. Szasz didn't do those things but the department did. It did a lot of shock. And I did shock."[84]

In any event, even on the intellectual level, the Szaszian heyday at Syracuse lasted only a few years. Paul Hoch, the Commissioner of Mental Health for New York State, sought to fire Szasz, on the grounds that someone who did not believe in the existence of mental illness was unfit to teach in the state-run mental hospital at Syracuse. Although Szasz managed to keep his job in the end, according to Breggin, "Hoch just totally devastated the department—he won. Syracuse now is this very ordinary department."[85]

A number of young psychiatrists around the country were deeply influenced by Szasz, among them E. Fuller Torrey, now an eloquent and able champion for the medical treatment of mental illness. Remarkably, Torrey's own sister was suffering from schizophrenia when he fell under Szasz's spell. (Normally there is no more effective antidote to Szasz than having a mentally ill relative.) Torrey is hard put to explain it now: "I never had to be involved in her care. It was somehow periph-eral. She was very seriously mentally ill. . . . But somehow I didn't make the connection."[86] Torrey wrote much of his anti-psychiatric polemic, *The Death of Psychiatry,* as a resident in psychiatry at Stanford in 1971 and finished it as an administrator at the National Institute of Mental Health. Szasz wrote a blurb for the cover, commending Torrey for his "reasoned review of the mythology of mental illness and the persecu-tory practices of psychiatry."

The Death of Psychiatry was a confusing book. Even then a close reader would perceive that Torrey was no true Szaszian, for he stated categorically that schizophrenia was an organic brain disease.[87] Most of the book was a cogent critique of psychiatry's application of the medical model to normal human problems. But Torrey also quoted Szasz liber-ally and sounded much like him in inveighing against "the medical model," denouncing involuntary commitment, and declaring—shades of Laing—that "we, who are psychiatrists and should know better, project our irrational impulses onto others whom we cannot under-stand, label them as mentally 'ill,' confine them, and feel better."[88] The endorsement from Szasz, the sweeping title and matching rhetorical style were responsible for the book's being viewed as an attack (which it was not) on the very existence of mental illness. Thus Michael Fleming and Roger Manvell in their study on the depiction of madness in films describe Torrey's book as "a stunning indictment of the obsolescence of psychiatry and the concept of mental illness."[89]

Of his views on involuntary commitment in *The Death of Psychiatry* Torrey now says simply, "I was wrong."[90]

Roots of Anti-Psychiatry in Psychiatry

Laing and Szasz both wrote their pioneering anti-psychiatric books in the 1950s, well before the campus ferment of the 1960s that was to give their works its impact. It is important to recognize that though Laing and (even more so) Szasz would find themselves isolated within psychiatry, their ideas actually stemmed from the psychiatric mainstream. Indeed, given the direction psychiatry had taken by the 1950s, it was probably inevitable that a challenge to the very existence of mental illness would arise within the profession itself.

In psychoanalytic thought the barrier between normal behavior and mental illness dissolves. As British psychiatrist John Wing notes, Kraepelin, the father of modern biological psychiatry, who always remained influential in Europe, had narrowed the range of social deviations that could be explained in medical terms. But Freud, who became father to American psychiatry, vastly extended the scope of behavior considered appropriate for doctors to treat, explaining mental illness in terms of the same psychodynamic processes as normal behavior.[91] Theodore Lidz, a psychoanalytically oriented psychiatrist whose writings were influential in the 1950s and 1960s, described how he and his fellow psychiatrists applied Freudian categories so as to uncover a specific crucial period in the development of schizophrenia. "At first we thought the development was related to the patient's progress from the oral to the anal to the phallic stage, to the whole process. Then we thought for awhile that the anal stage was more crucial."[92]

Supposed "advances" in studying the etiology of schizophrenia within the general framework of Freudian theory in the mid-1950s focused on family interaction, rather than early stages of childhood development. This still boiled down to blaming the family for the disease, but depending on the theorist, the *mechanisms* by which the family was held to have driven one of its members crazy varied. Bateson and his group in Palo Alto touted the famous "double bind," where parents imposed contradictory demands (or binds) on the child, while a third implicit demand prevented him from escaping the situation.

At Yale, Theodore Lidz (and co-workers) came up with two kinds of schizophrenia-producing parental relationships, "schism" and "skew": in cases of schism, parents were in open conflict, while in cases of skew one partner passively accepted the dominance of the other. (What this meant was that when parents argued a lot, they could be held responsible for schizophrenia, and when there was apparent harmony they could be held responsible as well.) The best consolation Lidz could offer the family was that they could do no differently: "their noxious influences upon the patient are not malevolent but rather the products of their own personal tragedies and egocentric orientations."[93]

A team led by Lyman Wynne at the National Institute of Mental Health posited "pseudo-mutuality." According to this theory, families could cover up, beneath an appearance of concord, the hostility and mutual destructiveness that led them to extrude one member; the family would label him sick so as to blame him for all the family tension.

No evidence ever emerged to support any of these theories, most based on laughably small samples, without control groups. Wynne's NIMH study analyzed four families. Lidz studied seventeen families (eight with "schism," six with "skew"). Indeed the theories turned out to be untestable. When replications were attempted, it was discovered there was no agreement on what a double bind was among the very "experts" who had advanced the theory![94]

Unaware they had been identified as pathological agents, families innocently agreed to participate in what they thought were scientific studies to help find a cure for schizophrenia. In one NIMH study, entire families agreed to live in the hospital for between six months and two years. No one has described the charade better than Peter Sedgwick.

> Hundreds of families have trooped into the laboratories of academic institutes and hospitals, there to have their entire verbal output tape-recorded over many sessions, their gestures and eye movements filmed and their biographies unearthed in depth by interdisciplinary panels of doctors, psychologists, sociologists and technicians.[95]

Sedgwick describes the researchers' cast of alleged villains. There was Mr. Doublebind, "a shifty, spineless, passive father," and Mrs. Doublebind, "a domineering dragon of a woman." There were the Doublebind children, "mentally unstimulating and mutually disloyal." And then there was the unlucky fall guy (or girl) of the house: Charles (or Clarissa) Doublebind, "a naive and dithering but basically rather sweet personality." The Doublebinds mount a vicious campaign, whose climax is reached when they decide

> to "elect" Charles/Clarissa as an insane mental patient, thereby expelling him/her from their totalitarian kingdom. The chorus of false attribution and impossible injunction, orchestrated by the monstrous Mrs. Doublebind . . . rises to a crescendo of rejection; at this point orthodox psychia-

try affixes the label of "schizophrenic" upon the family scapegoat, in a degradation ceremonial of hospital admission which inaugurates a lifetime's career as a mental patient.[96]

And this nonsense was funded at taxpayers' expense.

As a product of social interaction, schizophrenia began to look less and less like a real disease. It was inevitable that someone would raise uncomfortable questions. No one defines cancer or syphilitic dementia or diabetes as an effect of faulty family interaction. In what sense then was schizophrenia medical? It could only be a matter of time before some "expert" would declare: "The emperor has no clothes; there is no disease."

Laing merely carried the logic of family causation theorists one step further. Dr. Murray Bowen, one of the early NIMH researchers, saw schizophrenia as a process of diseased interaction involving an entire family over a number of generations. The patient was the member who overtly displayed the psychosis.[97] In *Sanity, Madness and the Family*, Laing eliminated schizophrenia altogether as an illness suffered by an individual; it became rather a communication syndrome of a family. The patient was no more disturbed than the rest of the family. Declared Laing: "Surely, if we are wrong, it would be easy to show it by studying a few families and revealing that schizophrenics really are talking nonsense after all."[98] (To be sure, Laing also portrayed schizophrenia as a voyage to "explore the inner space and time of consciousness,"[99] which suggested it *did* exist, even if its nature might be different from what was commonly believed.) Cooper declared that the family "in order to preserve itself in its inauthentic manner of living invents a disease."[100]

But that meant the psychiatrist was as culpable as the family. Psychiatrists had been able to avoid seeing themselves as part of the conspiracy against Clarissa/Charles precisely because they assumed the victim had been driven mad by his/her family, and madness was real, requiring the intervention of the psychiatrist. But if schizophrenia were *not* real, if, as David Cooper said, schizophrenia was merely "disturbed group interaction," then psychiatrists were in collusion with families to label and commit the unfortunate family scapegoat to the hospital.

From the family to the psychiatrist to society as the culprit—the sequence was inexorable. Once insanity lost content, it was easy to find we were all in the same "ship of fools" facing an alien (Keseyan) Combine. In the words of Laing's associate Joseph Berke: "We're up against a whole society that is systematically driving its members mad."[101]

Szasz Attacks Psychiatric Imperialism

If Laing carried to their logical end the theories of mainstream psychiatry in the 1950s blaming the family for the disease, Szasz responded at least in part to what he rightly condemned as imperialist trends in psychiatry. Under the influence of the Freudian view that mental illness and mental health formed a continuum, psychiatry had enlarged greatly the universe defined as mentally ill and the areas of behavior subject to psychiatric ministration. Thus, the widely publicized Midtown Manhattan Study of 1962 claimed that 80% of the population was psychiatrically impaired. A mere 18.5% were "well," while 23% were severely ill enough to require treatment.[102]

Psychiatrists did not hesitate to appoint as their province juvenile delinquency, school difficulties, problems of urban areas, community conflicts, marriage and family counseling. Some claimed psychiatric expertise extended to resolution of international conflicts. Szasz wrote with ample justification in 1970 in *Ideology and Insanity*: "It is no exaggeration to say that life itself is now viewed as an illness that begins with conception and ends with death, requiring at every step along the way, the skillful assistance of physicians and especially mental health professionals."[103]

The problem was that Szasz threw out the baby, bathwater, and tub. Instead of calling on psychiatry to define mental illness more narrowly (as Kraepelin had done) and its own expertise more modestly, he denied that mental illness existed. Szasz indicted the concept of mental illness for "obscuring the issue of man's responsibility for his actions."[104] In effect, as Krauthammer has pointed out, Szasz rejected mental illness on political grounds. If it exists, it shouldn't.

And so, what could have been a telling critique of psychiatric pretensions became instead an absurd and destructive attack. Szasz portrayed psychiatrists as key agents in a government plot to insinuate a totalitarian system of coercion through a therapeutic state. He thus reinforced the countercultural "anti-psychiatry" he professed to disdain, and he created for its core untruth—that there is no distinction between sanity and insanity—a credulous new audience on the Right among conservatives and libertarians.

Chapter 2

Mental Illness as Label

The Academy Joins Anti-Psychiatry

ALTHOUGH the most important individuals in the anti-psychiatry crusade were R. D. Laing and Thomas Szasz, a convergence of intellectual currents reinforced the movement. Peter Sedgwick rightly points out that the radicals' challenge to the validity of psychiatry would have been unthinkable without the enduring contribution of a critical sociology to the appraisal of psychiatric concepts.[1] For while Laing and Szasz were peripheral figures in their own field, anti-psychiatry became mainstream sociology—the wellspring of status and reputation in the field. Thus ideas that might otherwise have remained on the fringes of psychiatry and widespread only in the counterculture gained academic respectability.

For an influential branch of sociology mental illness became a societally constructed "label." Sociologists of the "labeling" school prominent in the 1960s focused on everything from heroin addiction to check forging, mental illness to gambling. Howard Becker, probably the best known proponent, summed up the perspective in his 1963 volume *Outsiders.*

> Social groups create deviance by making the rules whose infraction constitutes deviance and by applying those rules to particular people and labeling them as outsiders. . . . Deviant behavior is behavior that people so label.[2]

Sociologists moved the focus from deviant acts to those who labeled them, and emphasized the role of labels in turning individuals into "career" deviants. The net effect was to *relativize* deviance. It was in the eye of the beholder—or labeler—not in the behavior of the offender.

Again, despite the popularity of this theory of deviance on college campuses of the 1960s, its intellectual origins hark back a decade earlier. In 1951 Edwin Lemert published *Social Pathology,* in which he sought to move sociology toward a "value-free" approach to deviance. As Lemert saw it, primary deviations (intrinsic abnormalities) led to secondary deviations (the result of social response to the primary deviations). British psychiatrist John Wing has pointed out that in its "moderate" form labeling theory posed no difficulties. It made the unexceptionable point that certain forms of behavior (whatever their cause) brought people to public attention. The ensuing reaction defined the individual; when he internalized the definition he became a secondary or "career" deviant.

But sociologists soon ignored the abnormality that set the process in motion. The label became the sufficient explanation. Labeling theory became a rival to the medical explanation for major mental illness, providing both a substitute interpretation and approach to "treatment."

Erving Goffman and *Asylums*

Although technically not a member of the labeling school, Erving Goffman was the first to elaborate this approach to mental illness in detail. And while Laing and Szasz were scarcely staple fare in medical school in the 1960s, Goffman's *Asylums* was one of the most commonly assigned books in introductory sociology courses, let alone in courses on social deviance.

Published in 1961, *Asylums* was based on fieldwork Goffman had done in 1955–56 at St. Elizabeth's Hospital in Washington, D.C., then a federal institution with 7,000 inmates. Goffman was far from an unbiased observer: "I came to the hospital with no great respect for the discipline of psychiatry nor for agencies content with its current practice."[3] His experience at St. Elizabeth's did not change his mind.

Asylums is an anti-psychiatric polemic. Like Szasz's books, it derives much of its force from the apparent profundity of its specious comparisons. For Goffman, the mental hospital is only one of a number of noxious "total institutions," including army barracks, concentration camps, jails, nunneries, boarding schools, ships, and monasteries. Of course individuals enter most of these voluntarily. But Goffman likens these noncomparable institutions, so that the reader's antipathy is transferred from one to the other, building to a crescendo of revulsion against the "total institution" as such. Goffman moves from examples of "experiential mortification" in nunneries (a novice "begs soup" from the nuns), to mental hospitals (when electroshock is given, the inmate is forced to help hold down the patient, whose "convulsions resemble an accident victim in death agony"), to concentration camps (a Jew has to watch an SS sergeant torture his brother to death).[4]

Sociologists are typically acutely sensitive to social context, recognizing that the same behavior can have different meaning depending on the circumstances. But Goffman downplays the significance of social context in mental illness. In a 1964 essay Goffman writes:

> I know of no psychotic misconduct which cannot be matched precisely in everyday life by the conduct of persons who are not psychologically ill nor considered to be so; and in each case one can find a host of different motives for engaging in the misconduct, and a host of different factors that will modify our attitude towards its performance.[5]

Goffman calls decisions concerning inappropriate behavior "political," in that they express the special interest of some particular faction or persons, rather than interests above the concerns of any particular grouping, as in physical pathology.[6] In other words, Goffman, like Szasz, seems to feel that because mental illness involves *behavior,* it cannot be a medical illness.

Goffman goes even further. The institution *causes* the very deviant behavior it is meant to cure. The inmate is exposed to relentless "abasements, degradation, humiliation and profanations of self." Trapped, the inmate lashes out by acting out. "I want merely to add," says Goffman,

> that mental hospitals, perhaps through a process of natural selection, are organized in such a way as to provide exactly the kind of setting in which unwilling participants have recourse to the exhibition of situational improprieties. If you rob people of all customary means of expressing anger and alienation and put them in a place where they have never had better reason for these feelings, then the natural recourse will be to seize upon what remains—situational improprieties."[7]

Goffman notes that when the patient, in seclusion, tears up the mattress and writes with feces on the wall, these are viewed as psychotic symptoms. Actually, says Goffman, these are the patient's only means of asserting himself against the total institution.

To win release, or even to ease his life in the asylum, the individual must accept his place, that is, a "self-alienating moral servitude."[8] This confuses the inmate even more. He also experiences "deculturation"— the loss of or failure to acquire habits needed to survive in the wider society.[9] No wonder then that the mental patient becomes more deviant, and more incapacitated for life outside the asylum.

Goffman's exercise in participant observation (he served as assistant to the hospital's athletic director) had an enormous impact. His work was interpreted to mean that hospitals were responsible for most of the symptoms of their patients. It followed that eliminating mental hospitals would markedly improve their condition. The simple point raised by Martin Roth and Jerome Kroll highlighting the fallacy of the theory did not occur to those who rallied behind it: "If institutionalization created the schizophrenia-like picture of apathy, then prisoners and chronic schizophrenics would closely resemble each other after five to ten years of confinement."[10]

Actually Goffman was more cautious than most of those who quoted him. He writes: "Nor in citing the limitations of the service model do I mean to claim that I can suggest some better way of handling persons called mental patients." If all mental hospitals were closed down today, "tomorrow relatives, police, and judges would raise a clamor for new ones; and these true clients of the mental hospital would demand an institution to satisfy their needs."[11] But if Goffman did not know how to get rid of mental hospitals—he goes so far as to say that without some functional equivalent, it is hard to see how we could maintain a social order[12]—it was clear to him that they served no good purpose for their ostensible beneficiary, the patient.

By the time *Asylums* came out in 1961, the phenothiazines had revolutionized hospital treatment nationwide. In May 1954 Thorazine appeared on the market and within eight months had been administered to over two million patients. In 1955, when Goffman began his field work, New York became the first state to adopt a complete program of treatment with neuroleptic drugs in all its hospitals. Daniel Patrick Moynihan writes that he was present at the meeting in Governor Averell Harriman's office when it was decided to provide the new drugs to all patients system-wide.

> [I]n the spring of 1955, Harriman's Budget Director, Paul H. Appleby brought the new Commissioner of Mental Hygiene, Dr. Paul Hoch, in to see the Governor. I was in the room and was—I like to think—dimly

aware that something important was happening. Hoch reported that something called tranquillizers had been developed, that this seemed to work on experimental groups, and thus he wanted money to start using them on all patients, system-wide. Harriman was awfully tight with money. $1.5 million was involved. But he trusted Appleby and made the bet. (He would later explain that he was, after all, an investment banker.)[13]

Yet there is no mention of the phenothiazines in *Asylums*. Several articles by Szasz published between 1956 and 1960 are quoted liberally: Goffman does not ignore everything that happened after his stay in St. Elizabeth's. But, for him, the truly watershed pharmacological development might just as well not have happened.

Goffman ignores the neuroleptic drugs because they reinforce the medical model that he discards. Like Szasz, he seems to consider treatment a species of torture, an assault on the patient's physical integrity. This means that, for all his astute perceptions of patterns of interaction and the "underlife" of the institution (probably as accurate today as they were thirty years ago), Goffman has no sense of where the institution is going. He has no inkling that, within a short time, St. Elizabeth's will shrink dramatically in size. If he had recognized mental illness as a medical disease, he would have understood the importance of the new drugs, and seen the potential for the changes ahead.

Thomas Scheff and "Residual Rule-Breaking"

Goffman, primarily interested in studying forms of face-to-face interaction, soon moved on from the mental hospital. Sociologist Thomas Scheff, on the other hand, has built his entire highly successful career (he has edited a number of major sociological journals[14]) on the basis of bestowing academic legitimacy on anti-psychiatry.

Scheff's *Being Mentally Ill* first came out in 1966; a major new edition was published in 1984. Scheff defines mental illness as "residual rule-breaking." After crime, perversion, drunkenness, bad manners, there are always those diverse grab-bag violations for which the culture has no explicit label—the "residual rules" broken by those deemed mentally ill. Scheff further declares that "relative to the rate of treated mental illness, the rate of unrecorded residual rule-breaking is extremely high."[15]

Scheff (like Goffman) makes the crucial assumption that the amount of unrecognized ("unlabeled") mental illness is very high in proportion to the amount of behavior that becomes labeled. After all, if a relatively small number of people display strange behavior and are duly labeled mentally ill, there is not much reason to develop elaborate theories. Scheff cites as his basis for making this assumption the 1962 Midtown Manhattan study mentioned earlier, which had found 80% of the population to be psychiatrically impaired. Scheff further assumes that the labeling process was arbitrary, with some families demanding hospitalization for behavior that others easily tolerated.[16]

Given these assumptions, Scheff poses what he sees as the crucial question: Why do a small percentage of residual rule-breakers go on to careers as mental patients? His answer: the accident of labeling. Those brought by their families or other authorities into the purview of official agencies of control and treatment for so-called mental illness are stigmatized and isolated, committed and treated. Says Scheff: "Residual deviance may be stabilized if it is defined to be evidence of mental illness and/or the deviant is placed in a deviant status, and begins to play the role of the mentally ill."[17]

How does the deviant know how to play such a role? Scheff tells us that we have all learned how to do so in childhood from stereotyped imagery on the mass media.[18] But, as Roth and Kroll point out:

> It has never been explained by the social labelling theorists how people who do not know how to act in socially appropriate roles in the first place and are unable to behave according to normal social expectations become so proficient in sensing, learning and performing the deviant role that society suddenly expects of the "insane." If they are so adept at conforming to the roles assigned by society to the insane, imitating the conduct expected of those to be judged as cases of schizophrenic or manic illness, why could they not have learned socially appropriate roles in the first place?[19]

Scheff leaves such mysteries unresolved. He never says outright there is no such thing as mental illness. But he calls labeling theory the "antithesis" of the medical model and says the very term mental illness is "obfuscating for research and most other purposes."[20] Moreover, Scheff's remedy has a distinctly Szaszian flavor. It is to "normalize" rather than treat the illness, which means denying the reality of the illness on the assumption that if it is ignored it will go away.

The solution to schizophrenia, then, is not to study the malfunctioning brain, but the labelers. We should be investing our money in studying the "stereotypes" deployed by the allegedly normal. If labeling is to end, says Scheff, we must seek its roots not just in social structure but in individual psychology. One root is the repression of emotions:

decrease repression and individuals may feel less compelled to label others.[21]

Labeling theorist Kai Erickson has a yet more sinister view of the labeling process, for he views deviance as something society *needs* to maintain its stability. Arguing that deviant behavior enhances social stability by showing us "the difference between kinds of experience which belong within the group and kinds of experience which belong outside it," Erickson says there is an active recruitment process as "society as a whole actively tries to promote this resource."[22]

The radical countercultural assumptions sometimes break through the sociological veneer. In the 1984 edition of his work,[23] Scheff writes: "[T]he evaluation of conventional sanity as desirable and 'mental disease' (e.g., schizophrenia) as undesirable should be reversed."[24] In lines that could as easily have been penned by Laing twenty years earlier, Scheff declares: "Perhaps the time has come to consider the possibility that the reality that the so-called schizophrenics are out of touch with is so appalling that their view of the world may be more supportive to life than conventional reality."[25]

While criticizing psychiatrists for overextending their jurisdiction, labeling sociologists have shown marked tendencies toward hegemony themselves. Scheff is eager to apply labeling theory to international relations: to use "the kind of conceptualization of the status dynamics between nations that has been discussed here for mental illness."[26]

"Moral Imprisonment"

Nor were sociologists the only academics in the 1960s building reputations by assaulting the distinction between sanity and madness. Revisionist historians of social welfare turned traditional perspectives upside down, arguing that what appeared to be progress in the care of madness was in fact retrogression. Sociologists had dissolved the category of madness by treating it as the product of social labeling; there now arose those who affirmed the existence of madness, but claimed it was the *equal* of sanity, that unreason had as much dignity, vitality, and worth as reason. In this view, widely acclaimed for its alleged profundity, the original guilt lay with those who sought to convert the mad to reason.

It had been generally assumed that treatment of the mentally ill had become more humane in the two hundred years since Philippe Pinel, in the famous image, struck the restraints from fifty-three lunatics loaded with chains and shackled to walls and floor in the cells at La

Bicêtre asylum in 1793. Americans looked with pride upon Dorothea Dix, the frail schoolteacher who, beginning in the 1840s, singlehandedly moved the conscience of the nation (and several foreign nations) to erect state hospitals in the place of jails and almshouses for the insane.

In *Madness and Civilization,* published in 1961 (and translated into English in 1965), French historian and philosopher Michel Foucault turned this assumption on its ear. In instituting the famed "moral treatment" that sought to cure the mentally ill through firmness, kindness, education, and work, Pinel in France and Walter Tuke in England had *not* inaugurated a more humane era in the treatment of the mentally ill. Quite the contrary, said Foucault. Moral treatment was the cruelest and most insidious regimen of all. Chained though the madman had been earlier, he had been spiritually free, allowed his own voice and mode of perception. For Foucault, the new system rested on a "gigantic moral imprisonment," as wardens imposed their own morality upon the hapless psyche of their victims. There would be no escape—not even into madness. The new asylums instilled anxiety and guilt, substituting for "the free terror of madness the stifling anguish of responsibility; fear no longer reigned on the other side of the prison gates, it now raged under the seals of conscience."[27]

As John Wing has noted, Foucault saw madness as a form of opposition to *established* reason, possessing no less value and legitimacy. According to Foucault, prior to the rational-industrial era, Madness and Reason engaged in equal dialogue. But while madness may have been used as a literary device in the Renaissance, it is doubtful those suffering from severe mental illness fared better as a result, any more than when the counterculture of the 1960s celebrated madness as a rational alternative to "the establishment."

Foucault's theories rapidly became integrated into the anti-psychiatric canon. A young Communist-turned-anarchist (*Madness and Civilization* was his doctoral dissertation), Foucault suited perfectly the New Left *Weltanschauung.* "It is possible," said Foucault in a 1971 interview, "that the rough outline of a future society is supplied by the recent experiences with drugs, sex, communes, other forms of consciousness, and other forms of individuality." Foucault emphasized that the goal of his prison work was not to extend rights, but "to question the social and moral distinction between the innocent and the guilty."[28] Similarly, his writings on madness boldly equated sanity and madness.

A series of revisionist histories of the asylum followed, both in Europe and the United States, mixing in varying proportions Marxist theory, anti-psychiatry, and sociological notions concerning the madness-engendering institution. In 1969, Klaus Doerner in Germany published *Madmen and the Bourgeoisie,* purporting to show how mental hospitals had been used from the seventeenth century onward to suppress misfits and political dissidents. Some English and U.S. writers portrayed a whole panoply of nineteenth-century institutions, from the penitentiary to the poorhouse to the asylum, as capitalism's method of coercing and disciplining an unwilling work force.

The most influential study in this country was David Rothman's *The Discovery of the Asylum,* published in 1971. Ostensibly more moderate, Rothman took a curious position. He dismissed the view of the asylum as a tool of capitalist control as "too narrow."[29] But rather than starting with an examination of the reformers and their perspective, which would have emphasized their benevolent aims, Rothman worked backward from the untoward consequences to question their assumptions. Rothman notes that we look back "on the discoverers of the asylum with pride, placing them in our pantheon of reformers. We applaud the promoters of change, and are horrified with the result of their efforts."[30]

Rothman seems to hold the reformers at least partly responsible for the fate of their designs. They should have foreseen what would happen.

> The reformers' original doctrines were especially liable to abuse, their emphasis on authority, obedience, and regularity turning all too predictably into a mechanical application of discipline. And by incarcerating the deviant and dependent, and defending the step with hyperbolic rhetoric, they discouraged—really eliminated—the search for other solutions that might have been less susceptible to abuse.[31]

(Rothman does not specify what these solutions might have been, given the absence of any effective medical treatments in the nineteenth century.) The chief hopeful lesson of the nineteenth-century institution, according to Rothman, was that since it had been created by one generation, it could be eliminated by another.[32]

The Rosenhan Study

By the beginning of the 1970s, then, the anti-psychiatric case drew the support of a number of theorists from an array of disciplines, whose arguments, however fallacious, by mutually reinforcing one another, became overpowering. All that anti-psychiatry lacked was a study to provide empirical proof of its contentions. In 1973 *Science* published a report on an unusual experiment that clinched the anti-psychiatric argument for its advocates and gave it credibility among those who might normally have been skeptical. Indeed, that article, "On Being Sane in Insane Places," although the work of a psychologist, is probably the single most-quoted study in psychiatry over the last generation.

In undertaking the study, David L. Rosenhan, then professor of psychology at Stanford University, was influenced by Szasz, Goffman, Scheff, and Laing, all of whom he cites for their view that "psychiatric diagnoses . . . are in the minds of the observers and are not valid summaries of characteristics displayed by the observed." He contrasts this with the traditional psychiatric view that "patients present symptoms, that those symptoms can be categorized, and implicitly, that the sane are distinguishable from the insane."[33]

Rosenhan set out to perform a real-life experiment to resolve the dispute in favor of one or the other perspective. He would have normal people apply for admission to psychiatric hospitals and then see what happened. As Rosenhan saw it:

> If the sanity of such pseudopatients were always detected, there would be prima facie evidence that a sane individual can be distinguished from the insane context in which he is found. . . . If, on the other hand, the sanity of the pseudopatients were never discovered . . . such an unlikely outcome would support the view that psychiatric diagnosis betrays little about the patient but much about the environment in which an observer finds himself."[34]

Rosenhan sent eight pseudopatients (among them were three psychologists, a pediatrician, a psychiatrist, a painter, and a housewife) to gain admission to twelve different hospitals in five states on the East and West coasts. Each pseudopatient was to come to the hospital admission office complaining that he had been hearing voices. Asked what the voices said, the "patient" was to say they were unclear but seemed to be saying "empty," "hollow," and "thud." Apart from falsifying name, occupation, and employment, the patient was to report his life history truthfully. Immediately upon admission, the patient was to cease simulating any symptoms of abnormality.

The hospital staffs failed the test miserably, from the psychiatrists on down. Each patient was admitted without difficulty, receiving a diagnosis of schizophrenia except in one case, where, with identical symptoms, the individual was diagnosed as manic-depressive. Once in, the patients were never found out. Even the pseudopatients' constant notetaking did not make the staff wary: it too was interpreted as an aspect of their pathology. "Patient engages in writing behavior" was the daily nursing comment on one of the pseudopatients. The only people who detected the deception were the real patients. A substantial number challenged the pseudopatient: "You're not crazy. You're a journalist, or a professor (referring to the continual note-taking). You're checking up on the hospital." Patients were kept from seven to fifty-two days (the average was nineteen days) and all were discharged "in remission."[35]

What the pseudopatients recorded bore out the Goffman thesis of mental hospitals as agents of depersonalization and dehumanization. The pseudopatients found themselves powerless and invisible. ("A nurse unbuttoned her uniform to adjust her brassiere in the presence of an entire ward of viewing men. One did not have the sense that she was being seductive. Rather she didn't notice us. A group of staff persons might point to a patient in the dayroom and discuss him animatedly, as if he were not there.") The more status the staff person had, the less contact he had with patients. The mean amount of daily contact a patient had with psychiatrists, psychologists, residents, and physicians combined was 6.8 minutes. The nurses spent the overwhelming proportion of their time in the "staff cage."[36] Without doubt, Rosenhan's experiment proved that some hospitals were abominably run.

Rosenhan devised yet another method to show the unreliability and lack of validity of psychiatric diagnosis. He set out to discover if the tendency to diagnose the sane as insane could be reversed. The staff at a research and teaching hospital, which had heard about the results of the experiment and doubted such an error could occur in their hospital, were informed that at some time during the next three months, one or more pseudopatients would seek to be admitted into the hospital. Each staff member was asked to rate each patient who presented himself for admission according to the likelihood he was a pseudopatient. Judgments were obtained on 193 patients who were admitted for psychiatric treatment. While nurses and attendants were more likely to suspect pseudopatients than psychiatrists, twenty-three patients were considered suspect by at least one psychiatrist.[37] In fact, all were genuine patients, since Rosenhan had sent no pseudopatients to that hospital.

In the most charitable estimation, this was scarcely psychiatry's finest hour. Most psychiatrists waxed indignant, arguing the study only proved that psychiatrists, like other doctors (and people in general) could be conned by individuals out to make fools of them. But as John Wing has pointed out, if the conspirators really did confine their faking to one abnormal experience, this made the diagnosis of schizophrenia indefensible. Admitting them into the hospital was equally so, since treatment, given the minimal symptom reported, could equally well have been given outside.[38]

For Rosenhan, his study validated the entire anti-psychiatric case. In his view, the study showed that psychiatrists could not distinguish the sane from the insane. Rosenhan raised the frightening specter of massive false imprisonment. "How many people, one wonders, are sane but not recognized as such by our psychiatric institutions?" Were sane people being driven insane by the hospitals to which they were wrongly committed? "How many patients," Rosenhan asked "might be 'sane' outside the psychiatric hospital but seem insane in it . . . because they are responding to a bizarre setting?"[39]

In Rosenhan's view, labeling theorists were proved right, and traditional psychiatry wrong. Rosenhan reports that his pseudopatients found that bizarre behavior constituted only a small fraction of the behavior of their fellow inmates. What sense did it make then to label them as schizophrenic? "The sane are not 'sane' all of the time," says Rosenhan. Ordinary people become depressed. "If it makes no sense to label ourselves permanently depressed on the basis of an occasional depression, then it takes better evidence than is presently available to label all patients insane or schizophrenic on the basis of bizarre behaviors or cognitions."[40]

The impact of the Rosenhan study on the credibility of psychiatry for the general public was devastating. The public was already skeptical of psychiatric diagnoses from the familiar spectacle of psychiatrists testifying for opposing sides in the courtroom. The anti-psychiatrists could now claim their case was "proved." A scientific study in the premier journal of the scientific community had shown psychiatrists did not know the sane from the insane. Thus there *was* no real difference. Worse still, the experiences of segregation, powerlessness, depersonalization, mortification, and dehumanization that both Goffman and the pseudopatients sent by Rosenhan had found endemic to mental hospitals were enough to drive a normal person insane.

But, in fact, both Rosenhan and those who seized upon the study totally misinterpreted its meaning. Rosenhan had started out by asking "If sanity and insanity exist, how shall we know them?" His conclusion was that since psychiatrists could not distinguish between those feigning symptoms and those who really had them, insanity did not exist. But all the study showed was that psychiatrists could easily be fooled; once fooled, psychiatrists and staff could interpret all behavior in psychiatric terms. As Rosenhan put it: "The hospital itself imposes a special environment in which the meanings of behavior can easily be misunderstood."

The study shed light on the limitations of hospitals and psychiatrists, but none on the nature or reality of insanity. Rosenhan sent no patients feigning symptoms of heart disease or muscular dystrophy or epilepsy to internists; would he have concluded, had they been fooled, that this proved the nonexistence of these illnesses?

We noted that Rosenhan cited Szasz, Goffman, Scheff, and Laing, and that in fact he saw his experiment as a "test" of their theories. This illustrates an important point: those opposed to the medical model have drawn extensively upon each other's writing, claiming it as support for their own conclusions. Within a cozy, incestuous anti-psychiatric universe, Scheff draws liberally upon the writing of Szasz, Laing, Lemert, Foucault, Goffman, and Rosenhan; Laing draws on Szasz, Scheff, Goffman, Bateson, and Foucault; Goffman draws upon Szasz and Bateson; Leifer draws upon Szasz, Foucault, and Goffman. (Szasz is the only one to move out of the magic circle. While he quotes several of the labeling sociologists, in his early works he relied chiefly on language theorist Gilbert Ryle and, more recently, has depended upon pathologists— totally misinterpreting their findings.) The interdisciplinary influence and cross-fertilization were crucial to the success of anti-psychiatry. The misconceptions of one theorist underpinned and became "evidence" for the misstatements of the next.

The tremendously subversive implications of these ideas would only become fully apparent in the 1980s as insanity, chaos, and disorder came to occupy, physically, our public places. Public authorities were paralyzed. Their agents could not intervene to prevent appalling human degradation. To exert authority and force crazy people, however needy, into treatment was, or so the public was told, an unconscionable repression of human rights: the mad—if indeed there was such a thing as madness—had a civil right to their own reality, their alternative "lifestyle." Intervention was legitimate, said lawyers and judges, only when someone was an "imminent danger" to himself or others, and this was defined so narrowly that the individual had to be on the verge of suicide or murder.

Nor could police intervene to enforce standards of decent behavior in the public domain. "Homeless advocates"—supported by the courts—insisted the plight of these people was purely an economic one, for which the housed were responsible. A society that failed to provide jobs and homes could not take away the right of those in need to live and panhandle on subways and sidewalks, in parks, and transport terminals, whatever the impact on others who used these places. Repeatedly, judges insisted it was therapeutic for people to be forced to confront the face of poverty.

An advocate like Mitch Snyder, although he encountered the reality of mental illness daily in his huge Washington, D.C. shelter, hewed to the ideological orthodoxy of the 1960s. In their book *Homelessness in America,* he and Mary Ellen Hombs head the chapter on mental illness with the quote: "A psychotic episode is a socio-political event and not a medical event." In a melange of labeling theory and New Left radicalism, they claim that people are put in mental hospitals because they have "violated the ritual ceremonies that make up society's 'norms' as agreed upon by those who prevail (economically, politically, socially and otherwise)."[41]

In the intellectual confusion, American society found itself helpless to deal with an enormous social problem destroying the quality of life of its cities. The writer of a letter to the editor of *Commentary* declared: "We are losing the clarity of distinction between what is permissible and what is not, not only in the ethical sense of the distinction between good and bad, but in our very perception of reality. . . . The most pervasive and profound idea of the last three hundred years is that everything is permitted, and this includes being crazy."[42] This was of course arguably the most important and destructive legacy of the 1960s.

Radical Therapy and the Ex-patient Movement

Not surprisingly, a number of ex-patients responded enthusiastically to the anti-psychiatry movement. In daily life, they were shunned and stigmatized. Here was an ideology that cast them as romantic figures combating oppression, individuals whose perceptions of the world had equal if not greater validity than those of "sane" society. As anti-psychiatry gathered force, mental patient liberation groups sprang up. The Insane Liberation Front began in Portland, Oregon in 1970, followed by the Mental Patients Liberation Project in New York City, the Mental Patients Liberation Front in Boston, and the Mental Patients' Association in Vancouver, all in 1971. *Madness Network News,* the movement's journal, began publication in 1972.

As early as 1963, Thomas Szasz had called for the creation of such groups. He had noted that "mental hospital patients have consistently failed to hang together. As a result, they have indeed hanged separately." The solution was "psychotherapeutic efforts with mental patients." Such efforts, "directed at educating them to revolt for independence—might yet instill in them the understanding, and the hope, that their rights may be secured not only by assimilation into the more privileged majority but also by effective protest." Mental patients had to be inspired "to acquire the spirit of liberty and, indeed, of revolt."[43]

Such "psychotherapeutic efforts with mental patients" were not long in coming, although the libertarian Szasz could not have wholly approved the form they took. In the late 1960s an offshoot of SDS was established called Psychologists for a Democratic Society which published a journal called *Radical Therapist* (later to be called *Rough Times* and later still *State and Mind*). These practitioners saw themselves, according to an anthology produced by the *Rough Times* staff, as "part of a movement to build a revolutionary new world."[44]

There were heated debates among radical therapists as to whether therapy was appropriate at all. Some felt those labeled mentally ill should not be seen as sick, but as "oppressed people who must be liberated." Therapy, they argued, falsely transformed the sickness of society into the sickness of an individual, *preventing* the recognition of oppression.[45] Others condoned therapy only if done according to the "right" principles. Radical psychologists Michael Glenn and Richard Kunnes found the guide for the new therapy in "Marxist-Lenin-Mao Tse-Tung thought applied with a sound understanding of the principle of contradiction."[46] Phil Brown, part of the *Rough Times* group, advocated consciousness-raising collectives for those termed mentally ill, which would build on the "partial" contribution of anti-psychiatry to go forward to confront "the capitalist monster."[47]

While the contribution of radical therapists in the United States was chiefly rhetorical, in Europe the mixture of left-wing politics and anti-psychiatry proved explosive. In the venerable university town of Heidelberg, a Socialist Patients Collective, formed in 1970, rapidly transformed itself from a patients group to a political organization. It propounded such doctrines as "illness and capital are identical: the intensity and extent of illness multiply in proportion to the accumulation process of dead capital."[48] In her 1988 book *The Europeans,* Jane Kramer points out that most of the "second generation" of Baader-Meinhof terrorists came out of this group. She writes:

> They followed a psychiatrist guru by the name of Wolfgang Huber—a kind of Leninist R. D. Laing, who convinced the people in his charge that the society was their real disease, and apparently inspired a lot of them to try to cure it.[49]

In 1972 the collective was broken up by the police. Radical "therapists" Wolfgang and Ursula Huber received sentences of four and a half years imprisonment for activity in a "criminal association."[50]

In Italy, anti-psychiatric psychiatrist Franco Basaglia founded Psichiatria Democratica in 1974. With the backing of the Communist Party he secured passage in 1978 of Law 180, which banned any new admissions to state mental hospitals. Basaglia made clear that his purpose was at least in part political: on the street, mental patients would be a living example of the contradictions inherent in capitalism. According to Basaglia:

> The project [creating a new awareness of the social oppression inherent in mental illness] was therefore more akin to the political struggle which broke out in other areas of social life during the 1960s, breaking up established institutions and exposing their shortcomings, than to avant garde psychiatric experiments. . . . [51]

In the United States relations between politically radical therapists and the ex-patient movement grew increasingly uneasy. Initially there was close cooperation, with therapists traveling to state hospitals on weekends to organize the wards. In Boston, the Mental Patients Liberation Front first met in the offices of the *Radical Therapist*.[52] Of the initial group of eight editors of *Madness Network News,* the national voice of the ex-patient movement, six were radical therapists. The first national Conference on Human Rights and Psychiatric Oppression, held in 1973 at the University of Detroit, also included both sympathetic professionals and ex-patients.

But while many ex-patients subscribed to the anti-capitalist sentiments of their New Left therapist-mentors, primarily they saw themselves engaged in a civil rights struggle. Just as homosexuals, blacks, Hispanics, and women sought equal rights and recognition, so mental patients sought equal status— in this case, for their alternative perceptions of reality. As recovered ex-patient Judi Chamberlin put it: "We must work to eliminate the racism, sexism and mentalism which makes lesser people of us all."[53] Stereotyping people as mentally ill was "sane chauvinism." Said Chamberlin: "Defining the rebellious person as sick invalidates his or her perception of the situation. And the testimony of the 'sane' parties to the situation is accepted as reality."[54]

Anti-Psychiatric Perspectives Advance

Novels and films were vital in introducing the anti-psychiatric perspective to the general public. We have already mentioned Kesey's best-selling *One Flew Over the Cuckoo's Nest,* later an Academy Award winning film. Michael Fleming and Roger Manvell, authors of a book on the portrayal of insanity in feature films, claim that the movie version of *Cuckoo's Nest,* made over a decade after the novel, displayed greater recognition of the reality of madness in the patients than the book.[55] But this is questionable. Certain typical countercultural features are gone. There is no "conspiring Combine," and the psychedelic motif of the novel is absent. (Kesey actually sued the film's producers on the grounds they had neglected to show the responsibility of American institutions for the condition of their victims.[56]) But the messages that what patients really need is freedom, that psychiatric treatments are clinically worthless gratuitous cruelty remain. McMurphy, as a result of hospital "treatments," becomes a vegetable who can only be freed by being murdered—an act of kindness by Chief Broom under the circumstances.

The posthumous publication in 1972 of the autobiography of the film star Frances Farmer, *Will There Ever Be a Morning?,* buttressed the anti-psychiatric view. A leading lady in the 1930s and mistress of left-wing playwright Clifford Odets, Frances is portrayed as a high-strung young woman railroaded by her domineering mother into a Washington state hospital, where for a period of eight years she was beaten, raped, and tortured by electroshock treatments. Reporter William Arnold's 1978 book *Shadowland,* on which the movie *Frances* was based, depicted Farmer's hospitalization as the result of a McCarthyite conspiracy to punish her for her left-wing politics. Arnold (and the movie) threw in a lobotomy for good measure although Farmer, scarcely reticent about the mistreatment she suffered in the hospital, never mentioned this in her autobiography.[57]

Some feminist authors integrated anti-psychiatry with women's liberation. In her widely read 1972 book, *Women and Madness,* Phyllis Chesler complained that anti-psychiatry missed part of the picture, remaining "unaware of the universal and objective oppression of women and of its particular relation to madness in women."[58] Women who refuse to act out male-prescribed roles were called insane; those who angrily reject such roles "are isolated, strait-jacketed, sedated and given shock therapy."[59]

But how then is madness in men to be explained? According to Chesler, "What we consider 'madness,' whether it appears in women or in men, is either the acting out of the devalued female role or the total or partial rejection of one's sex-role stereotype."[60] Men who act like women and women who refuse to act like women are both labeled "mad." While Chesler is pessimistic about changing "in our lifetime" what oppression has wrought, her ultimate remedy for mental illness seems to be female empowerment.

All these cultural messages had a definite impact. By 1986, *Science* reported the results of a poll that found 55% of the public did not believe there was such a thing as mental illness.[61]

Psychiatry Finds No Defenders

Unbelievably, as the anti-psychiatric attack mounted, no one spoke up against it. The families knew that mental illness was real, none better. But in the 1960s and early 1970s, they were in the closet with their shame and guilt. Freudian psychiatrists blamed them for the illness; they not only devalued and demoralized but actually demonized families, especially mothers. The public also condemned the whole family as tainted. Much of the families' energies then were directed at keeping the presence of their mentally ill relative secret. If the latter remained out of sight in a mental institution, that eased the task.

Patients? Those who had recovered and were satisfied with the treatment they had received kept quiet. So did those who functioned, with medication, well enough to "pass." Their jobs and social relationships could be jeopardized if it were discovered they had ever been mentally ill. Those who remained ill more often than not denied the illness. By default, the role of spokesman for the mentally ill devolved upon a handful of recovered ex-patients whose bitterness motivated them to step forward.

That left only the psychiatrists to defend their profession. But psychiatry made unconscionably little effort to counter the onslaught. Indeed, most psychiatrists did not even seem to be aware there *was* an onslaught. Incredibly, in 1976, after more than a decade of anti-psychiatric attack, the American Psychiatric Association, at its annual meeting, praised the fiercely anti-psychiatric *Cuckoo's Nest* for its "timely relevance" and expressed "hope that it will break down some of the barriers that have made mental disease a hidden quality [sic] in American culture."[62]

Many young psychiatrists, in training when Szasz and Laing began to publish, were impressed with the revolutionary new ideas. Fuller Torrey says that his fellow residents in psychiatry at Stanford were, like himself, profoundly influenced by Szasz. (Torrey also points out that many of these young psychiatrists never saw seriously ill patients.) Laing's coterie at Kingsley Hall included a number of American doctors inspired by his ideas, among them Joseph Berke, Morton Schatzman,

Joseph Lins, and Leon Redler. In *Atlantic* in 1971 a young psychiatrist named James S. Gordon, who had just been appointed chief resident on a psychiatric ward in New York, wrote a reverent article on Laing, describing how deeply he had been affected by reading *The Divided Self.*

All this helps to explain why psychiatrists did not react more vigorously to the anti-psychiatric onslaught. A great many did not feel personally affected. Few seriously mentally ill patients could afford to see psychiatrists in private practice. They could not hold minimal jobs, let alone function in positions that would enable them to pay psychiatric bills. The state hospitals, which in the 1960s still cared for most of the severely disabled, then as now depended upon foreign doctors, many of whom spoke little English. (The situation has worsened since; the state hospitals have been able to hold on to these doctors only because they are not licensed to practice elsewhere.)

But most important, American psychiatry lost faith in its institutions. The great surge of asylum building in the nineteenth century had not come at the behest of psychiatrists (or alienists, as they were known then), but in response to the vision of a layman, Dorothea Dix, who had promised they would provide a rapid cure for mental illness. Not only was this promise not fulfilled, but the huge overcrowded system seemed incapable of providing even decent custodial care. As a result, the blows directed against institutions by anti-psychiatrists, particularly labeling sociologists, struck a responsive chord in psychiatrists, even the relatively small proportion who still worked in state mental hospitals.

This loss of faith explains the rapid dissolution of the existing system of care, despite the fact that some psychiatrists did document the limitations of drug therapy and the continued need for institutions. In a 1962 article studying the impact of the new psychotropic drugs in New York State (which had pioneered in their wide use), Deputy Mental Health Commissioner Henry Brill and statistician Robert Patton warned of the "dangers in overoptimism since this could lead to premature demobilization of our mental hospital facilities."[63] They estimated that state hospital populations could only be expected to decrease temporarily at the rate of 1% to 1.5% a year for a decade and then reach a plateau, as chronic cases continued to accumulate. With prescience, they warned:

> Any advance beyond the present rate seems to require either a newer and better technology or a newer administrative and organizational approach and it is to be hoped that no type of innovation will be applied on a large scale without provision for critical and adequate evaluation.[64]

Precisely what they warned against happened. Without evaluation or planning, without better drugs or a better "organizational approach," hospitals were emptied pell-mell. Indeed, efforts at the time to develop a better organizational approach were abruptly jettisoned. Psychiatrist Fritz Freyhan has described a comprehensive psychiatric center that he developed with associates at St. Elizabeth's Hospital in Washington, D.C., combining hospital and outpatient facilities to provide continuity of treatment. But "this kind of realistic clinical thinking," writes Freyhan, "had no chance in this country" for those in charge were simply intent on shutting down hospital beds.[65] Similarly ignored were the recommendations for transformation and renewal of the state hospital system by the congressionally funded Joint Commission on Mental Illness and Health.

Those within psychiatry who suggested reform of state hospitals were voices in the wilderness. The only possible obstacles to dismantling the institutional system—the psychiatrists and the families of the mentally ill who saw value in institutions as asylums—turned out to be no barrier at all. The mental health system proved a pushover. The apparently formidable institutional edifice of laws and hospitals and psychiatric authority crumbled with scarcely a sign of struggle.

PART II

*The Vision of
Community Care*

Chapter 3

Community Mental Health Centers

The Dream

IF psychiatrists abandoned asylums without a struggle, it was not because they no longer believed in psychiatry. Rather, they thought asylums were simply not *needed*. Psychiatry was in the grip of its own social delusion, which paradoxically would reinforce anti-psychiatry. Post-World War II American psychiatry was seized with megalomania. Intellectual leaders within the profession actually believed that they could end not only the scourge of mental illness but all social ills, from war to juvenile delinquency, through a new preventive community psychiatry. "They had lovely ideas," says sociologist Mort Wagenfeld, "that had absolutely no basis in reality."[1]

Many factors fostered psychiatry's delusion that preventive community psychiatry could eliminate mental illness. One was the conviction that there had to be an alternative to the thoroughly discredited state hospital. Shortly after World War II, a series of shattering exposés on state hospitals appeared. In 1945, Mike Gorman, just out of the army and a fledgling reporter for *The Daily Oklahoman,* embarked on a campaign, as he later put it, to wave "the reek and stench of our state mental hospitals under the public's nostrils."[2] In May 1946, *Life* magazine ran Albert Q. Maisel's withering report on the conditions in these institutions. In 1948 both Albert Deutsch's *Shame of the States* (like

67

Maisel's, accompanied by photos) and Gorman's *Oklahoma Attacks Its Snake Pits* were published.

These journalists compared some psychiatric wards to Nazi extermination camps, which newsreel footage had freshly seared in public memory. Maisel compared state mental hospitals to "concentration camps on the Belsen pattern." Similarly, Albert Deutsch wrote of

> scenes that rivaled the horrors of the Nazi concentration camps—hundreds of naked mental patients herded into huge, barnlike, filth-infested wards, in all degrees of deterioration, untended and untreated, stripped of every vestige of human decency, many in states of semi-starvation.[3]

The timing of the wave of exposés was not accidental. During the war, conscientious objectors (or "conchies" as they were familiarly called) were assigned to alternative service as attendants in state mental hospitals. The hospitals were in desperate straits. Funding for them had been cut in the Depression, and with the war, they lost most of their professional staff, especially psychiatrists, whose services were in high demand in the armed forces. Unlike the run-of-the-mill state hospital employees dependent on their jobs, the conchies were not disposed to remain silent about what they saw. They communicated with each other, assembled massive affidavits, and turned them over to politicians and journalists. By the end of the war, the conchies had formed their own network, which assembled over 2,000 eyewitness reports. Maisel quoted from some of them in his pioneering 1946 article.

Hoping that public indignation would force state legislatures to provide the funds to improve hospital conditions, psychiatrists corroborated the charges of the critics. Dr. Kenneth Appel, elected head of the American Psychiatric Association in 1953, drew attention to state hospitals in his presidential address: "Treatment can scarcely be said to exist for the majority. It is mostly care and custody. Mass methods, herding and regimentation, are the rule."[4] Even some of the hospital superintendents were outspoken. Dr. Mesrop Tarumianz, who for thirty years had presided over what Gorman called "one of the better state mental hospitals" (in Delaware), told a National Governor's Conference on Mental Health in 1954:

> Conditions in our state mental hospitals are rotten. For want of a more adequate word, and I don't know that I could find a more adequate word, I can only tell you the state mental hospital system stinks.[5]

Many were convinced the existing system was beyond reform. Gorman, who was to become a major figure in reshaping mental health policy as chairman of the National Mental Health Committee,[6] was among those who insisted it was necessary "to tear down the whole rotting structure and build afresh;" there was no possibility of preserving the state hospital "with its freightage of despair, defeatism, despondency, filth, futility and failure."[7] This view drew endorsement from the pinnacle of the psychiatric profession, when Dr. Harry Solomon said in his 1958 presidential address to the American Psychiatric Association:

[The state mental hospital] is antiquated, outmoded and rapidly becoming obsolete. We can still build them but we cannot staff them; and therefore we cannot make true hospitals of them. . . . I do not see how any reasonably objective view of our mental hospitals today can fail to conclude that they are bankrupt beyond remedy. I believe therefore that our large mental hospitals should be liquidated as rapidly as can be done in an orderly and progressive fashion.[8]

Faith in Psychiatry Grows

However negative they might be about the prospects for reforming mental asylums, psychiatrists in the 1950s had enormous faith in their own therapeutic powers and the need to exercise them in a much broader arena.

Psychiatry's status had gone up sharply during the war. At the battlefront, psychiatrists developed methods for treating servicemen suffering from "battle fatigue" quickly, and returning them to the front. Psychiatrists persuaded themselves—and others—that these methods could be carried over to treatment of the mentally ill, where they would prevent the development of chronic illness.[9] The war also suggested that vastly more people were psychiatrically impaired than hitherto realized: almost two million draftees were rejected for mental disorder or deficiency.[10] A study conducted in the 1950s in Stirling County, Nova Scotia, which concluded that only 17% of the population was mentally "well," lent added force to the view of endemic psychiatric illness. The equally misleading Midtown Manhattan study of 1962, mentioned earlier, appeared to validate the results of the Canadian study by coming up with almost the same figure, 18.5%, of mentally healthy individuals.[11] Even for those outside mental hospitals, the ministrations of psychiatrists appeared sorely needed.

The work of English psychiatrist Maxwell Jones seemed to prove that the kind of prompt, intensive treatment used at the front could be applied in mental hospitals. In April 1947 Jones opened an Industrial Neurosis Unit at Belmont Hospital in London in which he set out to create, as the title of his famous book put it, "The Therapeutic Community." The method involved restructuring the entire waking life of the patient, who was absorbed into a "Unit Community" that had its own distinctive staff-created culture. Group interaction and pressures enforced new social attitudes and a new level of performance.

Jones did not work with the most seriously ill, but with neurotic and character-disordered individuals who were unable to hold down jobs. He admitted, "We do not, however, accept cases which are frankly psychotic."[12] Nonetheless, Jones's work had a profound impact. It would lead some psychiatrists to focus upon "milieu therapy" within mental hospitals; others would draw from it lessons for a preventive community psychiatry outside hospital walls. As the foreword to Jones's book said, there was now the prospect of designing "a whole culture which will foster healthy personalities."[13]

The Revival of "Primary Prevention"

The idea of preventing mental illness through nurturing healthy personalities was not new. In *Nowhere to Go,* Dr. E. Fuller Torrey traces the origin of the preventive ethos to the turn of the century when William Crawford Gorgas eradicated yellow fever in the Panama Canal Zone, making prevention the dominant idea in American medicine.[14] Prevention became the dominant theme of the National Committee for Mental Hygiene (later the National Association for Mental Health) established by former mental patient Clifford Beers; its chief practical expression was the child guidance clinic. The hope was that treating emotional problems in children would stave off the development of mental illness later in life. But while a new population received mental health services in these clinics, there was no indication that they prevented the development of later psychotic illness. In any case, the first wave of preventive psychiatry had no impact on the mentally ill, who continued to be cared for in state mental hospitals.

The rebirth of community psychiatry, this time with profound consequences for the mentally ill, can be traced to the work of Erich Lindemann, who in 1943 studied bereavement reactions among the survivors of those killed in the Coconut Grove nightclub fire and established a community mental health program, the Wellesley Human

Relations Service, to implement his ideas for preventive intervention in crisis situations. It was Lindemann's disciple, Gerald Caplan, an English-trained psychoanalyst, who became the most influential theorist of preventive community psychiatry.[15] Like Lindemann, Caplan was a professor at Harvard, heading its School of Public Health's Community Mental Health Program.

The underlying problem in both the original and the second wave of community psychiatry was, as Torrey observes, that no one had the faintest idea how to prevent mental illness. Community psychiatrists misunderstood the nature of major mental illness as profoundly as the anti-psychiatrists who claimed it did not exist. They subscribed to the dominant Freudian orthodoxy of the time that mental illness was caused by pathological interpersonal relationships. Caplan and Lindemann were typical of Freudian-trained analysts of the period.[16]

Community psychiatry's major variation was in going beyond early childhood and the immediate family to explore the role of the broader community in allegedly producing mental illness. And while psychiatrists had focused on psychotherapy with the individual sick person, Caplan argued their task was to promote "mental health" in the entire community. Caplan explained:

> Primary prevention is a community concept. It does not seek to prevent a specific person from becoming sick. Instead, it seeks to reduce the risk for a whole population, so that, although some may become ill, their number will be reduced.[17]

How was this to be accomplished? In part, said Caplan, it was to be done by "modifying the network of emotional influences on an individual," in part by social action to obtain the "basic physical, psychosocial, and sociocultural supplies" necessary for mental health.[18] Caplan acknowledged that a psychiatrist's advice on social issues would be based on his political prejudices. Still, he believed the answer lay "in careful self-scrutiny and self-awareness," in "avoiding utopian efforts," and in "the restriction of social action to the righting of discrete, present wrongs."[19]

Others were less cautious. Psychiatrists at the University of Rochester, like Harvard a center for the new ideas, argued that only by changing pathogenic social institutions could the "flow of disorders" be cut down.[20] In 1962, even such a normally sober figure as Dr. Leon Eisenberg, then president of the American Orthopsychiatric Association, joined the social-action chorus: "As citizens, we bear a moral responsibility, because of our specialized knowledge, for political action to prevent socially induced psychiatric illness."[21]

For psychiatrists convinced of their special preventive mission, the task took on urgency in the 1960s when riots broke out in the black ghettos of American cities. Dr. Leonard Duhl, who became chief of planning at the National Institute of Mental Health (NIMH), described the city as an organism crying out for psychiatric intervention.

> The city . . . is in pain. It has symptoms that cry out for relief. They are the symptoms of anger, violence, poverty, and hopelessness. If the city were a patient, it would seek help. . . . The totality of urban life is the only rational focus for concern with mental illness. . . . Our problem now embraces all of society and we must examine every aspect of it to determine what is conducive to mental health.[22]

Not surprisingly, Duhl concluded "it is . . . the total society that needs a mental health treatment program."[23]

This was heady stuff, and there was little wonder psychiatrists were enthusiastic about community psychiatry as a way to move from the margins of medicine to a vanguard role in shaping society. Instead of patrolling the halls of remote state hospitals, if they followed Caplan's call, they would be coordinating the labors of "social scientists, economists, legislators, citizen leaders, and professional workers in the public health, welfare, religious and educational fields."[24]

Nor did there seem any reason to stop at the water's edge; psychiatrists were prepared to make the whole world well.[25] Dr. Harold Rome, who served as president of the American Psychiatric Association in 1965, used the language of community psychiatry in calling "no less than the entire world . . . a proper catchment area for present day psychiatry."[26] Psychiatry, wrote Rome, "need not be appalled by the magnitude of this task," for the same social conditions that

> display their pathology in the forms of mental illness . . . are expressed in the phenomena of discord, in wars big and little, in violence and ignorance, and in squalor and unemployment. All these complex elements that create anomie in a nation or a region or a ghetto or a family have to be seen as targets for active preventive psychiatry.[27]

Writing from the vantage of the 1980s, psychiatrist Donald Light aptly observes that psychiatry should have taken *itself* on as a patient. "Given the difficulty psychiatrists had in treating disturbed individuals, the assertion that it could also treat whole communities, carry out primary prevention, and eradicate mental illness was extraordinary."[28]

In retrospect, of course, the overweening—indeed ridiculous—pretensions of psychiatry reflected a utopian climate of thought within the social sciences as a whole: social ills from poverty to crime to racial prejudice were to be "socially engineered" out of existence.

The Joint Commission on Mental Illness and Health

Legislators and government officials had a more mundane interest in community psychiatry. State mental hospitals imposed an enormous and seemingly endless drain on state budgets. New York State in 1955 devoted 38% of its State's Purposes budget to pay for 90,000 resident patients in its state mental hospitals. Yet there seemed to be general agreement that these enormously expensive institutions were, as Mike Gorman put it, "abominable, undesirable and unfavorable to the recovery of patients."[29]

Gorman, for whom changing the mental health system had become a crusade, took a key role in mobilizing elected officials at both the state and federal level for undertaking a radically new approach. He persuaded a number of governors to call a Governors' Conference on Mental Health in 1954. Governor G. Mennen Williams of Michigan gave the opening address, in which he emphasized the need for change.

> [T]he cost of dealing with mental illness on the present basis is becoming too great to be borne. We simply cannot go on building more and more mental hospitals to house more and more patients. The burden upon taxpayers is already becoming intolerable, and there is no relief in sight.[30]

At the end of the conference, the governors adopted a ten-point set of recommendations, which focused on the need to prevent mental illness. However, a close reading of the recommendations indicates that what the governors had in mind was not "primary prevention" of the sort advocated by Caplan and his followers, but what psychiatrists call secondary and tertiary prevention. Secondary prevention refers to early treatment of mental illness, and tertiary prevention—which is not really prevention at all—is care of the chronically ill to minimize renewed psychotic episodes. Thus the recommendations identify "prevention" as requiring "facilities for early identification, for early treatment and for aftercare and supervision of those on leave from state hospitals."[31] The recommendations also called for increased research and training expenditures by states to find better treatments and to train more mental health professionals.[32]

The ferment caused even the president of the American Medical Association, traditionally little interested in mental illness, in his 1955 inaugural address to complain of hospitals in which the mentally ill "are virtually tossed on a human junk pile."[33] And Congress in that same year passed legislation requiring the National Institute of Mental Health to appoint a commission to reevaluate the nation's approach to mental illness. To conduct the study, for which Congress appropriated over a million dollars, NIMH selected the very group that had mobilized to lobby Congress for the legislation: the newly formed Joint Commission on Mental Illness and Health, which had been initiated by the American Medical Association and the American Psychiatric Association. NIMH chose psychiatrist Jack Ewalt, then Commissioner of Mental Health in Massachusetts, to head the commission's study.[34]

In *Nowhere to Go,* Fuller Torrey criticizes the Joint Commission report, *Action for Mental Health,* six years in the making, as "strange and confused," with something for everyone—"as if each of the forty-five individual members and thirty-six participating agencies had taken turns writing paragraphs."[35] His criticism is surprising, because the report did concentrate on the needs of the seriously mentally ill; had it been implemented, the worst public policy mistakes that ensued could have been avoided.

The report identified major mental illness as "the core problem and unfinished business of the mental health movement." While Mike Gorman, who took an active role in the commission, would later say that his "hidden agenda was to break the back of the state mental hospital,"[36] the Joint Commission report was not opposed to the *idea* of the hospital. On the contrary, it sought to transform and renew the state hospital system, making state hospitals, "in fact what they are now in name only—hospitals for mental patients."[37] No more state hospitals of over 1,000 beds were to be built and not a single patient was to be added to any existing hospital already housing 1,000 or more patients. The 1,000-bed limit was in itself a compromise, with many thinking this far too large. The theorists of "moral treatment" (an early nineteenth-century version of milieu therapy), whose ideas deeply influenced these would-be architects of a new system, had considered 200 beds an optimum size.[38]

In the model proposed by the Joint Commission, every patient would be treated where possible and for as long as possible in the psychiatric ward of a general hospital. If longer term care was necessary, he would be transferred to the small treatment-intensive hospital of no more than 1,000 beds. However, the Commission also recognized the continuing problem of providing care for chronic patients who failed to respond to treatment. The larger existing state hospitals should be converted into centers for the long-term and combined care of all chronic diseases, including mental illness.[39]

In addition the Joint Commission called for establishment of community mental health clinics, with one clinic for each 50,000 persons, which would serve as "a main line of defense in reducing the need of many persons with major mental illness for prolonged or repeated hospitalization." The principal functions of the clinic would be to care for persons with acute mental illness and to care for "incompletely recovered mental patients either short of admission to a hospital or following discharge from the hospital."[40] The report described the range of aftercare services, from halfway houses to social clubs to sheltered workshops, needed by mental patients—and the small numbers currently receiving such services.[41]

The Commission was emphatic in *rejecting* primary prevention. Primary prevention, said the report, "has remained largely an article of scientific faith rather than an applicable scientific truth." The efforts of the earlier mental hygiene movement had "diverted attention from the core problem of major mental illness. It is our purpose to redirect attention to the possibilities of improving the mental health of the mentally ill."[42] The mental health clinics were not even to engage in mental health education, which "should preferably be left to other agencies."[43]

The Commission urged the federal government to abandon its traditional insistence that services to the mentally ill were strictly a state responsibility and to provide funds to implement the report's recommendations. It urged that expenditures for public mental patient services be doubled in the next five years, and tripled in ten.[44]

Dissatisfaction with the Joint Commission Report

Not surprisingly, those in the vanguard of community psychiatry were unhappy with the report. Caplan wrote:

> I differ sharply from the point of view of the report of the Joint Commission. I believe that preventive psychiatry must include primary prevention as an essential ingredient and must promote mental health among members of the community who are currently not disordered, with the hope of reducing the risk that they will become disordered.[45]

Similarly, Emory Cowen, Elmer Gardner, and Melvin Zax, theorists of community psychiatry at the University of Rochester, accused the Joint Commission of "tunnel vision." They warned: "The overriding salience attributed by the report to the problems of major mental breakdown (i.e., psychosis) suggests a point of application in time for our mental health efforts, which may be much too late."[46]

More important, the leadership at NIMH was dissatisfied with the Joint Commission's emphasis on upgrading hospitals to a therapeutic level. Dr. Robert Felix, NIMH's director for its first two decades, was a major patron of preventive psychiatry.[47] Felix wrote the foreword to Caplan's *Principles of Preventive Psychiatry,* describing it as "not only a primer for the community mental health worker—it is a Bible."[48] In the Joint Commission Report, Felix charged, "considerably more attention could have been placed upon steps aimed at prevention of mental illness and upon maintenance of mental health."[49]

Felix was not alone in these views. Torrey points out that NIMH was enamored of preventive approaches from its inception in 1946.[50] By the late 1950s, there were more staff members at NIMH holding Master of Public Health degrees than in any other division of the Public Health Service.[51] Dr. Bertram Brown, who served as a deputy to Felix and became director of NIMH in 1970, says that at NIMH it was felt a radical departure was necessary[52]—a wholly new approach to treatment of mental illness.

The Joint Commission Report Ignored

John Kennedy, who became President in 1960, had a keen personal interest in enacting legislation in the mental health area. His sister Rosemary suffered from both retardation and mental illness. (Publicly, only her retardation was acknowledged, a tribute to the stigma surrounding mental illness.) Kennedy appointed a "Secretarys' Committee," consisting of the Secretary of Health, Education and Welfare, the Secretary of Labor, and others to review, with NIMH, the Joint Commission Report and propose actions that his administration might take based upon it.[53] The resulting report, prepared by NIMH, was called "A Proposal for a Comprehensive Mental Health Program to Implement the Findings of the Joint Commission on Mental Illness and Health." (A more candid title would have been "A Proposal to Ignore the Findings of the Joint Commission on Mental Illness and Health.")

The Joint Commission's central proposal, to create a new system of small treatment-intensive state hospitals, was ignored. Its warning that prevention was a chimera went unheeded. The NIMH review sent to the President in the spring of 1962 fastened on a single Joint Commission recommendation: that there be one mental health clinic for each 50,000 of population. This led to the review's urging that community mental health centers be established, each for "catchment areas" (geographic zones) of 100,000 people. However, the centers were to take a far greater role than the Joint Commission had intended the clinics to assume.

The new centers were to provide "comprehensive services," from regular inpatient hospital services to the obligatory prevention of mental illness. In the letter of transmittal to the President of the report, the "Secretarys' Committee" declared it was the committee's firm opinion that the emphasis should be on "strengthening of noninstitutional services, rather than massive subsidization of existing, anachronistic, State public mental institutions." Such institutions, the President was told, might be expected to "disappear from the scene" within twenty-five years.[54]

President Kennedy and his advisers found the idea of a bold new approach establishing a community-based system of care politically far more attractive than the original Joint Commission proposal to revitalize state hospitals. And so, in his special message on mental illness and retardation to Congress, President Kennedy welded together the goals of primary prevention and reduction in state hospital populations, falsely intimating that psychiatric knowledge had reached the stage where both could be achieved through community mental health centers.

Kennedy began with prevention:

> Here, more than in any other area, "an ounce of prevention is worth more than a pound of cure." For prevention is far more desirable for all concerned. It is far more economical and it is far more likely to be successful.[55]

Prevention would result from strengthening community, social welfare, and educational programs to correct "the harsh environmental conditions" that Kennedy declared "often are associated with mental retardation and mental illness."

Kennedy encouraged the belief that the major problem was the existing institutional care of patients, not the disease itself.

> I am convinced that, if we apply our medical knowledge and social insights fully, all but a small portion of the mentally ill can eventually achieve a wholesome and constructive social adjustment. It has been demonstrated that two out of three schizophrenics—our largest category of mentally ill—can be treated and released within 6 months. . . .[56]

He promised: "If we launch a broad new mental health program now, it will be possible within a decade or two to reduce the number of patients now under custodial care by 50 percent or more."[57]

Kennedy rejected the notion of trying to rehabilitate state hospitals: "Merely pouring Federal funds into a continuation of the outmoded type of institutional care which now prevails would make little difference."[58] State hospitals would receive $10 million in aid, but only so they could serve a "valuable transitional role,"[59] until their disappearance. The most quoted passage—which today has a bitter ring—promised that "reliance on the cold mercy of custodial isolation will be supplanted by the open warmth of community concern and capability."[60]

Bait and Switch? Selling the CMHC Act to Congress

The subsequent congressional hearings on the Community Mental Health Centers (CMHC) Act, emphasized the role of the proposed centers in caring for the severely and chronically ill patient, permitting state hospitals to fade away. In view of how little that promise was kept, Fuller Torrey has scathingly compared the testimony of NIMH and administration officials to the shoddy merchandising tactic of "bait and switch."

But the hearings (more than a thousand pages of them in House and Senate) suggest that if congressmen were deceived, they were partly to blame. They screened out what they did not want to hear, seized upon what they chose, and failed to ask the most obvious questions. For example, testifying before the House subcommittee, Boisfeuillet Jones, special assistant to Health, Education and Welfare Secretary Anthony Celebrezze, repeated the President's promise that the program would reduce the population of state mental hospitals by 50% within a decade or two. But he also declared: "The prevention of mental illness is as important as the care and treatment of the mentally ill." The centers, said Jones, were designed "to bring order to the existing chaotic situation by providing a coordinated system of services which efficiently and effectively ministers to the mentally ill and *to the entire community*."[61]

Rather than probing Jones and others for evidence—of which there was none—that prevention was an achievable goal, congressmen fastened on the goal of reducing state hospital populations. This was how Congressman Kenneth Roberts of Alabama summed up what he saw as the nucleus of Jones's presentation:

I take it that you envision replacement of the current state services which are in your opinion primarily custodial. . . . We will bring these services back to the grassroots, so to speak, or back to the hometown of the patient who is affected, and gradually large institutions that are concentrated maybe in one or two or more places in each state will be out of the picture, so to speak, as far as the overall treatment of this problem is concerned.[62]

Oren Harris of Arkansas, the chairman of the House committee conducting the hearings, was confused, as well he might be, by the discourses on "prevention." After Jones and Dr. Robert Felix and Dr. Jack Ewalt had all testified, he seized with obvious relief on the statement of Dr. George Ulett, head of Missouri's Department of Public Health: "We feel the only way we have of reducing or eliminating the large State hospital population in Missouri is by giving the people a chance for treatment at the community level in these comprehensive community health centers."

> Mr. Harris: Then what you hope to do with this program has not been brought home to me heretofore. . . . What you ultimately hope to accomplish by this program is to reduce the number of patients in the big State hospitals to a minimum, and ultimately down the line to more adequately take care of the patients in the local center, and thereby increase the opportunities or possibility of that patient then getting back into society instead of being sent to the State hospital where he becomes a life patient?
>
> Dr. Ulett: Yes; that is a very excellent summary of what we hope to do with this program.
>
> Mr. Harris: That is the most revealing information I have had about this whole problem. I only wish that every member of this committee could have heard this comment that you have just given about this program, and what we might ultimately expect or hope from it. . . . You have thousands of thousands in State after State. It seems to me it is really a problem that we should tackle. I don't care if it is from the Federal level or the local level.[63]

Content once they had obtained the responses they wanted, congressmen failed to ask the most obvious questions. Saul Feldman, for many years in charge of the community mental health centers program at NIMH, marvels: "No one asked the question 'Where will all those people live once they get out of the state mental hospital?'"[64] That omission was even more bizarre than it sounds today, because there were then no entitlement programs to sustain the mentally ill in the community: no Medicare or Medicaid to pay medical bills and no Supplemental Security Income (SSI) to provide living allowances for those unable to work.

One reason congressmen may have avoided questions that would have pointed up hidden additional costs was that they looked on the centers as a way to *save money.* (Remember, the Joint Commission had called for tripling funds spent on the mentally ill in a space of ten years.) Congress felt too much money was being spent on them already.

Like others who testified, Boisfeuillet Jones was pressed to predict that the centers would save states large sums of money currently being spent on state hospitals. At first, Jones tried to evade promises on this score, saying that the amount to be saved was "hard to predict" but that "it will make it possible for the funds now being spent at State mental institutions to be more effectively used in bringing better treatment to those who will necessarily remain in State mental institutions."[65] But Congressman Roberts, not to be deflected, pressed Jones until he received the response he wanted.

> MR. ROBERTS: So any way you look at it States are going to be relieved of a considerable amount of financial burden that they have been under for the last several years. Is that not correct?

> MR. JONES: That is the full and reasonable expectation demonstrated already in a few communities.[66]

Congress duly passed the CMHC legislation in October 1963, initially providing $150 million in construction grants, with staffing grants of $735 million enacted two years later. (Congress would ultimately invest over three billion dollars in them.)

The CMHC Regulations: Forgetting the Chronic Patient

After the hearings, NIMH could be in no doubt that as far as Congress was concerned, the chief purpose of the centers was to reduce existing state hospital populations. Yet, amazingly, in putting the CMHC program in operation, NIMH set about *eliminating* precisely those parts of the program that, in the planning stage, had been designed to serve the chronically ill.

The Joint Commission Report had said that "after-care and rehabilitation are essential parts of all services to mental patients, and the various methods of achieving rehabilitation should be integrated in all forms of service."[67] In NIMH's initial proposals, there were references to aftercare, with foster care, nursing homes, halfway houses, social clubs, vocational rehabilitation, sheltered workshops, and recreation defined as essential features.[68] The "Secretarys' Report" to President Kennedy defined eight essential services that would be provided by CMHCs, including rehabilitation programs and supervision of foster home care for discharged patients.[69] In his message to Congress, President Kennedy included rehabilitation and foster home care among the key elements of a comprehensive community mental health center.

But no sooner had Congress decided to fund community mental health centers than NIMH leaders lost interest in the needs of chronic patients. When NIMH drew up the final regulations, a CMHC had to provide only five services to qualify for federal funds: inpatient services, partial hospitalization (i.e., by day or night), outpatient services, twenty-four-hour emergency services, and consultation and education services. Services tailored to the chronic patient came under an optional second group of five services that would make a center "comprehensive." (As things worked out, many centers never would have the full complement of *essential* services, let alone those in the optional second group.)

Harry Cain, now a vice president of Blue Cross, was a young man fresh from an internship at the National Institute of Health when he worked on the regulations. He says: "I remember there were a number of arguments over what should be in the first five [required services] but I don't remember our having any fix on the chronic population in general. It was much more an orientation toward the new people."[70] In *Madness and Government,* Henry Foley and Steven Sharfstein (earlier an official at NIMH) declare: "CMHCs were originally intended more to serve new constituencies in their own communities than large numbers of a great under-constituency of patients discharged 'better but not well' from mental institutions into these communities."[71]

Dr. Lucy Ozarin, for many years in charge of program development at NIMH, blames the emphasis on prevention, noting that most of those at NIMH did not see the psychotic patient as of special importance. Dr. Ozarin had worked for many years in state hospitals (at one point during World War II, she found herself a single psychiatrist serving a thousand patients); however, she was an exception at NIMH. She points out that most of those in leadership positions had little clinical experience working with the patients who filled state hospitals.

Long-time NIMH executive Saul Feldman cites another pragmatic factor.

It may well be the omission of sheltered living arrangements as a required service could have been consciously or otherwise an acknowledgement that requiring such services might engender substantial community opposition and might have defeated the legislation.[72]

In any event, as Dr. Richard Cravens, who became branch chief of the CMHC program, now admits, CMHCs were not designed to serve chronic patients in the community. "To be quite honest, the CMHCs were not equipped to deal with them. . . . The people released needed a whole array of services; they needed income support, vocational training, housing. They would have had to provide a whole array of services."[73]

CMHC Regulations: No Coordination with State Hospitals

Incredibly, in the regulations governing the new CMHCs, the National Institute of Mental Health did not even mandate coordination with state hospitals. Without coordination, how could candidates for admission to state hospitals be routed, where appropriate, to their local CMHC instead? How were CMHCs to provide outpatient care for released patients?

Those who supervised the CMHC program at NIMH early in its history agree that the competition between state hospitals and the new CMHC program explains the otherwise inexplicable oversight. Dr. Cravens, a mental health administrator in Missouri before coming to NIMH, says: "The community mental health centers came on as a threat to the hospital superintendents. They thought of them as putting them out of business." And Cravens points out that the NIMH staff thought so, too. "They [the people at NIMH] thought with this new system they were creating there would just simply not be a need for state hospitals in time."[74]

Many apparently felt that under the new system the need for hospital beds would be minimal. Earlier we mentioned Dr. Fritz Freyhan's frustration at NIMH's lack of interest in the program he developed to provide continuity of treatment by combining hospital and outpatient facilities. Freyhan, in charge of clinical studies at NIMH's Clinical Pharmacological Research Center at the time, says he "was an eye and ear witness" to pronouncements from those in charge of creating the CMHC program that "what the future CMHC needs the least are beds." Each mental hospital bed, says Freyhan, "was seen as a threat to treatment and prognosis of future generations of patients."[75]

Under these circumstances, NIMH was understandably fearful of mandating a relationship between hospitals and CMHCs. Says Saul Feldman:

> If we had required some sort of contractual relationship between state hospitals and CMHCs in order to fund a CMHC, we would in effect have been holding the CMHC hostage to the will or whims of the state mental hospital.[76]

At the time, the issue of coordination did not even seem an important one. Harry Cain, whom former NIMH head Bertram Brown described to us as "the man who wrote the regs with me,"[77] told us:

> If you ask why didn't the regs specifically mandate a relationship, I'll tell you I don't remember, in anything I was ever involved in, even an argument over whether or not they should. . . . With a lot more age and experience, as I look back on that time, most of us involved were rather naive and really viewed the CMHC program as a break from the past, as a new beginning, and it doesn't really surprise me that we wouldn't have examined the question of whether or not to require a tie between the state hospitals and the CMHCs. From hindsight we should have. . . . I remember we were quite concerned about how community mental health centers would tie into other community institutions but not so much the state hospitals.[78]

NIMH looked on the centers as a break not only with state mental hospitals, but with the state-controlled system of care. Dr. Ozarin reports that when the CMHC law was passed, state mental health commissioners wanted to control the way the money was spent and were indignant when NIMH decided to fund local programs directly.[79] The strained relations with state mental health directors made cooperation with state hospitals even more problematic. In practice, says Ozarin, many people at CMHCs were not acquainted with state hospitals. "It was almost as if we had two totally different sets of people."[80]

Whither the Chronic Patient?

What then did those at NIMH think would happen to the discharged chronic patient? To a large extent they bought the anti-psychiatric argument that institutions *caused* the disabilities that were then falsely attributed to mental illness. Erving Goffman's *Asylums,* published in 1961, with its devastating critique of the "total institution," was in fact an NIMH-funded project.

Goffman's ideas were amplified by mainstream psychiatrists on both sides of the Atlantic. In England, Dr. John Wing wrote of the impact of "institutionalism," a syndrome characterized by lack of initiative, apathy, withdrawal, feelings of worthlessness and dehumanization.[81] The Joint Commission report quoted Dr. Robert Hunt, himself a superintendent of a large New York state hospital, who declared: "Hospitalization as such is an important cause of disability."[82] Preventive psychiatry's Gerald Caplan took up the theme:

> In the past twenty years, we have come to the realization that most of the symptoms of the chronic deteriorated psychotics who crowd the back wards of our mental hospitals are produced by the pathogenic environment in which we incarcerate them rather than by the mental disorder which led to their admission.[83]

Saul Feldman says there is no question but that these ideas had an impact. "There was the feeling, if not the mythology, that if you let people out of a bad place and give them their freedom—that in itself can make a substantial difference."[84]

In addition, the notion of "community" had a romantic aura in the 1960s, and its imaginary warmth was in itself seen as therapeutic. Charles Windle, at NIMH for many years and currently chief of services research, says: "There was enthusiasm for believing if you were just in the community, that would answer most of the questions and that you would do better."[85] Harry Cain concurs.

> There was a lot of wishful thinking along these lines. The community had a halo at the time. We were federal bureaucrats on an NIMH campus talking about the community, but really from some conceptual level as opposed to hands-on experience.[86]

The availability of neuroleptic drugs also encouraged optimism that CMHCs could maintain former patients in the community on the strength of a prescription.[87] Yet, as we have seen, studies had been published chronicling the limitations of the drugs. Brill and Patton, whose study of psychoactive drugs, referred to earlier, was quoted by the Joint Commission, emphasized that the drugs were much more effective in reducing "positive" symptoms of schizophrenia, such as delusions and hallucinations, than in the "negative" ones: "occupational inertia, vocational incapacity, and lack of initiative for constructive occupation." Psychiatrists insufficiently appreciated, they observed, that defects in this area "are not an accidental and secondary problem but a primary and central one directly related to mental illness and especially schizophrenia. . . ."[88]

It was their misplaced confidence in the efficacy of prevention of chronic illness that enabled NIMH leaders to shrug away such warnings. Richard Cravens recalls:

> At the time the centers were created, if you go back to Caplan's writings, there was an awful lot of emphasis on trying to identify those people whose coping skills were not strong and to work with them, the idea being you would prevent more serious decompensation later on. . . . The goal was early intervention and prevention and to make hospitalization either unnecessary or to make it necessary only for twelve to fifteen days and to provide that service in the community.[89]

And so those at NIMH were not preoccupied with the almost half million patients still resident in mental hospitals in 1963. These real people represented a legacy from the past. Unfortunately the eyes of those at NIMH were fixed on a mirage: an ideal social order, shaped by psychiatrists, where no one would feel the need for what Gerald Caplan called "regressive" escape into mental illness.

Chapter 4

Community Mental Health Centers
The Reality

ONE of the tenets of community psychiatry no one explained in the congressional hearings was the need to transform society as a precondition for securing mental health. In his writings, community psychologist George Albee had spelled out the anti-establishment implications, noting that if "mental disorder is eventually acknowledged to be largely social and cultural in origin, the consequences for action will be very serious, if not downright dangerous to the status quo."[1] In pursuit of this political mission several of the intellectual fathers of community psychiatry took up the challenge of reforming society.

The Rise and Fall of Social Activism in CMHCs

The two most famous examples of centers that pursued mental health through political protest were the Lincoln Hospital Mental Health Services in New York City, which opened in 1963 and was initially funded by the Office of Economic Opportunity,[2] and the Temple University Community Mental Health Center in Philadelphia, which opened in 1966. In the end social activism led to the internal upheaval and collapse of both.

The two centers resembled each other in many respects. Both were led by intellectual architects of community psychiatry, the Temple

University center by Dr. Elmer Gardner, who had been a theorist of community psychiatry at the University of Rochester, and the Lincoln center by Dr. Harris Peck.[3] Both programs generated enormous enthusiasm in their staff. Dr. Anthony Panzetta was one of the former students Gardner brought with him from Rochester to serve as unit heads in the center. Panzetta remembers:

> When the CMHC Act developed and there was this thing called a CMHC, I knew I had to be part of it. . . . This was in 1966. What was clear to me was that we were attracting the brightest and the best. All kinds of terrific people were being attracted to the field. Those early days were very heady, full of naive expectations.[4]

Both the Temple and Lincoln centers served the most blighted areas of their cities, with the highest rates of crime, infant mortality, substandard housing, and unemployment. Both programs hired community activists as nonprofessional staff, and set up shop in storefronts, or row houses, to make services more accessible to the community.

Above all, both centers interpreted their mandate to prevent mental illness broadly. Says Panzetta:

> We supported a rent escrow drive to force landlords to do better by their tenants. We were part of marches. . . . We thought we'd prevent mental illness somehow by doing the sort of things we were doing.[5]

There was constant pressure, Panzetta reports, "to get to the cause of mental illness" through dealing with social issues. The rationale came out sounding like: "If we can influence oppression, poverty and overcrowding, then there will be less depression and alcoholism."[6]

Girding up for battle against an oppressive "establishment," these psychiatrists were stunned to find themselves defined as the oppressors. In the case of the Lincoln Hospital center, the catchment area was largely Puerto Rican, with a substantial black minority. The white (chiefly Jewish) psychiatrists had been active in the civil rights movement; as Seymour Kaplan and Melvin Roman, associate directors of the program, observed in their chronicle of events at Lincoln Hospital, they "felt a special kinship for the black struggle."[7]

But these doctors displayed little understanding of community politics. Dr. Peck, the program's director, was elected to serve on the board of the Hunt's Point Community Progress Center. He supported a black candidate as director over a rival Puerto Rican candidate, though he owed his presence on the board to the vote of Puerto Rican leaders.

They perceived the director as an entirely political choice and could not comprehend Peck's action.[8]

In retrospect, Kaplan and Roman saw the CMHC's growing emphasis on the "culture" of the black civil rights movement in a program serving a primarily Puerto Rican community as a significant factor in its downfall. Suspect as far as Puerto Rican leadership was concerned, the program's directors later lacked their strong backing when they came under attack from the black community activists they had hired as mental health workers.

Before long, the program was seething with tensions. A black staff member produced a newsletter attacking the center's leadership, calling six of the professionals "useless as human beings" and warning them to get out "while they had the choice to walk away." The writer accused blacks in the program of being "Uncle Toms" and "house niggers." The individual who wrote the newsletter was fired—then reinstated with back pay, and went right on distributing the newsletter![9]

Finally in March 1969, the dismissal of a few workers triggered a revolt, and between 50% and 70% of the staff occupied the administration building, locked out the directors, and appointed a nonprofessional, who designated himself the new director of Lincoln Hospital Mental Health Services. There were now two, rival Lincoln Hospital mental health centers claiming legitimacy, with several psychiatrists and a number of other professional staff having allied themselves with the rebels. Signs went up declaring the new group a "People's Mental Health Center." Mark Rudd of Columbia student revolt fame visited, and the Black Panthers also lent their support to the rebels. One community organizer remarked: "Baby, this is some people's revolution. You got white shrinks from Westchester, the VC [Vietcong] flag, posters of Che and Malcolm, but there ain't a Puerto Rican button in sight."[10]

The media did not delve into the inter-ethnic subtleties. Journalists used the terms of those who staged the takeover: it was a struggle for "community control" of the center. And they caused the ultimate embarrassment to the community psychiatric gurus at Lincoln Hospital by ridiculing their plight. Thus in its report of the takeover, the *New York Times* asserted:

> Dr. Harris B. Peck, director of the Lincoln Hospital Mental Health Service, used to pound the table at staff meetings and call for a "revolution." He urged community workers, one of them recalled, to wrest control of their South Bronx mental health project from him and other professional administrators and put him out of a job.
> Yesterday, they did.[11]

At roughly the same time, the Temple University Mental Health Center was self-destructing. Like the Lincoln Center psychiatrists, those at Temple found themselves castigated as representatives of an oppressive establishment. Dr. William Hetznecker, a student of Gardner at Rochester, was recruited to head the child and family unit at the Temple center. He recalls:

> We thought we were going to change the system, grand phrases like that, and weren't really trained to deal with complex social and political institutions and did not appreciate the issues we were dealing with as middle-class professionals dealing with poor populations, who saw us at times as colonialists. . . . This was also the time of a strong black nationalist identity, so I think people who were at the forefront trying to do something about community issues were the most easily available and accessible targets for the long-standing resentments and anger, that were justified, against institutions that were predominantly white and predominantly professional and served underclass people poorly.[12]

Panzetta says:

> The center divided itself into two camps, one clinically oriented, that wanted to take care of the day-to-day walking wounded, focusing on the most seriously ill. The other camp wanted to get more and more preventive, and be involved in social mission. They felt the limited resources of the center were being squandered on the clinical side.[13]

Soon members of the staff were accusing each other of racism. "How much was there? Who was guilty of it? Against whom?" There were all-day meetings with charges, countercharges and bitter recriminations, emergency executive council sessions, fair play committees. The focus of therapy became the staff itself.[14] Says Panzetta: "It burned us out, as well as wasting our abilities."[15] The center limped on (as indeed did the Lincoln Hospital CMHC), but by 1969, Panzetta observes, it was so polarized that most of the psychiatrists who formed the backbone of the program left.[16]

Their activities—and disintegration—alike highly publicized, the Lincoln and Temple centers served as object lessons to others. In 1964, NIMH held out the new-born Lincoln Hospital Center as one of eight model programs around the nation.[17] In 1968, it received the American Psychiatric Association's Silver Achievement Award for "its innovative efforts" in "demonstrating how to reach the unreachable."[18] That same year NIMH awarded the center a federal staffing grant.[19] Yet within a year an NIMH inspection team, reviewing the Lincoln CMHC's operations in the wake of the upheaval, announced that "an identifiable community mental health center . . . does not exist fiscally, administratively or programmatically."[20]

On sober reflection, it was absurd to believe that if psychiatrists and patients organized together against landlords, the sum total of mental illness would be affected in the slightest. But once caught up in the fashionable utopian enthusiasms of the 1960s, psychiatrists did not pause to reflect. They hurled themselves into what was considered the noblest and most urgent task of the time—social action to remake an unjust society—and called it psychiatry. Fortunately, the debacle at the Lincoln Hospital and Temple centers helped to discredit global prevention as part of a community mental health center's mission. By the mid-1970s, sociologists Mort Wagenfeld and Stanley Robin found so little evidence of activist orientations among CMHC staff that they concluded: "[T]he activist, community-oriented, socially ameliorative community mental health concept envisioned by many of its founders never really existed—at least in the beliefs and day-to-day activities of community mental health center staff."[21]

What Was the Mission of CMHCs?

If they were not to abolish mental illness through ending social injustice, what were CMHCs to do?

In 1967, a team from the Joint Information Service (set up by the American Psychiatric Association and the National Association for Mental Health), led by former journalist Raymond Glasscote, visited eight of the first centers to be funded. The team reported its regret at not having asked "Why was this CMHC established?"

> [W]e ourselves felt that we understood the answer and therefore felt that others would consider the question fatuous and the answer self-evident. In retrospect, we wish that we had asked.[22]

The team had obviously looked at the hearings.

> From the legislative history, it is clear that the community mental health center was represented to Congress as a facility capable of supplanting the state mental hospital. . . . However much mental health centers may accomplish in other ways, they will not accomplish the goal for which Congress established the program unless they can stem the flow of the mentally ill to the state hospitals.[23]

But what was self-evident to the visiting team was far from obvious to the center staff, and with good reason. Two weeks after the passage of the CMHC Act in 1963, Dr. Robert Felix, chief architect of the CMHC program and in his last year as NIMH director, defined the tasks of CMHCs as including

> not only the reduction of those factors which tend to produce mental and emotional disturbances, but also the provision of a climate in which each citizen has optimum opportunities for sustained creative and responsible participation in the life of the community, and for the development of his particular potentialities as a human being.[24]

NIMH official Alan Levenson wrote: "The purpose of a center is to provide the full range of mental health services needed by the residents of the community."[25] Jack Ewalt, who had directed the Joint Commission, said CMHCs "should serve the troubled, the disturbed, the slow, the ill, and *the healthy* of all age groups."[26] (Italics added.)

Saul Feldman says there was a reason for such vague pronouncements.

> It would be fair to say different people had different ideas. To a significant extent that was not an accident. NIMH in the early days did not do a great deal to be specific about what the operational objectives were. In fact, Stan Yolles, who was director of NIMH at the time the legislation was enacted, said that as communities differ from each other, so should their CMHCs. In fact, if you assume that a major objective of the CMHCs was to provide services responsive to the people they were to serve, if the needs of people in one area were different from another, those objectives and services should be different.[27]

Those at the centers visited seemed more familiar with the broad mandates coming from NIMH than with the text of the hearings. The team found that only three of the eight centers were making a serious attempt to serve the chronically ill population. *All* the centers sent patients they believed would require long-term hospitalization to the state hospital: in one center long-term treatment was defined as anything over seven days. More people were being sent to the state hospital from the catchment area served by one new CMHC than had been going before the center was established. Yet half the center's own inpatient beds were not filled! (The center's staff explained it didn't want to clog up beds with long-term cases.[28]) In another center, being in need of inpatient care and unable to pay meant instant transfer to the state hospital.

In November 1967, following the site visits, heads of the CMHCs that had been visited, the Joint Information Service team, staff people from the American Psychiatric Association, and officials from NIMH held a conference in Washington, D.C. (NIMH had provided most of the funds for the on-site visits and several of its officials had accompanied the survey team.)

At the conference, the center heads were challenged with their failure to serve chronic patients. Glasscote, who had headed the team, observed:

> If one goes to a public general hospital and is bleeding and doesn't have any money, that hospital will have to take care of him. But with the community mental health center, do we know just how many can be sent away unserved? If one is allowed to send alcoholics, children, old people, and chronic patients out of the community, then what is being provided locally comes down pretty much to the acute psychotic and the neurotic. . . . When you have stripped off all of the special problem groups you may have a more or less comprehensive spread of services to a quite uncomprehensive spread of consumers.[29]

In response, some of the assembled leaders of community psychiatry offered a chastened view of its potential to make a difference in chronic illness. Dr. Edward Beaghler, the director of the Central Utah Community Mental Health Center in Provo, said:

> People can deteriorate as easily in the community as in state hospitals. We have seen this in Utah with some of the nursing home placements that have been used to get rid of chronic schizophrenic patients. They are returned to us, and we see that we should not have sent them out in the first place.[30]

Dr. H. G. Whittington, who ranks as one of the half dozen intellectual architects of the community psychiatry movement, and headed a CMHC in Denver, was equally skeptical.

> There's adequate evidence that we could close up all the state hospitals and do everything they're doing in the community. But it may not be economical nor the most effective way. . . . There is evidence that many of the people we could treat in the community are probably better off at this point in time being treated in a state hospital.[31]

When the center heads were pressed by Dr. James Sussex, a member of the Joint Information Service team, to say whether they even saw it as a realistic goal to change the locus of treatment from the public mental hospital to a community facility, Dr. Whittington was the only one who gave a direct reply. He said it was an attainable goal but warned:

> The major challenge is not to set up a new institution that will keep people in the community. It's to see that they are *better off* in the community, and that the community is better off because they are there.[32]

He feared reproducing "at the community level the same kind of monstrous non-patient-directed messes that some state hospitals are."[33]

There was some irritation at the way the Joint Information Service team kept harping on the chronically ill. Dr. John Cody, director of the High Plains Mental Health Center in Kansas was blunt: "I wonder why we're focusing so much on chronic schizophrenics."[34] Dr. Whittington concurred:

> Right—the chronic schizophrenics are a small proportion of the concern of the center. . . . If all we do with community mental health centers is create little state hospitals in the community, we're wasting our time, because they're not going to work there any more than they worked anywhere else.[35]

If the testimony at Congressional hearings a few years earlier had been so candid, it is doubtful the centers would ever have been funded.

The Needs of the Chronically Ill

Some of the CMHC heads saw the need for different kinds of agencies to care for the chronically ill. According to Dr. William Hart of the Rochester Mental Health Center in New York State, not only mental health centers but a complete range of agencies was necessary.

> I think the mental health center can peel off some chronic patients, but there must be systems to get them back into the community—rehabilitation and work-adjustment programs and socialization programs. These seem to be developing separately from the community mental health center system, and perhaps appropriately so. A fully adequate system will have to be massive.[36]

This touched upon the absence of aftercare in the CMHC structure. Dr. Whittington observed: "For chronic schizophrenics, we begin to see a need for rehabilitation, or habilitation, or education, or training— emphases that don't at all fit the functional definition of most comprehensive community mental health centers."[37] Dr. Elaine Cumming, a sociologist who was a member of the Joint Information team, made the same point:

> I wonder if the concept of the mental health center has left out—perhaps rightly, perhaps not—the notion that there are many people whose major need is rehabilitation, which isn't one of the essential services. . . . In some sense, the mark has been missed in defining the nature of the illness to be dealt with.[38]

Implicitly this was a devastating indictment of NIMH, which had promised Congress an alternative to state hospital care and then *deleted* the required services.

The CMHC directors acknowledged that their own programs were deficient. When they were asked, at the conclusion of the conference, for ways they thought the regulations governing the centers should be changed, the following dialogue ensued.

> DR. WHITTINGTON: I'd like to suggest that aftercare be included as an essential service, but under a special provision whereby NIMH would match state contributions to community services. The state hospitals pride themselves on how quickly they discharge patients, but really they dump some patients back in the community little better off than when they went into the hospital.

> DR. SUSSEX: [a member of the Joint Information team]: Do those of you here agree at least in principle that aftercare services for discharged mental hospital patients should be an essential service of community mental health centers?

> VOICES: [Agreement]

> DR. SUSSEX: No one disagrees.[39]

The Joint Information Service endorsed this consensus. The evidence was abundant, the team concluded, that mentally ill persons could live at least partially satisfying lives in the community if supports were available.

> This would include halfway houses, sheltered workshops, job training, social retraining, and activity centers among other things. Such facilities are prescribed in the federal regulations as part of a *comprehensive* mental health center program—but they are optional, not *essential*. And they are precisely what will be required if the centers are to accomplish the original goal of transferring the care of the mentally ill from the state hospital to the community.[40]

Although NIMH's purpose in funding the survey team was to identify "solutions to problems" so that newer centers could "avoid some of the problems that early-established programs experienced,"[41] NIMH did not change the regulations so that CMHCs would address the needs hospitals had met for housing, help with tasks of daily living, and social interaction. Those in charge of the program at NIMH, committed to preventive psychiatry, simply did not see care of the chronically ill as the CMHC's major responsibility. Even today, Saul Feldman says:

> To provide care for that population at the expense of providing it to people who are neurotic or who have less persistent mental disorders, or even the worried well seems to me will only increase the number of chronically mentally ill. . . . Mental health problems generally don't go away and if they are not treated they get worse. If there are no resources and no services to treat people to prevent mental illness . . . what we may be doing in effect is creating a whole new army of chronically mentally ill people because we're not spending money on preventing chronic mental illness; we're spending all the money on people who are already chronically mentally ill.[42]

Dr. Bertram Brown also retains a naive faith in prevention. He told us: "I think the current look at neuroscience and biology as going to solve [it] is nonsense; there's still the social, political, poverty, and other forces that are as critical as ever."[43]

Apparently those who guided the CMHC program at NIMH have *still* not learned what Anthony Panzetta ruefully recognized after his experience at the Temple CMHC: "When we in psychiatry wave our preventive banners, we must look ridiculous to even the gods on Mount Olympus who once held the key to the causal mysteries of human events."[44]

Finally, in 1975, Congress mandated aftercare as a CMHC service. But by then care of discharged state hospital patients was only one of seven additional services Congress required of CMHCs, and as Mort Wagenfeld points out, there was scarcely a CMHC in the country in compliance with the regulations. One NIMH official said the CMHC had become like a dinosaur, unable to support its own weight.[45]

The Average CMHC: Psychotherapy Triumphant

What *were* CMHCs doing? In 1980 Dr. Donald Langsley, a former president of the American Psychiatric Association, observed that they had moved "into a social service model. . . . Primarily they seem to feature counseling and crisis intervention for predictable problems of living."[46] The centers offered psychotherapy: ten million sessions in 1978, the last year for which data were compiled. Torrey points out that "these sessions, according to NIMH data, did not include 'medication or drug maintenance,' and only a small proportion of them were for individuals with serious mental illnesses."[47] Even Saul Feldman, who says that Torrey's criticisms are "overblown," admits:

> It certainly was true there were a number of centers whose program was more or less dictated by what their staff liked to do and what their staff liked to do was dynamically oriented analytic psychotherapy. People who had interesting dreams.[48]

CMHCs also provided inpatient treatment for those in short-term crisis, and to some extent provided ongoing supervision of chronically ill in the community. Nonetheless, as the pace of deinstitutionalization accelerated sharply in the 1970s, CMHCs devoted proportionately *less* of their attention to state hospital patients. The longer a CMHC was in operation, the smaller the percentage of its referrals from these hospitals. Torrey writes:

> In 1976, for example, CMHCs that had been operational for one to two years had 5.5 percent of their admissions referred from state mental hospitals, whereas CMHCs that had been operational for six to seven years had only 2.6% of their admissions referred from public mental hospitals.[49]

Moreover, as time went by, the proportion of patients suffering from serious mental illness served by CMHCs decreased. Between 1970 and 1975 the proportion of those suffering from schizophrenia at CMHCs declined from 15% to 10% and the proportion suffering from depression from 20% to 13%. In those same years, the proportion treated suffering from no mental disorder at all more than quadrupled, going from 5% to 22%.[50]

Embarrassed by these figures, several researchers at NIMH published a paper arguing they were deceptive because the *number* of patients with schizophrenia treated at CMHCs had increased in those years, going from 50,000 to 91,000. The proportion had fallen because the number of patients treated at the centers had almost tripled, going up to 919,000.[51] But this was a weak argument. The need for community treatment of the chronically ill had soared in those years, and CMHCs were treating less than 10% of those now estimated to be in the community suffering from severe chronic illness. If addressed, the needs of that population would have absorbed most of a center's energies. As Anthony Panzetta observed cogently in his 1971 book on CMHCs:

> [D]oing a good job of comprehensive and continuous care of the psychotics and mental retardates of a base population group of from 75,000 to 200,000, may very likely absorb every available manhour of resource . . . and then some.[52]

By 1977 a Federal General Accounting Office report made official what had been obvious for a decade: not only had the centers developed without connection to the state hospitals but they were often not even in communication with each other. The report concluded that "CMHCs attracted a new type of patient who was not very ill and [was] not a candidate for hospitalization in a state institution."[53]

In practice the most severely ill were often made to feel unwelcome. One mother in Wisconsin told us that in the local CMHC her son and other severely ill patients had been told to use a different waiting room: it was feared their presence would drive away the "better class" of client, that is, those who were not seriously ill. Many staff members considered taking care of the chronically ill an onerous, unrewarding task. Dr. James Beck, one of the NIMH representatives in the 1967 Joint Information Service survey team, put it bluntly: "Many people can't tolerate working with chronic schizophrenics. Doctors and nurses don't like to treat patients who don't get well."[54]

NIMH's Charles Windle observes that the seriously ill who were served tended to be less impaired than those who went unserved, and even then were inadequately treated.

> When they were really hopeless they were in the nursing home, or they didn't stay very long in the CMHC because it didn't have a way to serve them, so those kinds of patients didn't stay around long and didn't glut up the system too much. Or they were inadequately served—they just came in for medicine.[55]

The CMHC program was so poorly supervised by NIMH that many centers failed to provide the specified services. In March 1990 a congressional committee issued a report estimating that CMHCs had diverted between $40 and $100 million to improper uses, and that a quarter of all CMHCs had so thoroughly failed to meet their obligations as to be legally subject to immediate recovery of federal funds.[56] Centers in Minneapolis, Boston, Orlando, and many other cities built swimming pools with their CMHC federal construction money. Orlando Regional Medical Center, in addition to a pool, built tennis courts with its federal construction grant and used a federal staffing grant to hire a gardener, lifeguard, and swimming instructor.[57]

In response to the many criticisms, defenders of the CMHC program have emphasized its achievements. In an overview, David Dowell and James Ciarlo conclude that its greatest success was in increasing the range and quantity of public mental health services. CMHCs have served the poor and minorities. As a result of the centers, psychotherapy is no longer an upper- or middle-class term.[58] Lucy Ozarin emphasized to us that CMHCs pioneered partial hospitalization and twenty-four-hour emergency services. CMHCs were also responsible for increasing the number of psychiatric beds in general hospitals, since a number of hospitals took advantage of the construction grants in the CMHC program for this purpose. Acutely ill psychotic patients needing only brief treatment were often well served by CMHCs. The CMHC is now serving as a model for the private sector, as a number of those who once worked in CMHCs, like Anthony Panzetta, are pioneering programs for insurance carriers that use services like partial hospitalization to cut down surging mental health costs.[59]

Dr. Charles Ray, who formerly worked at a center in Kansas City, and now represents the National Council of Community Mental Health Centers, defends the CMHC's treatment of a broad range of clients. He observes that the pain of "the worried well" in the face of a life crisis is as real as that of the mentally ill.[60] That may be so, but Congress—and taxpayers—did not intentionally fund a national counseling service; it intended to fund a program to substitute for state hospitals in caring for the severely mentally ill.

The Lowell CMHC: What Might Have Been

Despite NIMH's failure to serve as guide, there were a small number of CMHCs that took as their mission service to the chronically ill. Centers like the Solomon Community Mental Health Center in Lowell, Massachusetts, illustrate what CMHCs that focused on this population could accomplish.

The Lowell Center's first director was J. Sanbourne Bockoven.[61] In some respects Bockoven was a conventional psychiatrist, subscribing to what he called the "modern" view that an individual's mental illness "cannot be understood without taking into account his interactions with his family and with society."[62] But in other ways, Bockoven was anything but conventional, arguing that psychiatry and psychiatric education had digressed from their fundamental task—to care for those most seriously damaged by mental illness. Accordingly he welcomed the opportunity of heading a state-funded community mental health center in the Lowell area, which opened in 1966.[63] (A few years later it would receive federal staffing grants as a CMHC.)

Even before the center's inpatient beds were ready, Bockoven sent nurses to the wards of Worcester State Hospital where they became acquainted with Lowell area patients. As soon as the inpatient unit opened up, reports Dr. Jerome Klein, a long-time staff member of the center:

> Backoven sent a bus up to Worcester and brought back nine patients, chronic patients, and filled up the spanking new unit with patients from Worcester. Most of the CMHCs were going out counseling bartenders to teach other people how to counsel drunks, running divorce mediation units and all that great stuff. They didn't open up their units with chronic patients from the state hospital. . . .
>
> And so, by 1974, we had emptied out the whole [Lowell] population from Worcester. . . . We were the only mental health center who'd done that. We had to reeducate families. We had to tell Worcester . . . don't accept patients [from the Lowell catchment area] from anybody but us. We're it now, if you live in Lowell and the surrounding towns.[64]

Says Klein: "We are the state hospital. We're a community mental health center but we are the state hospital. So our difficult patient is the chronic state hospital patient. Or a difficult patient no one else wants to tackle because of violence." Klein says that 98% of the center's resources go to serve the chronically ill.

> The nature of the delivery system here is geared around the sickest chronic patient. Our emergency service is geared to that. Our community support service is geared to that. Maybe in the beginning people had notions about getting the bartenders in and all that silly stuff, but the superintendent [Dr. Bockoven] . . . said that the main business of the center is going to have to be the chronic patient. He saw where it was going and he was right.[65]

Unwilling to dump long-term chronic patients into a community where they could not function independently, the center over the years funded or fashioned ties to a whole array of supportive services. Says Klein: "We have a certain number of residential beds, halfway houses, quarterway houses, rooming houses with staffing." There are also a social club and a sheltered workshop.

But the Lowell Center was an anomaly as far as the universe of community mental health centers was concerned. There were other similar exceptions: Torrey cites a CMHC in Sacramento that reduced admissions from its catchment area to state mental hospitals from 1,100 per year to 4.[66]

CMHCs Bypassed

In the mid-1970s, NIMH established the Community Support Program, thereby implicitly recognizing the failure of the CMHC program to provide adequate services to the nearly two million persons outside of hospital settings NIMH estimated to be "severely mentally disabled" by chronic mental illness. NIMH officials explained the need for the program as if CMHCs had never been established.

> In a previous era, the mental health system, through its institutions, took responsibility for meeting *all* the needs of people with long term mental disability. . . . At present, responsibilities are fragmented at the state and community levels. No single agency has clearly been charged with comprehensively assessing and monitoring the community support needs of the mentally disabled or with planning and carrying out assistance programs for them.[67]

A number of places to find people needing services were identified: hospitals, private practitioners, outpatient clinics, rehabilitation centers, other mental health or human service agencies, nursing homes, boarding homes, SROs, families, and consumers themselves (who might know of others).[68] CMHCs were not even singled out as a place to *find* severely ill patients. Torrey observes:

> Rather than try and correct the CMHC program, the NIMH simply gave up and started another program instead. One may argue with the wisdom of replacing a Mercedes that is not working with a Hyundai rather than repairing the Mercedes. The logic becomes more strained when one continues to make payments on both cars.[69]

For psychiatrists too, the glamor of CMHCs soon wore off. By 1970 it was clear that psychiatrists were not going to be philosopher-kings supervising society's battle against racism, poverty, and oppression. As federal funding dried up (the proportion of funding to be supplied by local sources grew with each year of a CMHC's existence), psychologists and social workers replaced psychiatrists, who were increasingly relegated to the role for which they were legally indispensable: writing prescriptions. From 1970 to 1975, the number of psychiatrists at CMHCs fell by half. The narrower their role, the more disaffected psychiatrists became, and soon CMHCs were in the same position as state mental hospitals: they were forced to rely increasingly on psychiatrists who were foreign-born and foreign-trained.[70]

CMHCs Take "Credit" for Deinstitutionalization

At NIMH the chronically ill assumed center stage when it was time to obtain renewed funding from Congress. NIMH officials then spoke of the "unquestionable" role played by CMHCs in lowering state hospital censuses. Testifying before Congress in 1969, Stanley Yolles, who replaced Robert Felix as head of NIMH in 1964, said: "Largely because of the impetus of community mental health centers we have seen a startling reduction of patients in the mental hospitals of the United States."[71] In 1972 then-NIMH head Bertram Brown told Congress: "We had 557,000 in mental hospitals in 1957. We are down to 308,000 in 1971. That is the kind of progress that you can see."[72]

In fact, CMHCs had little impact on reducing state hospital populations. Studies by Charles Windle and others comparing areas with and without CMHCs found little difference in the use of state mental hospitals: examining data from sixteen states over five years, they found there was no impact on the number of *residents* in state hospitals, but "there may be a tendency for centers to lower state hospital *admission* rates."[73]

Moreover, as psychiatrist David Musto pointed out as early as 1975, before the era of massive numbers of mentally ill street people, CMHCs should have shunned credit for what was occurring. Elderly patients were being packed off to nursing homes, where they often received care worse than in the average state hospital. Others drifted to sleazy hotels, going, as the phrase went, "from the back ward to the back alley."[74] Even Robert Felix, chief architect of the CMHC program, had second thoughts:

> Many of those patients who left the state hospitals never should have done so. We psychiatrists saw too much of the old snake pit, saw too many people who shouldn't have been there and we overreacted. The result is not what we intended. . . .[75]

Of far greater impact on deinstitutionalization than the CMHCs were the lawsuits, to be described in the next chapter, brought by public interest lawyers imbued with the ideas of anti-psychiatry. In response to their determined challenge, politicians took the easiest way out: they emptied the hospitals. The government programs encouraging this process were Medicare and Medicaid, both passed in 1965, and Aid to the Permanently and Totally Disabled (APTD) whose benefits were extended to mental patients in 1962.[76] In 1972 Congress replaced APTD with SSI (Supplemental Security Income) under the Social Security Administration: it went into effect in 1974. But, except for those over age sixty-five, the federal government would only provide benefits to persons *not* in state hospitals. To shift the financial burden to the federal government, states had to send patients into the community.

From 1955 to 1965, the first decade after the introduction of anti-psychotic drugs, the average annual decrease in resident state hospital populations was 1.75%. However from 1970 to 1975, while government benefits were being put in place and major lawsuits decided against state hospitals, making them vastly more expensive to operate, state hospital populations decreased by a dizzying average of almost 11% *per year.*[77] Yet no better treatments had been discovered: rather, as we shall see, existing effective treatments had been abandoned.

Can Psychiatry Slough Off Responsibility?

Most psychiatrists have shrugged off all responsibility for the disaster that befell the chronically ill—and the families who cared for them. Even a psychiatrist noted for his concern for this population, Dr. John Talbott, in his presidential address to the American Psychiatric Association in 1985, spoke of deinstitutionalization as "a 30-year-old failed public policy which we had so little power to influence." According to Talbott,

> the presence of thousands of severely and chronically mentally ill and gravely disabled Americans wandering aimlessly across our nation's landscape attests to the failure of our state governments' policy of mental hospital depopulation.[78]

He complains that the "precipitous attempt to move large numbers of their [state mental hospital] charges into settings that in fact did not exist must be seen as incompetent at best and criminal at worst."[79] To have expected severely disabled patients suddenly to be able to obtain for themselves the professional and custodial services they took for granted in the hospital, writes Talbott, "seems the stuff of sheer fantasy."[80]

But psychiatry bears far more of the responsibility for this situation than Talbott is willing to acknowledge. Psychiatrists at NIMH were giving CMHCs credit for the rapid discharge of patients Talbott deplores and obtaining money from Congress on the strength of it. More important, *in every treatment arena psychiatrists had abandoned the seriously ill.* As late as World War II most psychiatrists worked in state mental hospitals. Psychiatrist Paul Appelbaum observes: "Post-war enthusiasm for psychiatry created a tremendous market for private psychotherapeutic services. Psychoanalysis was at its peak of influence and not interested in the public sector. The whole focus of the profession was away from the public sector."[81]

Donald Light points out that much of the appeal of Freud's theories was that they took psychiatrists out of the asylum, giving them a social base in the upper class of society, with patients who could pay. Psychoanalytic interpretations of personality became the doctrines in which everyone was trained and by which other therapies were measured. An effort in the 1960s to use psychiatric residents to test scales measuring competing orientations in psychiatry ran into the problem that there were too few subscribing to anything but the psychoanalytic model to test them![82]

If most psychiatrists had little interest in the public sector, those who took the lead in this area pursued the will o' the wisp of prevention. As psychiatrist Fritz Freyhan points out, community psychiatry became committed to a "new myth of social curability."[83] In the nineteenth-century version, superintendents had claimed enormous therapeutic powers for the asylum. Now the asylum was excoriated and the same therapeutic powers once claimed for it transferred to "the community." There was even less excuse for the new cult, for it rested on no evidence at all. Even community psychiatric advocate Dr. John Cumming noted in 1963, the year the CMHC legislation passed: "There are at the moment, as far as I know, no American studies that demonstrate that, when the quality of care is held constant, community-based treatment facilities function any better than those located in large hospitals."[84]

Ignoring the absence of empirical evidence for their theories, community psychiatrists sold community psychiatry to Congress largely on grounds in which they themselves did not believe. Dorothea Dix and the early asylum superintendents genuinely believed what they told state legislatures—that asylums were a good financial investment because they could cure mental illness, especially if the patient was treated promptly. But community psychiatrists persuaded Congress to pay for CMHCs by claiming that they would restore *existing* chronic patients.

They themselves did not believe this; to care for the chronic patient they were privately counting on the very hospitals they publicly condemned. The 1967 Joint Information Service survey team noted: "Everywhere we went we found the state hospital being relied on as the principal facility for long-term patients, including some who were labeled 'chronic' merely because they had had a previous hospitalization."[85]

Even among psychiatrists, only a small minority believed in the untested theory of prevention. The Joint Commission explicitly rejected it. Yet a small number of the faithful in key positions at NIMH implemented a national program based on its premises. Now Saul Feldman criticizes the behavior and ethics of mental health administrators at NIMH who promoted the policy. On one hand, Feldman sees what he calls the "oversell and overkill process" as inevitable.

> Very few bills that get introduced get enacted into law. Those that do must have certain characteristics that I call oversell and overkill. You have to absolutely laud the program you want legislation passed for, and ascribe to it the most wondrous sorts of characteristics. If it's only enacted, it will solve lots of problems of mankind. At the same time you have to overkill what already exists as being absolutely terrible, and so on.[86]

While oversell and overkill may be required to get legislation passed, Feldman acknowledges that the combination of "hype and hope, deception and dedication" has potentially harmful consequences.

> The superlatives that were designed for a particular purpose—to gain support for a program and to get a bill through the Congress—radiate out, become generalized, and are absorbed into societal values and beliefs. The oversell and slogans, inherent parts of the ritual of legislation, come slowly but surely to shape professional and public expectations. . . . And thus we become victims of our rhetoric, in part because we want to believe it so badly.[87]

Feldman notes that in the case of the CMHC legislation, "success" for a mental health administrator became defined by the number of patients discharged from hospitals.

> And so the census continued to drop, the number of homeless former patients continued to increase, and the profession achieved what could be considered the ideal state of grace—doing good, looking good, and feeling good.[88]

Community Psychiatry Reinforces Anti-Psychiatry

The effect of community psychiatry then, was to promote the goals of anti-psychiatry—"liberating" patients from institutions to the spurious freedom of the streets and enslavement by their illness.

The convergence between the two movements is not as anomalous as it might appear. On the surface, there seems an enormous gap between anti-psychiatry, with its denigration—even vilification—of the psychiatric role and community psychiatry, with its grandiose visions of psychiatrists-as-kings. Yet the underlying premises of the two were very similar. We have already noted the influence of Goffman's ideas on community psychiatrists. The latter lent their support not only to the argument that state mental hospitals were terrible places, which in many cases was true, but that they served no important function, which was not. They undercut the Joint Commission proposal for renewing state hospitals. Like anti-psychiatrists, community psychiatrists regarded institutions as evil per se. As Fritz Freyhan pointed out, for community psychiatry there was "no such thing as chronic schizophrenic illness—there is only hospitalism, a social but not a medical phenomenon."[89]

Like anti-psychiatry, community psychiatry was anti-medical in its orientation; indeed, there were those in the movement who said it was "in certain respects, incompatible with the medical model."[90] The whole notion of mental illness as something to be prevented by environmental action, whether community organization to reduce poverty and racism, or family therapy, lent credence to the anti-psychiatric dogma that mental illness did not really exist, that it was merely a label attached to deviant behavior by an intolerant family or oppressive society.

Today, those who served as leaders of community psychiatry in the 1960s blame events they did not anticipate for the hundreds of thousands who wound up in the streets, in sordid rooms, or in jail. Bertram Brown says:

> They [the CMHCs] were overwhelmed. . . . Major external phenomena that were unanticipated took place. They were the advocacy—civil rights thing—that whole thrust, people "dying with their rights on." And the states suddenly seeing a way to get this off their back and dumping them on the street. . . . [91]

Similarly, in *Madness and Government,* Henry Foley and Steven Sharfstein say that the CMHCs were "overtaken" by the urgent needs of patients with chronic illness.[92]

But if the leaders of American psychiatry were taken aback by the pace of deinstitutionalization, they themselves had prepared the way for its pacesetters. If community psychiatrists decried mental hospitals as intrinsically destructive, how could they combat the civil rights lawyers who took up the same theme? Community psychiatrists had said mental illness was merely a response to unjust or unhealthy social conditions. Did it not follow that the answer was in changing those conditions, rather than locking up the victims against their will? Community psychiatrists had declared CMHCs would take over the task of caring for the mentally ill in the community. How could they now say the centers were not doing the job? The disjunction between the needs of former hospital patients and CMHCs was obscured by the ideology of the community mental health movement. The myth had more influence than the facts of the matter.[93] In this sense, it was as an *idea* that the CMHCs played their most important role in fostering deinstitutionalization: because they were there in theory for the mentally ill, state officials could empty hospitals in good conscience.

In the end, CMHCs furthered goals precisely opposite those community psychiatrists had sought. They had argued that prompt intensive care in the community would prevent the development of chronic illness and thus obviate the need for state hospitals. Bertram Brown had said the goal was "care for the mentally ill close to home, with continuity and compassion, early enough rather than too late."[94]

But as the victories of anti-psychiatric lawyers mounted, the goal of early treatment—indeed of any treatment—receded. Psychiatry would lose its most basic tool for treating the severely ill: involuntary civil commitment. "Dangerousness," not severity of illness, would become the legal standard for imposing care on those whose disease, in many cases, led them to deny their need for treatment. Hundreds of thousands of young severely ill chronic patients, many of them *never* treated, would roam the streets, fill the jails, vegetate in the homes of their increasingly desperate parents. Pursing the chimera of preventive psychiatry, community psychiatrists had paved the way for the triumph of anti-psychiatry.

PART III

The Law Becomes Deranged

Chapter 5

The Rise of the Mental Health Bar

B Y the end of the 1960s, anti-psychiatry had begun to enlist what would turn out to be by far its most important recruits: lawyers. A group of young public interest attorneys established an informal "mental health bar," or more precisely, a mental patient liberation bar. They had no knowledge of, or interest in mental illness as such. Rather, they saw themselves on the frontier of the civil rights movement, white hats riding to free the most overlooked of this country's oppressed social groups. Their goal was sweeping—the elimination of involuntary civil commitment. And since they saw involuntary commitment as the keystone of the state hospital system, they believed its end would spell the demise of state mental hospitals.

These young public interest attorneys incorporated anti-psychiatric doctrine with amazing casualness. The "father" of the mental health bar, still a relatively young man, is Bruce Ennis, who was frank in explaining to us how his views on mental illness were formed. In 1968, recently graduated from the University of Chicago law school, Ennis applied for a job as staff attorney at the New York Civil Liberties Union.

> I was told there were no openings for staff attorneys but that the New York Civil Liberties Union was thinking of starting a special project on the rights of the mentally handicapped and would I be interested. My initial reaction was "I don't know anything about that and I don't know if I'd be interested or not." I went home and then I went to a library and I looked under "law and psychiatry" and found some books by a man named Thomas Szasz which I found interesting from a civil liberties perspective

and I read more and I realized this was a very, very big problem about which most people, including myself, knew nothing. I decided it was an important enough subject to devote a lot of my time and life to, so I did.[1]

Although the ACLU provided part of the funding for the New York Civil Liberties Union project, Ennis had a more radical agenda than the parent organization, whose model law underpinned the District of Columbia law passed by Congress in 1964.[2] In 1969, after the project had been in existence only a year, the New York Civil Liberties Union passed a resolution denouncing involuntary hospitalization as incompatible with the principles of a free society.[3] And Ennis, with the support of a handful of other sympathetic lawyers, set out to create a cadre of attorneys who would work to end it.

While an initial effort, in 1971, to organize a conference on "The Rights of the Mentally Handicapped" in New York had to be canceled for lack of interest, a second effort in 1973 drew over 500; three other conferences quickly followed in Pittsburgh, Dallas, and San Francisco.[4] Two major successful suits by patients' rights attorneys in the courts in 1972, one in Alabama, one in Wisconsin, did much to account for the rapid growth of interest. In a 1974 interview Ennis explained:

> During these four conferences we have contacted about 1,000 lawyers and distributed course materials to them and had training sessions, etc. . . . If half those lawyers file one test case in the next year, by this time next year we'll have 500 test cases. . . . The impact on the system could be devastating, because the system rests on a rotten foundation.[5]

In 1972 Ennis and three other young attorneys (Charles Halpern, Paul Friedman, and Margaret Ewing), then working on the Alabama case, known as Wyatt v. Stickney, formed the Mental Health Law Project, which rapidly became—and has remained—the ideological and logistical center of the mental patient liberation bar.

Ennis himself seems to have adopted Szasz's conclusions without accepting his premise. Szasz argued there was nothing to treat because there was no disease. Ennis told us he believes in the reality of mental illness as a biochemical disease but that from a civil rights standpoint it makes no difference.

> I'm simply a civil libertarian and in my view you don't lock people up because they've got a problem. You don't lock people up because they've got a heart problem. The fact a person has a mental illness rather than a heart illness doesn't justify locking them up. It's just never really been

very important to me if there is or is not mental illness. My response would be the same.[6]

The problem, which Ennis blithely ignores, is that when the diseased organ is the brain, the afflicted individual cannot make the reasoned decisions regarding treatment that a cardiac patient can be expected to make. Nor does heart disease produce the disordered, sometimes dangerous behavior characteristic of mental illness.

Whatever his private views on the nature of mental illness, Ennis's 1972 book *Prisoners of Psychiatry* reflected anti-psychiatric perspectives. Thomas Szasz wrote the preface, and in it praised Ennis for recognizing "that individuals incriminated as mentally ill do not need guarantees of 'treatment' but protection against their enemies—the legislators, judges, and psychiatrists who persecute them in the name of mental health."[7] In the book, which describes a number of his major cases, Ennis portrays psychiatry as a means to control or dispose of people who annoy others. Ennis writes: "How would we tame our rebellious youth, or rid ourselves of doddering parents, or clear the streets of the offensive poor, without it?" For Ennis, hospitals are places "where sick people get sicker and sane people go mad."[8]

In *Prisoners of Psychiatry* Ennis appears ready to accept involuntary commitment for persons who had recently committed or threatened substantial physical harm. But two years later, in an interview published in *Madness Network News,* Ennis stated: "My personal goal is either to abolish involuntary commitment or to set up so many procedural roadblocks and hurdles that it will be difficult, if not impossible, for the state to commit people against their will."[9]

Previous Reform Efforts

If the mental health bar had been content simply with tightening commitment standards, it would have been following a well-worn tradition. Depending on whether optimism about the effectiveness of therapy or suspicion of psychiatric abuse of authority was uppermost in public opinion, state legislatures have oscillated for a hundred years between tightening and relaxing commitment laws. But prior to the emergence of the mental health bar, the fundamental assumptions of the system were not challenged: mental illness existed, and severely ill patients had to be treated, involuntarily if necessary.[10]

In the 1840s, when the "cult of curability" was at its height, commitment procedures were informal. They were tightened in the

1860s as a result of the impact of an English novel—*Hard Cash*—and a famous insanity trial, the Packard case: both fueled fears that sane people were routinely shut up in mental hospitals. *Hard Cash,* the *One Flew Over the Cuckoo's Nest* of its day, described the travails of Alfred Hardie, an academically brilliant and athletically gifted Oxford student who is railroaded into a series of asylums by his wicked father, fearful that his honorable son will disclose how he has cheated a sea captain (father of the girl the son loves) of his entire life savings. The author, Charles Reade, insisted he had uncovered many similar real life cases that had never come to light because, even when justice was ultimately done, the cases "are nearly always accompanied with a stipulation of secrecy; so terrible, so ineradicable is the stigma."[11]

The case of Elizabeth Packard highlighted fears of unwarranted commitment in the United States. The mother of five children, the youngest still an infant at the time of her commitment in 1860, Mrs. Packard spent three years in the Illinois State Hospital for the Insane. She claimed that she was falsely charged with insanity by her husband, a minister, because their religious beliefs differed. Whether Mrs. Packard was mentally ill at the time of her commitment is open to question. Albert Deutsch has pointed out that as a young girl she had briefly been confined at Worcester State Hospital in Massachusetts and seemed to suffer from delusions, asserting at one time that she was the third person in the Holy Trinity and the mother of Jesus Christ.[12] In any event, Mrs. Packard's ideas did not interfere with her functioning, and she proved to be a strikingly effective advocate.

Acquitted of insanity in a famous jury trial, she campaigned for both substantive and procedural changes in the law. She wanted insane "ideas" (without accompanying irrational behavior) eliminated as a basis for commitment and mandatory jury trials in every commitment proceeding. While only a few states passed the "personal liberty" bills for which she lobbied, the wave of public sentiment she created led to the passage of stricter commitment laws in a number of states.

Ironically, compulsory jury trials turned out to be a miserable remedy and were detested by families and physicians alike. The trials forced families to testify against patients in open court, a humiliating procedure. There were complaints that patients went untreated in the early, more treatable, phase of their illness as the family sought to postpone the stigmatizing ordeal. Nor did juries prove reluctant to commit patients. State hospital superintendents claimed more sane persons were found insane by jury trials than had ever been wrongfully committed under the earlier system.[13]

At the end of the nineteenth century, the pendulum began to swing once more. In the Progressive era the psychopathic hospital was born, designed for quick, early intervention in cases of mental illness. Mental health reformers now viewed procedural safeguards as roadblocks that prevented prompt treatment in the community.[14]

Yet another wave of faith in the powers of psychiatry followed World War II. In 1952, a draft act proposed as a state model by the recently created National Institute of Mental Health proposed extremely loose commitment criteria—those committed should be "in need of care or treatment." And, in fact, there was a further relaxation of commitment laws in some states. Pennsylvania permitted commitment of anyone suffering from mental illness that "so lessens the capacity of a person to use his customary self-control, judgment and discretion in the conduct of his affairs and social relations as to make it necessary or advisable for him to be under care." Massachusetts provided that a person could be committed who was "likely to conduct himself in a manner which clearly violates the established laws, ordinances, conventions or morals of the community."[15]

There were then grounds for reformers to seek tighter standards once again, so as to prevent the potential for abuse in such vague statutes. And exposés of appalling conditions in mental hospitals by Albert Deutsch and others in the late 1940s and early 1950s helped to create a climate of opinion opposed to liberal commitment laws.

Mental Health Bar Launches All-out Attack on Psychiatry

But the members of the mental health bar were abolitionists, not reformers, who challenged every assumption of the mental health system. Its members launched a two-pronged attack, assailing the system's intellectual foundations in law journal articles and bringing a series of major lawsuits. The strategy worked synergistically, the articles becoming the acknowledged underpinning for judicial decisions in the lawsuits. Neither Szasz nor the labeling theorists of mental illness were bedside reading for judges who decided the major cases. Anti-psychiatric theories became the basis for judicial decisions by way of law journal articles that rested upon their assumptions. Indeed, anti-psychiatry so dominated the perspective of articles on mental illness in law journals in the 1970s that it was rare to find an article with a different viewpoint.

The intellectual assault on psychiatry was a total one. A prescient article in the *UCLA Law Review* in 1967—before the takeover by the mental health bar—warned: "If ever it be proven that psychiatry is not reliable, there will be created a doctrinal abyss into which will sink the whole structure of commitment law, not just those portions that deal with the harmlessly insane."[16] It was precisely toward creating that doctrinal abyss that the mental patient liberation bar directed its energies.

Entire issues of law journals were devoted to demolishing all psychiatric claims. A series of articles in the May 1974 issue of the *University of California Law Review,* for example, attacked psychiatry for everything from incompetence to sex bias. Bruce Ennis and Thomas Litwack, a psychologist and attorney, co-authored the most quoted article in the issue: "Psychiatry and the Presumption of Expertise: Flipping Coins in the Courtroom." The article argued that psychiatrists could not even diagnose mental illness, let alone predict who was dangerous. Relying on psychiatric expertise, wrote Ennis and Litwack, was *worse* than relying on chance. "It is inconceivable that a judgment could be considered an 'expert' judgment when it is less accurate than the flip of a coin." Consequently, Ennis and Litwack maintained, "psychiatrists should not be permitted to testify as expert witnesses" in civil commitment hearings.[17]

One by one, the major treatment advances of the previous two decades were debunked. In an influential 1977 article in *Northwestern University Law Review,* "Limiting the Therapeutic Orgy: Mental Patients' Right to Refuse Treatment," Robert Plotkin castigated the major psychiatric treatments, not only psychosurgery and electroshock therapy (both by then familiar targets) but the psychoactive drugs, psychiatry's proudest achievement. In Plotkin's analysis, the benefits of the drugs—never described—are secondary to their side effects, which he painstakingly details. For Plotkin, "the primary reason for the continuing extensive use of these drugs. . . . is the control of institutional patients' behavior."[18] Not surprisingly, Plotkin advocates the patient's right to refuse any and all psychiatric treatments.

Some grounds for attack were ingenious. A 1974 article in the *Yale Law Journal* by an anonymous state legislator declared: "The *sine qua non* for mental illness to qualify as a suspect classification is numerical domination of legislatures by persons not mentally ill." Since all legislatures fell into this category, before devising statutes governing involuntary commitment of the mentally ill, they had the burden of proof "to demonstrate sheer perfection in classification." Dangerous to others? People who are not mentally ill are just as dangerous, so it is discriminatory to institutionalize only the mentally ill prior to actual commission of a crime. Dangerous to self? Normal people may neglect their health—smoke cigarettes for example—without state intervention. In short, all involuntary commitment standards evaporated once mental illness was recognized as a "suspect classification."[19]

Similar attacks continue in legal journals. In 1988, the *Rutgers Law Review* published a lengthy diatribe against all forms of treatment, from psychotherapy to psychotropic medications.[20] The article was riddled with the standard anti-psychiatric assumptions, including the discredited shibboleth that institutions "create" mental illness.

Government Funds the Mental Health Bar

In addition to assaulting the intellectual foundations of psychiatry in law journals, members of the mental health bar brought a series of lawsuits designed to end involuntary commitment. They were able to do so because of the creation in the late 1960s of government programs that paid their salaries. (The most important was the legal services division of the Office of Economic Opportunity—part of President Johnson's War on Poverty—which in 1974 was reconstituted as the Legal Services Corporation.) Influenced by the campus rebellions of the 1960s, many of the young attorneys who joined legal services offices around the country harbored strong anti-institution and anti-authority sentiments. They gave up the higher remuneration offered by private law firms to work for legal reform through government subsidized legal aid. And viewing the mentally ill through the distorting lens of anti-psychiatry, legal services attorneys were convinced the chief benefit they could render those clients was to obtain their freedom.

The Federal Civil Rights Law of 1964, and accompanying changes in 1966 in procedural rules, provided another funding vehicle for the mental patient liberation bar. Suits could now be brought on behalf of hospitalized mental patients under the so-called "1983" provision of the civil rights act. If a lawyer claimed the civil rights of mental patients had been violated, and won the suit, his fees would be paid by the losing government agency. Private lawyers took a big gamble with such cases, for they might lose and recover nothing, and even if they won, payment was slow. But the "1983" provision spurred legal services programs, since salaries of these lawyers were in any case paid by the government and the programs might also collect under "1983."

Richard Cole, working for Greater Boston Legal Services, brought a case establishing the right of hospitalized mental patients to refuse treatment, in which over a million dollars in attorney's fees were recovered. Says Cole: "This is the largest fee award I know of nationally in any civil rights case."[21] (Since one government agency is usually suing another—in this case a federally funded legal services program sues the state mental hospital system—the taxpayer pays for both sides of the case and then, also, pays the legal fees assessed against the losing party!)

In addition, individual states in the 1960s and early 1970s established programs providing legal advocacy for inmates in state hospitals. New York pioneered with its Mental Health Information Service in 1965. In 1974, Ohio established a Legal Rights Service, and New Jersey's Office of the Public Advocate also set up a mental health section. The very next year the latter brought the first right to refuse treatment suit. According to an attorney who worked on the New Jersey case: "We stopped counting the cost when we passed a million dollars."[22] (The Office of the Public Advocate did not sue under "1983" to recover costs because, in this case, one branch of state government was suing another, which would have made a third raid on state funds for the same case politically embarrassing.)

Private foundation funds have supplemented government programs. The Mental Health Law Project, the intellectual fulcrum of the mental health bar, has benefited from both. Primarily funded by foundations, for some years it served as a Legal Services Corporation backup center, providing training and expert advice to local legal services groups on cases involving mental illness. The National Institute of Mental Health funded the Mental Health Law Project's study on mental health law (which predictably included proposals for further tightening commitment laws).[23] Today, it acts as a training center for government Protection and Advocacy programs, to be discussed later.

Of course, all this legal activity would not have had the impact it did, were it not for a receptive judiciary. In *The Tempting of America,* Robert Bork explores the role the judiciary has taken in the general politicization of culture that has occurred in the last decades. Judges, says Bork, have treated statutes, and the Constitution itself, as "malleable texts that judges may rewrite to see that particular groups or political causes win."[24] They thus arrogate to themselves a legislative power superior to that of any legislature, because the innovation is announced in the name of the Constitution: in fact, the Constitution has little or nothing to do with it. The Fourteenth Amendment, mandating due process of law, is a particular favorite of the judicial activists, who interpret "due process" not merely as *legal procedures* but as "substantive due process." Here, the substance is whatever the judge fabricates on the basis of the political or intellectual fashions he espouses.[25]

The willingness of judges to create new law flows from misguided faith in what law can do. In 1976, chronicling a problem that has since only become worse, sociologist Nathan Glazer pointed out that judges "increasingly are intrigued by the opportunity to go to the root of the problem" despite the fact that "in many of these areas of social policy there is no clear knowledge of what the root of the problem is."[26]

Bork observes that judges are deeply influenced by the culture of the law schools, which is of course reflected in the law journals they produce. Mental patient liberation attorneys, in law journal articles, assured the courts that the root of the problem of mental illness lay in the coercive powers of psychiatry, not in the disease itself. The "solution" was to free the prisoners of psychiatry from mental hospitals to pursue unimpeded their alternative lifestyle in the community. In the course of achieving this end, judges uncovered a series of dubious, often contradictory, "constitutional rights." These included a right to treatment, a right to psychotic thought, even a right to panhandle in subways (the latter two rights based on a tortuous interpretation of the First Amendment).[27]

The Perversion of Reform Efforts: Restoring Competency

A series of well-meaning reforms proposed or actually carried out in the early 1960s aided the efforts of the mental health bar immeasurably. These were intended to reduce stigma, tighten commitment standards, and stop warehousing of patients in hospitals by guaranteeing actual treatment. In the 1970s and 1980s, the mental patient liberation bar subverted all such reforms, turning them into roadblocks to treatment.

The Senate Subcommittee on Constitutional Rights, meeting in 1961, had no idea that it was to begin a process of legal unraveling, whose end product would be legions of homeless mentally ill. The committee took pride in examining "one of the most neglected of all legal fields," and hoped to pave the way for "sound, effective legislation . . . so that the patient's constitutional rights can be protected without unduly hampering his medical needs."[28] Albert Deutsch, whose 1948 *The Shame of the States* had evoked a public outcry at the conditions in state hospitals, summed up the background for the hearings in his testimony: "In a period when civil rights for minority groups constitute a major national issue, theirs remains the most ignored and neglected of all."[29]

According to those who testified both in 1961 and in follow-up hearings in 1963, one of the most vexing civil rights issues was the mental patient's loss of rights upon commitment. By law in some states, by custom in others, individuals committed to mental hospitals were automatically deemed to be "incompetent"—to write a will, marry, dispose of property, enter into contracts, vote, even to drive a car. Several witnesses put special emphasis on the hardships worked by the loss of a driver's license. Colman Stein, the spokesman for the Mental Health Association, described the Catch-22 situation of a former mental patient in the District of Columbia. When he tried to regain his driving license, the form asked if he had ever been in a mental hospital. If he said no, he had perjured himself, and if he said yes, he would probably be denied a license. Stein pointed out that this cut recovered patients out of a great many jobs.[30]

The psychiatrists who testified uniformly urged that commitment laws be changed to allow mental patients to retain their civil rights. To them this was a reform that would *encourage* treatment. As one psychiatrist told the committee, the stigma attaching to mental illness would thereby be reduced and the patient would no longer fear what his hospital stay would "do to his employment record, to his general position in the community."[31] The American Psychiatric Association's Dr. Zigmond Lebensohn said that mental hospitals should be "looked upon as treatment centers for sick people in the same sense that general hospitals are still viewed," and it was only when mental patients had the same civil rights as general patients that this would be possible.[32]

The model bill that the Senate drafted in 1963 specified that the mentally ill patient would lose no civil rights on commitment, and the District of Columbia adopted it in modified form in 1964. Within little more than a decade, virtually every state followed suit. The individual involuntarily committed on the basis of mental illness was now assumed to be competent in all other respects. The model bill also provided that "dangerousness" to self or others be the sole criterion for commitment.[33] While the intent was to plug loopholes for abuse left open by vague commitment criteria, the senators made it easier for the mental health bar to controvert the purpose for commitment, namely treatment.

The Perversion of Reform Efforts: The Right to Treatment

The mental health bar would successfully confound the intent of yet another reform goal—giving mental patients a legal "right to treatment." One of those who testified at the 1961 Senate hearings was Dr. Morton Birnbaum, who had introduced the concept of the right to treatment a year earlier in an article published in the American Bar Association's journal.

Trained as both an attorney and a physician (not a psychiatrist), Birnbaum hit upon the idea when he was studying in a Harvard program for social scientists in medicine in the late 1950s. As Birnbaum himself admits, many look upon him as a modern Don Quixote, a lone figure battling over many decades to invoke an elusive, perhaps indefinable right. A simple, even humble man, whose Harvard stay made no dent in his strong Brooklyn accent, Birnbaum, now in his sixties, has a modest geriatric practice in the run-down Bedford Stuyvesant section of Brooklyn. Arthritic, with thinning silver hair crowning a long face, he perseveres in his driven, selfless quest. In the evenings and on weekends, he works on right to treatment suits he continues to bring in New York State. Birnbaum explains wryly: "I make my living as a doctor and throw it away as a lawyer."[34]

But for all his quixotic idealism, Birnbaum conceived the right to treatment as a pragmatic solution to the hitherto intractable problem of securing decent care for mental patients. Periodically, there would be exposés of dreadful conditions in state hospitals. Public wrath would force improvements for a while. Then the situation would revert to its previous state. The neuroleptic drugs did eliminate wards like the one with hundreds of naked men described by Deutsch (at Byberry Hospital in Philadelphia), but patients continued to be warehoused, often for life, in huge, often antiquated, hospitals with tiny professional staffs.

Birnbaum wanted to find a way to produce changes that would outlast fickle public indignation. If the right of a mental patient to treatment were somehow to be enshrined in law, it could then be enforced in the courts. Birnbaum came up with a simple enforcement device. The courts would rule "that if an inmate is being kept in a mental institution against his will, he must be given proper medical treatment or else the inmate can obtain his release at will in spite of the existence or severity of his mental illness."[35]

In view of the impact Birnbaum's article would have, it is interesting that his idea initially met with very little interest. Birnbaum recalls his disappointment.

> I sent the article off. It seemed to me absurdly simple. I couldn't understand that no one would accept it. I could show you maybe fifty rejections. I sent it off to the *New England Journal of Medicine*—it came back. I sent it to the *Journal of the American Medical Association;* it came back.

American Journal of Psychiatry, it came back. I sent it to *Harvard Law Review, Yale Law Review.* They didn't even send it out for peer review lots of times. One journal sent it back with a note saying "This is preposterous." I sent it out for a couple of years.[36]

When the article finally appeared in 1960 in the *American Bar Association* journal, it was accompanied by an editorial endorsing Birnbaum's idea. And in its Sunday edition, the *New York Times* published an article about this novel idea of a "right to treatment." (Birnbaum explains that he served as his own promoter, running to the paper and hand-delivering the article.)

Even then not much happened. Says Birnbaum:

I thought once it got published the doors would break down and everyone would say what a wonderful idea, you discovered a new penicillin. But nobody broke down the doors. What amazed me was the only real comments I got on it were from two patients in state hospitals. One was Donaldson in Florida and the other was a guy Stevens in New York.[37]

Birnbaum took on the cases of both at his own cost—and pursued them with his customary tenacity. Fifteen years later, O'Connor v. Donaldson became a landmark Supreme Court ruling.

But the impact of "the right to treatment" was felt much earlier. As a result of Birnbaum's 1961 testimony, the Senate subcommittee introduced into the first draft of its model bill a provision to recognize and enforce the right to treatment. By the time the bill was enacted in 1964, only a phrase was left referring to the right. While Birnbaum was disappointed, concluding that "it was only intended to be a moral right to treatment and not a realistic legal right," the U.S. Court of Appeals for the District of Columbia in 1966 recognized the right on the basis of that hesitant reference in the 1964 bill.[38]

As we shall see, in the hands of the mental patient liberation bar, the right to treatment would become a battering ram for deinstitutionalization. This was far from Birnbaum's intention. On the contrary, Birnbaum declared in 1961 that he did not expect any major decrease in the number of hospitalized patients. The neuroleptic drugs, Birnbaum recognized, had produced only a slow and irregular drop in the patient population; patients continued to relapse despite the drugs; and no new methods of treatment were on the horizon.[39]

Birnbaum excoriated community psychiatrists who advocated discharging patients despite the lack of community alternatives, and who overlooked the reality that discharged, seriously ill patients often wound up in situations where they received neither treatment nor rehabilitation. Naively, as it turned out, Birnbaum thought that if the public discovered that the courts were discharging severely ill patients from hospitals because of inadequate treatment, it would react "to force the legislatures to increase appropriations sufficient to make it possible to provide adequate care and treatment so that the mentally ill will be treated in mental hospitals."[40]

Lanterman-Petris-Short: The Magna Carta of the Mentally Ill

The mental health bar's campaign against involuntary commitment was boosted by the passage in California in 1967 (to take effect in 1969) of a revolutionary new program designed to transform the care of the mentally ill. Dubbed "the Magna Carta of the mentally ill," the Lanterman-Petris-Short (LPS) Act created the first state mental health system to be deeply influenced by anti-psychiatry. The LPS Act was passed as a result of an odd coalition of believers in community psychiatry, anti-psychiatry, and fiscal savings.

LPS began with a 1966 study commissioned by the California mental health subcommittee that drafted the legislation. Called *The Dilemma of Mental Commitments in California,* the study drew on research by Social Psychiatry Research Associates of San Francisco, which did not conceal its anti-psychiatric bias. The group described itself as "researchers engaged in a series of social surveys generally focused on the community careers of persons *labeled as deviant.*"[41] (Emphasis added.)

The Dilemma quoted Szasz and Laing (whose work was described as "authoritative"), but its main sources were labeling sociologists (especially Scheff and Goffman) and a group of community psychiatrists who saw hospitals as cause rather than cure of mental illness. For example, the study quoted Dr. Werner Mendel, a psychiatrist whose study of almost 3,000 schizophrenic patients had led him to the same conclusions as Goffman. According to Mendel, "patients hospitalized for long periods show a clinical picture which erroneously has been attributed to the disease process. . . . We must seriously question the present conceptualization of the hospital as a method of treatment in the chronic schizophrenic patient."[42]

Even sharper words came from one Arlene Daniels, a consultant to the U.S. Army Psychiatric Residency Training, who wrote to the subcommittee: "It is possible that hospitalization is not only incorrect treatment but in some cases dangerous to any hope of future recovery."[43] (It is interesting, in light of the tremendous emphasis placed on the alleged role of hospitals in creating symptoms which are then erroneously attributed to the disease, that a 1985 study of matched long-term inpatients and outpatients published in the *British Journal of Psychiatry* found this to be a myth: the authors report that "long-term hospital care and social environment do not have a significant influence on the deficits of chronic schizophrenia."[44])

The Dilemma called for a bold new system in which patients could be held involuntarily for a maximum of seventeen days. Only those judged "dangerous" or "gravely disabled" (defined as "so incapacitated as to be unable to communicate or feed, clothe or shelter themselves") could be held even for those seventeen days. The study promised that "when these steps have been taken, state hospitals as we now know them, will no longer exist."[45]

The LPS Act embodied most of the recommendations of the draft study. Supported by the idealistic and the tight-fisted—who anticipated massive savings—the bill passed unanimously. This was largely because its anti-psychiatric thrust appealed to several of the professional groups that constituted the "attentive public" for the legislation. As Eugene Bardach points out in *The Skill Factor in Politics,* an in-depth study of how the LPS Act came to be passed, psychologists and social workers were jealous of psychiatrists' controlling role in management of mental illness. The address to the California State Psychologists Association in 1967 by its president was frank on this point. "As members of a younger professional group on the outside of organized medicine's attempts to pre-empt all 'medical' fields (including and especially mental health) . . . I think psychologists find themselves in a philosophic position very close to that of . . . Szasz. Maybe as an emergent group we even secretly gain solace and sustenance from these views."[46]

More surprisingly, psychiatrists were generally supportive. Although Bardach has pointed out that the LPS Act was "an attack on the medical model in nearly all its dimensions,"[47] community psychiatrists were willing to overlook this. Other psychiatrists were mollified because the Act freed them from burdensome court procedures during the initial seventeen-day period, and they had authority to administer intensive treatment. (There were steady procedural inroads on this right, and by the mid-1980s, the mental health bar would successfully sue for a "right to refuse treatment" in this seventeen-day period.)[48] Most psychiatrists were indifferent, since they had no contact with severely, chronically ill patients. There was no serious challenge by organized psychiatry to the utopian premise, flouting all previous experience, that the mentally ill, at the end of seventeen days, could be universally counted upon to accept treatment voluntarily in the community.

Paradoxically, the most telling criticism came from the *UCLA Law Review,* which asked what would happen to "persons who do not seek treatment because they do not recognize that they are ill."[49]

While the new law had a dramatic impact, it did not fulfill the hopes of many of its supporters that it would eliminate state hospitals. The length of time involuntary patients stayed in hospitals of course plummeted, the average stay dropping from 180 to 15 days. (The period voluntary patients stayed in hospital dropped also, although not as sharply, going from 75 to 23 days.)[50] But by 1973, when LPS had been in force only four years, then-Governor Reagan had to abandon his plan to close all state mental hospitals by 1982 except for small forensic units for the criminally insane. Protests came not only from unions of state employees but from an alarmed general public, concerned for public safety.[51]

As it turned out, the LPS Act had a provision that became the key to keeping the system functional. (Those who hoped LPS would eliminate state hospitals complained it undermined the purposes of the Act.[52]) This provision permitted "conservatorship" for those who were "gravely disabled" by mental illness. The background document on the Act indicates that the purpose of conservatorship was to provide continuing assistance in managing the affairs of gravely disabled patients beyond the two-week treatment period.[53] But the Act permitted court-appointed conservators to make treatment decisions for their conservatees, including long-term hospital placement. The vast majority of those who remained in hospitals more than seventeen days under LPS were there as gravely disabled conservatees.

Such an extensive use of conservatorship had not been foreseen by LPS backers, who had finally compromised on permitting ninety-day extensions for "dangerous" individuals (those presenting an "imminent threat of substantial physical harm to others").[54] But it was not on grounds of dangerousness that the mentally ill remained in California state mental hospitals. Five years after LPS took effect, a California Department of Health study revealed that in the 1972–73 fiscal year, of over 6,000 people kept for seventeen days (that included a three-day evaluation hold and a fourteen-day intensive treatment certification) *only eighteen* were kept for an additional ninety days because they were considered dangerous. But in that same period 3,296 individuals were kept as conservatees after being declared "gravely disabled."[55] Long-term involuntary commitment had been smuggled in through the back door.

One of the findings of the 1965 *Dilemma of Mental Commitments* study that had shocked legislators was that California commitment hearings lasted an average of only 4.7 minutes. This study, similar to one done by Thomas Scheff in Wisconsin, was made much of by labeling theorists. They contended that a carelessly applied label, based on no more than a few minutes in a courtroom, determined an individual's entire future as a career deviant (mental patient). Now, a study of court hearings to establish conservatorship revealed they were of even shorter average duration![56] In neither case was this in itself evidence of railroading of "inconvenient" people into mental hospitals. By the time individuals came to court, they had usually given ample evidence of serious mental illness. In the case of conservatees the decisions had been made earlier by psychiatrists and a specifically appointed conservatorship investigator; the court hearing did indeed become a formality. Actually, conservatorship investigators in most cases applied the criteria to establish "grave disability" so rigidly that a great many people severely disabled by their illness did not obtain treatment.[57]

Chapter 6

Hospitalization
Under Attack

The Major Legal Cases

THE emergent mental health bar found the Lanterman-Petris-Short (LPS) Act a valuable model in many respects. However, it did not like those features that postponed court involvement and relied on medical judgment for the two-week treatment period: for the mental patient liberation bar, these were serious drawbacks. So rather than attempt to replicate LPS procedures in state after state, the mental health bar sought both to transform commitment standards (which California had done) and to make *courts,* acting under strict procedural guidelines, the only avenue for commitment.

The mental health bar was granted a major weapon by a Supreme Court decision in the apparently unrelated field of juvenile delinquency. In 1967, after a hard look at the juvenile justice system, the Supreme Court ruled in *In re* Gault that the system's benevolent intentions were irrelevant. The juvenile was stigmatized and deprived of his liberty; he was therefore entitled to the due process protections of the adult system of justice.

Mental patient liberation lawyers looked at civil commitment in the same light: those "accused" of mental illness deserved at least the same due process protections accorded criminals, particularly since they had not committed crimes. And if the therapeutic objectives of the juvenile court could not obviate the need for due process, then why should those of the state hospital system abrogate the due process rights of the so-called mentally ill facing imprisonment?

In 1972 the mental health bar mounted its first major successful legal challenge to a state's civil commitment system. Milwaukee Legal Services brought a class action suit under the "1983" provision of the Civil Rights Act (giving it the opportunity to collect legal fees if successful) in federal court on behalf of Alberta Lessard and all those committed involuntarily under Wisconsin statutes, arguing that the state's commitment statutes were invalid because they lacked the safeguards of criminal law.

To the police who picked up Lessard and the judge who committed her, it must have seemed a routine case. Following a purported suicide attempt, the police took Lessard to a Milwaukee mental health center where, after psychiatric examination, she was said to suffer from schizophrenia. Wisconsin's mental health laws in 1972 were typical of the era of therapeutic optimism, providing that a mentally ill person, defined as someone who "requires care and treatment for his own welfare, or the welfare of others in the community" could be committed if "a proper subject for custody and treatment."

While legitimately calling for tightening of this vague statute, Milwaukee Legal Services demanded besides that Wisconsin's civil commitment laws provide the mentally ill with the same protections accorded the criminal suspect: effective and timely notice of the "charges" against him; mandatory notice of right to a jury trial; a right to appointed counsel; a right to remain silent; a right of counsel to be present at psychiatric interviews to guarantee the patient understood the privilege against self-incrimination, exclusion of hearsay evidence, and a standard of proof beyond a reasonable doubt.[1] Strict implementation of these requirements would indeed have achieved the mental patient liberation bar's goal of eliminating involuntary civil commitment.

The district court's judgment in the Lessard case, which quoted critics of psychiatry ranging from Mrs. Packard to Bruce Ennis, obviously reflected anti-psychiatric influence. The court endorsed virtually all the demands made by Milwaukee Legal Services, rejecting only the one requiring the presence of an attorney during the psychiatric examination. In addition, it set a dangerousness standard narrower than anything seen before: "there is an extreme likelihood that if the person is not confined he will do immediate harm to himself or others."[2] The court saw civil commitment primarily as what it called "a massive curtailment of liberty." *There was no recognition that a disease process had already curtailed the individual's liberty and that treatment might be necessary to restore the person's autonomy in any meaningful sense of the term.*

The case wended its way to the Supreme Court, which, clearly unhappy with the decision of the lower courts, vacated and remanded it twice, in 1974 and 1975. But the lower courts made only minor changes ("imminent" was substituted for "extreme" likelihood). The Wisconsin legislature then amended its statutes to bring them into accord with the court's decision. Thanks in part to the Lessard decision, the percentage drop in resident patients in Wisconsin's mental hospitals has been larger than in any state except Arkansas.

The Lessard decision went further than LPS in attacking the "medical model" of mental illness. Under LPS, those who met the severe criteria of the Act could at least be intensively treated for seventeen days. Under the Lessard decision, an individual could only be held for seventy-two hours on an emergency basis before a court applied a standard of proof based on procedures used in criminal law. In practice most people were released after seventy-two hours.

The court did not recognize that, unlike criminal incarceration, involuntary treatment for mental illness offered *benefits* to the patient, and that unlike criminal and jailer, doctor and patient had a common interest in securing the patient's improved health. When someone has heart disease, no one calls for a lawyer to be present when a doctor questions the patient, although he might be "incarcerated" in a hospital. Mental illness is different only in that the brain is the diseased organ, leading many of those most severely affected to deny the existence of the illness. Blinded by anti-psychiatry, the Lessard court treated a disease as if it were a criminal deed. The effect was to *increase* rather than reduce the stigma associated with mental illness.

Facing a rash of similar suits by the mental health bar, other state legislatures followed Wisconsin in changing their statutes to apply criminal standards to mental illness, although few adopted all the procedural protections of Wisconsin. (Only a minority, for example, included a right to remain silent during psychiatric evaluation.[3]) In this way, policies made by the judiciary *seemed* to obtain democratic sanction as legislatures were impelled to incorporate them into statutory law.

The effect was to deprive many of life in the name of liberty. Darold Treffert, a psychiatrist who was then head of the Mental Health Institute in Winnebago, Wisconsin, began to compile reports of cases in Wisconsin (and around the country) of patients who, as he put it, "died with their rights on." This, even though Wisconsin did far better than most

states in providing alternative services in the community for the seriously mentally ill.

Wyatt v. Stickney: Strange Bedfellows

As psychiatrist and writer Alan Stone has astutely noted, the effort
to make dangerousness the sole criterion for civil commitment is not
reform but *abolition* disguised as reform. Not content with their success
in this effort, liberation advocates worked along other fronts simultaneously. Procedural changes primarily prevented people from being
admitted to hospital. But the mental health bar also wanted to empty out
hospitals of patients already there. In light of this goal Morton Birnbaum's claim for a constitutional "right to treatment" began to seem a
useful tool. It was largely thanks to the liberation bar's drive to *end*
treatment that the "right to treatment" became the major mental health
issue of the early 1970s.

The mental health bar was at first dubious about using the issue.
Talking to *Madness Network News,* Ennis explained his initial refusal to
handle right to treatment cases.

> I refused to do so because I was afraid that if they were successful . . . it
> would become a legitimizing stamp on involuntary confinement, another
> basis for depriving people of their liberty. . . . In other words I don't really
> believe in the 'right to treatment' concept.[4]

Yet the right to treatment had an advantage in carrying moral weight. It
could win the support of a broad spectrum, including psychiatrists,
other mental health professionals, and the general public. (In the early
1970s families of the mentally ill were still in the closet and did not
constitute a separate factor.)

In the end, the mental health bar decided to become involved in
the major "right to treatment" case, Wyatt v. Stickney, in Alabama. Ennis
explained his reasoning. There was "advance information" that the
judge "would not only say there is something in the abstract called the
'right to treatment,' but that he would set standards so high that the State
of Alabama literally would not be able to meet them." This meant the
state "was going to have to discharge many of the residents in its
institutions." Winning "the right to treatment" would thus serve, said
Ennis, "as the best method for deinstitutionalizing thousands of persons."[5] This was why, said Ennis, he decided to become involved in
Wyatt v. Stickney. Thus, those seeking treatment and those seeking to
end treatment joined forces in an anomalous alliance.

Wyatt v. Stickney originated with a cut in Alabama's cigarette tax. In the resulting budget shortfall, over a hundred employees at Bryce Hospital in Tuscaloosa, Alabama lost their jobs, twenty of them professionals (psychologists, social workers, and occupational therapists). The Department of Psychology at Bryce spearheaded the suit for reinstatement brought by those laid off, and for tactical reasons added a patient, Ricky Wyatt, the nephew of one of the laid-off employees.[6] While Federal Judge Frank M. Johnson held that the Alabama Department of Mental Health had the right to lay off employees, he consented to hear the part of the suit dealing with the patients' grievances.[7] (The suit alleged that patients' treatment suffered as a result of the layoffs.) The attorney for the employees, a well-known trial lawyer named George Dean, decided to forge ahead on the basis of Morton Birnbaum's theory of a right to treatment, and Birnbaum himself became co-counsel.

As more and more national organizations lined up behind Dean, the case looked like a conflict between the forces of humanitarian liberalism and red-necked conservatism. The ACLU, professional organizations, even the American Psychiatric Association came in on behalf of Dean. On the other side was Alabama's mental health commissioner, whose very name harked backwards—Stonewall Beauregard Stickney. Birnbaum describes him as "a big husky guy with a Van Dyke beard. He looked like Stonewall Jackson with a gray hat, a Confederate general." Behind Stickney was Alabama's Governor George Wallace, then a symbol of a populist Far Right. The system they were defending had little to recommend it. The hospital was shamefully overcrowded and the staffing pitiful. There was a single psychiatrist for 5,000 patients, and psychologists and social workers were correspondingly scarce. Physical plant, clothing, food—budgeted at 50 cents a day—all were woefully inadequate.

But the situation was more complex than it appeared. Alongside those ostensibly seeking to improve conditions in Alabama's hospitals (the suit was extended to include both state mental hospitals and the institution for the retarded) were those who aimed to close them down: initially, though, such allies in the suit as the American Psychiatric Association were unaware of this. On the other side, Stickney was actually sympathetic to the declared purpose of the suit—obtaining more money from the state legislature so as to improve treatment in Alabama's hospitals. Birnbaum speaks warmly of him: "He didn't have to work there. He worked there because he wanted to help the people of Alabama."[8] At the outset Stickney conceded the opposition's case: patients *had* a right to treatment.[9]

Judge Frank Johnson, widely known for his liberal views, un-hesitatingly endorsed the existence of a previously unsuspected consti-tutional right to treatment and defined it in Birnbaum's terms: by "objective" criteria. Paradoxically, this meant the right to treatment did not refer to *treatment* at all; it was defined purely by such things as staffing ratios and physical amenities, with the assumption that if these were in place, therapy automatically took place. (Stickney would point out tellingly that some of the staffing ratios—i.e., so many Masters of Social Work, so many Ph.D psychologists—catered more to the prestige needs of the professions involved than to the needs of patients.[10]) Judge Johnson not only stipulated the required proportion of psychiatrists, nurses, psychologists, etc., to patients, but dictated the number of chaplains, messengers, dietitians, and maintenance repairmen needed. He stipulated how often linen had to be changed, how many showers a patient should receive, and what furniture should be in the dayroom.[11]

Wyatt v. Stickney: Rifts in the Alliance

Those allied in bringing the suit fell out as the prospect of victory highlighted their opposing agendas. Where would the personnel and money come from? Nowhere, rejoiced the members of the mental patient liberation bar involved in the case. Ennis observed that there were not enough psychologists in the state of Alabama to staff the institutions for the retarded alone. Unable to meet the standards, Ala-bama would have to discharge thousands from state institutions. But Birnbaum, genuinely concerned with the right to treatment, looked to the federal government. Birnbaum wanted to challenge the constitu-tionality of the 1965 Medicaid legislation that excluded state mental hospital patients under age sixty-five from Medicaid benefits. Because of Medicaid's matching provisions, he calculated that if Medicaid included state mental hospital patients, Alabama would be able to quadruple its expenditures on these patients without increasing state appropriations.

It was the strategy of Ennis and the mental health bar that won out. Birnbaum describes what happened:

> Dean . . . decided not to challenge the constitutionality of the Medicaid exclusion. He believed that the state mental institution system was ba-sically bad and should be done away with in favor of alternative commu-nity facilities. My arguments that a sufficient number of alternative facili-ties were not available were of no avail. I then decided not to participate any further as co-counsel for plaintiffs and attempted to interest various groups participating as amici curiae in this challenge of the Medicaid

exclusions. They believed, however, as did Dean, that the state mental hospital system should be abolished and that increased funding would only perpetuate an evil.[12]

The amici curiae to whom Birnbaum refers are, of course, organizations represented and guided by members of the new Mental Health Law Project, which itself was established by Ennis and other young public interest attorneys working on the case.

In a twist, Birnbaum then turned to his ostensible opponents in the suit. "I said maybe you're interested. They're going to give a judgment against you, you'll need the money. For $100 of Alabama funds, you'd get $300 of federal funds. Without it you're going to get nothing." Stickney was responsive, promising to talk to Governor Wallace. As Birnbaum tells the story: "I couldn't believe it. I have a letter somewhere. He says the governor wants to come in." Birnbaum recalls calling F. Lewis Bartlett, a Pennsylvania state hospital psychiatrist politically to his left: "And I said Lew, who have I ended up with? I'm in the same bed with Wallace." Bartlett reassured him: "Those patients are living in shit. Do you think they care about politics? Anyone who will help."[13] But the unusual incipient alliance ended abruptly when Governor Wallace, at the time campaigning for the Presidency, was shot and paralyzed.

In 1972 Birnbaum bowed out of Wyatt v. Stickney to initiate a separate challenge in federal court in New York to the Medicaid exclusion. Sixteen organizations filed amicus briefs, ranging from the American Medical Association and the American Psychiatric Association to all the major black civil rights groups. (The suit emphasized that blacks were disproportionately treated in state mental hospitals while whites were more likely to be treated—with Medicaid funds—in private hospitals.) But the ACLU and the Mental Health Law Project refused to participate, because, said Birnbaum, "it is their goal to destroy the state mental hospital system."[14]

In the end, it was the agenda of mental patient liberation attorneys that advanced most. Birnbaum lost his suit to force Medicaid to include state mental hospital patients. And as the mental health bar anticipated, despite a major recruitment effort, Alabama could not meet the personnel requirements imposed by Judge Johnson (and which the state agreed to meet in a consent decree). *Psychiatric News,* the official newsletter of the American Psychiatric Association, was sufficiently embarrassed by the unwillingness of psychiatrists to take the advertised new positions that it published an editorial appealing to its members to come forward. While more maids and attendants were hired, and the standard of food and clothing improved in the state hospitals, the main result of Wyatt v. Stickney was that Alabama rapidly emptied its state mental hospitals. Indeed, fourteen years later, in 1986, when a settlement was signed in the Wyatt case that finally ended the prolonged litigation, Judge Johnson's requirements had still not been met.[15]

Fearing the precedent of costly improvements that had been set, other states accelerated deinstitutionalization after 1972, since it was clearly the cheapest way to achieve improved ratios of staff to patients. The mental health bar had merely to set up shop to spearhead an exodus from state hospitals. An attorney for the Mississippi Mental Health Project, set up in 1974 at Mississippi State Hospital by a local (federally funded) legal services program, boasted in *Madness Network News* that the project had reduced the number of residents at the hospital in a single year by over a third, through a series of lawsuits and threatened lawsuits.[16]

The Donaldson Case: Suing Psychiatrists for Failing to Treat

A second suit had a major impact in accelerating the emptying of hospitals. On the surface the Donaldson case was simple, and the outcome a cause for rejoicing. The right to freedom of a man long confined in a mental hospital was affirmed by a jury, a federal appeals court, and finally the Supreme Court. But by merging the conflicting agendas of right to treatment and liberation advocates, it caused immense confusion and produced a series of ill-considered court rulings.

In December 1956, a judge told Kenneth Donaldson that he was committing him to Florida State Hospital: "A few weeks up there. Take some of that new medication—what's the name of it?—and you'll be back."[17] (Thorazine was just then being widely introduced.) Unconscionably, Donaldson remained in the hospital at Chattahoochee for fourteen years. While Donaldson did suffer from paranoid delusions on entering the hospital—and as his subsequent writings make obvious, continued to do so—his illness did not impair his functioning in other areas. He showed no signs of being dangerous to anyone; he had consistently been able to support himself (for years he supported a wife and three children); he made friends readily; and he showed a high degree of motivation, persistence, and intelligence. There were repeated offers, both from a halfway house in Minneapolis and a friend of Donaldson's in Syracuse, to provide a home and supervision for him.[18]

The case was brought as a right to treatment suit. Yet as Donaldson makes clear in his book *Insanity Inside Out,* he was convinced he had been fraudulently railroaded, and there was "nothing to treat." His case became entangled with Birnbaum's principle of a right to treatment after Donaldson read the 1960 *New York Times* story about Dr. Birnbaum mentioned earlier and wrote to him asking for help. Birnbaum suggested that he base his next petition for a writ of habeas corpus on the hospital's failure to provide his "constitutional right to treatment."[19]

In fact, Donaldson himself was so opposed to treatment that he chose to remain in the hospital indefinitely rather than accept it. Shortly after being committed, Donaldson was summoned by the hospital psychiatrist who told him that his mother had written to the hospital urging that he be given electroconvulsive treatment (ECT). Donaldson's first serious episode of mental illness occurred in 1943, when he was thirty-four, married, and working for a General Electric defense plant in Syracuse. Hospitalized at Marcy State Hospital, he had been given twenty-three shock treatments. Since the treatments worked—he was released from the hospital and resumed his married life—his mother presumably hoped that they would be effective once again. But Donaldson, who had hated the treatments, told the psychiatrist: "I can tell you this—you won't give me more than one." Told it was either ECT or the General Wards (i.e., the back wards of the hospital) Donaldson replied: "I'll take the General Wards even if it's twenty years."[20]

The hospital then sought to persuade Donaldson to take medication. When his parents visited him in 1958, his father told him the doctor said he would have to take a course of medication before he could leave. Donaldson replied: "That's ridiculous—I don't need pills." Six years later, in 1964, the hospital's doctors were still trying to persuade Donaldson to accept treatment. Donaldson reports the following exchange:

DR.: Would you rather stay here year after year than take some medication—even if you knew you could get out if you took some?

ME: Why should I take medication if I don't need it? . . .

DR.: Supposing you were told that you couldn't leave unless you took some medicine?

ME: That would be blackmail!

DR.: Yes—but if it meant you must stay here many more years?

ME: Bullshit! Pills don't cure anything.[21]

Donaldson viewed anti-psychotic drugs as destructive for any patient. "For a rare few of us," Donaldson wrote, "the absence of 'prescribed' medication meant our chance for survival."[22] (Donaldson insisted that the vast majority of the 10,000 patients he encountered in the hospital were basically normal, and that only three were schizophrenic.)

Donaldson was equally opposed to "talk" therapy. He reports the effort, the following year, of a new doctor to engage him in group therapy.

> DR. CHACON: I am having a group of four, twice a week—to discuss your problems and see what's wrong. You're the first one I've called. We're going to straighten out your thinking and get you out of here.

> ME: There was nothing wrong with my thinking when I was put in here. I don't want any group therapy.[23]

It is interesting that although Donaldson was committed at a time when enthusiasm for the new neuroleptic drugs was at its height, and no one even dreamed of a right to refuse treatment, Donaldson's wishes were honored throughout the fourteen years of his incarceration, except for a two-week period when a doctor new to his case, eager to release him, and whom Donaldson liked, forced medication on him.

Birnbaum took the case because for him, as Donaldson wrote, it "was part of a broad offensive to improve the state hospital system." When Donaldson told him that he neither wanted nor needed treatment, Birnbaum assured him that by using the right to treatment argument he would be helping thousands of other inmates. And so in Birnbaum's briefs the *failure* to treat was emphasized. "What member of this court would not consider it a tale of horror if he or a member of his family were to be involuntarily committed to a mental institution where there were only one doctor to more than 950 inmates?"[24] To Donaldson, it would have made no difference if there had been one doctor for every five inmates: in his own view, he was and always had been mentally well.

The paradox was not lost on Julian Davis, one of the psychologists who examined Donaldson in the hospital. Davis, who had repeatedly urged that Donaldson be released, told him: "As I understand it, there are two parts to your case—the Right to Treatment and the fact that you don't need treatment." Davis probed uncomfortably. "What kind of treatment do you think you should have, if you were to have some treatment?" Donaldson reports that he realized this was dangerous

ground for him, and responded: "There is no point in making a hypo-
thetical choice." Davis came back: "But you told the court you wanted
your release because you were getting no treatment, didn't you?" Donaldson replied: "I don't want any."[25]

The real reason he was held so long, in Donaldson's (probably
correct) view, was because he refused to play games. He explained how
other patients managed to get out: "They tell the doctor how pleased
they are because he has got them well. Then the doctor lets them go."[26]
One of the doctors, telling him he had the votes to get him out, tried to
coach him prior to bringing him to staff. "You must not show any
hostility. . . . Don't argue with the doctors." But Donaldson, with stubborn integrity, refused to compromise his principles.

Repeatedly brought before staff in the ritual that served as prelude
to release, Donaldson would go on the attack, telling those assembled
that the fraud and lies of psychiatrists had brought him into the hospital
and that he was not and never had been mentally ill.[27] The doctors
would duly note his "lack of insight" and refuse to let him go. One
doctor told him angrily: "I've tried to help you. I've said all along you're
only stubborn. That's the only thing that is wrong with you."[28] Donaldson further antagonized the staff by his constant petitions and appeals outside the hospital. In the end, Donaldson won release on his
own terms, refusing the furlough that was eventually offered him (a
probationary kind of release) and holding out successfully for a full
"competency" discharge.

The Mental Health Bar Takes Over Donaldson's Case

As in the Wyatt case, Birnbaum's agenda was displaced by that of
the mental patient liberation bar. Birnbaum's time and resources were
limited—he was raising five children on his modest medical practice.
And so he drew the key members of the Wyatt team into the Donaldson
case, notably George Dean and Bruce Ennis, the latter eventually assum-
ing the leading role. For Ennis, the case provided an opportunity to
establish a right to freedom for all nondangerous individuals, and to
frighten hospital administrators into discharging patients by making
them personally liable for failure to do so.

And so late in 1972, a jury in Tallahassee was asked to rule on
Donaldson's suit against two doctors at Florida State Hospital for failing
to treat him. The suit sought damages from Dr. J. B. O'Connor—whose
retirement in 1971 had finally paved the way for Donaldson's release—
and from his assistant, Dr. John Gumanis. Dr. Birnbaum says he was

horrified. "When I heard that I felt terrible. I said the doctors are working, they're killing themselves; they think they're helping the people of Florida and they're held personally liable."[29] Although at this point there was no such thing in law as a "right to treatment," the judge instructed the jury that it should rule for Donaldson if it found he was not given such "treatment as will give him a realistic opportunity to be cured or to improve his mental condition." The jury ruled Donaldson had indeed been denied the right to treatment and assessed damages of $38,500 against O'Connor and Gumanis.[30]

How could Donaldson, having tenaciously rejected all treatment, win a case based on his "right to treatment?" In the trial, the "treatments" Donaldson had been denied were specified: ground privileges, occupational therapy, and psychotherapy.[31] But there was no reason to believe that ground privileges or occupational therapy would have any effect whatever on paranoia. As for talk therapy, a famous study by Dr. Philip May comparing the effectiveness of neuroleptic drugs, ECT, and psychotherapy had appeared four years earlier; May and his team had found drugs the most effective, ECT second, and psychotherapy virtually useless in achieving improvement in hospitalized psychotic patients.[32] Donaldson had refused both ECT and medication, the treatments most effective in countering paranoid delusions. The notion that the other "treatments" Donaldson had been denied would have "cured" him, or given him "a realistic opportunity to be cured," was laughable. Nonetheless, the U.S. Fifth Circuit Court of Appeals upheld the decision of the trial court, affirming that the "patient had constitutional right to such treatment as would help him to be cured or to improve his mental condition."

The Donaldson decision then served as the basis for the same court to uphold Judge Johnson's decision in the Wyatt case. It had sat on Alabama's appeal of that decision for two years. But upon deciding in 1974 that there *was* a right to treatment in the Donaldson case, the Fifth Circuit promptly affirmed the Wyatt decision on that basis.[33]

The U.S. Supreme Court showed little better grasp of the issues in the Donaldson case. In fact, it deliberately skirted them on the grounds—typical for courts—that larger issues should not be considered if a case can be decided on narrow ones. In July 1975, in a unanimous decision, the Supreme Court declared the case raised "a single, relatively simple, but nonetheless important question concerning every man's constitutional right to liberty." The grounds for freeing Donaldson were so strong that the Supreme Court was off the hook. The court temporized: "There is no reason now to decide whether mentally ill persons dangerous to themselves or to others have a right to treatment upon compulsory confinement by the State, or whether the State may compulsorily confine a nondangerous mentally ill individual for the purpose of treatment."[34]

But of course Donaldson's attorneys had originally brought the case precisely to obtain answers to the questions the Supreme Court set aside. Birnbaum was the most frustrated. "The first time they had the issue squarely before them, they sidestepped it. . . . What about the sick patients who are rotting in crowded warehouses without proper food and with no psychiatric care? Can't these jokers see that this inhumane issue must be attacked?"[35] Ennis was disappointed that the court had failed to proclaim that all nondangerous mentally ill persons had the right to freedom. Only Donaldson's delight was unqualified, if illogical: "I always felt that the right to proper treatment amounted to the same thing as the right to freedom."[36]

In a separate, concurring opinion, then Chief Justice Warren Burger zeroed in on conceptual problems inherent in "the right to treatment," problems that Birnbaum—by focusing on staffing ratios rather than treatment methods—had sought to mask. On the one hand, said Burger, the right to treatment would make commitment too difficult: "Given the present state of medical knowledge . . . few things would be more fraught with peril than to irrevocably condition a State's power to protect the mentally ill upon providing of 'such treatment as will give a realistic opportunity to be cured.'" On the other hand, said Burger, the right to treatment could make commitment too easy. "To the extent that this theory may be read to permit a state to confine an individual simply because it is willing to provide treatment, regardless of the subject's ability to function in society, it raises the gravest of constitutional problems . . . ."[37]

The chief impact of the Donaldson case was not in enshrining a right to treatment, but, as the anti-psychiatric mental health bar had hoped, in *spurring deinstitutionalization*. While the $38,500 in damages assessed against O'Connor was whittled down to $20,000 in a consent decree in 1977, the principle of the personal liability of psychiatrists in state hospitals had been established. For psychiatrists, it was far easier to release patients than to run the risk of damage suits.[38]

Peonage Suits

Liberationist attorneys found another method to induce state officials to empty state mental hospitals: the peonage suit. When the cult of curability finally disappeared late in the nineteenth century, the annual reports of state mental hospitals turned from emphasizing discharge rates to the productivity of patient labor. Some of the large hospitals produced much of their own food, clothing, and linen and even maintained small industries. Patients performed most of the housekeeping functions of the hospital. No one questioned the value of this from the standpoint both of the institution and the patient, for from the pristine days of moral treatment, labor was considered the capstone of therapy. Emil Kraepelin, the father of biological psychiatry, summed up the long-held general view: "Every experienced alienist soon recognizes the worth of meaningful activity, especially farming and gardening, in the treatment of mental patients."[39]

Unquestionably, there were abuses. In many cases patients worked long hours for many years at menial tasks for no more reward than a few special privileges on the ward. Good workers might be kept in the hospital long after they could have been discharged.

Members of the mental health bar seized upon the issue of patient labor (first taken up by Birnbaum's friend Dr. F. Lewis Bartlett) as a way of making large state hospitals both uneconomic and unmanageable. The Wyatt case provided a precedent by outlawing unpaid patient labor. (There was a specific exemption allowing the patient to make his own bed.) Moreover, Judge Johnson had ruled that a patient's wages could not be used to offset the costs of his care, that is, the hospital could not pay with one hand and withhold the money with the other.

Advocates brought a series of cases charging patient peonage in the early 1970s. One prong of attack, used by mental patient liberation bar member David Ferleger in Pennsylvania, argued that the Thirteenth Amendment outlawing slavery should be applied to unpaid patient labor. Another line of attack, pursued by the Mental Health Law Project, was based on 1966 congressional amendments to the Fair Labor Standards Act and subsequent interpretations by the Department of Labor that extended coverage of minimum wage laws to institutions for the mentally ill.[40]

Outlawing patient labor proved easy to achieve. The case brought by Ferleger was settled out of court, with the state agreeing that any patient who worked would be paid the minimum wage. According to Ferleger, in Pennsylvania, the number of patients working immediately sank from 6,000 to 600. The Mental Health Law Project's 1973 case against the Secretary of Labor effectively ended patient labor nationally. Paradoxically, now that they had outlawed patient labor, some members of the mental health bar sought to impose it: In New Jersey the Office of the Public Advocate brought suit to force hospitals to employ patients at prevailing commercial wage rates. While a consent degree was obtained, nothing happened. An attorney who worked on the case said: "The problem was there was no money and we didn't get any enforcement."[41]

Outlawing patient labor had enormous impact on the running of state hospitals. Maintenance costs soared, and the difficulty of managing institutions with huge idle populations became much greater. When a New York State Commission on Quality of Care for the Mentally Disabled visited the state's nine state hospitals (euphemistically restyled "psychiatric centers") in 1985, it complained most of the "total lack of occupation" on the wards. According to the Commission report: "The norm of patient idleness was, in many ways, further reinforced by the unwritten proscription on almost all wards against patient participation in the daily maintenance of their ward environments."[42] While the Commission declared that hospital administrations had "overreacted" to peonage suits, it was little wonder, with members of the mental patient liberation bar prowling the hospitals, eager to find ever new grounds for suit.

Nowhere to Go

The cumulative effect of the hundreds of suits brought by the mental health bar at the beginning of the 1970s was vast. There has been an ongoing dispute as to whether the neuroleptic drugs or the ideology of community care or federal disability benefits were chiefly responsible for deinstitutionalization. But this debate overlooks an equally important factor—the liberation lawsuits. The figures are certainly suggestive. In the fifteen-year period from 1955 (when state hospital populations reached their peak and the neuroleptics were widely introduced) to 1970, resident state hospital populations fell from 559,000 to 339,000. In the decade between 1970 and 1980, however, the decade of the precedent-setting lawsuits to force deinstitutionalization of state mental hospitals, they fell to 130,000, a drop of equal magnitude in a considerably shorter period. After 1974, the availability of federal Supplemental Security Insurance for the mentally disabled, in conjunction with the lawsuits, provided a classic "push and pull" situation. The lawsuits made it impossible to keep patients in hospitals, while SSI made it possible for states discharging them to pass the financial burden for their care to the federal government.

Moreover, during the early years the patients who were the best candidates for community living were released. These were the patients with somewhere to go, who had families to take them in or could function independently.[43] In the first decade, also, many elderly patients were transferred to nursing homes. (In the latter case deinstitutionalization is better described as "transinstitutionalization.") Between 1970 and 1980, under pressure of the mental health bar, it was those who had, in Torrey's phrase, "nowhere to go," who were released.

Equally significant, it was in the first decade of the mental health bar's major lawsuits that the front doors of the state hospitals slammed shut. From 1955 to 1970, although the *resident* population of state hospitals declined sharply (i.e., long-term patients) total *admissions* doubled. While this famous revolving door was widely viewed as marking a failure of the mental health system, it offered a safety valve. Chronically ill individuals who became acutely ill could return, usually for brief periods, until they were better once again. But between 1970 and 1980, even admissions fell significantly, in some states going down by half. (In California admissions fell from 42,000 to 19,000 and in Massachusetts from 13,000 to 6,000).[44]

The suits brought by the mental health bar ended all prospects for an orderly reduction in state mental hospital populations. Since emptying the hospitals was the goal of the lawyers who brought the suits, they made no attempt to stem the stampede. The only organized groups to protest were state employee unions, and because their self-interest was obvious, their protests carried no moral weight.

For state hospital populations to be reduced humanely, adequate alternative community programs had to be in place to provide housing, ensure medication compliance, and provide social supports. But the mental patient liberation bar did not put comparable effort into suits seeking to force establishment of community programs. It succeeded in consecrating the principle that patients had to be treated in "the least restrictive alternative" in the law of a number of states.[45] Yet this principle in most cases became merely another means of securing "freedom," and not better treatment for the mentally ill.

Paul Friedman, an early director of the Mental Health Law Project, has written frankly of the doubts civil libertarian lawyers felt about community treatment. On its face, the notion of treatment in the least restrictive alternative was hard to quarrel with. But members of the mental health bar, Friedman noted, worried that "because the deprivation of liberty is less in community-based treatment than in total institutionalization . . . the resistance against state intrusion will also be less and the lives of many more persons may ultimately be interfered with by the state, even if to a lesser extent."[46]

Accordingly, while the mental health bar sometimes sought to establish community services in tandem with closing hospitals—for example, a suit in western Massachusetts to force the closing of Northampton State Hospital resulted in a consent decree through which a network of community services was in fact established—overall, it did not push for such programs with anything like the zeal it directed toward depopulating hospitals.

Thus, patient liberation advocates, supposedly engaged in a movement of reform, left nothing in their wake but hordes of severely ill people abandoned to the vain "freedom" of the disease that enslaved them. Secure in their anti-psychiatric dogma that mental illness was a fiction, or at most an artifact of the mental institutions that made people sick, the mental health bar committed patients to the streets in the best of conscience.

Congratulating themselves on their expansion of "human rights," members of the mental patient liberation bar now directed their energies toward the second phase of their war against psychiatry: securing the right to refuse treatment.

Chapter 7

From the Right to Treatment to the Right to Refuse Treatment

From the beginning, it had not been the right to obtain, but the right to reject treatment that had been the hidden agenda of the mental health bar. In the 1974 interview with *Madness Network News* quoted earlier, Ennis had been forthright: "I don't think it makes sense to talk about a 'right to treatment' for involuntary persons. I think that the only thing that makes sense is to talk about a 'right to refuse treatment.'" But Ennis warned: "I think we are a long way from getting the judges to go that far."[1] The interviewer, former patient Leonard Frank, was disappointed, arguing it "would be much more effective if you began to deal with such realities as 'therapeutic tortures.'"[2]

In fact, judges were much closer to going "that far" than Ennis realized. Within three years of the interview the first two major suits that would establish *a right to refuse treatment* had been brought in New Jersey (Rennie v. Klein) and Massachusetts (Rogers v. Okin). The Rogers case in Massachusetts resulted in the largest award—over a million dollars—ever given to attorneys bringing suit under the "1983" civil rights provision of federal law. Thereafter a series of suits would establish the right in states from California to Vermont.

It is no wonder that even Ennis was taken by surprise by these developments. Despite the anti-psychiatric bias permeating a major 1974 review of civil commitment law in *Harvard Law Review,* the article nonetheless declared that treatment was inherent in the decision involuntarily to commit a mental patient—it would be incongruous if an individual could frustrate the very reason for the state's action by refusing treatment.[3] Judges in the 1960s showed scant patience when a hospital used a patient's unwillingness to be treated as grounds for its failure to treat. The Massachusetts Supreme Court, the very court that would pioneer the right to refuse treatment, in 1969 had condemned as poor practice a state hospital's failure to medicate a patient involuntarily.

Similarly, a New York court in the same year granted an ex-patient $300,000 damages on the ground that if he had been treated adequately he could have been released in two years, not the twelve years for which he was actually confined. The court scornfully dismissed the hospital's argument that the patient had refused all medication. That argument, said the court, was "illogical, unprofessional and not consonant with prevailing medical standards."[4]

How could the right to refuse treatment become a broadly accepted right within a decade of such decisions? In part, state legislatures prepared the way by making dangerousness the sole standard for commitment. If the basis for commitment is the patient's need for treatment, it makes little sense not to treat him. But as psychiatrist Thomas Gutheil observes: "If you split off dangerousness only, then the person is 'quarantined' because he is dangerous."[5] At that point, says Gutheil, the state's right to impose a further demand for treatment upon a nonconsenting individual becomes a separate issue.

Even more important was the "sleeper" effect of the reform, discussed earlier, that won universal approval in the 1961 Senate hearings: *the separation of commitment from competency.* This reform, designed to make the mentally ill and their families seek treatment earlier by reducing stigma, became the lever by which the mental health bar prevented treatment of seriously ill patients.

By the mid-1970s, the statutes of virtually all states provided that hospitalized mental patients remained legally competent unless specifically judged otherwise by a court. The mental health bar could now argue that the right to informed consent enjoyed by competent patients in regular hospitals applied to patients in mental hospitals. A patient could refuse a coronary bypass operation or chemotherapy, even though his doctors were confident such procedures would prolong his life. Indeed, under the law, forcing unwanted medical procedures upon a competent patient was considered assault and battery.[6] Since the involuntarily committed patient was assumed by law to be as competent as the heart or cancer patient, why should his right to refuse treatment be any different?

The Birth of Substituted Judgment

Judicial decisions in right to refuse treatment suits were also influenced by a series of suits in the early and mid-1970s focusing on the "right to die." Several courts resorted to the concept of "substituted judgment" to decide if terminal comatose patients, kept alive by advanced medical technologies, should be allowed to die. Substituted judgment was invoked in a New Jersey court's decision to permit removal of life supports from Karen Ann Quinlan, a young girl who had lain for over a year in a vegetative state in Newton Memorial Hospital in New Jersey. The court attempted to determine what Karen Ann, had she been competent, would have wanted under the present circumstances. According to her parents, she had spoken of her distaste for having her life artificially prolonged in such a situation.[7]

But what was to be done in the case of individuals who had never been competent? In 1976 Joseph Saikewicz, a severely retarded man who had lived in state institutions for most of his sixty-seven years, was dying from leukemia. Although chemotherapy could prolong his life for some months, it was argued that he would suffer distressing symptoms without understanding why. The Massachusetts Supreme Judicial Court decided Saikewicz should be allowed to die without chemotherapy. And it did so on the basis of a tortuous definition of substituted judgment:

> In short, the decision in cases such as this should be that which would be made by the incompetent person, if that person were competent, but taking into account the present and future incompetency of the individual as one of the factors which would necessarily enter into the decision-making process of the competent person.[8]

In other words, how would an incompetent person decide if he were competent taking into account the fact that he is incompetent? Note the court is not asking what an incompetent person would do if he were competent. The court had already concluded that competent persons overwhelmingly chose to take chemotherapy under the medical circumstances in the case. And the court was ruling *against* chemotherapy for Saikewicz. The court was saying a judgment had to be made on the basis of what a competent person would do if he were incompetent, a contradiction in terms. Yet this sophistry of substituted judgment became the basis for the same court's ruling in what was to become the most influential right to refuse treatment case.

Richard Roe III and the Right to Refuse Treatment

Interestingly, the critical case in establishing the right to refuse treatment was not the multimillion dollar federal Rogers suit in Massachusetts or the equally expensive Rennie case in New Jersey; it was a minor, initially unremarked case in a state district court entitled "In the Matter of Guardianship of Richard Roe III."

Richard Roe III (a pseudonym) had been a bright and popular boy, twice elected vice president of his junior high school class. He became withdrawn in his first year at a private residential prep school, and began to drink and use drugs. Expelled, he went to public high school, leaving before graduation. His behavior became increasingly uncontrollable. He lashed out at his sister, assaulted both his parents, and threatened to kill his mother.

Richard was diagnosed as schizophrenic at Northampton State Hospital following his arrest in the summer of 1979 on charges of receiving stolen property. On his release, he continued to show bizarre behavior, according to the court records "wearing a fur coat for hours on extremely hot days and standing for prolonged periods of time with a water glass poised at his lips." Within a few months he was arrested again, this time charged with attempted unarmed robbery and assault and battery. In the hospital for observation, he was assaultive, attacking another patient for no apparent reason.[9] Although, according to Dr. Jeffrey Geller, then a psychiatrist at Northampton State, Roe responded well to medication, he now refused both medication and psychotherapy.

In April 1980, the hospital prepared to release Roe, untreated and still severely ill, to his parents' care. According to Mark Berson, an attorney who represented the Roe family, Roe was formally a "voluntary patient," and the hospital would not make him an involuntary one. Says Berson: "Northampton State at one time had 600 patients; now it has a quota of 65. You almost have to be in the act of committing suicide before they will commit you."[10]

Richard Roe's parents were prepared to take him back into their home, but wanted to make sure that if he became assaultive, the hospital could make him take medication as an outpatient. The family was asked to go through what the hospital administration said would be a simple process of getting court approval to secure this goal.

The hospital assumed this would be a simple matter because of the federal district court's decision in the Rogers case, then under appeal to the U.S. Supreme Court. The district court had ruled that "competent" mental patients (and all mental patients were assumed to be competent) had the right to refuse treatment. But what of patients found in a special court hearing to be incompetent? The court ruled that for such persons, the decision whether or not to take prescribed medication could be made for them by a court-appointed guardian.

Psychiatrists at Northampton Hospital saw in this a basis for treating Richard Roe, since it was clear to them that he was incompetent. However, the federal court's decision applied to patients at Boston State Hospital, and Richard Roe was going to be an outpatient. So the hospital told Richard Roe's family to bring a case to make Richard's father his guardian with the power to decide if he should take medication prescribed for him. And at first, things went according to plan. The probate judge ruled that Roe was mentally ill and incompetent, appointed his father his guardian, and agreed that under "Rogers" he had the authority to determine his son's treatment. But the case was appealed by the "guardian ad litem" who had been appointed to represent Richard Roe. The Massachusetts Supreme Judicial Court produced a decision that was an anti-psychiatric mishmash—and a triumph for the patient liberation bar.

The Massachusetts Supreme Judicial Court conceded that "the evidence is more than adequate" that Richard Roe was incompetent to manage his own affairs. Even the psychiatrist brought in by the guardian ad litem admitted Richard was incapable of carrying on a reasonable conversation and unable to live in the community by himself. All the psychiatrists talked of his inability to control his anger, and the court said it was convinced Richard's judgment was so severely impaired that there was a strong likelihood he would inflict serious injury on himself or others. The judges concluded Richard needed a guardian and his father was the appropriate choice.

However, the judges ruled that he could not make the decision whether Richard should take the medications his psychiatrist prescribed for him. They declared that Massachusetts law made a "profound distinction" between commitment and incompetence, and even if a patient were found incompetent, only a court could conduct the "detached but passionate investigation" (the same phrase they used in Saikewicz) necessary to decide if Richard should take medication or not. Moreover, it should not decide on the basis of what was medically in the "best interests" of Richard Roe. Presumably this would result in his taking the prescribed medication so that his competence would be restored. Instead the judges said, invoking Saikewicz again, the court's task was to decide what the incompetent mental patient would want to do, if he were competent (taking into account the fact that he is incompetent).[11]

How were judges to decide what an incompetent mental patient would want? The Massachusetts Supreme Judicial Court declared that they should determine his values and preferences. The attitude of family members was a relevant factor, but only if the patient desired to minimize the burden he placed on them.[12]

The Massachusetts Supreme Judicial Court's decision stood on its head John Donne's famous dictum "No man is an island." As psychiatrist Alan Stone points out, the result of its decision is to render the person an island.[13] It never seemed to occur to the judges that Richard Roe's family, despite his serious illness, wanted to take care of him and that making it feasible for them to do so should be society's concern. On the contrary, his parents' effort to pursue Richard's best interests, and ensure the family's survival as a functioning unit, *disqualified* its members from decision-making! Said the court:

> We intend no criticism of the guardian [Richard's father] when we say that few parents could make the substitute judgment determination—by its nature a self-centered determination in which the decision maker is called upon to ignore all but the implementation of the values and preferences of the ward—when the ward, in his present condition, is living at home with other children.[14]

In making this profoundly anti-family ruling, the judges of the Massachusetts Supreme Judicial Court displayed reasoning no less disordered than that of Richard Roe. For them, Richard Roe's father lacked the necessary "detachment" to decide whether his son should take medication. But of course, it was precisely that lack of detachment that made Richard Roe II a desirable guardian of his son's interests. He *cared* what happened to his son. He wanted him restored to competence.[15] And the whole family had an interest in eliminating the psychotic thought processes that had led Richard in the past physically to attack them and that could make living with him intolerable. The judges refused to consider that other children in the family had a legitimate interest in living without fear of violence from a severely ill, uncontrollable family member. Such interests were viewed as "selfish." For the judges, only the preferences of Richard Roe III had value—to be discovered, in their words, with "objectivity and selflessness." Thus, society must selflessly yield to the selfish, deranged desires of Richard Roe III.

Underlying the Massachusetts court's decision in the Roe case was what Robert Bork has described as a "position of extreme individualism, which amounts necessarily to an attitude of moral relativism," that has also characterized Supreme Court decisions. Yet, Bork points out, this undercuts the very basis of law. If all that counts is the gratification of the individual, then morality is completely privatized and society may make no moral judgments that are translatable into law.[16]

Anti-Psychiatry Disguised as Substituted Judgment

As Paul Appelbaum and Thomas Gutheil have pointed out, "substituted judgment" really means the substitution of the preferences of the decision-maker for those of the incompetent person.[17] In the Roe case, the judges of the Massachusetts Supreme Judicial Court were implementing *their own false anti-psychiatric theories,* derived from law journal articles that transmitted the Szaszian notions of the mental health bar to the bench. In the Roe decision, the judges repeatedly quoted from one of the most egregious of these articles, Robert Plotkin's "Limiting the Therapeutic Orgy," mentioned earlier. (Plotkin was a staff attorney for the Mental Health Law Project when he wrote the article.)

The judges described the drugs—ordinary, routine treatment for psychosis—as "extraordinary" medical treatment. They warned darkly that "the impact of the chemicals upon the brain is sufficient to undermine the foundations of personality." Nay more, the medications were "powerful enough to immobilize mind and body"; they were "mind-altering."[18] (They quoted the federal court in the Rogers case which similarly described the neuroleptics as a form of "involuntary mind control."[19])

It is hard to imagine a more distorted view of anti-psychotic drugs. As Appelbaum and Gutheil point out, the drugs reduce hallucinations, disordered thought processes, agitation, withdrawal, and other psychotic symptoms. They are not "mind-altering" in the sense of changing the content of a patient's beliefs, as the judges clearly thought. They don't change rebels into conformists or Democrats into Republicans.[20] As the American College of Neuropsychopharmacology said tartly in its amicus brief in the Rogers case: "Psychotic disease alters the minds of afflicted patients; antipsychotic medication is mind-restorative."[21]

Laboring under their own anti-psychiatric delusions, the judges of the Massachusetts Supreme Judicial Court declared, "We treat these drugs in the same manner we would treat psychosurgery or electroconvulsive therapy." (In other words, the judges viewed *all* somatic treatments for mental illness with equal suspicion.) With Plotkin as their source, they launched into an exhaustive account of possible side effects of the anti-psychotic drugs, ignoring that most are controlled by additional medication prescribed with them. If "the intended effects of anti-psychotic drugs are extreme," the judges warned, "their unintended effects are frequently devastating and often irreversible."[22] By almost totally ignoring the proven role of medication in controlling the symptoms of mental illness, the judges undermined the very objectivity they claimed for the substituted judgment decision.

In theory, after the Roe decision, the family could have applied for a substituted judgment decision whereby the court would order their son to be medicated involuntarily. Demoralized, they did not. According to their attorney, Mark Berson, the family gave up. "It was clear the drugs would not be given, so why go on with it? The family had put so much time and effort and money trying to get the kid back to normalcy. After they lost they just didn't have the energy. It blew the family to pieces. The husband and wife divorced." Asked what happened to Richard Roe, Berson replied: "Nothing good. He became a semi-street person and has been constantly involved with the law with minor infractions."[23]

Impact of the Roe Case

The Roe case had an impact that extended far beyond Richard Roe III and his family. After the Massachusetts Supreme Judicial Court issued its ruling, the U.S. Supreme Court decided to remand the Rogers case to be decided in light of Roe. The Supreme Court did so on the grounds that the judges in Roe had carved out a right to refuse treatment on the basis of state law that went beyond anything it could find on the basis of U.S. constitutional law. And so, in the end, the "major" federal Rogers case was decided on the basis of the "minor" state Roe case.

There was a more sensible model which, surprisingly, had less impact. The New Jersey right to refuse treatment case, Rennie v. Klein, had resulted in a decision by the Third Circuit Court of Appeals which provided for a second medical opinion when an incompetent person refused medication.[24] The U.S. Supreme Court accepted Rennie for review at around the same time it granted certiorari for Rogers, but in the end decided neither case. Remanding Rogers in light of Roe, it remanded Rennie in light of its own decision in Youngberg v. Romeo. Because the latter concerned a severely retarded young man's "right to treatment," it was not altogether clear what its implications were for a case involving a mentally ill individual's right to refuse treatment.

Since the Supreme Court, in Youngberg, supported the right of professionals to make the difficult judgments involved in a case like

Romeo's, it seemed to back the Third Circuit Court of Appeal's decision that New Jersey's provision of a second professional opinion in cases of patient refusal was adequate. And that was indeed how the Court of Appeals interpreted the decision when the case was remanded. Studies showed that the way the New Jersey model worked in practice was to lead to more "negotiations" between patient and psychiatrist, that is, psychiatrists were more ready to listen to the patient's complaints about medication and adapt to them, sometimes with lower doses, sometimes with trials of alternative medication.

Despite the Supreme Court's backing for the professional judgment standard and the example of New Jersey, many courts lined up behind Massachusetts. New York, Oklahoma, Colorado, Wisconsin, Indiana, South Dakota, Minnesota, Washington, and California all followed Massachusetts in requiring court hearings before incompetent patients who refused medication could be treated. Other states, among them Vermont, New Hampshire, Alaska, Florida, and Arizona, changed their procedures without waiting for court rulings.

In Harper v. the State of Washington (which was appealed to the Supreme Court), the Supreme Court of Washington went even further than Massachusetts in establishing rigorous criteria before an incompetent patient can be forcibly medicated. In a 1988 decision, it ruled that a court could order anti-psychotic drug treatment—in this case for a prisoner—only if the state could prove by a "clear, cogent, and convincing" standard of evidence "a compelling state interest to administer antipsychotic drugs" and that "the administration of the drugs is both necessary and effective for furthering that interest."[25]

The Costs of the Massachusetts Model

Studies in Massachusetts and New York of the impact of requiring judicial hearings before a nonconsenting mental patient can be treated illuminate the costs: inexcusable waste of scarce mental illness dollars, long delays in treatment, and inappropriate discharge of refusing patients.

A study by the Massachusetts Department of Mental Health found that in the eighteen-month period from 1986 to 1987, roughly 1,500 cases of patients who refused treatment resulted in court hearings. More than 4,800 clinical staff hours were spent on these cases, all of them taken from patient care. The chief beneficiaries were the lawyers and paralegals who filled the new jobs that were opened up by the mandated court procedures. In 1986 alone, the Massachusetts Department of Mental Health had to allocate $800,000 for additional attorneys to deal with these cases. More than 3,000 paralegal hours were spent on them.[26] And the net result was that in 98.6% of the cases, the court ruled the individual should be medicated.[27]

This is only a fraction of the cost. In Massachusetts, on average, fourteen days intervened between the filing of a petition and the court hearing. A study at New York's Manhattan State Hospital found the process took an average of 5.8 weeks.[28] Psychiatrists had to complete an eight-page form on each refusing patient; the hospital then had to file four separate legal documents with the court. Acting-out, untreated patients clogged hospital wards, squandering taxpayer dollars, and made life on the wards more hazardous for staff and fellow patients alike.

From the standpoint of psychiatrists and other clinical staff, the paperwork and time involved in these judicial procedures are wasteful and onerous. Release of patients to streets or shelters, or leaving patients untreated, becomes a very attractive alternative. Julie Zito, who has studied the way the right to refuse treatment works out in practice, notes that in Minnesota, which had an in-house review procedure for patients who refused treatment, roughly 18% of patients refused, and went through the procedure. Yet in New York she found a documented refusal rate of less than 2%. Zito (who is in sympathy with the right to refuse) believes the real refusal rate is similar in both places: what happens is that in New York psychiatrists only initiate the paperwork for court reviews in a small minority of cases.[29] Practically speaking therefore, winning judicial review in right to refuse treatment cases is a bigger victory for the mental health bar than the statistics on judicial endorsement of psychiatric decision-making suggest.

Moreover, the need for judicial hearings is not necessarily confined to those who refuse treatment. All patients too psychotic to make a "competent" decision concerning their own treatment must be brought to court under the rules of some states.

The chief victims are not an inconvenienced professional staff but the patients themselves, discharged without treatment, or deteriorating on the wards. A reporter for the *Seattle Times* investigating the impact of the state supreme court's ruling in the Harper case found the use of seclusion and leather restraints *up sharply*. At Harborview Hospital the reporter found "an emaciated young man propped up on a gurney, a green feeding tube running into his nose, his arms and legs bound with cloth." In response to a psychiatrist's questions, "the man mumbles incoherently and continues staring into space without a glimmer of recognition." He had been held like this for two weeks awaiting a hearing on whether he could be treated.[30] At Northwest Evaluation and Treatment Center in Seattle, the reporter found a man who refused to eat, urinated on himself, and hid under his bed or in a closet. According to Leo Perry, the center's clinical director: "The man is too psychotic to give us permission so we're frightened to give him medication. He's been reduced to being an animal while we wait for a court decision."[31]

The Right to a *More* Restrictive Alternative

Because their real agenda is to destroy psychiatric authority, patient liberation activists seemingly do not care that the right to refuse undercuts two other principles they have entrenched in law: the right to treatment and the right to treatment in the least restrictive alternative. The court in the Roe case professed itself unable to decide whether "mind-altering drugs" or institutionalization was more restrictive. Presumably, the individual has the right to a physically restrictive alternative as a way to avoid internally restrictive drugs. *Then, rather than being obliged to provide treatment, the institution becomes an alternative to treatment.*

Because it rejects the immense benefits treatment can offer, the right to refuse treatment is nihilistic. In his brief in the Rogers case, Greater Boston Legal Services attorney Richard Cole did not take the conventional position of anti-psychiatry that there is no such thing as mental illness. Rather, his argument, unusual for the mental health bar, was that mental illness was so hopeless a disease, there was no point in treating those who suffered from it! Cole argued that most of those who live in the community after leaving hospital "continue to be unproductive and are often a burden to their families. Many individuals released to foster homes or to other sheltered environments are as dependent and alienated as those confined to an institution."[32] The Rogers case, in which seven patients at Boston State Hospital filed suit to stop administration of anti-psychotic medication to patients without their informed consent except in narrowly defined emergencies, had developed out of the organizing efforts of the Mental Patients Liberation Front within the hospital; the Front denied the existence of mental illness. Yet it could cooperate with Cole because the end result of both arguments was rejection of treatment.

The chief hope for stemming the tide of court rulings setting up elaborate obstacles to treatment lies in federal courts. In 1988 the U.S. Court of Appeals for the Fourth Circuit ruled that Michael Charters, a prisoner at the Federal Correctional Institution at Butner, North Carolina, could be medicated against his will on the basis of the professional judgment of medical personnel. The two-stage plenary proceeding in district court demanded by the mental health bar, the judges ruled, was a misuse of the courts.

> With this would go all the cumbersomeness, expense, and delay incident to judicial proceedings every time an involuntary medication decision had to be made for any inmates.[33]

Moreover, the judges pointed out, courts would be confronted with the conflicting testimony of institutional medical personnel arguing for treatment and outside expert witnesses "whose testimony surely can be anticipated," arguing against it. That would cast the court "in the role of making the primary decisions on purely medical and psychiatric questions."[34]

In 1990 the U.S. Supreme Court overturned the Supreme Court of the State of Washington's 1988 decision in the Harper case. In a 6-3 decision, writing for the Court, Justice Anthony M. Kennedy ruled that the Washington court had erred in stating that the Constitution required the state to prove it had a "compelling interest" in medicating a prisoner and that the drugs were "necessary and effective" in furthering that interest. The inmate's interests, Kennedy maintained, were "adequately protected, and perhaps better served, by allowing the decision to medicate to be made by medical professionals rather than a judge."[35]

The Supreme Court decision will not affect other states whose courts have already ruled that judicial hearings are necessary before patients can be medicated. For example, Paul Appelbaum says, "Here in Massachusetts I think we're impacted by this not at all." Appelbaum notes except for Washington, state supreme courts "have been very careful to say we are making this decision on independent state law grounds"—not on federal constitutional grounds.[36] In this way they have precluded appeal of their decisions to the Supreme Court. Nonetheless, Appelbaum believes the decision may have an effect on states whose courts have not yet ruled on the right to refuse treatment. The enthusiasm of state courts for making the judiciary the arbiter of psychiatric decisions may wane as a result of the Supreme Court's decision in Harper.

Dangerousness Standard Survives

For all its victories, the mental patient liberation bar has not accomplished its original purpose—abolishing involuntary civil commitment. Having narrowed the criterion for commitment to dangerousness, it had hoped to invalidate that last ground on both constitutional and practical grounds. The constitutional argument was summed up in a 1973 article in the *Santa Clara Lawyer:* confinement for "dangerousness" was "an arbitrary and unreasonable deprivation of liberty contrary to the precepts of procedural due process." Therefore, involuntary commitment was "incompatible with the tenets of liberal democracy and more particularly with the constitutional order."[37]

The mental health bar's second major argument was that psychiatrists in any case were unable to say who would be dangerous. Earlier we referred to Bruce Ennis and Thomas Litwack's scathing dismissal of psychiatric predictions as "flipping coins in the courtroom." Surveying all extant studies in 1969, civil libertarian attorney Alan Dershowitz concluded that psychiatrists seriously overpredicted dangerousness.

An article in the *University of Pennsylvania Law Review* a year earlier showed why that was—and remains—true. When predictions of rare events (with low base rates) are attempted, overprediction is inevitable. Suppose, say the authors, one person out of a 1000 will kill and a 95% accurate test for predicting who would do so existed. That would mean that if 100,000 people were tested, out of the 100 who would kill, 95 would be detected. But alas, an additional 4,905 people who would not kill would also be identified as potential killers.[38] Violence among the mentally ill, like violence among the general population, has a low base rate. Since psychiatrists cannot hope for better than a 60–70% rate of accuracy, they must inevitably overpredict dangerousness in applying the standard in civil commitment. Ennis dismisses the entire effort: "There is nothing in the education, training or experience of psychiatrists to enable them to predict violent acts."[39]

In attacking psychiatric ability to predict dangerous behavior, the mental health bar wound up with a surprising ally in much of the psychiatric establishment. In part, psychiatrists were motivated by self-interest: the assumption that they could predict dangerousness opened them to malpractice suits. The Tarasoff case in California sent tremors throughout the psychiatric profession. The parents of Tatiana Tarasoff, a University of California coed murdered by her mentally ill, rejected boyfriend, successfully sued a college psychiatrist for failing to warn her of his homicidal fantasies. The boyfriend had confided his murderous impulses to the psychiatrist. The psychiatrist had notified the campus police, urging that the boyfriend be hospitalized. Although it was the police, operating under the rigors of California law, who refused to hospitalize him, the court ruled the *psychiatrist—not* the police—could be held liable.[40] Following the 1976 Tarasoff decision, psychiatrists were even less eager to be cited as experts on predicting dangerousness.

But many leading psychiatrists went beyond the issue of prediction to object to the dangerousness standard on philosophical grounds. Making dangerousness the standard for commitment turned doctors into jailers. It forced the mental health system to devote most of its efforts to those least likely to benefit from them. Alan Stone points out that with courts demanding that patients be both mentally ill and dangerous, a new class of mental patients fills state mental hospital beds. These are "males between age 20 and 40, who move back and forth between prisons and mental hospitals, who have serious character disorders bordering on schizophrenia, who are more violent, and who are resistant to neuroleptic treatment."[41] Paul Appelbaum makes the same point even more vehemently. "The dangerousness standard makes no sense whatever. It makes no sense on policy grounds because it is not at all clear that you should be using your mental hospitals for the purpose of detaining people who are dangerous rather than treating people who need treatment."[42]

Despite this unusual concordance between the mental health bar and psychiatrists, the dangerousness standard has held firm. Seeing the standard as a protection for society, legislators and judges are unwilling to give it up. Alan Stone notes acerbically: "When the Supreme Court acknowledges that it is difficult to decide who is dangerous, but tells courts to make such decisions anyway, it embraces incoherence."[43] And it is of course on psychiatric testimony that the courts rely in making such decisions.

The Triumph of Thomas Szasz

In making the family impotent to secure treatment, and in making dangerous acts the sine qua non for commitment, the mental health bar has substantially realized the vision of Thomas Szasz. As early as 1963, in *Law, Liberty and Psychiatry,* Szasz had seen clearly that treatment—involuntary treatment if necessary—was the key to permitting a family to keep close ties with its mentally ill member. Szasz urged sacrificing the family on the altar of individual autonomy, precisely the course chosen by the Massachusetts Supreme Judicial Court in the Roe case. In 1980 Berel Caesar, a lower court judge in Philadelphia, deplored the damage wrought by the laws he was called upon to uphold. Wrote Caesar: "That the family has an interest in preserving its 'familyhood' is disregarded and that the respondent has an interest in preserving a support system is legally irrelevant."[44]

To a large degree, Szasz's dream of turning the mentally ill over to the criminal justice system has also become a reality as dangerousness has replaced the need-for-treatment standard. Moreover, because the standards for entry into the mental health system are more stringent than the standards for admission to the criminal justice system, it is easier to put the mentally ill into jails than it is to secure treatment for them. Psychiatrist and forensic expert Robert Sadoff observes that "in Pennsylvania, where a threat is considered to be an assault, i.e., a crime, it is often easier to take into custody an individual who threatens another and have him charged with a crime than it is to apprehend and confine a mentally ill person who 'only threatened.'" It is easier, says Sadoff, "for a psychiatrist to recommend to a family concerned about a relative who is acting bizarrely, and who has a history of mental illness, to seek help for their relative through the criminal justice system- . . . rather than through the restrictive, often odious measures instituted under the mental health system."[45]

Not surprisingly, jail and prison officials complain of experiencing a sharp increase in seriously mentally ill inmates. Easy targets for a criminal population, the imprisoned mentally ill are tormented and often sexually abused. In a powerful NBC documentary on mental illness, "They Have Souls Too," a severely ill young man named Bobby is shown cowering in a prison cell. Bobby, whose mental disorder was first diagnosed when he was eight, is in a Richmond, Virginia prison on a first offense. He describes being gang-raped in the jail:

> Over half the tier, over half the tier that was there, over half of them were in that. It's too hard for me. And I'll tell you, even sometimes I feel like— feel like taking my own life, because the way people do me, treat me is just not fair, and it's never been right.

Robert Winston, the sheriff of Richmond County, Virginia, agrees. He says someone like Bobby "needs professional care and he needs it constantly. But we don't have that, and we don't have the wherewithal to provide it."[46] Ironically, it is in the name of preserving Bobby's "liberty" that the mental health bar has denied him that care.

The Real Victims

Hospital personnel may not like the system the mental health bar's lawsuits have created but they adapt to it. Alan Stone observes:

> There is a pervasive conviction in public mental hospitals that the law has made it impossible to treat people who don't want treatment, so why bother. Being a psychiatrist seems to require acts of civil disobedience which few are willing to perform. Instead, psychiatrists merely go through the motions without feeling responsible.[47]

As psychiatrists spend ever more time on paperwork and court appearances, state hospitals become even more unattractive to U.S. psychiatrists. The field is left to foreign doctors trapped in them because they are not licensed to work anywhere else.

The real victims of the system are the mentally ill and their families. In the name of the least restrictive alternative, patients are condemned to a prison of psychosis. Robert Jackson, a reedy, very tall, bearded black man of forty who had spent many months on the streets of New York and Philadelphia, described that internal prison to us.

> I'd hear voices. The voices are very horrible. I stopped brushing my teeth because I'd think that if I brushed my teeth it'd bring on the voices. They would tell me to do certain things . . . and I'd like, you know, fight it off, just staying in my room.
>
> But sometimes I would trust the voices because they were my only companion. Sometimes it would get ridiculous. They would tell me to do something foolish like jumping out the window. They'd say walk out and don't come back to the house. It's a very scary thing. Even if I had a token, I'd walk long distances until my feet needed surgery. They had to cut my callouses off; they had to break a couple of my toes and take out some bones in my feet. Because I would just walk. The voices would tell me.[48]

While many of the severely ill, like Jackson, reject hospitalization, denying their illness, those who seek treatment do not fare much better. If they are not "dangerous," hospitals are reluctant to accept them. A Philadelphia social worker told us she was criticized by her superior for telling a newspaper reporter that it was easier to get into Harvard than to gain admission to the local state mental hospital.[49]

The presumption of dangerousness has become a pervasive feature of the system. Edward and Ellen Holder, a Virginia couple in their eighties, told us of the humiliation they and their gravely disabled middle-aged son Arnold had recently suffered. Arnold, in his mother's words, "is as dangerous as a one-year-old infant." Nonetheless when they followed procedural requirements for their son's admission to a hospital by calling for emergency service, the unit tore into the hotel lobby where they had arranged to wait, cleared the lobby of its surprised occupants, handcuffed their son, and dragged him off. His parents report that Arnold was so angry that although he had agreed to accept treatment, he signed himself out the next day.[50]

In the name of liberty, the mental health bar destroys lives. Its lawyers take pride in their success in outwitting psychiatrists in the courtroom and freeing their clients from mental hospitals. They take no responsibility for what happens afterward. Joel Klein, a "convert" from the mental patient liberation bar who once worked for the Mental Health Law Project and in recent years has fought a mostly losing battle in right to refuse treatment cases as attorney for the American Psychiatric Association, says:

> Lawyers are not "morning after" people. They're people who are wonderful the night before in life and then they go their own way and say to the psychiatrists and patients, "Now you people work this out."[51]

Indeed, the morning after, the family may be burying the "liberated" patient.

This is precisely what happened in the case of Catherine Henley, whose story Bruce Ennis relates in *Prisoners of Psychiatry.* A graduate of Wellesley College, the mother of three small children, Catherine Henley became depressed in 1969. Ennis reports that her sister became concerned that Catherine "had been neglecting the children—not feeding them or herself properly—and that she spent most of the day crying and walking aimlessly around her small apartment on East Fourth Street [in Manhattan]."[52] She arranged for Catherine to be hospitalized involuntarily at Bellevue.

Catherine contested her commitment and was represented by an attorney from New York State's Mental Health Information Service. Her entire family—mother, sister, and husband—opposed the discharge. The judge ruled that Catherine be transferred for six months, as her family desired, to New York Hospital's psychiatric division in Westchester County. At this point, Catherine's Mental Health Information Service attorney asked Ennis to take over, and Ennis successfully blocked Catherine's transfer and obtained her freedom by demanding a jury trial. Ennis notes:

> Although every patient has a theoretical right to a jury trial, in New York there are never more than four or five a year; for most psychiatrists, a jury

trial is such a nettlesome and time-consuming affair that the mere demand for one is usually enough to effect the patient's release.[53]

Not content with this achievement, Ennis sought (vainly as it turned out) to have New York's highest court rule that her original hospitalization was illegal. And what happened to Catherine Henley while Ennis continued jousting in the courts on her behalf? He tells us himself:

> Soon after her release from Bellevue, Catherine Henley found a job. A few weeks later she was recommitted—I do not know the circumstances. Once again, the Mental Health Information Service tried to get her out, and once again her family opposed. This time, however, the MHIS was successful and she was discharged. One week later, Catherine Henley threw herself in front of a subway train and died.[54]

Ennis expresses no regret here at her death, or at the role he played. What makes Catherine Henley's death especially tragic is that of all the serious mental illnesses, depression responds best to treatment. Catherine Henley was never given her chance to resume a normal life, and her children and family bore the grief of her death—while Ennis moved on to his next client.

Nothing Is the Hardest Thing to Do

The chief legacy of the mental health bar has been to prevent families, faced with a devastating illness, from doing anything. Earlier we mentioned Elizabeth Hilton, who heads a network to find homeless and missing children of the National Alliance for the Mentally Ill, and whose own son has been intermittently on the street for the last eleven years. Although her son responds to medication, he refuses to take it. She wrote a poem about her frustration entitled "Nothing Is the Hardest Thing to Do."

Mrs. Hilton explains: "There was nothing I could do when he was in the house. There was nothing I could do when he left, when he stood in front of me and told me he was leaving. There was nothing I could do when he was on the road and he would call me sometimes and ask me where he was."[55] She learned to ask the long distance operator what state and city the collect call was coming from, so she could tell her son where he was. Each day she dreads a call in the night. And since her son loses or discards any identification, Mrs. Hilton is tormented by the realization that should he die, she may never know.

Community psychiatrist Richard Lamb insists there can and must be another way.

> Suppose you or I were acutely or chronically psychotic . . . and let's say we are living on the streets, vulnerable to every predator, eating out of garbage cans and in and out of jail. I think we, or at least I, would desperately hope that the agent of society who saw my plight would not simply tell me that I have a right to live my life that way, but would instead do something to rescue me. . . . I believe that the mentally ill have another crucial right, in addition to all the rights we've heard about. When because of serious mental illness, the mentally ill present a serious threat to their own welfare . . . I believe they have a right to involuntary treatment. A very important right that I believe needs to be recognized.[56]

The mental patient liberation bar has established a new, cruel system for the mentally ill. The right to treatment has become the right to no treatment, the right to freedom is now the right to deteriorate on the streets and die in back alleys. In an obscene parody, the attorneys who have created the dreadful new cityscape continue to parrot the rhetoric of civil rights. In self-righteous satisfaction, they ignore the fact that, in Judge Caesar's words, "we have consigned many persons to lives of quiet desperation, have destroyed the mental and emotional health of those who love and care for them, and destroyed families—to the ultimate detriment and even destruction of the disabled person."[57]

PART IV

The War Against Treatment

Chapter 8

The Rise of the Ex-Patient Movement

THE onslaught on civil commitment and involuntary treatment foreshadowed something more fundamental: an attack on treatment itself. To claim that the psychiatric treatments that had revolutionized care of the mentally ill over the last fifty years were valueless—or worse, harmful—was a logical extension of the anti-psychiatric perspective. In Thomas Szasz's words, psychiatry was "a form of quackery because it offers cures for which there are no diseases."[1]

Szasz ignored psychiatric treatments in his writing. He repeated loftily his single theme: "[I]f there is no disease, there is *nothing* to treat; if there is no patient, there is *no one* to treat."[2] But his politically activist followers were not satisfied with such Olympian rhetoric. They were determined to halt—or where that was not possible, at least impede—the psychiatric treatments being administered to patients in the real world.

In the early 1970s, an alliance of a small number of ex-patients and a few disaffected psychiatrists spearheaded the assault on treatment. These ex-patients, who lived for the most part in the San Francisco area, were motivated by their bitter resentment—sometimes justified—of psychiatric treatment they had received. Through their journal *Madness Network News,* they forged an ideology that bound together a variety of similar ex-patient groups then forming around the country. Starting in 1973, they began to network annually in the North American Conference on Human Rights and Psychiatric Oppression. Psychiatrists who joined forces with them consisted of political radicals and students or disciples of Szasz.

Attacks on Treatment Coincide with Major Medical Advances

From a scientific point of view, the assault on all forms of somatic treatment could not have been timed more strangely. While the activists were gearing up to deny the value of treatment, scientists were explaining how the neuroleptic and anti-depressant drugs actually worked.

The psychiatric properties of these drugs were discovered by serendipity, so initially their mode of action was unknown. This permitted psychoanalytically oriented psychiatrists, at their peak of influence when the first of the anti-psychotic drugs, chlorpromazine, was discovered in 1952, to discount the subversive implications of these drugs for theories of family causation. They regarded the anti-psychotic drugs as powerful tranquillizers that calmed patients sufficiently to allow the real work of psychoanalysis to proceed and uncover—in the environment—the "root cause" of the problem.[3]

In the early 1960s, Swedish scientist Arvid Carlsson published classic papers advancing the hypothesis that the neuroleptic drugs blocked dopamine receptors in the brain. In May 1973, within months of the first meeting of the National Conference on Human Rights and Psychiatric Oppression in Detroit, Solomon Snyder and Candace Pert, the first a professor of neurochemistry, the second a doctoral student at Johns Hopkins University Medical School, proved that receptors in the brain did in fact exist. A year later Snyder, working with two postdoctoral fellows, found receptors for dopamine in the brains of rats. The scientific support mounted for Carlsson's theory that neuroleptics influenced the way receptors in the brain responded to dopamine, one of the key neurotransmitters.

But while the mode of action of the neuroleptics had been clarified, questions about schizophrenia remained. Was there too much dopamine in the brains of schizophrenics? Or was the problem rather an excess of receptors for dopamine? Or was the problem that the brains of schizophrenics were too sensitive to dopamine? Could there be—as some recent research suggests—not a dopamine excess but a dopamine *insufficiency* in the brains of schizophrenics?[4] To what extent was the brain's dopamine system the problem and to what extent was the dysregulation of dopamine only a symptom of a more fundamental problem in brain chemistry?

While all too many questions remained, one thing did become clear. As Dr. Terence Early, psychiatry professor at Washington University in St. Louis, points out: "A condition like schizophrenia is an illness that is first and foremost a brain disease."[5] With this recognition, the balance of power in psychiatry changed. Departments of psychiatry in major medical schools had been dominated by psychoanalytically oriented psychiatrists. Now these positions of influence increasingly went to psychiatrists who did research on the biological basis of mental illness.

Beginning in the 1970s, new technologies permitted scientists for the first time to look into the living brain. The search for differences between the brains of normal individuals and those suffering from schizophrenia had a long and unproductive history, so much so that the search had come to be considered the graveyard of once promising careers. That search had necessarily been a post mortem one. But now, through PET (position emission tomography) scans, differences could be seen in the distribution of blood flow to different regions of the brain as well as in the way the brains of schizophrenic and normal subjects functioned when the same task was set to them. EEG studies (of electrical transmission in the brain) have suggested that schizophrenics have slower activity in frontal regions of the brain.

One of the most important studies using the new brain-imaging techniques—in this case magnetic resonance imaging, or MRI—examined the brains of identical twins, only one of whom suffered from schizophrenia. A number of earlier studies using MRI had revealed enlarged ventricles and cortical atrophy in patients suffering from schizophrenia, suggesting that at least some schizophrenics might have abnormal brain structure. The difficulty was that normal brains vary widely so that many features seen in the brains of schizophrenics were also seen in people without the disease. But in examining identical twins, the study had a built-in genetic control.

The findings were dramatic. So strong were the differences, that simply by visual inspection researchers were able to identify the twin with schizophrenia in twelve of the fifteen pairs of twins. Brain volume was smaller in a number of areas associated with thinking, concentration, memory, and emotion, all of which are affected in schizophrenia. Those suffering from schizophrenia had larger ventricles, cavities within the brain filled with fluid, suggesting missing tissue in the brain had been replaced by cerebrospinal fluid. They also had wider cortical sulci, spaces in the foldings at the surface of the cortex, suggesting atrophy or failure of brain cells to develop. Fourteen of the fifteen affected twins had a smaller left anterior hippocampus and thirteen had a smaller right hippocampus. No such differences were found in seven sets of normal twins who served as a comparison group. The study concluded that "when appropriate controls are available, subtle anatomical changes can be detected in most patients with schizophrenia and are probably characteristic of the disease."[6]

Marsel Mesulam, a neurologist at Harvard Medical School, declared the study offered "definitive evidence that schizophrenia is a brain disease and that it involves more than genetic susceptibility." In addition to genetics, researchers would now be looking at a variety of potential contributing factors, from viral infections to trauma leading to early loss of tissue in neural development.[7]

In the 1980s huge strides were also made toward closing in on the genes that made individuals vulnerable to major mental illness. Biologically oriented psychiatrists had long recognized a genetic component in these diseases, which ran in families. Moreover, if one identical twin became schizophrenic, the chances were upwards of 50% that the other would be afflicted with it. To be sure, this indicated that simply having the predisposing gene (or genes) did not guarantee that it would be "expressed" in the form of illness. (Genetically loaded diseases typically do not have 100% expression and the figures for schizophrenia in identical twins are similar to those in such illnesses as diabetes and rheumatoid arthritis.)

Consequently there was considerable excitement in 1987 when scientists in the United States studying a group of Old Order Amish families in Pennsylvania said they had discovered a genetic marker for manic-depressive illness on chromosome 11 and a month later scientists in Israel found a marker for the same illness on the X chromosome. In 1988, Hugh Gurling in England announced he had found the first genetic marker for schizophrenia on chromosome 5. (Finding a genetic marker—*not* the gene itself, but a fragment of DNA whose presence coincides with the presence of an inherited disease—is a first step toward locating the actual genes.)

It since appears the researchers may have been overoptimistic about their findings. A research team, including some of the original investigators, on reanalyzing the Amish pedigree, concluded that while the evidence for a genetic marker in the Amish remained strong, it was probably not on chromosome 11. Neither Gurling's study nor the Israeli one has been replicated. Yet even those most critical of these initial studies are confident the predisposing gene (or more likely, genes) for these illnesses will eventually be found.[8]

With the 1989 decision of the National Institutes of Health to undertake the mammoth project of mapping the human genome (the complete set of instructions for making a human being), the prospects for locating the genes responsible for the major illnesses have come much closer.

Radical Ex-Patients: Getting Even

The ex-patients who formed the "mental patients liberation" groups were not deflected by scientific discoveries concerning the biological basis of major mental illness. Most were extremely bitter as a result of personal experiences; a few talked explicitly of obtaining vengeance. Ex-patient activist Judi Chamberlin reports that even when she was locked up "I knew I would get even." Forming a link in a human chain of ex-patients demonstrating against a meeting of the American Psychiatric Association in San Francisco, she found that Sally Zinman, standing next to her, was experiencing the same thing. Sally told her: "I used to say to myself when I was in that dungeon, that they didn't know who they were doing this to—that I would get even."[9]

In some cases there were ample grounds for resentment. Ex-patient activist Ted Chabasinski was taken to Bellevue Hospital in Manhattan in 1944 at the age of six. At the time shy and withdrawn, Chabasinski believes he was considered crazy because his mother had been a mental patient and the social worker who supervised him in his foster home was "looking for symptoms." He was kept at Bellevue for five months and given twenty electroshock (ECT) treatments by Lauretta Bender, a famous child psychiatrist. Chabasinski says he was terrorized by the treatment.[10] (The treatment would not be considered appropriate for a young child today.)

But Chabasinski's ordeal had just begun. After five months in his foster home, still just seven years old, he was put in Rockland State Hospital and remained there for the next ten years.

It is a mark of Chabasinski's resilience that he went on to graduate from City College magna cum laude and later to study toward a doctorate in psychology. In 1973 he moved to the West Coast in order to work full time for the ex-patient movement. His chief contribution would be in organizing the coalition that in 1982 won passage of a referendum banning ECT in Berkeley. (The ban was promptly overturned by the courts.) In 1987, at the age of fifty, Chabasinski passed the bar exam. The mental health bar had demonstrated how useful the law could be in destroying the mental health system, and Chabasinski sought to serve the movement even more effectively as a lawyer.[11]

Leonard Frank, eloquent and gray-bearded—Chabasinski describes him as "looking and sounding like an Old Testament prophet"—is an equally effective anti-psychiatric advocate. Frank grew up in a prosperous family in New York and at the age of twenty-eight went to San Francisco to work as a real estate salesman. Shortly thereafter he quit work, became immersed in studying religion and philosophy, and grew a long beard. His parents came out to California and had him committed to a series of hospitals in the San Francisco area in 1962.

Frank was diagnosed as paranoid schizophrenic, although the medical records which he later published in *Madness Network News* give no indication that he suffered from the symptoms required for that diagnosis under psychiatry's *Diagnostic and Statistical Manual for Mental Disorders,* 3rd edition, revised (DSM III R). He was given fifty insulin coma treatments and thirty-five electroshock treatments: while he was in a coma induced by insulin he was given ECT. (This was not an uncommon procedure in the period when insulin shock was still used as a treatment for schizophrenia.) These treatments, given in a short time frame—today a course of ECT rarely exceeds eight to ten treatments—dramatically affected Frank's memory.

> The last shock treatment was like an eraser going across a blackboard. . . . When I got out I went into this room and stayed here and reacquired the information I'd lost. There were big chunks of my memory that were gone. My college and high school education was wiped out.[12]

For the next eight years Frank lived quietly on a stipend his parents provided him. He started an art gallery in 1970 but closed it in 1974 to go into ex-patient movement work full time. With another ex-patient, Wade Hudson, he started the Network Against Psychiatric Assault as a political action spinoff from *Madness Network News.*[13]

Of all the leaders of the ex-patient movement, Sally Zinman had the most bizarre experiences. She had literally been in a "dungeon," as she told Judi Chamberlain. The daughter of a wealthy banker, Sally Zinman attended Sarah Lawrence College and the University of Pennsylvania. At the age of thirty-three she was teaching English at Queens College in New York when she awoke one day feeling disassociated from her past: she no longer felt she was Sally Zinman. This is the only symptom of her illness Zinman herself describes.[14]

Her father turned for help to Dr. John Rosen, a psychiatrist who belonged to his country club.[15] Rosen had achieved considerable attention in psychiatric circles as a result of his claim to have found a cure for schizophrenia through "direct analysis," which involved assaulting the psychosis verbally.[16] However dubious his success with patients, he unquestionably had a way with wealthy families, Annenbergs and Rockefellers among them, who entrusted family members to his care.

Never admitted to a hospital, Sally became subject to Rosen's extraordinary methods of treatment. Her father flew her down in a private plane to one of Rosen's treatment residences in Boca Raton, Florida. When after a month she asked to become an outpatient, according to Sally, Rosen first agreed but later in the day, when she sought to leave, tore off all her clothes except her underpants and, while an aide held her, began beating her on the face and breast, leaving her with a black eye and bruises. She was then placed on a bed, still without clothes, and tied hand and foot.[17] She escaped to Pennsylvania but was returned to Rosen's control by her parents and driven, screaming all the way, to Rosen's Bucks County facility. There she lived for two months in a "dungeon," a cellar room without windows, furnished only with a mattress on the floor and a bucket as a toilet.[18]

It subsequently transpired that compared to some of Rosen's other patients Zinman had escaped lightly. In 1981 Janet Katkow sued Rosen for damages in six figures, charging that he had forced her into performing oral sex, anal sex, homosexual acts, and at least sixty-five group sex sessions over nine years of supposed therapy. Another patient, Claudia Ehrman, a thirty-one-year-old artist from New York City, died as a result of injuries inflicted in the course of "therapy" by two of Rosen's aides. Rather than stand trial, Rosen surrendered his medical license in 1983 and settled the claims against him out of court.[19]

Not all those who became activists in the ex-patient movement had terrible experiences with psychiatry. Wade Hudson, one of the original editors of *Madness Network News,* spent less than three weeks in mental hospitals. He wrote warmly of the Woodlawn Hospital in Dallas, where he spent most of that time, and especially of his psychiatrist there, whom he described as "very sharp and very sensitive" and a "good friend."[20] But most felt like Sally Zinman: "I got involved because of my experiences, which were so horrible."[21]

The writings of Thomas Szasz became immensely important to the ex-patient movement, for they provided a reasoned theory with which to back up emotional rejection of the mental health system. Again and again the founders of the movement refer to Szasz's influence on them.

Leonard Frank writes: "Early in 1964 I ran across an article by Dr. Thomas S. Szasz in *Harper's Magazine*. I was surprised and encouraged to find brilliantly articulated in this article a number of my own views on psychiatry which were then only loosely formed."[22] Sally Zinman reports that after she escaped from Rosen's control, "I read a lot of Szasz and was very, very influenced by him."[23]

Madness Network News Frames Ideology

The ex-patient movement brought to an ideology compounded of Szasz and R. D. Laing[24] the hard edge of passionate anger. But they differed from these mentors by focusing upon treatment. While the movement sometimes said that it only opposed forced treatment, its publications and activities make clear that treatment as such was the target: *all* treatments were evil. According to *Madness Network News*, "once those who are labelled with phony illnesses are committed, psychiatrists begin to terrorize them with phony treatments."[25] As one writer put it forthrightly "Treatment invariably means TORTURE."[26]

Vituperation was heaped upon all psychiatric treatments. ECT? The Network Against Psychiatric Assault called ECT "one of the grossest, most violent, dehumanizing techniques ever devised by man."[27] Drugs? David Richman, a psychiatrist who wrote a regular column for *Madness Network News* under the pseudonym "Dr. Caligari," attacked the neuroleptics singly and collectively as dangerous drugs with little or no therapeutic value. Anti-depressants were no better. According to "Dr. Caligari," "It's a question of 'choose your poison.'"[28] Lithium? Dr. Caligari called this natural salt, which has made it possible for many thousands of people suffering from manic-depression to lead normal lives, "the great pretender."[29] The most urgent task of movement people, wrote Canadian activist Don Weitz, was to "DEMYTHOLOGIZE ALL MEDICAL-PSYCHIATRIC TREATMENTS AND LABELLING OF PEOPLE BY PUBLICLY EXPOSING THESE PSYCHIATRIC 'TREATMENTS' AND LABELS AS INHUMANE ATROCITIES BY ANY MEANS NECESSARY."[30] (Capitalized in original.)

Nor was there any possibility that better treatments could be developed. An article in *Madness Network News* announced emphatically: "Someday there may be a cure for cancer, but there will never, ever be one for mental illness. . . . There is no cure, because there is no disease."[31] Mental patients, said the writer, need lawyers, not doctors.

Such disagreement as there was in the movement revolved around the role of capitalism in the oppression of mental patients. Some of the groups saw psychiatry as a capitalist plot. The following declaration, printed in *Madness Network News,* was typical of this perspective.

> We of the Mental Patient Liberation Front [the Boston ex-patient group] contend that *all* "treatment"—whether it be drugs, seclusion, electroshock, psychosurgery, behavior modification, or even psychotherapy—are used to coerce us into conforming to the narrow competitive, individualistic, sexist, racist, classist roles which are deemed acceptable by capitalist society and which drove us "crazy" in the first place.[32]

Perhaps the most extreme formulation of this perspective came from a movement member who wrote in to protest the paper's position that if a person was violent, he should be the concern of the criminal justice system.

> We need to abolish *all* repressive institutions, including the prisons, courts and police, as well as the mental hospitals and repressive psychiatric system. The answer to worries about violent acts committed by ex-patients is to call for the abolition of the society that creates those acts.[33]

But most movement members argued that the enemy was not primarily capitalism but psychiatry, which could thrive under any political system. This majority attitude was reflected in a 1975 article in *Madness Network News:* "For too long we, who have been branded as 'mental patients,' have been spat upon, oppressed, humiliated and subjugated by America's updated version of the Gestapo, more familiarly known as Organized Psychiatry."[34] The ex-patients saw themselves, as one activist put it, as "liberation fighters . . . struggling against psychiatric oppression, tyranny and murder."[35] When President Carter became involved in an effort to improve services for the mentally ill, the North American Conference on Human Rights and Psychiatric Oppression sent him a resolution saying what was needed was not more attention to "mental health" but a tribunal to investigate "psychiatric crimes against human rights" and to make judgments against "these criminals."[36]

The most complete summation of the ex-patient movement's ideology was the Declaration of Principles drawn up by representatives of various mental patients liberation groups during the Tenth Conference on Human Rights and Psychiatric Oppression in 1982. The Declaration, which opposed all civil commitment and involuntary treatment, rejected "the medical model of 'mental illness' because it dupes the public into seeking or accepting 'voluntary' treatment." The psychiatric system, said the Declaration, "cannot be reformed but must be abolished."[37]

Movement Activities

The ex-patient groups made up in energy and imagination for what they lacked in numbers. They demonstrated, staged guerrilla theater, organized boycotts and sit-ins (including a month-long occupation in 1976 of then Governor Jerry Brown's offices in California), initiated legislation, and organized political referenda.

Their protests, staged so as to attract media attention, focused on all the major forms of treatment. The first national protest, in 1977, struck out at psychosurgery, with demonstrations in several cities. The action was in response to a favorable report issued by the National Commission for Protection of Human Subjects, which had performed an in-depth study of psychosurgery for Congress.

A year later, the North American Conference on Human Rights and Psychiatric Oppression, meeting in Philadelphia, demonstrated at the offices of Smith, Kline and French, makers of Thorazine, demanding an end to the production of Thorazine and other "mind controlling chemicals."[38] In 1982, the ex-patients dragged a huge posterboard needle labeled "Thorazine" to the Sheraton Centre Hotel in Toronto, where the American Psychiatric Association was meeting. The needle was used to "attack" some of the marchers, who fell over "dead" with signs posted over them "Cured by Psychiatry." The ex-patients then staged a sit-in at the hotel until they were taken away by police.[39] In 1983 the ex-patients organized a North American Day of Protest against ECT with guerrilla theatre and demonstrations against hospitals in a number of cities.[40]

The movement had no hesitation in making its "abolitionist" perspective clear. Marching on the Massachusetts Mental Health Center in 1976, participants from the North American Congress on Human Rights and Psychiatric Oppression (meeting in Boston that year) presented their "demands." "We demand the total abolition of psychiatric institutions, since the function they serve is to imprison, torture and dehumanize people and not to help them."[41]

Ex-Patient Movement Finds Allies Within Psychiatry

Despite its venomous attacks on psychiatry, the ex-patient movement found allies in a number of young psychiatrists influenced by the left-wing radicalism of the 1960s. *Madness Network News* was founded by radical psychiatrist David Richman and his wife, Sherry Hirsch, a social worker. Richman declared that he wanted to use the journal to forge a broader coalition of those who saw the struggle against institutional psychiatry "as a part of a larger and broader movement to make basic changes in the nature of our world, country, society, communities, homes, etc. (one being the de-institutionalization of life)."[42]

As the ex-patients grew in numbers and self-confidence, relations with "radical therapists" grew increasingly tense. The crisis came to a head at the third meeting of the Conference on Human Rights and Psychiatric Oppression held in San Francisco in 1975 under the sponsorship of the *Madness Network News* spinoff, the Network Against Psychiatric Assault. The Network had put a number of professionals on workshops and panels; the ex-patients in attendance felt excluded and "put down," especially when they vented their emotional rage against psychiatry. They formed their own caucus and put a "Keep Out" sign on their meeting room for anyone who had not "done time" in a mental institution.[43]

From then on, the ex-patients decided that annual meetings of the Conference would be closed to professionals (except for those specially invited as being in full accord with ex-patient goals). Activist Judi Chamberlin explained:

> Sincere radical therapists have a big job—reforming the institutions and professions of which they are a part, or abolishing them in favor of humane alternatives. They should be too busy to have the need to "lead" mental patient groups. Those radical therapists who see the mental patients' movement as their arena are the ones we most need to keep away from.[44]

In 1976, as part of the ouster of professionals from leadership roles, David Richman was forced out as editor of *Madness Network News*.

More than a simple power struggle was involved. The ex-patients felt that radical therapists did not espouse liberation movement goals. Indeed, many of the ex-inmates came to believe that radical therapists were even worse than establishment psychiatrists in being hypocrites. Judi Chamberlin noted that the Italian anti-psychiatrists who boasted of ending admissions to state mental hospitals admitted that they used drugs in their community centers.[45] And ex-patients discovered that the same anti-psychiatrists who denounced all somatic treatments in the United States might raise no objections to electroshock, for example, in Cuba.

Accordingly, when the International Network: Alternatives to Psychiatry, composed of radical therapists from around the world, met in San Francisco in 1980, the Network Against Psychiatric Assault handed out a leaflet complaining that while the ex-patient movement focused on ending "brutal and coercive psychiatric 'treatments,'" there were anti-psychiatric leaders who actually used ECT and drugs in their own clinics. An anti-psychiatry movement dominated by psychiatrists, said the pamphlet, in fact represents "torturers pretending to be philosophers of liberation."[46]

Radical psychiatrists had little direct impact on American psychiatry. Since the alleviation of mental illness had to await the destruction of capitalism, the proper focus for action was in the political sphere, not the narrow mental health arena. Radical therapists continued to publish journals and met as a radical caucus at the annual meetings of the American Psychiatric Association; they heard speeches with titles like "Theoretical, Ideological and Methodological Issues of Psychology from a Marxist Perspective—A Summary of a Conference at the University of La Habana, Cuba."[47] It is easy to sympathize with the ex-patients' complaint that when shrinks dominate anti-psychiatry, the focus shifts "to esoteric and obscure discussions of Freud, language, and the nature of society and the mind."[48]

Psychiatrists Denounce Psychiatry

There were a handful of psychiatrists (and neurologists) who were considered true allies by the ex-patient movement. Their importance to the ex-patients was in lending credibility to what would otherwise have been dismissed as ravings of a literally lunatic fringe. These medical professionals focused on halting psychiatric treatments, and did not, as Judi Chamberlain said of the Marxist therapists "talk of radicalism (but who knows what they do)."[49] David Richman, despite his "deinstitutionalization of life" rhetoric, remained close to the movement because he agreed that all the medications—neuroleptics, anti-depressants, lithium—used in the treatment of major mental illness were harmful.

In their antagonism toward psychiatry, these medical allies outdid many in the ex-patient movement. For neurologist John Friedberg—himself an ex-patient—the ex-patient movement did not go far enough. He complained that the introduction to ex-patient Leonard Frank's indictment of ECT, *The History of Shock Treatment* did not make sufficiently clear that shock treatment was "the logical consequence of the premises of all of psychiatry."[50] Psychiatrist Jeffrey Masson, a latecomer to the group, argued that psychotherapy was as dangerous and destructive as the somatic therapies.[51]

Dr. Peter Breggin, a former student of Szasz in Syracuse, has repeatedly likened psychiatric treatments to Nazism. In a 1973 speech on psychosurgery, he compared psychiatry's "menticidal programs" (mind murder) to Nazi Germany's genocidal programs.[52] By 1988, he was holding psychiatry chiefly responsible for the Holocaust. According to Breggin, "psychiatry was the first group to propose the systematic mass extermination of a group of people," and it was psychiatry that "developed the medical umbrella for killing in the extermination centers." Without that umbrella, according to Breggin, the Holocaust would not have happened.[53] (In fact, while German psychiatrists played a shameful role in the Nazi regime, failing to oppose and cooperating in the mass murder of mental patients, psychiatry did not instigate the Holocaust.[54])

Breggin, easily the most effective of the group, is to the attack on treatment what Szasz is to the attack on the idea of mental illness. If Szasz seems to enjoy showing off his skills as a dialectical debater, Breggin identifies more with the ex-patient role. In a revealing speech in 1988 to a largely ex-patient audience, Breggin declared he was probably not an ex-patient only because he "never sought help when I was in my worst condition."[55] To us, Breggin explained the anti-psychiatric direction he had taken in terms of his experiences in the Harvard-Radcliffe mental hospital volunteer program he started while a Harvard undergraduate.

> That's what got me in my direction, not meeting Szasz. I worked in a mental hospital for four years from 1954 to 58 and came to the conclusion there wasn't a lot of difference between me and the patients. . . . I had my picture in the *Saturday Evening Post* in those days. We got thirteen out of fifteen patients out of the hospital and that was before drugs.[56]

Like Szasz, Breggin is a skilled publicist, appearing on scores of radio and television shows. A veritable fountainhead of conspiracy theories, Breggin provides good television with his nugget phrases and simplistic attacks on his own profession. On the Oprah Winfrey show, Breggin explained why biological theories of major mental illness had become dominant.

> We got more competition from social workers and clinical psychologists and counselors and other people doing 'talking.' So the question became: How can psychiatrists, faced with all this competition and loss of funds, regain their authority and their status? The decision was the New Psychiatry, to emphasize that all these problems are biological. We'll repeat it in the newspapers, we'll repeat in the magazines: Depression's biological, schizophrenia's biological. . . . And it's all lies.[57]

With each television appearance, there was a new plot. Again on Oprah Winfrey, Breggin declared that psychiatrists prescribed drugs because the American Psychiatric Association was in the financial pocket of the drug companies, which, for example, bought ads in the association's journal.

> We are dependent on the drug companies financially now. We can't survive. Our journals, our lobbying efforts, our public relations. . . . We need a Psychogate investigation of this. Congress should investigate this, Oprah.[58]

Like the handful of other professionals close to the ex-patient movement, Breggin has joined the small band who have made national reputations by attacking the scientific consensus in their own field. Like most of the scientists who have taken this course, Breggin has not made contributions that would win him recognition among his peers. But his slashing attacks—"it's all lies"—on those who *have* made the major scientific breakthroughs in the understanding and treatment of mental illness in the last decades have earned him fame and status his professional work could not. Television talk shows are eager to provide people like Breggin with a platform. Because discussion programs are visually unstimulating, their hosts are on the lookout for theatrical participants who will provide heat rather than light.[59]

Less intellectually gifted than Szasz, Breggin has been more active politically, testifying tirelessly in hearings at both the federal and state level, serving as "expert witness" in a stream of lawsuits, and working with legislators. He has mounted a series of highly effective political campaigns against each of psychiatry's somatic therapies. The first campaign, against psychosurgery, would lay the groundwork for those that followed.

Chapter 9

Psychosurgery
The First Domino

Pˢʏᴄʜᴏsᴜʀɢᴇʀʏ was the first and easiest target of those op-posed to all psychiatric treatments. The crude early operations had a significant mortality rate and often had a severe negative impact, some-times so severe as to produce a "vegetable personality"—people who were left without awareness or initiative, and would vegetate on the back wards of hospitals for the rest of their lives. Today, the term "lobotomy" arouses almost universal revulsion.

But Peter Breggin's campaign against psychosurgery, launched in the 1970s, attacked an *old* treatment at the very time when vastly refined techniques had eliminated its defects and improved understanding had narrowed its use to small subgroups of patients most likely to benefit. Breggin's attacks have made such surgery almost impossible to obtain in the United States. Psychiatrists failed to come to the defense of the new psychosurgery, many of them identifying it with the old lobotomies, which they viewed as barbaric and outmoded. They did not perceive that psychosurgery was merely the first target in what was from the outset a war against all somatic treatments for major mental illness.

The birth of psychosurgery can be traced to an international neurological conference in London in 1935 at which neurophysiologist John Fulton presented the results of experiments he and his colleague at Yale, Carlyle Jacobsen, had conducted with two chimpanzees, Becky and Lucy. The two chimps had been trained to solve elaborate problems in order to obtain food and became upset when they were frustrated in their efforts, shaking and kicking their box, pulling their hair, even throwing their excreta at the scientists. But after Fulton and Jacobsen removed their frontal lobes, the animals became immune to frustration. While their skill in handling the tests had diminished somewhat, they were no longer upset by their failures.

In the audience were two figures who would become the giants of psychosurgery: Egas Moniz and Walter Freeman. Moniz was a distinguished Portuguese scientist, already celebrated for developing cerebral angiography. Fulton reports that after he had read his paper, "Dr. Moniz arose and asked, would it not be feasible to relieve anxiety states in man by surgical means?"[1] Freeman, a young American neurologist, would later modify and disseminate widely the technique that Moniz developed.

Only two months after the London conference, Moniz guided the first surgery on human beings. (The actual operation was performed in Lisbon by a young neurosurgeon, Almeida Lima.) Instead of removing the frontal lobes, as Fulton and Jacobsen had done, Moniz cut fibers connecting the frontal lobes to other areas of the brain. He called the operation "leucotomy" (after the Greek words "leucos" meaning white and "tomos" meaning cutting) and developed a special surgical tool, the leucotome. The leucotome's shaft (cannula) would be inserted into the brain and when it reached the desired plane of section, the surgeon would depress a plunger; a wire looped out and was rotated, cutting a core of brain tissue.

Psychosurgery Comes to the United States

In the United States Freeman, with the aid of neurosurgeon James Watts, pioneered the operation and renamed it "lobotomy," because nerve fibers of a lobe of the brain were cut. As Freeman explained to a group of skeptical psychiatrists: "The [delusional] idea is still there, but it has no emotional drive. . . . I think we have drawn the sting, as it were, of the psychosis or neurosis."[2]

In his own way a community psychiatrist, Freeman felt his life mission was to empty the back wards of state mental hospitals. He recognized that the existing operation could never achieve that end, because it was expensive, requiring the skills of a neurosurgeon, and not likely to be available to patients in the great custodial warehouses maintained by the state. So by the end of 1945 Freeman was looking for a new kind of operation, one, moreover, that would do less extensive damage to personality. Freeman perfected an operation devised by the Italian surgeon A. M. Fiamberti,[3] which reached the frontal lobes from a different direction, avoiding the need for boring holes through the skull. Freeman called the operation, which did not even require an operating room, transorbital lobotomy. His initial operating instrument was in fact an icepick taken from his kitchen drawer.

Freeman, using electroshock in lieu of anesthetic, drew the upper eyelid away from the eyeball to expose the tear duct and then tapped the pick with a hammer to drive through the orbital plate. He would oscillate the instrument to sever fibers at the base of the frontal lobe. The patient would wake up with black eyes but could return immediately to his home or hospital ward "with no restrictions" on his activities, as Freeman would tell the family. Watts, who performed traditional lobotomies, was outraged by the new technique, which he felt diminished the dignity of neurosurgery.[4]

Transorbital lobotomies—or icepick lobotomies as they were dubbed by critics—could be easily performed in state hospitals. It is estimated that by 1955 over 40,000 had been performed in the United States, most of them between 1945 and 1949. Freeman *alone* performed or supervised over 3,500 of the operations in nineteen states and ten foreign countries.[5] Ordinary doctors at backwater state hospitals could master the simple technique. In 1957, science popularizer Paul DeKruif wrote an enthusiastic book about Jack Ferguson, a country doctor (not a psychiatrist) working at Traverse City State Hospital in Michigan, where he was trying the then brand-new, anti-psychotic medications. A few years earlier Ferguson had worked at the state hospital in Logansport, Indiana, where he had pored over Freeman's writings, and then modified the procedure so that it could be completed in three minutes! Ferguson performed hundreds of these operations and told DeKruif that while perhaps two-thirds of the patients behaved better after the operation, "they couldn't plan ahead."[6]

The public image of these procedures did not gain much from Freeman's habit of calling the patients upon whom he had operated "trophies," or terming his mammoth journeys to follow up on what had happened to them "head-hunting expeditions." Yet this effort, which Freeman's one-time partner, James Watts, called his "magnificent obsession"[7] was a laudable one. Even in his old age, Freeman would drive 26,000 miles on a single journey,[8] combing the country in search of his former patients, and keeping meticulous records of their progress. (These records, which to this day have not been studied, are kept at the Himmelfarb Health Sciences Library at George Washington University in Washington, D.C., where Freeman taught for many years).[9]

The discovery of anti-psychotic drugs ended the era of lobotomies and by 1960 hospitals no longer permitted even Freeman to operate. Many have condemned the psychiatric profession for permitting such operations, but as Desmond Kelly, an English psychiatrist and expert in modern psychosurgery, points out, the context in which the operations were performed needs to be kept in mind.

> It is very easy to look back and to say it was an evil thing, but when you're there it's different. Although there were major personality changes, it enabled an awful lot of schizophrenics to leave psychiatric hospitals . . . but at a price. The difficulty was all the successes were in the community and they didn't tell anyone they had the operation and all the failures were in the hospitals as tombstones of the negative effects of surgery.[10]

The Development of Limbic System Surgery

Lobotomies in their heyday enjoyed widespread public acceptance. It was after they had been discarded, and far superior neurosurgical procedures developed in their place, that modern psychosurgery came under vigorous assault. The *new* operations, emerging in the mid-1960s, were attacked on the basis of the failures of the *old* techniques. As psychiatrist Stewart Shevitz has pointed out, it's as if we were to reject current surgical approaches to coronary heart disease because of the difficulties encountered with the first human heart transplants.[11]

The foundation for modern limbic system surgery was laid in the late 1940s as a result of progress on a number of fronts: in surgical techniques, in identifying the anatomical basis of emotion, and in narrowing the criteria for selecting patients. In 1947 Ernest Spiegel and Henry Wycis at Temple University in Philadelphia pioneered stereotactic surgery. Using three-dimensional brain maps as a guide, they applied a fixating apparatus to the head, which allowed greater precision and far smaller lesions than in the old, blind, freehand operations.[12] At the same time John Fulton, whose chimpanzee experiments had triggered Moniz's first surgery, published the results of his study—based on post mortems of lobotomized individuals—on how the site of the lesion related to the effects of the operation. He concluded that lesions should be confined to one quadrant of the frontal lobe.[13] With stereotactic techniques, it was possible to make the lesion exactly in the area pinpointed by Fulton.

In the late 1940s, Paul MacLean confirmed the existence of the "Papez circuit," named for James W. Papez, a neuroanatomist at Cornell whose 1937 paper "A Proposed Mechanism of Emotion" postulated— with very little evidence at the time—that the anatomical basis for emotion lay in an ensemble of structures deep within the brain: the so-called limbic system. (Limbic means "forming a border around" and these structures border the brain stem.) From now on, neurosurgeons would move in two directions: in one, selected fiber tracts connecting the frontal lobes and specific limbic structures were cut; in the other lesions were made in the limbic structures themselves, such as the cingulum, midline thalamic areas, and the amygdala. How precisely the surgery worked was not known: brain chemistry might be affected, or interrupted abnormal nerve pathways replaced by normally functioning ones.

The means for making lesions ranged from electrodes to radioactive rods to ultrasound. The new operations had far less risk of complications than the old and did not have their damaging effect on personality or intelligence. By the late 1960s, in the view of California neurosurgeon M. Hunter Brown, limbic system surgery had the "highest benefit to risk ratio of any procedure in neurological surgery."[14]

Spurring development of limbic system surgery in the mid-1960s was the growing recognition that the medications that at first had made psychosurgery seem obsolete did not help everyone. By now psychiatrists and neurosurgeons also had a better understanding of the kinds of patients most likely to be helped by surgery: those, as Robert Arnot pointed out as early as 1940, suffering from a "fixed state of tortured self-concern."[15] Psychosurgery had been used extensively in schizophrenia because of the severity of the illness, but drugs were far more successful in treating psychosis. Severe chronic anxiety, agitated depression, and obsessive compulsive behavior, on the other hand, responded well to surgery.[16]

By 1970 there was enough progress for a Second International Congress on Psychosurgery (the first had been in 1948) to be held in Copenhagen.

Breggin Mounts His Campaign

It was at this promising juncture that Peter Breggin began his fanatical crusade against the principle somatic treatments for the mentally ill. According to Breggin:

> I was sitting in my office in 1970 when I opened up *Psychiatric News* and saw a headline, which read—it was very close to this—"Psychosurgery Said to Be Effective in Certain Neuroses," or something like that. . . . And

it was about an international meeting of psychosurgeons in Copenhagen and how psychosurgery was coming back, a second wave. And I was appalled. . . . And I said to myself, someone has to do something about this.[17]

Breggin explains that he wrote to all those mentioned in the article, said he was writing a review of psychosurgery "and would love to include them." In this way he obtained information to be used in his campaign against the treatment, a campaign that would take him to Congress and the media, to law courts, state legislatures, and endless conferences. Breggin adds: "And it's never stopped since then. Because it became obvious that psychosurgery was nothing more than the ultimate expression of biological psychiatry. That all the treatments damaged the brain; all the treatments worked by destroying function."[18]

Breggin's "research" paper on psychosurgery which was entered into the *Congressional Record* in February 1972 and his testimony in congressional hearings (chaired by Senator Edward Kennedy) early in 1973 relied far more on hysteria than on science. Breggin proclaimed: We are in danger of creating a society in which everyone who deviates from the norm will be in danger of surgical mutilation." Psychosurgery, Breggin warned, was a new form of "totalitarianism," and if America ever became a police state, it would be armed with "lobotomy and psychosurgery."[19] (This was too much for another witness at the Kennedy hearings, Dr. Willard Gaylin, president of the Hastings Institute, who said dryly: "It seems unlikely, if there were some plot to take over the country . . . that psychosurgery would be the method of choice. I doubt that they would find the most efficient technique for mass control would be planting electrodes on a population of 200 million, or psychosurgery, when they have access to a limited national television, and to schools with compulsory education, to psychological inputs and to drugs . . . .[20])

Breggin described psychosurgery as no more than senseless mutilation of the brain, whose effect, *by definition,* had to be harmful, for "improvement in function cannot follow mutilation of the functioning brain."[21] But as British psychiatrist Dr. Desmond Kelly points out:

Peter Breggin's contention is that you are destroying normal brain tissue and my contention is that these are some of the sickest people I've ever seen in psychiatry and they are so grateful when they come through because although it [the brain tissue] may appear normal under the microscope, it certainly isn't functioning normally. Obsessives are crucified by their illnesses; they may spend sixteen, eighteen hours a day washing, cleaning, their various rituals. They can't work, they can't do anything except ritualize until they finally fall asleep from sheer fatigue, and if that is viewed as the functioning of a normal brain that certainly isn't my definition.[22]

Paul Bridges, consultant psychiatrist at the psychosurgical unit at Brook General Hospital in London, told us that he had invited Breggin, when he was in England, to come and see his patients for himself: "He didn't have time or something like that."[23]

Breggin was no more to be tied down by clinical realities than by scientific evidence; like his mentor Thomas Szasz, he offered rhetorical arguments and denunciation by analogy. From then on, Breggin's attacks on other forms of treatment would consist primarily of equating them with the long-discarded lobotomy. All limbic system surgery was lobotomy. ECT was another type of lobotomy and treatment with neuroleptic drugs "chemical lobotomy."

In his effort to obtain a congressional ban against limbic system surgery, Breggin's initial strategy was to focus on black congressmen. Neurosurgeons Vernon Mark and William Sweet and psychiatrist Frank Ervin, all associated with Harvard Medical School, had sent a foolish joint letter to the *Journal of the American Medical Association* in 1967, at the time of the riots in black ghettoes around the country, citing "medical evidence" that violence was due to biological, not environmental factors, and suggesting psychosurgery as a remedy for the violent behavior of some rioters.

In 1970 Ervin and Mark published *Violence and the Brain,* in which they again suggested that criminal violence could be sharply reduced by psychosurgery. Later one of the authors would agree with the consensus in his field that psychosurgery was appropriate for treatment of aggression only in the presence of a specific brain disorder.[24] But the damage was done: Breggin could plausibly argue that nothing less than "political psychosurgery" was being advocated, and line up black congressmen on the grounds that psychosurgery might be used to control blacks in the ghetto.

While Breggin did not achieve his goal of a legislative ban on psychosurgery, he was successful in obtaining what was then viewed as a prelude toward that end, establishment by Congress in 1974 of a commission to investigate under what circumstances "if any" the continued use of psychosurgery might be appropriate. Breggin boasts of his role in creating the commission. "I created the psychosurgery commission. I lobbied; I sat down in my living room and created that with chief assistant to Senator Glenn Beall from Maryland."[25]

But this particular move backfired. The commission contracted for two studies, conducted by separate teams of scientists and clinicians from MIT and Boston University. The MIT study evaluated eighty-five patients who had received cingulotomies (surgery performed by Dr. H. Thomas Ballantine of Massachusetts General Hospital that makes a lesion in the cingulum, one of the structures in the limbic system), while the Boston University study examined fifty-two patients, who had been ill an average of twenty years, some of whom were evaluated both before and after surgery. Each patient received one of four different limbic system surgical procedures. Both studies, using interviews and objective tests, came to the same conclusions: more than half the patients improved significantly following psychosurgery and *none* of the patients suffered significant neurological or psychological impairment.[26] The results were particularly impressive because only those who were severely disabled and failed to respond to all other treatments had been accepted for surgery.

Although most of the commission's eleven members had approached their task biased against psychosurgery, their report, as critics noted angrily, fell only slightly short of an endorsement. The chairman of the commission explained:

> We looked at the data and saw they did not support our prejudices. I, for one, did not expect to come out in favor of psychosurgery. But we saw that some very sick people had been helped by it, and that it did not destroy their intelligence or rob them of feelings. . . . The operation shouldn't be banned.[27]

The report was the more remarkable in that the commission undertook its work in a climate poisoned by near hysteria. The media, uncritically enthusiastic about lobotomies in their heyday, had become extremely hostile now that the risk-benefit ratio had radically shifted in favor of surgery. *Ebony Magazine* published a quote from Dr. Alvin Poussaint, a black psychiatrist at Harvard, that whites believed blacks so "animal and savage that whites have to carve on their brains to make them human beings. . . . "[28] Surgeons who performed the operations were intimidated. Breggin boasts: "There were people picketing these guys' [neurosurgeons] houses, picketing the hospitals, women reporters calling them on the phone."[29]

When the commission held public hearings in San Francisco on the commission's recommendation that institutional review boards monitor the surgery, demonstrators stood outside the meeting hall chanting "It didn't end with the Second World War/Eichmann's alive on the fifteenth floor." An article in *Madness Network News* bragged that the commissioners were forced to flee and would probably never return.[30] The Church of Scientology, through its Citizens Commission on Human Rights, also threw itself into the anti-psychosurgery crusade with demonstrations, and pickets. Breggin notes that the Church of Scientology has always been an outright enemy of psychiatry, seeing it as competition for its *own* theory of "psychosis" and treatments.[31] (Scientologists teach that individuals can free themselves of abnormal thought processes through "auditing," a process of tracing past lives, and through the use of an "E-meter"—a battery-powered galvanometer that uses a needle dial wired to two tin cans—can reach a "Clear" status.[32])

Despite the furor, the Commission recommended that psychosurgery continue to be available, and although it opposed such surgery for prisoners, it urged that the operations not be limited to patients able to give informed consent, since this would deprive some seriously ill individuals of a valuable treatment. Indeed the only disappointing finding, from the standpoint of neurosurgeons who performed the operations, was that the commission continued to define psychosurgery as "experimental" rather than as a well-established procedure. Dr. Ballantine complained: "If I've done the same operation for seventeen years and 70–80 percent show useful improvement, I don't see how it could be called innovative."[33]

But if the Commission withstood pressure fairly well (its final report in 1977 was more qualified in its support than its initial 1976 report, presumably in response to the outcry evoked by the latter), Department of Health, Education and Welfare Secretary Joseph Califano wanted nothing to do with such a political hot potato. Limbic system surgery could not be banned in the wake of the report, but Califano did not recommend that the operations be available to those too ill to give informed consent; nor did he follow through on the recommendation that review boards be established to monitor the surgery and that comprehensive scientific studies of its effectiveness be undertaken. Both would have given limbic system surgery more legitimacy.

The Kaimowitz Case

Although Breggin's hoped-for congressional ban did not materialize, the courts dealt psychosurgery a heavy blow. In 1973 Gabe Kaimowitz, an attorney with Legal Services in Michigan, brought suit to prevent performance of an amygdalotomy on "John Doe," who had been in an institution for the criminally insane for seventeen years.

(Doe's real name, Louis Smith, became known during the trial.) While in a mental hospital for psychiatric evaluation, Smith had murdered a student nurse and raped her dead body.

There were many problems with the proposal to perform surgery on Smith. The only clear criterion for surgery in cases of aggression is evidence of temporal lobe epilepsy, which was not present in his case. Moreover, while the original intent was to study twenty-four criminal sexual psychopaths in the state mental health system, comparing the effects of surgery (an amygdalotomy) with the effects of a drug (cyproterone acetate) in providing relief from aggression, it was found that Smith was the only appropriate candidate in the system for surgery.[34] The value of the experiment in the absence of any other subjects was dubious.

Although technically speaking he had no client (both Smith and his parents had consented to the operation), Kaimowitz brought suit on the ground that the coercive atmosphere of a prison made it impossible for an incarcerated individual to give informed consent to psychosurgery. The case continued despite the fact that the issue, at least in so far as it concerned Louis Smith, had dissolved. The three-judge panel in Wayne County hearing the case set him free on the ground that the "criminal sexual psychopath" statute under which he had been incarcerated was unconstitutional. Once free, Smith decided he did not want psychosurgery. Local newspapers reported he was "looking for an apartment and planning to attend community college."[35] (Within a few months he was back in prison, arrested for stealing women's clothes from a store; he was wearing nineteen pairs of women's underpants and ten slips.[36])

The judges ruled that it was impossible for a prisoner to give informed consent to psychosurgery because the risks surrounding it were so great as to make "knowledgeable consent to psychosurgery literally impossible." Breggin was delighted with the outcome. "The judges wrote their opinion and it practically looks like my testimony. They cite the Nuremberg code; they said psychosurgery was destructive of the creative process and described the lobotomy syndrome."[37]

On the other hand, the losing attorney, S. I. Shuman, observes that because the judges in the Kaimowitz case were in effect serving as a medical review committee for a whole field of medicine, they were dependent on the quality of the expert witnesses who testified. Says Shuman: "The medical scientist who gains access as an expert to the institutionalized judicial decision-making process has a professional and political obligation to perform as a scientist and not as a political huckster." Yet, Shuman points out, "the effectiveness of Dr. Breggin's advocacy is in large part due to the fact that it is not scientific."[38]

While members of the mental health bar were delighted that the court had ruled against psychosurgery, the decision's implications made them uneasy. Informed consent, said the judges in Kaimowitz, required not only knowledge, but also voluntariness and competence to make a decision, and these were also absent in the inherently coercive environment of a state mental hospital. (Breggin had told them state mental hospitals were like concentration camps and "that if you're in this oppressive, humiliating, debilitating situation and somebody says he'll volunteer for a freezing experiment, it's only because you're afraid you'll go to the ovens."[39]) Did that mean the involuntary patient could not consent to *any* treatment? What would happen to the "right to treatment" under those circumstances?[40]

Even more serious was the court's ruling that the very fact of institutionalization, by depriving the individual of his sense of self-worth, diminished his competence. The suits brought by the mental health bar depended heavily upon the presumed *competence* of mental patients. Were the judges resurrecting by a back door the old rules that treated mental patients as legally incompetent?

These fears proved unwarranted because other courts never followed up on these elements of the decision. The case only served as precedent for further decisions favorable to the patient liberation bar. For example, the Kaimowitz court decided that psychosurgery violated the First Amendment's guarantee of freedom of speech: by limiting the ability to produce new ideas, it undercut the basis of free expression.[41] This notion would soon be employed by the mental health bar in right to refuse anti-psychotic medication cases. It would be alleged that psychoactive drugs, by interfering with psychotic thought processes, deprived individuals of their constitutional right to freedom of thought and speech.

The Kaimowitz decision had a major impact in discouraging psychosurgery. Breggin boasts that the case brought to an end operations in state mental hospitals. "Up to that point, for example, they were operating in Missouri and I'd go to Missouri and talk on radio and television. Then they would stop it in Missouri and I'd hear about it in California. This really put a blanket on it."[42] Oregon in 1973 and California in 1977 established mandatory psychosurgery review boards whose practical effect was to eliminate the treatment.[43] (Two of the best known neurosurgeons in the field, M. Hunter Brown and Peter Lindstrom— Ingrid Bergman's first husband—were in California.) Neurosurgeons everywhere were reluctant to perform surgery that a court had ruled "clearly experimental," fearing that malpractice suits might be more easily brought—and won—in the wake of the decision.

Victims of Kaimowitz—Other Patients

The real victims of Kaimowitz were not the neurosurgeons—limbic system surgery counted for a tiny percentage of the practice even of those most active in the field—but the severely mentally ill people who responded to no other treatment and whose suffering stood an excellent chance of being alleviated by it. John Gavin, Jr., whose operation was scheduled at the time of the Kaimowitz case, suffered from the kind of tortured self-concern that psychosurgery was best suited to relieve. He first became ill at the age of fifteen, and from the age of seventeen spent half of each year in the hospital, the rest at home on convalescent leave. He became increasingly self-destructive, blinding himself in one eye and badly injuring the other. When he was out of restraints he would poke whatever he could find into his eye or ear. He developed meningitis after puncturing an ear drum with a pencil point; he would run full speed into a wall and bang his head against it.[44]

Gavin did not respond to drugs and a team of psychiatrists at the Medical College of Virginia determined that psychosurgery stood a good chance of helping him. Gavin consented to the operation as did his parents. His mother said: "We couldn't stand to see him tear himself apart piece by piece."[45] Neurosurgeon Donald P. Becker, who was to have performed the surgery, had participated in surgery in a similar case in which, following the operation, the individual became in Becker's words, "incredibly rehabilitated."[46] Becker did not undertake the surgery lightly: "I personally consider this operation only when a patient's life is so miserable for himself and those in his environment that there is no alternative. Furthermore, I insist on psychiatric evaluations by three separate board-certified psychiatrists."[47]

Gavin was transferred to the University of Virginia hospital in Charlottesville for the operation and Dr. Becker remembers that the morning it was scheduled, while he was having breakfast with his house staff, he was called to the phone. The individual at the other end warned him, "If you do this procedure, I'll kill you." Since it was not an emergency, Becker canceled the operation, hoping to reschedule it.[48] But his caller also phoned the *Washington Post* and other papers and the Virginia Attorney General's office, which announced an investigation into the legality of the operation.[49] Gavin was sent back to the Medical College of Virginia.

While one can only speculate on the difference limbic system surgery would have made in John Gavin's life, the difference it has made in the life of many tormented individuals can be documented. In November 1986, Dr. Ballantine received a letter from a fifty-three-year-old woman he had operated on seven years earlier: "On June 29, 1979, a very important day in my life, I was one of the privileged few to have the cingulotomy operation. I celebrate this day yearly as my re-birthday. For many, many years before this day, I was plagued with severe depression and was in and out of mental wards and hospitals many, many times."[50]

We talked to Paula Perlstein, another former patient of Dr. Ballantine. Paula Perlstein is her real name: she asked that it be used. "If I hide behind a pseudonym we are telling the world that I have something to hide. I'm proving I have had an illness; I'm not a criminal who has to hide my past."[51] Black-haired and diminutive, with large deep-set dark eyes, Paula Perlstein at thirty-eight is a dynamic and highly intelligent woman, whose demeanor and speech give no hint of the terrible illness that dominated her life prior to surgery.

Paula's first hospitalization, in New York State, came when she was thirteen; it lasted for nineteen months. At fifteen, diagnosed as schizophrenic, she was hospitalized again. She says the voices began when she was fifteen and a half or sixteen: "I was very paranoid. I felt like I wasn't human, and I was very self-destructive and suicidal." She went from High Point Hospital in Port Chester (private) to Creedmoor (public) to the Psychiatric Treatment Center in Manhattan, a private hospital no longer in existence that specialized in adolescents. Of the Psychiatric Treatment Center, Paula says: "I was very heavily medicated there, and I had private nurses twenty-four hours a day—and I even managed to break windows with the private nurses!"

The next fifteen years went by with on-again, off-again hospitalizations in an endless series of private and public institutions in both New York and Massachusetts. All the therapies—recognized and not recognized by psychiatry—were tried: medications, electroshock, psychotherapy, megavitamins. (In megavitamin therapy, whose effectiveness has not been validated in double-blind studies, very large doses of certain vitamins are taken.) At some points all were being tried at once; while she was in Fuller Memorial Hospital in Massachusetts, according to Paula, "I was getting shock treatment, medication, megavitamins, aversive conditioning, adrenal cortical extracts, you name it, I had it." In all, beginning when she was eighteen, Paula received at least two hundred electroshock treatments. She says: "I don't know why because they didn't do me much good."

At nineteen Paula was back in Creedmoor where she almost died.

> I was in a seclusion room and I don't remember this, this is what they told me. They had bars on the window but I noticed there was a piece of broken glass behind the bars. I reached for it and slit my throat and they found me lying there and they had to stitch me up and I was in intensive care.

But Paula's drive to hurt herself could not be controlled, and she began to burn her arms. Says Paula: "It started with cigarettes and then it graduated to matches." Ultimately she would have to undergo painful skin grafts.

Enormous doses of combined medications had no effect on Paula. "I was taking 800 mg a day of Mellaril, 75 mg a day of Nardil, and a fairly high dose of Moban. But I was not sedated at all."

In 1973, when Paula was twenty-one, she had her first limbic system surgery: a cingulotomy performed by Dr. H. Thomas Ballantine. Paula describes her condition at the time. "I was very bad then. I've read some of the records and I was in restraints." When the first operation did not help her, Dr. Ballantine performed a second one. Paula explains: "It's the same procedure except they go a little deeper each time. A little more tissue is destroyed. There's a better chance that it will work."

The second operation made a dramatic difference. Says Paula: "I signed myself out of the hospital early in March of 1974 and then I started blossoming like a flower. I could concentrate. I could read. All the time I was sick I wasn't able to read; I wasn't even able to watch TV." But the effect did not last, and Paula underwent a third cingulotomy in 1975. For the next five years she was able to remain outside the hospital, an enormous improvement given her history of constant rehospitalization.

Eager to create a normal life for herself, Paula set out to become a psychiatric nurse. In 1980, after taking a series of college courses, she enrolled in nursing school at the age of twenty-eight. The stress proved too much for her, and she became ill again. "I'd walk into the dining room and hear everyone talking about me, looking at me. I couldn't concentrate, I was sleeping two or three hours a night." She dropped out of school, and the pattern of repeated hospitalizations began again.

Finally, she was referred to neurosurgeon Dr. Charles Fager of the Lahey Clinic in Burlington, Massachusetts. In November 1981, he performed a bimedial leucotomy, also known as "the Poppen operation" after the surgeon who devised it, the most radical limbic surgery done today. According to Dr. Fager, the operation "involves cutting the medial tracts between the portions of the frontal lobe and the thalamus." For Paula, "that was the miracle. I immediately responded to it." She has not been in the hospital since.

Because she had schizophrenia, Paula was an unusual candidate for psychosurgery, which is used for individuals suffering from severe affective or obsessive compulsive disorder (and in the United States— but not in England—for people suffering from intractable pain). In Paula's case the enormous agitation that accompanied her illness (what Robert Arnot had called "tortured self-concern"), along with the failure of all other treatments, led to the decision to try surgery.

But precisely because Paula was an exceptional candidate, her story illustrates both the strengths and limitations of limbic system surgery. Paula must still take anti-psychotic medication, although in vastly reduced dosages. Says Paula: "Medication works wonders for me now. Prior to the surgery no medication in any dose would touch me. It did nothing." But if surgery did not "cure" Paula, it brought her relief from fifteen years of terrible suffering. "All the symptoms which plagued and controlled me vanished."

Moreover—and here Paula's experience was typical—the surgery had no harmful effects on her personality, although she had four operations, very rare today. We asked Paula if there had been changes.

> I am much more outgoing than I was. That's not a negative side effect, that's a positive one. As a matter of fact, [before] I was afraid to say boo to anybody. If I had to ask a question, I'd ask my parents to ask the person. Since that time I've made speeches in different parts of the country.

One would think that contact with this vibrant woman—now resident services coordinator at an apartment complex for recovering mentally ill people in Hyannis, Massachusetts—would alter entrenched prejudices. But Paula reports her experience to the contrary. She is friendly with the family of a severely ill young man who suffers from the same compulsion for self-mutilation that she did and has also failed over the years to respond to any of the standard treatments. Paula suggested to the mother that they think of surgery. Her reaction was one of horror: "Oh Paula, you're just lucky you didn't become a vegetable."

While all limbic system surgery addresses the same tortured self-concern, different operations seem to be especially effective in particular disorders. English psychiatrist Desmond Kelly feels limbic leucotomy, the operation he helped to develop in the 1970s, is the best operation for obsessive compulsive disorder. But, he says, "If I had depression I would go to Brook General [hospital] for their operation [stereotactic subcaudate tractotomy]."[52] Dr. Ballantine finds his cingulotomy procedure more effective in depression than in obsessive compulsive behavior, for which he feels Dr. Kelly's operation may be more effective.[53]

Limbic system surgeons are eager for double blind studies that could scientifically establish the value of these operations. In the past the obstacles to such studies have been overwhelming, because subjecting individuals to surgery, which always carries risks, without actually performing the therapeutic procedure is not considered ethical. But now a technique has been developed in Sweden by neurosurgeon Lars Lecksell that requires no incision; the "gamma knife" focuses three beams of gamma rays emitted from a radioactive cobalt source. Each of the rays is too weak to harm tissue by itself: only as they focus together at the desired spot in the brain is tissue destroyed. The technique, which is also used to destroy brain tumors, epilepsy-causing lesions, and deadly arterio-venous masses, makes a double blind study feasible. What stands in the way is the political obstructionism that has so far made all rational consideration of limbic system surgery impossible.

Limbic System Surgery Driven Underground

The commission established by Congress to investigate psychosurgery estimated that in 1971 and 1972 approximately 140 neurosurgeons performed between 400 and 500 operations a year. (Even then, at a time of resurgence of interest in limbic system surgery in the United States, the operations were being performed at only half the rate they were in England and a third the rate they were in Australia.[54]) By 1988, when Thomas Ballantine retired, the number of neurosurgeons performing them was so small that those we spoke to—including Dr. Ballantine—could not even make an estimate of their number. Dr. Charles Fager, who performed Paula's operation, said he did no more than one a year, and believed only a handful of operations were being done in the United States. Asked if there was any group of doctors who kept each other informed, Dr. Ballantine said: "No. There was in the early 1970s. It's almost a sub rosa procedure."[55]

There is no training whatsoever in medical schools. Dr. Fager says: "The current generation of psychiatrists wouldn't even consider it. The acceptance level has fallen to practically zero."[56] Paul Bridges came from England to give a paper on limbic system surgery at a Philadelphia conference on resistant depression. "They were interested but I had the distinct feeling they were not going to take it on board because of the hassle in America."[57] Dr. Ballantine says: "When you think of the number of patients completely disabled by their affective illnesses, there is an important role for this type of surgery. If it were not for the negative image, a lot more of the surgery would be done."[58]

Breggin's Luddite boast to us was clearly not an idle one. With Dr. Ballantine's retirement, said Breggin: "I think there is no really active psychosurgeon in the United States. I'm sure there are some people doing it but they won't publish because they don't want me to see their publications. They don't want Peter Breggin finding out they're doing it."[59] And indeed one neurosurgeon refused to discuss the operations he had performed with us on the grounds that "it is not professionally safe."

Chapter 10

Electroconvulsive Therapy
The Second Domino

THE chief importance of the battle over limbic system surgery was in paving the way for the campaign against electroconvulsive therapy (ECT). ECT has been described as "one of the most effective treatments in all of medicine—with a therapeutic efficacy, in properly selected cases, comparable to some of the most potent and specific treatments available, such as penicillin in pneumonococcal pneumonia."[1]

Limbic system surgery makes a huge difference in a few lives. Without the campaign against it, more than the four to five hundred people a year estimated to be receiving the surgery at the opening of the 1970s surely would now be having it. But the numbers would not have risen dramatically, for the operations are confined to severely ill individuals in limited categories who respond to no other treatment. The campaign against ECT affects hundreds of thousands of lives.

The Origins of ECT

The history of electroconvulsive therapy is often traced by looking at early efforts to use electricity in the treatment of mental illness. As ECT expert Dr. Richard Abrams points out, this misses what is crucial to the therapy, which is the convulsive *seizure* the electricity produces; the seizure can and has been achieved in a variety of other ways. Indeed, the

194

treatment goes back to the sixteenth century when Paracelsus administered camphor to produce convulsions in lunatics. But because others did not follow up, Hungarian psychiatrist Ladislas von Meduna was unaware of the existence of predecessors when in 1934 he injected camphor-in-oil in a schizophrenic patient who had been in a catatonic stupor for four years, not moving or eating, incontinent and tube fed. The patient fully recovered.[2] Meduna subsequently substituted the chemical metrazol to induce the seizures.

As is often the case with major medical discoveries, the theory behind the discovery was wrong. Meduna believed incorrectly that individuals who suffered from epilepsy did not become schizophrenic. (In fact, epileptics are more liable than others to suffer from psychosis.[3]) Wagner von Jauregg had won the Nobel Prize for introducing malaria therapy for general paresis—mental disease caused by syphilis—and Meduna reasoned that inducing epileptic fits might work a similar cure in schizophrenia.

In Italy, Ugo Cerletti, director of the University Clinic in Rome, realized that it would be much easier to induce seizures with electricity than by injection with chemicals; he was at that time using electricity to induce convulsions in animals in connection with his studies of epilepsy. The difficulty was that in his clinic's experiments, half the animals died. Lucio Bini, Cerletti's assistant, figured out the source of the problem: in their experiments one electrode was customarily put into the mouth and one into the anus, passing electricity through the heart. Bini came up with an answer: he applied the electrodes to the animal's temples, so that the current passed from one side of the brain to the other, sparing the heart.[4]

In April 1938, the first electroshock treatment was performed on a catatonic man, around forty years old, his identity unknown, who had been found in the Milan train station without a ticket and spoke an incomprehensible gibberish. After a series of nine treatments, he improved markedly, rejoined his wife, and resumed his engineering career.[5]

Electroshock quickly replaced metrazol. It also replaced, although less rapidly, insulin coma therapy, which had been developed by Austrian physician Manfred Sakel in 1933, just a year before the introduction of chemically induced convulsive therapy by Meduna. The effectiveness of insulin as a treatment for diabetes had been discovered in 1927 and Sakel, who was not a psychiatrist, was experimenting to see if insulin would help morphine addicts. He discovered that some chronic mental patients, given insulin to relax them and help them gain weight, were sensitive to the drug, went into a coma and awoke improved. He developed a technique of giving schizophrenic patients daily comas.[6] For some years insulin was used in combination with electroshock—as in the case of Leonard Frank, who as late as 1962 received both treatments. Eventually, unfortunately, it was abandoned altogether.[7]

Not surprisingly then, the 1930s were a time of enormous therapeutic optimism in psychiatry. Dr. Lothar Kalinowsky, who was on Cerletti's staff when ECT was developed, became the leading exponent of ECT in the United States. He reports that when he started out in the admitting ward in a German mental hospital in the late 1920s, the staff would give each patient a spinal tap looking for general paresis, for only then could they offer useful malarial treatment.[8] Within the space of a few years the situation had changed radically. In rapid-fire succession came psychosurgery, insulin coma therapy, and the shock treatments: metrazol followed by electroshock.

The spread of these therapies was in part determined by the flight path of scientists from Nazi-dominated Europe. Dr. Lothar Kalinowsky, whose mother was Jewish, left Hitler's Germany in 1933 for Italy where he joined Cerletti's staff. After the 1938 Axis pact calling for forcible return of German Jewish nationals to the Nazis, Kalinowsky fled Italy, taking the diagrams for the ECT machine with him. He told us: "I stopped in Paris and introduced the technique during a short stay and then the same in Holland and then in England. Then in 1940 I came to the Psychiatric Institute at Columbia and for several years I treated three days a week at the Medical Center [at Columbia] and three days a week at Pilgrim State Hospital [Long Island]."

We interviewed Dr. Kalinowsky in 1987, just short of the fiftieth anniversary of the treatment. White-haired and elegant at the age of eighty-nine, leaning on his cane, Dr. Kalinowsky could still be found early on every Monday, Wednesday, and Friday morning, administering ECT at Gracie Square Hospital in New York. (Since then failing eyesight followed by a stroke has forced the retirement of this remarkable pioneer of biological psychiatry.)

It is noteworthy that Dr. Kalinowsky was quickly invited to give ECT at Pilgrim State Hospital. Many state hospitals were then in the forefront in using the new treatments. Dr. Kalinowsky points out that insulin coma therapy had been introduced at Harlem Valley State Hospital in 1938 where Sakel himself gave a course on the treatment attended by people from all the New York state hospitals. Similarly, New York state hospitals were the first to introduce chlorpromazine (the first of the anti-psychotic drugs) on a large scale in the mid-1950s. Dr. Nathan Kline of Rockland State Hospital pioneered in the use of reserpine and of iproniazid, an anti-depressant originally used in the treatment of tuberculosis. (Unfortunately, state hospitals were also the first to succumb to the pressures of the anti-psychiatry movement, and since the 1970s have become for the most part therapeutic backwaters.)

Convulsive treatment was originally introduced as a treatment for schizophrenia. Dr. Kalinowsky observes: "It was only four years later [in 1938] when it was realized that it is also for depression. People now think it is specific for depression but it is not. But since depression is a less dangerous sickness than schizophrenia, the results are better in depression."[9]

Problems in Early Use of ECT

In the fresh flush of therapeutic enthusiasm ECT was overused. As one writer observed: "When any new treatment comes along, it is tried on every disease from alcoholism to zoophobia, and so it was with ECT."[10] Even when ECT was used appropriately, for schizophrenia and the affective illnesses, in the first two decades there were undeniably problems associated with its use. The experience of ECT was nothing like that of metrazol, which in the period between injection and convulsion produced sensations so terrible that it was called "a roller coaster to hell."[11] But, without anesthetic, incomplete seizures from subconvulsive stimuli occurred frequently.

When ECT was administered properly, even in the treatment's first years, the experience was benign. Producer-director Joshua Logan described receiving ECT for his manic-depressive illness in the period before anesthetic and muscle relaxants:

> I could see his hand move to pull the switch, but I never saw him complete the action. In a fraction of a second, I was in total oblivion, having felt nothing. . . . I was no longer angry with the poor nun or the people who had dragged me back to the hospital. All I wanted to do was lie there and enjoy this cool peace that was flowing through me. If this was electric shock, then I wished I had it years ago.[12]

But when there were "missed" seizures, the experience was frightening. The reaction of the catatonic man in Milan who received the first treatment would turn out to be typical. Cerletti reported that initially he used insufficient electricity to induce a convulsion; as he prepared to try a second time, the man, who had been incapable of coherent speech, suddenly said: "Not a second. Deadly."[13] According to Kalinowsky's wife, when her husband came home after first witnessing the treatment, he told her: "I saw something terrible, I never want to see that again."[14] Sylvia Plath, the young poet who suffered from depression and eventually took her own life, recounts her own experience of ECT, which matches clinical descriptions of incomplete seizures.

> Then something bent down, and took hold of me and shook me like the end of the world. Whee-ee-ee-ee-ee, it shrilled, through an air crackling with blue light, and with each flash a great jolt drubbed me till I thought my bones would break and the sap fly out of me like a split plant.[15]

Nor were subjective feelings the only problem. Compression fractured vertebrae occurred in up to a third of patients, especially in young men, as a result of the force of the convulsion.[16]

Finally, the treatment was misused. Excessive numbers of treatments were given to some patients. While engaged in a 1960s study in England on the effects of anti-psychotic medications, Dr. Sydney Brandon discovered accidentally that there were some patients in the hospital who had been given over a thousand ECT treatments.[17] In other cases ECT treatments were given too close together. In the late 1950s, as part of a research project, Dr. Ewen Cameron and associates performed what they called "depatterning treatment" on chronic paranoid schizophrenic patients, which involved giving them twelve electro-shock treatments *per day* for a total of up to sixty treatments. Patients became profoundly disoriented, incontinent, in need of continuous nursing care. A majority reported "persisting amnesia retrograde to the depatterning . . . ranging in time from six months to ten years."[18]

Some hospitals took up the method. The Hartford Retreat (now the Institute for Living), a private hospital in Connecticut, adopted it to buttress misguided psychoanalytic theories. The notion was that if a patient regressed to an infantile state through ECT, the psychoanalyst could then restructure his personality.[19]

By the mid-1960s, however, major problems associated with ECT had been overcome. In the early 1950s, techniques were developed for using a muscle relaxant accompanied by anesthesia (with oxygen), and within a decade these were in almost universal use. Fractures and frightening experiences from missed seizures were eliminated. So major were the changes that the new procedure was called "modified ECT" to distinguish it from the original treatment.[20] Individuals reported nothing worse than a headache and most rated the treatment less formidable than a trip to the dentist.[21]

The only serious side effect remaining is memory loss, and for many patients this too can be minimized. In traditional "bilateral" ECT, where electrodes are placed on both sides of the head, all patients suffer temporary memory loss, and the effect is cumulative, so that the more treatments, the greater the loss. Tests of memory after ECT suggest that it is generally restored within around six months.[22] However, a significant number of patients complain of permanent, if spotty, memory loss for autobiographical events, especially for the months directly preceding the treatment. And while few mind forgetting the period immediately preceding ECT when they were profoundly depressed, acutely psychotic, or both, a small number complain of severe, long-term memory deficits.

It was discovered in the mid-1950s that memory deficits could be sharply reduced by placing the electrodes so that electricity passed through only one, nondominant, side of the brain—so-called "unilateral" ECT. However, this did not prove to be an "answer" to the problem of memory loss in the sense that muscle relaxants are to the problem of fractures. While few clinicians are as blunt as Dr. Kalinowsky, who says, "my experience is completely negative,"[23] surveys in the 1970s found that most psychiatrists used *only* bilateral ECT because in their clinical experience it is more effective.[24]

This is deplored by such experts on ECT as Max Fink and Richard Abrams. Conceding that from 10% to 20% of patients respond only to bilateral placement, Dr. Fink believes that because memory loss is so much reduced with unilateral placement, it should be tried first, except in special circumstances (for example, when the individual is actively suicidal).[25] Dr. Abrams has recent data suggesting that unilateral can be as effective as bilateral ECT if the electrical dosage intensity is raised to approximately two and a half times threshold (the minimum electrical dosage necessary to obtain a seizure).[26]

Ex-Patients Focus on ECT

From its inception the ex-patient movement concentrated on ECT. (None of the activists had undergone psychosurgery but a number had received ECT.) *Madness Network News* provided a constant stream of articles and editorials—even whole issues—devoted to ECT. Its spinoff, the Network Against Psychiatric Assault (NAPA), described ECT as "a bogus, barbaric and destructive technological weapon,"[27] and devoted most of its energy to lobbying and demonstrating against it.

As in the case of psychosurgery, the Church of Scientology was also active, and there were activists who worked with both groups. John Friedberg and Lee Coleman, physicians close to the ex-patient movement, also served on the national advisory board of Scientology's Citizens Commission on Human Rights.[28]

The ex-patient movement's effort to mobilize public opinion against ECT was given a major boost in 1975 when the filmed version of *One Flew Over the Cuckoo's Nest* (appearing thirteen years after the book) won the Academy Award as best picture of the year and Jack Nicholson won an Oscar for his portrayal of Patrick McMurphy. ECT is portrayed as a form of torture, administered to the hero to subdue, not treat him. And although modified ECT had been standard for over a decade (and specifically so at Oregon State Hospital where it was filmed), *Cuckoo's Nest* shows the writhing, convulsing body of McMurphy. In real life, only his toes would have moved. For McMurphy, ECT is prelude to the dreaded (and, at the time of the film, long obsolete) lobotomy, which transforms him into a vegetable.[29] (As noted earlier, the American Psychiatric Association witlessly praised this film for its "timely relevance.")

The ex-patients worked with a small circle of medical professionals, at the outset chiefly with then neurology resident John Friedberg. As a college student Friedberg had a brief mental hospitalization in New Haven and although he never was given ECT, felt he only narrowly escaped it. While serving as a medical resident at Pacific Medical Center, Friedberg worked closely with the Network Against Psychiatric Assault (NAPA), which he criticized for being insufficiently anti-psychiatric! The Network cooperated with a few radical psychiatrists, and Friedberg objected: "Good shrinks or bad shrinks—they all make money off human suffering. If NAPA must use them, use them like poison."[30]

Friedberg put an advertisement in the *San Francisco Examiner*: "Electric shock therapy is not good for the brain. I would like to hear from anyone who has received these treatments." His book on ECT, which he gave the same title as the first sentence of his ad, was published by the countercultural Glide Publications late in 1975. In the same year *Psychology Today* gave Friedberg's views on ECT wide circulation by publishing his "Electroshock Therapy: Let's Stop Blasting the Brain." Even the *American Journal of Psychiatry* included one of his anti-ECT articles in a 1977 special section on ECT.

In whichever forum Friedberg wrote on ECT, his work offered little science or scholarship, but much passionate rage. The book consisted of seven of the fifteen interviews obtained in response to his anti-ECT ad, scarcely a random sample. His 1975 article in *Psychology Today* announced—without offering any evidence—that ECT was "demonstrably ineffective" and declared "ECT perpetuates a long tradition of beating up those labeled insane." The claim that modified ECT had solved problems associated with the earlier treatment? According to Friedberg: "These 'improvements' are like the flowers planted at Buchenwald."[31]

Friedberg's article in *The American Journal of Psychiatry,* while more objective in tone, was equally distorted. For example, as proof of alleged "brain damage" caused by ECT, Friedberg cited Lucio Bini's 1938 report that mouth to rectum electrode placement in dogs produced "widespread and severe brain damage."[32] But the brain damage had resulted from circulatory failure, and Bini's crucial contribution that made ECT possible was to realize that placing electrodes on either side of the head would avoid the often fatal passage of electricity through the heart. In a commentary accompanying Friedberg's article, Dr. Fred Frankel, head of the American Psychiatric Association's 1978 Task Force on ECT, termed it "inaccurate," "careless," and "indiscriminate," and noted that it presented "personal opinions" as if they were scholarly decisions.[33]

Friedberg was soon joined in his efforts by Peter Breggin, fresh from his victory against psychosurgery. Breggin's *Electroshock: Its Brain-Disabling Effects* was published in 1979. The book's thesis was that ECT "worked" by damaging the brain in the same way as a blow on the head.[34] The "improvements" psychiatrists claimed to see in their patients merely reflected the characteristics of a damaged brain: "the apathy, docility, suggestibility, and helplessness that so often follow brain damage, as well as the tendency to hide symptoms and complaints."[35] In Breggin's formulation, ECT could not possibly emerge as an effective treatment. If the individual seemed to make a dramatic recovery, it was the temporary euphoria of brain damage or a pretense by the patient to make the psychiatrist stop the treatment.[36]

ECT expert Richard Weiner of Duke University Medical School has pointed out the absurdity of Breggin's argument. Breggin claims that ECT "*always* produces serious brain damage as manifested in the acute organic brain syndrome." But *anyone* wakening from general anesthesia has such a syndrome. "Such a statement," says Dr. Weiner, "suggests that a couple of martinis or a few beers, in producing a delirious state, always leads to serious brain damage. The logical fallacy in this type of argument is apparent."[37] Nonetheless, because the book was published by a reputable house, the Springer Publishing Co., and supposedly "proved" that ECT was a barbaric treatment, it was a powerful tool for the anti-psychiatric movement.

Changing California Law

In its very first year the Network Against Psychiatric Assault achieved a remarkable coup. A member of that group drafted a bill outlawing all involuntary somatic treatments. Joe Kennedy Adams, a radical therapist active in *Madness Network News* in its first years, persuaded California State Assemblyman John Vasconcellos—a close ally of the ex-patient movement to this day—to introduce the bill in the state legislature.[38]

Much to the surprise of the ex-patients themselves, the bill, amended to permit the continued involuntary administration of anti-psychotic drugs and (under highly restrictive conditions) ECT, sailed through both houses of the legislature with only one dissenting vote.[39] (The ex-patients were aided by domination of the key committees by individuals with anti-psychiatric perspectives, a holdover from the passage of the Lanterman-Petris-Short Act in 1968, described earlier.) Even when a patient wanted ECT, the new law imposed confusing procedures and severe penalties—including revocation of the psychiatrist's license—for failing to follow them.

Asleep at the switch when the law was passed, psychiatrists belatedly awoke to its implications. Psychiatrist Gary Aden brought suit, claiming the law was unconstitutional in limiting the patient's right to consent to medical procedures. For once the mental health bar's own arguments boomeranged. Patient liberation attorneys argued that freedom of speech had no meaning without freedom of thought and that psychiatric treatments, by altering (insane) thought patterns, interfered with free speech. But the court ruled that the state was violating voluntary patients' First Amendment rights by putting obstacles "in the path of those who both need and desire certain forms of treatment, and in that way their freedom of thought remains impaired because they cannot get treatment."[40]

Struck down by the courts, the 1974 law was replaced in 1976 by one somewhat less restrictive. Under this law, still in effect in California, an individual wishing to take ECT and able to give informed consent experiences delays and unnecessary added costs. But the real brunt of the 1976 law falls on persons too sick to give informed consent. In theory a prompt judicial hearing is provided in such cases, and if the judge finds the individual is too ill to give informed consent, a guardian or family member may give substituted consent. In practice, some courts throw up so many roadblocks in the path of the most severely ill patients—even when they consent to the treatment—that only 3% of those who have received ECT since the passage of the law have been people incompetent to make a decision, that is, those most in need of treatment.[41]

In 1981 two California psychiatrists published case histories from their own practice documenting long delays that unnecessarily prolonged the suffering of patients and added enormously to the cost of treatment. In one case, a twenty-one-year-old young man who suffered recurrent manic episodes had agreed with his psychiatrist and his family that if he became ill again he would take ECT. (In between episodes he lived at home, went to college, and worked parttime.) But when he next became ill, it took twenty-two days to get the court competency hearing.[42] In the meantime he spent much of the time in restraints, with round-the-clock nurses to contain him. When he was not shouting and fighting, he was in a state of panic. After he finally received ECT, he was back to normal within three days of the start of treatment.

Even worse, the hospital failed to transport a twenty-three-year-old girl, also manic-depressive, to repeatedly rescheduled court hearings because of her "aggressive uncontrolled delirium." The small university unit, unwilling to keep her any longer, sent her to a state hospital where she died within a month of cardiac arrest, apparently as a result of a rare reaction to anti-psychotic drugs.[43] Since she never received ECT, what would have happened had she done so cannot be known. However, all studies show that delusional affective disorders respond well to ECT.

One obstacle to treatment is that while judges are only supposed to determine if the individual is capable of giving consent, some rule on the merits of giving ECT. This is especially true in northern California, where the influence of the ex-patient network is strong. Glen Peterson is a psychiatrist in the San Francisco area, and until recently was the executive secretary of the International Psychiatric Association for the Advancement of Electrotherapy (now the Association for Convulsive Therapy). He explained:

> Sometimes they're referred [for ECT] on the point of death. They have to be so sick that the public defender and the judge will agree that even though ECT is a horrible, ominous treatment and abusive of their civil rights, I guess maybe it's better than death. . . . I get referrals from one of the county hospitals in our area, but in order to persuade their local judicial people and public defenders, they don't send these people till

they've already been back and forth to the medical ward a few times due to starvation or pneumonia or both, had tube feedings and so on.[44]

Following California's lead, twenty-five states passed legislation singling out ECT for special restrictions. In some cases, courts went further than legislatures. Wyatt v. Stickney, famous as a "right to treatment" suit, vis-à-vis ECT was an abolition of treatment case: the court, in 1975, issued fourteen rules whose combined effect was to virtually ban the use of ECT in the public system.[45] The Supreme Court of the State of Washington in 1986 set up elaborate legal obstacles, making it almost impossible to give ECT to a nonconsenting patient.[46]

ECT's Use Plummets

As in the case of psychosurgery, the anti-ECT campaign, aided by a consistently hostile media, was enormously effective. The biggest drop in the use of ECT occurred in states that passed stiff regulatory laws. By the latter part of the 1970s, ECT was being used only half as much in California as in Massachusetts, where, too, use of ECT dropped by almost 50% between 1974 and 1980.[47] A study of ECT in California from 1977 (when the new law went into effect) to 1983 found that ECT virtually disappeared in state and Veterans Administration hospitals.[48] In some counties, especially in the northeastern part of the state, ECT was unobtainable.

But if California led the way, the rest of the country was not far behind. ECT expert Max Fink has pointed out that from the late 1960s until the late 1970s, "ECT was a treatment that was hardly taught in the United States."[49] According to a study by James Thompson and Jack Blaine of the National Institute of Mental Health's Division of Clinical Research, the use of ECT plunged 46% nationally between 1975 and 1980. They concluded that only a little more than 33,000 patients received ECT in 1980, representing 2.4% of all patients hospitalized in psychiatric facilities.[50]

In the last two decades, the vast majority of those receiving ECT have been middle-class whites suffering from a depressive episode, whose stay in private hospitals is paid for by insurance. (Two-thirds are women, reflecting not—as Breggin claims—disrespect for female brains, but the fact that women are twice as likely to suffer from depression.) And even in private hospitals there was a 75% drop in the use of ECT between 1970 and 1980.[51]

In the 1970s, state hospitals—which had the most seriously ill patients—saw the steepest decline in use of ECT, to the point where only one third of one percent of patients received the treatment. In contrast, even at its lowest ebb, ECT was given to 4.6% of mentally ill patients in private general hospitals.[52] A 1977 study found that although 79% of all patients in VA hospitals suffered from depression, the illness most responsive to ECT, only 3.1% of patients with that diagnosis received the treatment.[53] By 1980 the situation was even worse: VA hospitals reported that only 0.3% of their almost 159,000 admissions received ECT, a mere 526 patients.[54]

The decline of ECT in the public system is illustrated by a 1974 letter in the *American Journal of Psychiatry* from Herbert Silverberg, an attorney who describes his efforts to obtain ECT for his client, a severely depressed divorced woman, whose children were at college. After she tried to hang herself in a public park, she was brought to St. Elizabeth's, the District of Columbia's public hospital. At the commitment hearing it was revealed that she had been given ECT five years before, and it had cleared up her depression. Silverberg reports that a "senior and very well respected member of the private psychiatric community" happened to be present and whispered to him that if she was not given ECT "it would amount to medical malpractice." Nonetheless, when Silverberg pressed the St. Elizabeth's staff to give his client ECT, which she wanted to take, he was told it was a symptomatic treatment, insufficiently understood, and she would have to come to grips with the source of her illness through psychotherapy and medications. Within a week, she had escaped from the hospital, jumped off a bridge, and died.[55]

Even in the private sector, obtaining ECT can be difficult. Kathleen O'Brien is a widow whose two sons became ill twelve years apart. In 1970, at the age of fifteen, her son Joseph became convinced that his mind was controlled by radio waves emanating from the head of his grandfather, who lived with them. He lost weight rapidly, and was unable to study at school or sleep at night. When he obeyed the commands of voices to run naked down their suburban street, Mrs. O'Brien took him to a nearby private general hospital with a psychiatric unit. Diagnosed as paranoid schizophrenic, Joseph was given large doses of Thorazine over a six-week period. Mrs. O'Brien says he was calmer and gained weight but still believed in his delusions. The psychiatrist recommended ECT and, after twelve treatments, Joseph was free of his bizarre ideas. The illness never recurred. He graduated from engineering school, married, and has two children.

Her second son Michael, three years younger than Joseph, became ill twelve years later and was admitted to the same hospital. When he was also diagnosed as paranoid schizophrenic, Mrs. O'Brien immediately asked about ECT. But the doctor who had treated Joseph had retired, and the young psychiatrist in charge of Michael's case was flatly opposed. "He said it was his clinical judgment it was not an appropriate treatment for Michael. I discovered later the hospital no longer even gave ECT."

After being discharged, Michael stopped taking his medication and took off, wandering the country for over a year. He returned home, filthy, emaciated, and delusional. Mrs. O'Brien says: "By now I was absolutely determined that we try ECT and Michael didn't object." Even so, it took weeks before she finally found a psychiatrist who told her that because his brother had responded to the treatment there was a good chance Michael would too. He took the treatment as an outpatient, and now works as a paralegal.

Her experiences have left Mrs. O'Brien at once grateful and horrified. "ECT would never have occurred to me in Michael's case, if it hadn't been for Joseph. I haven't the least doubt he'd be another homeless statistic now. When Joseph was so ill I remember thinking: if only this had happened ten years from now, they'd have a cure. What I found out was that there'd been a big step backward."[56]

Outlawing ECT

Energized by their success in reducing the use of ECT, the activists sought an outright ban. In California, the Citizens Advisory Council (established to advise and assist the legislature and the State Department of Mental Health on mental health issues) unsuccessfully urged a statewide "moratorium" on ECT in 1981.[57] This was followed two years later by a successful referendum, coordinated by the movement's Ted Chabasinski, which outlawed ECT within the city limits of Berkeley. The highest anti-ECT vote came from the black areas of the city, where the ex-patient activists, according to their own reports, had purposely concentrated their leafleting.[58] But while the activists aroused blacks by claiming ECT was used disproportionately on them, in fact ECT is disproportionately *denied* blacks. California law requires that each ECT treatment be reported, and the statistics are compiled annually by the Department of Mental Health. These show that blacks, who make up 7.6% of California's population, receive only 1.6% of ECT treatments given in the state. Hispanics are similarly denied treatment: though they constitute 16% of the state's population, they receive only 3.2% of ECT treatments.[59] The white middle class in private hospitals obtains ECT: minorities, overrepresented in the public sector, are the chief victims of anti-psychiatry.

The Berkeley ban was overturned by the courts, the judge ruling it was an "unwarranted local infringement on a matter of exclusive state-wide concern."[60] Even calling in such heavy guns of the mental health bar as David Ferleger did not save the situation, and the ex-patients gave up their efforts to appeal the ruling in 1985 when the California Court of Appeals affirmed the lower court ruling.

Nonetheless, the Berkeley effort reaped enormous national publicity and encouraged similar efforts elsewhere. The ex-patient Vermont Liberation Organization sought to make Vermont the first state to ban ECT. But while the state senate's health and welfare committee held hearings on the bill, it never came out of committee.[61] In Toronto, an Ontario Coalition to Ban Electroshock brought suit to declare ECT a form of psychosurgery, which would have all but eliminated the treatment.[62] That failed: after what amounted to a "trial" of ECT, complete with Breggin as expert witness, the judge ruled that it would be completely unacceptable and an infringement of the right to treatment of severely ill patients if the use of ECT were to be denied on the basis of "semantic manipulation."[63] Despite this setback, the Coalition achieved a victory when the provincial legislature took away the power of review boards to order ECT for objecting patients. (However, a substitute decision-maker may still decide on ECT for an objecting patient whom the court determines to be unable to make an informed treatment decision).[64]

The FDA: An End-Run Attack on ECT

In 1984, anti-ECT activists came up with yet another strategy, zeroing in on the medical device used to administer ECT. In passing the Medical Device Amendments of 1976, Congress gave the Food and Drug Administration responsibility for the safety and effectiveness of medical devices. Devices already in existence when the law was passed had to be assigned to one of three classes: Class I devices needed only "general controls"; Class II devices were safe but needed "performance standards"; and Class III devices appeared to present an "unreasonable risk of illness or injury" and were to undergo the same "pre-market approval" process as a new device coming on the market. In 1979 the FDA put the ECT device in Class III, in theory requiring pre-market approval, although in practice existing devices were not required to go through the process.

In 1982 the American Psychiatric Association petitioned the FDA to reclassify ECT devices to Class II, and in 1983, following hearings, the FDA published a notice of intent to do so. According to Joseph Sheehan, chief of the FDA's regulation desk for medical devices, most of the pre-1976 devices that remain in Class III are implantable devices (including pacemakers) which may break apart within the body.[65] X-ray machines, for example, are in Class II: because of the danger of radiation, they are required to meet a performance standard. It is hard to see why ECT devices, with their long record of safety and effectiveness, should be in a higher risk group than X-ray machines. As the American Psychiatric Association saw it, the high-risk classification acted as a barrier to the development of a new type of instrument, since manufacturers would be deterred by the expensive pre-market approval process for Class III devices.

The campaign to force the FDA to rescind its plan to reclassify ECT devices was led by Marilyn Rice, an ex-patient in Washington, D.C. She formed an organization called the Committee for Truth in Psychiatry, whose entire purpose was to combat the reclassification.

A decade earlier a *New Yorker* article, "As Empty as Eve," had related Mrs. Rice's story. An economist with the Department of Commerce, Mrs. Rice, in 1972, had gone to an orthodontist for realignment of several teeth affected by a gum condition. The bungled orthodontic work, which made her unable to close her mouth or chew food, triggered a depressive episode. Mrs. Rice's weight sank to eighty-nine pounds; she was unable to sleep, unable to eat. At her doctor's urging, she entered a private hospital early in 1973 and, despite initial reluctance, finally consented to a course of eight ECT treatments. But while the treatments were successful in reversing the depression, on returning to her job Mrs. Rice discovered "all my beloved knowledge, everything I had learned in my field during twenty years or more, was gone. I'd lost the body of knowledge that constituted my professional skill."[66] She felt unable to continue with her job and took a disability retirement. She sued the doctor who had prescribed ECT for her, and despite the testimony of Drs. Breggin and Friedberg on her behalf during the jury trial, lost the suit and her subsequent appeal.

Mrs. Rice has consistently claimed—and did so to us—that she is not seeking to ban the treatment. But it is difficult to avoid the conclusion that like so many other of the activist ex-patients, she cloaks abolitionist goals in the more respectable mantle of informed consent.

In speeches Mrs. Rice has described ECT as "just brain damage"; if something is "just brain damage," it is difficult to see what justification there is for continuing it. Moreover, the proposed informed consent statement Mrs. Rice wants the FDA to make mandatory for all patients is a diatribe against ECT. The section of her committee's petition to the FDA, "How Does ECT work?" says:

> ECT is one of a number of drastic psychiatric treatments, including insulin coma and psychosurgery, that relieve suffering temporarily. All of them "work" by destroying brain tissue. That is their common denominator. . . . For some still unknown reason, reducing the size of the brain not only reduces the amount of stored memory but also counteracts states of physical pain and any kind of emotion.[67]

In fact, there is no scientific evidence that ECT reduces the size of the brain.

Actually, the leading anti-ECT activists are good advertisements for ECT's failure to cause long-term harm. Both Leonard Frank and Marilyn Rice, "worst cases" in experiencing what they describe as devastating memory loss, are extremely intelligent, effective advocates, whose work shows every evidence of a well functioning memory. An excellent public speaker, Frank has also compiled a fascinating volume, *The History of Shock Treatment,* intended as a resource for anti-ECT activists, but useful to anyone interested in the treatment. Whatever the effect of ECT on Marilyn Rice's memory for the facts she had learned at the Department of Commerce, it has not interfered with her ability to learn and remember research material on ECT. Indeed, it was Marilyn Rice's pioneering work in researching and assembling the early animal studies on ECT that laid the groundwork for Breggin's book. Her presentations to the FDA are models of clarity and effective argumentation.

Why should ex-patients care in which class the FDA puts ECT devices? ECT devices are presently in Class III and the treatment continues to be given. And even Marilyn Rice does not argue that the devices themselves are unsafe. Rather, activists see the classification issue as a rearguard way to eliminate the treatment. As the FDA's Sheehan points out, pre-1976 devices in Class III are supposed to be subject to the same pre-market approval process as new medical devices. While in theory the FDA could withdraw its proposal to reclassify and leave things as they were, in fact Sheehan observes that it is very doubtful that would happen. The ex-patient movement would promptly push for the pre-market approval process to begin. That process is very expensive for the manufacturer; it can cost upwards of $3 million. As Sheehan points out:

"There's hardly a big market for ECT devices and they are fairly simple and not expensive. As medical equipment goes there's not much money in it." The mere fact of requiring manufacturers to undergo premarket approval could drive the devices off the market (and at minimum would steeply raise the cost of treatment).

Psychiatrists Fight Back

Even before the rise of the ex-patient movement, psychiatrists were deeply divided concerning ECT. As early as 1964 a review article lamented a strong desire within the profession to eliminate the treatment entirely.[68] In 1965 a psychiatrist who took ECT for his own depression wrote: "I have heard fellow psychiatrists decry this form of treatment as a brutal attack upon the person, and I have known them to withold it from patients to whom no doubt it would have brought great relief, or in whose case it might have been a lifesaving measure."[69] Yet ECT continued to have its supporters, and they mobilized to defend the treatment.

In 1975, Gary Aden, the California psychiatrist who brought the successful suit to overturn the 1974 law drafted by a Network Against Psychiatric Assault activist, joined together with a number of like-minded colleagues to form The International Psychiatric Association for the Advancement of Electrotherapy. It sought to combat the attacks on ECT and encourage psychiatric programs in medical schools, many of which ignored ECT, to include the treatment in the curriculum once again.[70]

That same year, also in reaction to the 1974 California law, the American Psychiatric Association appointed a Task Force on ECT, which presented its findings in 1978. The report affirmed the value of ECT, declaring there was no division of *informed* opinion concerned the efficacy of the treatment in appropriate cases. (However, as the task force's own survey of psychiatrists showed, there was still plenty of *uninformed* opinion within psychiatry itself, with 32% of those polled uncomfortable with its use.[71])

Not until 1984 did a major review of the literature on ECT seek to counter the distortions of Breggin and Friedberg. In connection with the American Psychiatric Association's petition to have the ECT device transferred to Class II, ECT expert Dr. Richard Weiner undertook the review, which was published in the international journal *The Behavioral and Brain Sciences* (accompanied by twenty-two peer commentaries).

Weiner dismissed the animal studies from the 1940s which Breggin offered as "proof" that ECT caused massive brain damage. Actually, Weiner pointed out, those studies showed little evidence of damage, were not applicable to modern modified ECT, and in any case were so methodologically flawed as to be irrelevant to present day ECT.[72] More recent sophisticated studies, which Weiner examined in detail, showed no evidence of damage.

Weiner also provided a lengthy evaluation of studies of memory disturbance, noting the failure of most objective tests to show long-term loss, but conceding that better tests might be needed, especially of autobiographical memory. Since there was no evidence for structural brain damage in ECT, Weiner speculated about mechanisms to explain memory loss, including a disruption of protein synthesis (it is not unlikely memory is coded in some type of protein structure), changes in neurotransmitter systems linked to memory, and the transient breakdown of the blood-brain barrier in ECT.[73]

Weiner drew cautious conclusions: he said the evidence for brain damage was "weak," but called "for further, more definitive research."[74] This led fellow expert on ECT Max Fink, one of the peer commentators on the article, to complain that Weiner "genuflects to avoid criticism" and that, given the body of the article, the summary should properly have read: "A reasonable scientist finds that the search has been extensive, the methods diverse, and the evidence of damage so sparse as to make the likelihood so remote as not to be a significant factor in the clinical decision to use ECT."[75] Another peer commentator argued that it was time to stop expending so much effort on searching for damage, for which evidence was so scanty, and to investigate instead "the *changes* in the brain . . . produced by ECT that are causally associated with its therapeutic efficacy."[76]

By 1985 even the National Institute of Mental Health had been drawn into the struggle, sponsoring a consensus conference on ECT. This was a significant breakthrough because NIMH had been notorious for ignoring the treatment. In 1972 and 1973, out of NIMH's $9.9 million in grants for research into somatic therapies less than $5,000 went to ECT, and NIMH published its first paper on ECT over forty years after its discovery![77]

While the conference supported the effectiveness and safety of ECT, in its futile attempt to appease anti-ECT activists, it paved the way for future problems. NIMH put Leonard Rubenstein, the attorney who heads the anti-psychiatric Mental Health Law Project, on the planning committee for the conference. He, in turn, was instrumental in inviting

Breggin to lecture the panel on "Neuropathology and Cognitive Dysfunction" from ECT and in arranging for a "survivors' panel" in which
ex-patient activists raged against the treatment.[78] The panel then bent
over backwards to include criticisms and began its concluding summary
with the statement: "Electroconvulsive therapy is the most controversial
treatment in psychiatry."[79] (Such was the success of the anti-psychosurgery campaign that the panel's members had presumably forgotten that
psychosurgery existed or did not consider it alive enough to rank as
controversial.)

Breggin was delighted, feeling the activists had gained a potential
basis for court actions on the issue of informed consent.

> You see, now when we go to court we can say the consensus conference
> says first of all that shock is the most controversial treatment in psychiatry
> today. Did you tell your patient that? It says you have memory loss for an
> average of six months prior to the treatment and two months after. Did
> you tell your patient that? And it says it doesn't do any good past four
> weeks as far as we can tell. Did you tell your patient that?[80]

(In fact, there is enormous variability in patient response, with some
patients relapsing quickly, while others remain well for many months or
years and still others never experience another episode. A study at Duke
University found that over two-thirds of patients reported the benefits of
ECT lasted over a year.[81])

Lay Activists for ECT

Although not organized or as numerous as the radical ex-patients,
there have also been energetic lay activists *for* ECT. In 1976, at the age of
forty-five, Norman Endler was at the height of his career. He was
chairman of York University's psychology department, the largest in
Canada, and the author of many articles and books that had given him an
international reputation in his field. In the fall of 1977 he experienced
what he would later realize was a manic episode followed by depression. By the spring of the following year he found it difficult to read or
concentrate, never smiled, rarely even spoke.

Endler went to a psychiatrist who prescribed anti-depressant medications, which did not help him. When the psychiatrist recommended
ECT, Endler reports, "I was aghast." But becoming increasingly desperate as his depression worsened—"I honestly felt subhuman, lower than
the lowest vermin"—Endler finally agreed to take ECT as an outpatient.
After the sixth treatment he felt fine. "A miracle had happened in two

weeks." Endler had a second episode a year later, and took a second series of eleven treatments. Since then he has taken lithium to maintain his stability and the illness has not recurred. He has resumed his busy writing and teaching schedule. Nor have the treatments affected his memory: "Neither the depression nor the ECT produced any memory loss. I had a super memory before; I still have one now."[82]

What was extraordinary about Norman Endler was not his experience, but his determination to stand up publicly on behalf of the treatment which had helped him. He did so despite the urgings of friends, one of whom warned him that going public could ruin his career.[83] Nonetheless, Endler in 1982 published *Holiday of Darkness,* a book about his experiences.

So concerned was Endler about the misconceptions that had been fostered concerning ECT that in collaboration with Emanuel Persad, the psychiatrist who had treated him, he wrote *Electroconvulsive Therapy: The Myths and the Realities.* Published in 1988 by Hans Huber, the book sought to dispel the phobic fears that had come to surround the treatment. There had been a number of technical books on ECT by psychiatrists for psychiatrists, but Endler and Persad provided an overview accessible to lay readers.

An equally impressive, if less well-known advocate for ECT has been Ted Hutchinson. Heavyset, with twinkling blue eyes, Hutchinson retired in 1989 from Rockwell International, where he worked as an engineer. In 1977 a member of his family recovered from a three-year bout of mental illness after a series of ten electroshock treatments. The attacks on ECT were at their height in California, and disturbed by what he heard and read, Hutchinson determined to learn more about the treatment. It had worked—in that sense he began with a prejudice in its favor—but was it brain-damaging?

In combing the literature, Hutchinson was struck by two things: the strength of the evidence that ECT caused no structural brain damage and the confusion within psychiatry itself on this issue. Even the animal studies of the 1940s, upon which Breggin depended heavily in his indictment of ECT, upon critical examination did not bear out his thesis. Hutchinson discovered that a group of neuropathologists led by William F. Windle in 1950 had reviewed the existing studies, and concluded that other investigators had mistakenly attributed to electroshock what were actually postmortem artifacts of their faulty methods of preserving animal tissue.[84] Windle's group developed new methods of preserving and preparing animal brain tissue (which have since become standard)[85] and in their own studies found no differences between the brain tissue of control and electroshocked animals.[86]

Hutchinson was also impressed by the epilepsy studies. Researchers studying epilepsy who *wanted* to produce brain damage in animals through electrical seizures found to their disappointment that "seizures lasting less than 30 minutes are not followed by permanent neurological disability or pathological evidence of brain damage."[87] Moreover, autopsies of people who had suffered from epilepsy showed two principal patterns of brain damage: neither was found at autopsy in individuals (not suffering from epilepsy) who had been given ECT during their lives.[88]

What gave Hutchinson special confidence was that neuropathologists and epileptologists (experts in the study of epilepsy) had no career interest in ECT. They could not be accused of a self-serving conspiracy to conceal its harmful effects.

Hutchinson was also struck by a report in the *British Journal of Psychiatry* on a woman whose records showed she had been given a staggering total of 1,250 ECT treatments. Autopsy showed her brain structure to be completely normal, with less atrophy than usual for a woman of her eighty-nine years.[89]

Yet Hutchinson found that writers of psychiatry texts seemed to be more influenced by the inflammatory charges against ECT than by the literature that refuted them. In his local university medical library he found an otherwise excellent 1982 textbook on clinical psychiatry that devoted eleven pages to raising doubts about ECT and recommended it only as a last resort. Another text by Stanford University professors expressed "concern about sustained brain damage from ECT" and noted the "dilemma" this posed for psychiatrists. Says Hutchinson: "They damned with faint praise. I was very uncomfortable with what I considered the failure of the psychiatric establishment to refute what I thought were really spurious allegations."[90]

Hutchinson was convinced that such misinformation led to under-utilization of ECT—he discovered the nearby University of California at Irvine in 1979 did not use ECT once in its sixty-bed psychiatric unit—and to its omission from the training of psychiatric residents. Stanford University Medical Center discontinued use of ECT in 1977. (It would not resume it until 1988.[91])

And so, in late 1984, Hutchinson prepared his own summary of the neglected studies, which he sent to Dr. Delmar Gregory of the California Department of Mental Health and to a number of psychiatrists expert on

ECT. Unbeknownst to Hutchinson, Richard Weiner had been assembling the first comprehensive review of the literature on brain damage at the same time. Although it would be considered the definitive review on the subject by the psychiatric profession, Weiner himself wrote to Hutchinson: "You will probably note that in some respects your references appear to be more complete than those that I used."[92]

When Hutchinson learned that Peter Breggin would be presenting a paper at the June 1985 NIMH-sponsored Consensus Development Conference on ECT, he sent the panel members his refutation of Breggin's attributions of brain damage based on early animal studies. And he was delighted when the Consensus Conference (despite its concessions to activists mentioned earlier) repudiated charges of brain damage: "In studies that have been controlled for . . . methodological problems, neuronal cell death has not been detected."[93]

Hutchinson has been indefatigable in California, battling not only the ex-patient movement and its allies in the legislature, but a Department of Mental Health intent on mollifying them. (By 1985 the department's letters spoke of sifting proposed ECT regulations through "the legal, medical and patients rights discipline"—as if agitation against treatment was a field having the stature of law and medicine![94]) He has prodded administrators at university hospitals that for years all but ceased giving ECT.

In the 1980s, under pressure of the activists, the California Department of Mental Health repeatedly proposed regulations to obstruct access to ECT even further. One proposed regulation would have provided that the mandatory informed consent form include notice of the patient's right to speak to a "patient's rights advocate" (many of whom would try to talk him out of taking the treatment). Hutchinson's written comments in the rule-making file dissuaded the Department from forwarding some proposed regulations and led to disapproval of others by the California Office of Administrative Law on the grounds they contradicted statutory law.[95]

For all his file cabinets full of correspondence with bureaucrats and the voluminous research he has conducted, Hutchinson believes that his most important contribution has been to put some starch into psychiatrists.

> What I've been trying to do is give psychiatrists some encouragement that some of us believe in the treatment and are willing to speak up for it. Mostly to give them a little courage, because they seemed so sensitive to criticism.

Hutchinson, who is active in the California Alliance for the Mentally Ill, an organization of families of mentally ill people, also believes it is important to reach family members.

> To the extent that I can talk to parents and families I emphasize that ECT is safe; it really is safe; and whether they use it or not, they should judge it on the basis of symptoms and the response. They should consider it like any other treatment. It's not a panacea. But in all too many places, ECT is not even considered.[96]

Why Are ECT Advocates So Few?

Hundreds of thousands of individuals—and their families—have benefited from ECT. Yet only a small number have come forward publicly. If ECT is such an effective treatment, why are the vocal opponents more numerous than the vocal supporters? The major reason is the stigma associated with mental illness. (Not long ago individuals who had suffered breast cancer would not speak publicly of their experiences for the same reason.) In the case of ECT, the treatment itself is stigmatized, producing a double reluctance to come forward. Those who have benefited from ECT run the risk both of jeopardizing their careers and horrifying their friends if they come forward publicly. The same considerations do not influence those in the ex-patient movement who have chosen to make a "career" from the ex-patient role.

Family members too may be more influenced by the widespread negative view of ECT than by their own experience. We interviewed the brother of a woman who received ECT for delusional depression thirty years ago, as a sophomore at Bennington. He recounts that she went on to finish college, marry, raise three fine children, become a "crackerjack artist," a leader in her church, and do extensive volunteer work with prison inmates. (Her only further clinical depressions followed the birth of each of her children, and were controlled by medications.) Yet he remains to this day "perturbed that my parents had agreed to shock treatment which I felt was something one did as a last resort." He was convinced that "it knocked some of the spontaneity out of her";[97] apparently, it did not occur to him that her depression, rather than the treatment, was responsible. But Lorraine Richter of the National Depressive and Manic-Depressive Association, composed of individuals suffering from these diseases, told us: "There are many, many people who are controlled [by medications] but never really regain that zip they had. I don't think it's clearly understood but it's sort of like a chronic semi-depression."[98]

The National Alliance for the Mentally Ill, as well as its member chapters, have largely ignored ECT, focusing almost exclusively on drug therapies. The mentally ill relatives of those who belong to the organization tend to be the most seriously ill: they suffer from schizophrenia or manic-depression. Since ECT in the last two decades has been given overwhelmingly for depression (chiefly to the elderly who are most likely to suffer serious side effects from anti-depressants), most families have had no experience with ECT.

NAMI's lack of interest is doubtless influenced by E. Fuller Torrey's otherwise excellent manual for families *Surviving Schizophrenia,* a standard reference for the family movement, which cavalierly dismisses ECT. Incredibly, it is included in the section on "Ineffective Treatments," along with psychoanalysis, group therapy, and megavitamins. Equally remarkable, in explaining the alleged "ineffectiveness" of ECT, Torrey writes that because its use "has been vigorously opposed by ex-patient groups in the United States," it is "therefore" not a realistic therapeutic alternative for schizophrenia.[99] In other words, a vocal minority's misguided opposition becomes the reason to abandon a valuable treatment.

Revival of ECT

Some psychiatrists believe that the use of ECT has gone up since 1980. Citations in the psychiatric literature have doubled since 1980, and the first journal devoted exclusively to ECT, *Convulsive Therapy,* was started in 1985. In 1990 the American Psychiatric Association published the report of its second Task Force on Electroconvulsive Therapy (the first was in 1978) ascribing an important role for ECT in modern psychiatric practice.

However, it is not yet clear to what extent these encouraging signs have up to now been translated into greater use of the therapy. Expert estimates of current usage range from 30,000 to 100,000 patients a year,[100] indicating the high level of uncertainty as to the extent to which ECT is in fact given. In so far as the use of ECT has gone up, it is primarily in the private sector; public hospitals for the most part lack the capacity to give ECT, sending out patients for treatment to private hospitals in the rare cases they decide it is needed.

Psychiatrists are beginning to advocate a larger role for ECT, making it a front-line, rather than a last resort treatment in some conditions, and expanding its use in schizophrenia and manic-depressive disorder, for which it had been largely discarded in the 1970s. Dr.

Max Fink notes that studies show ECT to be much more successful than drugs in delusional depression, so that this condition should be a primary indication for ECT; weeks should not be wasted going through the rigmarole of drug therapy.[101]

Recent studies indicate that many patients may have been poorly served by a too-exclusive reliance on drugs. One 1978 study compared hospital charts of patients who had received ECT before the discovery of anti-depressants, and who, years later, received drugs for a different episode of illness. Complete recovery occurred in 94% of the episodes treated with ECT, compared with 53% of those treated with anti-depressants.[102]

While psychiatrists agree that ECT is most effective in depression, some now feel it was too hastily discarded for other major mental illnesses. Thus Dr. Steven Potkin, professor of psychiatry and director of research at the University of California at Irvine, says: "ECT is a marvelous treatment for depression; the best treatment we have." And he adds: "It's not usually recognized, but ECT is also a wonderful treatment for mania."[103] A recent study of manic patients randomly assigned to lithium and ECT confirmed this, finding that ECT produced greater improvement.[104]

As for schizophrenia, the most important major study *discouraging* the use of ECT was published in 1968. In it, Philip May and associates, as noted earlier, assessed the efficacy of five treatment approaches in schizophrenia. While the study is chiefly famous for discrediting the use of psychotherapy in schizophrenia, it also found that ECT was less effective than drugs. May concluded that ECT could not be considered a serious rival to neuroleptics, except for those who "develop toxic side effects or who fail to respond [to drugs]."[105]

But ECT's midpoint position between drugs and psychotherapy in the study concealed a curious finding: ECT worked almost as well for *men* with schizophrenia as did drugs alone (91% vs. 95%).[106] This was surprising because women were known to respond extremely well to ECT in depression. Although May himself said that "further research study of this matter would seem to be indicated,"[107] no subsequent studies were made to determine if this gender gap could be replicated. Instead, the May study has been repeatedly cited in the psychiatric literature to dismiss ECT as a treatment for schizophrenia.

What has also been disregarded is that *May changed his mind about the effectiveness of ECT in the treatment of schizophrenia.* In 1981 the May team published the results of its three to five year follow-up on the patients in the original study. While psychotherapy continued to come off badly, of ECT they wrote:

> Patients who had been treated with ECT fared, in the long run, at least as well as those given drug therapy, and in some respects even better, but not to a statistically significant extent. It seems that the status and role of ECT in the treatment of schizophrenia merit serious objective study.[108]

A particularly interesting finding was that patients who had been treated with ECT received anti-psychotic drugs significantly less frequently than the other groups in the follow-up period.[109] A major reason for relapse and rehospitalization of patients who respond well to drugs is that they cease to take them. If ECT obviates or lessens the need for medication in a sizable proportion of patients, this alone is a major factor in its favor.

The reason ECT does well in both delusional depression and some cases of schizophrenia is illuminated by Dr. Pamela Taylor, an English expert on the use of ECT in schizophrenia. She observes:

> ECT is particularly successful in relation to delusions. It doesn't matter if they are depressive delusions or not. The greatest agreement would be over the treatment of depressed people who also have delusions. But it's also quite clear from the schizophrenia work, although it's rarely summarized in this way, that it is actually the delusional and the more frankly psychotic symptoms that respond.[110]

Psychiatrists have found that the more an affective illness resembles schizophrenia (with delusions as well as mood disorder), and the more a case of schizophrenia resembles affective disorder (with such "vegetative" symptoms as loss of sleep, motor retardation, etc.) the more likely it is to respond to ECT.

Furthermore, it has long been known that in its first stages schizophrenia—particularly where there is acute, rapid onset of illness—responds well to ECT. But in the neuroleptic drug era few patients have been given ECT in that period when the response is likely to be best. British ECT expert Sydney Brandon thinks this is a mistake:

> I think there's accumulating evidence, and that's why I'm in favor of using ECT in schizophrenia, of a kindling process. The more frequent and the more prolonged the episodes, the greater the likelihood of subsequent episodes and further damage. So there's a great deal to be said for early termination.[111]

On account of the "kindling process," says Dr. Brandon, "patients who do not respond rapidly to neuroleptics should have the benefit of ECT, because it terminates illnesses that may otherwise tend to become chronic." But, in fact, according to Dr. Jeffrey Geller, Director of Public Sector Psychiatry at the University of Massachusetts Medical Center, it is rare today to encounter a young chronic patient who has been given a trial on ECT.[112]

Belatedly, in the United States, awareness may be dawning of the magnitude of error this omission represents. In 1989, Dr. Richard Wyatt, chief of the neuropsychiatric branch at NIMH, said that in reappraising studies from the 1950s, he had been struck by the superiority in long-term outcome of patients treated with ECT on their initial schizophrenic break over those treated with neuroleptic drugs.[113] That this acknowledgment should come from a researcher at NIMH, which had so consistently neglected ECT, was striking; even more surprising, Wyatt was addressing the American Academy of Psychoanalysis.

Also, some young patients with schizo-affective disorder (in which there are schizophrenic and affective symptoms) respond particularly well to ECT.[114]

Even the use of ECT in chronic schizophrenia has come under new scrutiny. An epidemiological study was done in England in the expectation that most of those receiving ECT suffered from depression. But, says Brandon,

> this proved to be less so than we realized because we found there were a group of schizophrenic patients who were being referred, and many of these had in fact some evidence of chronicity. To our surprise, we found when we analyzed the results, that for many of them there was a very marked benefit.

Dr. Brandon sums up: "I'm sure we're underusing ECT in schizophrenia in this country and that's certainly true in the United States."[115]

Chapter 11

Psychoactive Drugs
The Last Domino

BY 1980 the anti-psychiatric movement had chalked up major successes in its war against treatment. Psychosurgery had virtually been driven underground. ECT had survived, but largely as a voluntary treatment for drug-refractory depression in the private sector. If some psychiatrists came to the defense of ECT, others, in Max Fink's words, considered it "inelegant, bizarre, dangerous, antithetical to the prevailing philosophy, and even expensive."[1]

Believing that anti-psychotic drugs obviated other treatments, many psychiatrists distanced themselves readily from psychosurgery and ECT. In 1976 the Los Angeles *Herald Examiner* quoted the boast of the acting director of Metropolitan State Mental Hospital that the hospital had not given ECT in three years: "We don't have to scramble and cook people's brains any more like they used to before we had good medicines."[2]

But to Peter Breggin and the radical ex-patient movement, psychosurgery was merely the prototype of *all* somatic treatment in psychiatry. ECT produced its effect "in the manner of a lobotomy."[3] Drugs were a chemical lobotomy. Not comprehending that psychiatry itself was under attack, psychiatrists were shocked to discover that success in stifling other treatments had only encouraged anti-psychiatric activists to storm the last bastion of biological psychiatry.

The extraordinary success of the activists in equating psychoactive drugs with psychosurgery and ECT is apparent in court decisions. In 1988 a Minnesota court ruled that anti-psychiatric drugs were as intru-

sive as both psychosurgery and ECT, and therefore warranted the same
rigorous due process before they could be administered.[4] In the same
year, the Washington State Supreme Court quoted its own 1986 decision
upholding the right to refuse ECT in ruling that a judicial hearing was
necessary before anti-psychotic drugs could be given involuntarily.

> We noted that the right to refuse ECT was especially important because
> ECT is a highly intrusive medical procedure. . . . Like ECT, antipsychotic
> drug therapy is a highly intrusive form of medical treatment.[5]

Balance of Power Shifts Against Psychiatry

By the time the war against drugs moved into high gear in the
mid-1980s, the balance of power had shifted markedly in favor of the ex-
patient movement, whose impact psychiatrists badly underestimated.
Even such a normally astute observer as Paul Appelbaum told us:

> For better or worse I think the consumer movement is going to have
> much less effect on development of policy than any of the other actors in
> mental health. They're stigmatized by virtue of being crazy in the public
> mind. Even if they're right they're not going to be listened to very much.[6]

Psychiatrists failed to recognize not only the growth of the movement and the talent and vigor of its leaders, but also its ability to forge
alliances with the mental health bar and with professional groups eager
to challenge psychiatry's pride of place in treating mental illness. The
last weapon for waging a successful campaign came from the federal
government, which in 1986 began to fund the warriors against treatment with millions of dollars through its new Protection and Advocacy
program. (State governments channeled funds to the opponents of
treatment even earlier.)

A mark of the ex-patient movement's vitality was the split that
occurred within it in 1985. Joseph Rogers had joined the movement
because, in his words, "those were the only people out there." But he
became dissatisfied, telling us: "If someone came along who was actively psychotic . . . he was usually excluded. If you were truly mentally
ill you were rejected by this group." Rogers felt that the movement's
leaders, such as Judi Chamberlin and the group around *Madness Network News,* were "a pretty elite kind of group, mostly people who had
been misdiagnosed, not really suffering from a serious mental illness,
although they had been treated in state hospitals which I consider an
abuse." While Rogers feels they had a right be angry, he observes: "Most

consumers were not fighting psychiatric oppression. They were fighting a mental illness." Rogers began to seek out what he called "a group of consumers who were not really heard, who were using programs and were not complaining as much."[7]

The end result was the creation of two organizations: the National Alliance of Mental Patients (NAMP), composed of the traditional leaders, and the challengers, who formed the National Mental Health Consumers' Association (NMHCA). Even the titles were significant: the old-line leaders were patients, inmates, or—most favored within the inner circle—"survivors." (Indeed, in 1989 NAMP changed its name to the National Association of Psychiatric Survivors.) These leaders hated the term "consumer" with its assumption that patients wanted and chose services. But this was precisely what the new organization wanted to emphasize—that psychiatry offered a range of treatments and services from which those who wanted them should be allowed to choose.[8]

In some respects Rogers proved a devastating critic of anti-psychiatric orthodoxies. He scorned the notion, popular in the movement, that psychiatrists had invented mental illness. "I was crazy before any psychiatrist met me, so if it's psychiatric oppression they have real good secret ways of doing it."[9] There was nothing romantic, inspiring, or wonderful about mental illness, said Rogers. "It is horrifying, terrifying, and destructive to the soul." Those of us who have suffered from serious illness, said Rogers, "need to speak out against those charlatans in our movement who claim that somehow our pain and our despair can be translated into the language of fairy tales."[10]

Rogers also acknowledged the value of anti-psychotic drugs and with considerable courage, given the popularity of Breggin in the ex-patient movement, attacked him publicly. Breggin appeared at a psychosocial rehabilitation conference in Philadelphia, denying as usual that mental illness was a disease and denouncing fellow psychiatrists for "lobotomizing" the mentally ill with "brain-damaging" drugs. Rogers stated flatly in an interview in a local paper that Breggin's ideas were "a lot of hot air designed to sell his books" and that he was "making bucks off the pain and suffering of mental illness."[11]

Still, when it came to the war on treatment, there was much common cause between Rogers' organization and the radical National Association of Psychiatric Survivors. Both Rogers as an individual and his National Mental Health Consumers' Association participated in the campaign against ECT. In January 1985 Rogers brought what *Madness Network News* described as a "vanload of homeless friends" from Philadelphia to demonstrate against the first International Conference on ECT held at the Barbizon Plaza hotel in New York City.[12] In October 1988 Rogers' organization led a protest demonstration against Friends Hospital in Philadelphia which was sponsoring a fiftieth anniversary symposium on ECT. The flyer carried the photo of a woman shrieking in agony and the logo "Electroshock is a Crime Against Humanity." (Marilyn Rice's insistence that her group, the Committee for Truth in Psychiatry, is not trying to eliminate ECT is belied by its participation in the "Coalition for Reject," which endorsed the protest.)

Rogers responded to sharp criticism of him by radicals in the movement with an admonition to "watch what I do, not what I say." In 1988, he wrote to *Dendron,* the anti-psychiatric ex-patient journal that replaced the defunct *Madness Network News:* "The truth is that, if you look at what actual actions are taking place—actions in the courtroom and in legislative forums—the National Mental Health Consumers' Association has taken a very strong approach to the question of involuntary or forced treatment."[13] And Rogers' point is well taken: his National Mental Health Consumers' Association has filed amicus briefs on behalf of the right to refuse medication, supported the right of Joyce Brown (who became better known as Billy Boggs) to remain undisturbed on her Manhattan steam grate when she was brought to Bellevue hospital for treatment, and fought changes in commitment laws that would make it easier to treat severely ill patients. The Rogers-led organization differed from the more radical groups in being willing to permit involuntary treatment "in very extreme and rare cases" (i.e., of imminent suicide or imminent threat of bodily harm to others).[14] The rival National Association of Psychiatric Survivors opposes involuntary treatment under *any* conditions.

Rogers emphasized that it was the means and not the goal that separated him from the more radical groups. "I feel very strongly that this is the most effective course at this present time. I think we have to be strategic in our approach by attacking the problem of involuntary treatment where we are in our present standard of law and steadily moving it toward what we all desire, which is the elimination of the need for any form of involuntary treatment."[15] It appeared then that while Rogers was prepared to accept the scientific evidence that severe mental illness is biologically caused, he was unwilling to conclude that this carried any implications for public policy.

What accounts for this attitude toward involuntary treatment on the part of the supposedly "moderate" ex-patient organization? One factor is that Rogers has had to take into account the hostility toward psychiatry of many in his own organization who were also members of the National Association of Psychiatric Survivors. Typical of such people is a board member of Rogers' organization who in 1988 wrote in to *Dendron:* "My philosophical standing is with NAMP [the National Alliance of Mental Patients, which had not yet changed its name], but I feel the reality of these times dictates my accessing the resources of NMHCA [the National Mental Health Consumers' Association]."[16] Rogers lost out to the extremists in 1989 and was replaced as head of the NMHCA in 1990 by anti-psychiatric activist Paul Dorfner. (The ideology of the National Association of Psychiatric Survivors was now the ideology of *both* organizations.)

There also seems to be a feeling that involuntary treatment derogates from the status of mental patients. This is made explicit by Jay Centifanti, who had been well-launched on a brilliant career when manic-depressive illness almost destroyed his life. One of the first students to graduate simultaneously from Harvard Law School and Harvard Business School, Centifanti joined a large Philadelphia law firm. In 1975, in the grip of his illness, he lost his job and his wife left him; he then shot her several times on a Penn Central commuter train. (Fortunately, she survived.) Eluding a major police hunt for months, Centifanti eventually turned himself in, and was imprisoned for a little more than two years in Norristown State Hospital.

Centifanti's license to practice law was suspended and to this date has not been restored. As a result, his redoubtable legal talents have been made available at very low cost to the ex-patient movement. While his name appears only as "law clerk" on Rennie v. Klein, New Jersey's major right to refuse treatment case, Centifanti did much of the legal work. Since then he has prepared the amicus briefs filed by the National Mental Health Consumers' Association in right to refuse treatment cases. A small round-faced man brimming with charm and energy, Centifanti takes lithium, which, he is quick to say, he considers vital to prevent a recurrence of his illness. In his own words: "In my case, give me lithium or give me death: I'd rather be *dead* than be the way I was."[17]

Despite his recognition of the importance of treatment for his own well-being, Centifanti believes firmly in the right to refuse treatment. He insists that only a judge should be permitted to decide whether a patient incompetent to make a decision can be treated—despite the fact that judges are poorly equipped to make medical decisions. His emphasis on judicial review seems to derive from his sense that when judges are involved, society places importance upon the issue. Conducting a workshop on the right to refuse treatment at a conference of the National Mental Health Consumers' Association, Centifanti referred to a famous multimillion dollar will contested by the deceased man's children: "Remember Johnson and Johnson? . . . Millions and millions of dollars were involved. When it's important, who decides whether someone's competent? You know the right to die cases? . . . Who decides about whether to pull the plug?"[18]

Forging Alliances with Professional Organizations

But it is not just an enlarged and diverse ex-patient movement that makes the campaign against treatment a formidable force in the 1980s. The ex-patient movement has been able to build alliances with a variety of voluntary associations. Joseph Rogers has worked closely with the National Mental Health Association, started by Clifford Beers early in the century to promote a loosely defined, generic "mental health" in the population. Professional associations of psychologists and mental health workers have also become part of the anti-psychiatric coalition. Even the American Orthopsychiatric Association, an interdisciplinary organization that includes psychiatrists along with other mental health professionals, has entered the lists against treatment.

For these organizations, the uppermost consideration is improving the status of their own specialties by curtailing the primacy of psychiatry. Anti-psychiatric psychiatrist Lee Coleman, in his introduction to Leonard Frank's book on ECT, declared that the resurgence of organic treatments in psychiatry was simply a method by which psychiatry could enjoy a haven from nonmedical interlopers.[19] This attitude was widely shared. Earlier we referred to the frank statement by the president of the California State Psychologists' Association in 1967:

> As members of a younger professional group on the outside of organized medicine's attempts to pre-empt all "medical" fields (including and especially mental health) . . . I think psychologists find themselves in a philosophic position very close to that of Szasz.[20]

Anti-psychiatric activists were open in their appeals to the self-interest of members of the "caring professions." At the 1988 IAPSRS conference (International Association of Psychosocial Rehabilitation Services) in Philadelphia, Peter Breggin told a packed meeting hall that his efforts to "demolish the entire medical model and medical authority . . . can only be a boon to those of you who are in psychosocial rehabilitation."[21] And many in these professions have responded. Radical ex-patient activist Jay Mahler says that in California his network of activists finds allies in the California Psychological Association, the

California Association of Rehabilitation Agencies, and organizations of patients' rights advocates.[22]

The Government Funds Anti-Psychiatry

Beginning in the 1980s, public funds began to reach anti-psychiatric organizations, primarily through the National Institute of Mental Health's Community Support Program. In 1983, California's Department of Mental Health provided $20,000 of NIMH money for Network Against Psychiatric Assault activists to create a statewide network of mental patients to provide a "unified view" on mental health policy. By 1987 the organization thus created, the California Network of Mental Health Clients, had received $350,000 from the state.[23] The salary of Paul Dorfner, then head of the Vermont Liberation Organization, now also president of the NMHCA, came from state funds. Federal money likewise went to the ex-patient movement in Vermont and other states through NIMH's Community Support Program.[24]

A few of the ex-patients were uneasy about these developments. Ted Chabasinski saw the money as a crass effort to buy off the movement.

> NIMH wants us to waste our time. After the shock ban, the response of the mental health establishment was to start spending money right and left subsidizing all these groups. . . . They got all this money to go to conferences and have teleconferences. . . . What you have now is this small group of two hundred people who get their way paid to this, that, and the other conference.[25]

Long-time activist Lenny Lapon in *Madness Network News* expressed his "sorrow and anger and alienation" at the movement's taking funds from "the genocidal National Institute of Mental Health." Wrote Lapon:

> They know what they are doing. They will never, in any large-scale way, fund our rebellion, our fight against them and their murderous policies.[26]

But most were confident, quite correctly as it turned out, that they could use government funds to promote their anti-psychiatric ideology with impunity. Paul Dorfner replied to Lapon's article:

> Now given that we live in a condition of twentieth-century slavery, what are we to do? If we don't or can't turn their money and systems against them, what do we do? How do we fight them?

Dorfner considered government funds a challenge, not a threat.

> It seems to me that by taking their money we are taking them on and we
> are in the world where we can prove that we are right and they are wrong.
> I like to attend their conferences because I feel that I can fight them more
> directly then. And I can fight them with more than words.[27]

Breggin Assails Drugs

The growth in support for anti-psychiatry within mental health's
"attentive public" meant that when, in 1983, Peter Breggin, fresh from
his victories against psychosurgery and ECT, published his onslaught
upon anti-psychotic drugs *Psychiatric Drugs: Hazards to the Brain,*
there was a sizable audience receptive to his message. The assault drew
legitimacy from Breggin's again obtaining the reputable Springer as his
publisher.

Breggin's technique—attack by analogy—is modeled on that of his
mentor Thomas Szasz. As we have seen, much of Szasz's work consists of
extended comparisons between the "myth" of mental illness and slavery, the Spanish Inquisition, and belief in witches. Breggin adapts this
method, repeatedly describing drugs as a form of lobotomy, a "chemical
lobotomy."

According to Breggin, modern psychiatric drugs, far from being
psychiatry's finest achievement, have created "a public health menace of
great proportions." The drugs, writes Breggin, "permanently damage
the higher centers of the brain, producing irreversible psychoses, apathy, generalized brain dysfunction, dementia and other effects similar to
those resulting from lobotomy." Moreover, Breggin declares, "brain
dysfunction is not a 'side effect,' but the primary, overriding effect. The
apparent improvement that patients show is actually a disability, a loss of
mental capacity inflicted by the drugs."[28] All the major psychiatric drugs
now in use do no more than "provide a sophisticated, disguised blow
on the head."[29] (This is of course the same argument advanced by anti-
psychiatric activists against ECT: what are beneficial, it is claimed, *are*
the brain damaging effects. Destroying brain function makes the individual feel better temporarily.)

Breggin insists that *all* the major drugs are brain disabling—
lithium and the anti-depressants, no less than the neuroleptics, produce
"severe disruption of the mental faculties."[30] Far from improving mental
function, Breggin declares, "drug-induced mental and physical dysfunction may be a major reason for the high recidivism rate."[31] This is a new

twist. Labeling theorists had held institutions responsible for creating the disease they were meant to cure. But now Breggin places responsibility for the stubborn chronicity of mental illness on the very drugs that make it possible to release people from institutions.

Breggin does not concede that drugs have any benefits. Expert on psychopharmacology Dr. Leo Hollister has summed up the clinical evidence: "The extensive literature of evaluative trials, constituting the most massive scientific overkill in all clinical pharmacology, has demonstrated the value of anti-psychotic drugs in all forms of schizophrenia, at all ages, at all stages of illness, and in all parts of the world."[32] But for Breggin, the drugs merely reduce "all verbal communications . . . with many patients becoming relatively mute."[33] Searching for the metabolic processes by which the drugs work makes no more sense than the search for a key metabolic process in electrocution.[34]

Breggin does not hesitate to make wild, outlandish charges. Millions of patients "throughout the world are being saddled with permanent lobotomy effects, irreversible drug-induced psychoses, chronic organic brain syndromes, and ultimately, dementia."[35] Breggin writes: "If it sounds as if no prudent individual would voluntarily submit to the major psychiatric drugs after these warnings, this reflects on the treatment itself."[36]

What then should be done to relieve the suffering of the millions of people who suffer from major mental illness? Although he criticizes Szasz for being "so narrowly focused on freedom that he overlooks the human angle, the pain, the complexity,"[37] Breggin offers nothing more to the mentally ill than his mentor. What is psychosis? According to Breggin, it is "utter irresponsibility for one's own thought processes and personal conduct. It is the ultimate expression of personal failure or abject psychological helplessness."[38]

Breggin's real message to the mentally ill is that they ought to pull themselves up by their own bootstraps. If they fail, Breggin, like Szasz, would let them go to the wall. "The main issue is whether anyone ever should be hospitalized or treated against his or her will. My answer to this is *no!*"[39] Breggin complains that for Szasz, "Everything goes. Do anything you want to anybody. If someone wants to kill himself, give him the pills. Give him the knife."[40] But it is hard to see how Breggin's message differs.

Far from isolating him within the universe of those who work with the mentally ill, Breggin's intemperate attacks on drugs have made him a favored speaker among mental health professionals. At the IAPSRS conference in Philadelphia in 1988 mentioned earlier, which brought together 1,700 mental health workers, Breggin was the *only* speaker in the workshop on drugs (which he ran twice in the course of the conference); there was no one to counter his wild distortions. The enthusiasm of the standing-room-only audience clearly surprised even Breggin, who began his talk warning that many in the audience would disagree with him.

Riese v. St. Mary's Hospital: The Anti-Treatment Coalition in California

The alliance of government-funded advocates, voluntary and professional organizations, and ex-patient groups in the war against treatment is illustrated by a key California right to refuse treatment case, Riese v. St. Mary's Hospital.

At first glance, California was not a promising state in which to introduce the right to refuse treatment. In passing the then-revolutionary Lanterman-Petris-Short (LPS) Act in 1968, the state legislature had attempted to strike a balance: the commitment period would be brief, but psychiatrists would be allowed to treat the patient in that time span. The law was specific on this point: a person detained for evaluation and treatment (the three-day hold) "shall receive whatever treatment and care as his or her condition requires for the full period that he or she is held."[41] The legislature's intent is so clear on this point that patients' rights groups opposed 1986 amendments to the LPS Act that required giving patients detailed information on side effects of drugs: they complained that the bill did not create any right to refuse treatment even for "competent involuntary patients."[42]

As we noted earlier, however, right to refuse treatment suits around the country, by positing the legal competence of mental patients, have been able to subvert the intent of the 1960s reform, which hoped that preserving patients' legal competence would *encourage* treatment. Because the LPS Act did not specifically negate patients' competence, California law offered the same crucial lever against involuntary treatment that other state laws provided: the presumption that the patient was legally competent.[43] Moreover, in a 1972 case, the California Supreme Court ruled that informed consent to medical treatment was a constitutional right that could only be denied if a patient were *incompetent.*[44]

Riese v. St. Mary's, like other right to refuse treatment cases around the country, was an anti-treatment case cloaked in the guise of enforcing a patient's civil rights: in this case the right to informed consent for medical treatment during the seventeen days the LPS Act permitted dangerous and gravely disabled persons to be involuntarily committed (and treated). Mort Cohen, who had brought an earlier right to refuse treatment case in federal court for the ACLU (resulting in a multimillion dollar system of second medical opinions in state mental hospitals[45]), recognized that state courts had become a more promising venue. The Massachusetts state court decision In the Matter of Guardianship of Richard Roe III, discussed in Chapter 7, had been followed by a number of similar decisions in other state courts—what one attorney has dubbed "the lemming school of jurisprudence."

Accordingly, Cohen brought a class action suit in California state court in the name of Eleanor Riese. Riese had been hospitalized for chronic schizophrenia in 1968, responded to the anti-psychotic drug Mellaril, and upon discharge in 1969 had moved into her own apartment. In 1981 she ceased taking her medication and was hospitalized again, initially as a voluntary patient. When she refused medication, her status was changed to that of an involuntary patient.[46] Cohen's suit demanded for Eleanor Riese—and all involuntarily committed patients—the right to refuse medication unless ruled incompetent by a court of law. Even if a patient were ruled incompetent, the suit demanded that a "substituted judgment" (what the person would have wanted, if competent) rather than a best interest standard be applied to decide whether or not the individual should be treated.

Unsuccessful at the trial level, Cohen won at the appellate level. California's Court of Appeals in 1987 ruled in Riese v. St. Mary's Hospital that except in an emergency, a judicial hearing was necessary before a patient could be treated involuntarily. The court specifically ruled that in the case of anti-psychotic drugs the procedures used for giving ECT involuntarily must be followed—cumbersome procedures, as we have seen, that have made involuntary ECT comparatively rare.

As Ted Hutchinson has pointed out, if those bringing the suit genuinely sought informed consent to psychiatric treatment (rather than to subvert treatment), existing administrative procedures could have been used. The LPS Act provides that each patient on a three-day hold receive a prompt, "multidisciplinary" evaluation of any "medical, psychological, educational, social, financial, and legal conditions as may appear to constitute a problem."[47] The question of whether one has the capacity to give informed consent is clearly a legal condition that may constitute a problem. Existing law thus offered a framework for addressing the issue of informed consent ostensibly at the heart of the Riese case. In cases where the evaluation team found the capacity to give informed consent lacking (informal estimates suggest the proportion of such cases is very high),[48] a substitute decision-maker, preferably a family member, could be appointed to discuss the treatment plan with the psychiatrist. Hutchinson points out this would ensure informed consent (or a substitute decision-maker) for *each* mentally ill person, not just those who refuse treatment.[49]

But if the goal is not really ensuring informed consent, but rather creating roadblocks to treatment, judicial hearings are far more effective. Given the inevitable delays of an already overwhelmed judicial system, mandatory judicial hearings for refusing patients would in most cases amount to a right to refuse treatment. Even in states without a time limit on holding patients, we have seen that psychiatrists are reluctant to spend time on court appearances and paperwork. If an individual can only be held fourteen days anyway, the temptation becomes even greater to release the refusing patient in favor of someone else who can be treated.

Back to Bedlam

The California Court of Appeal's decision in Riese v. St. Mary's Hospital was in turn appealed to the California Supreme Court, which, in the end, allowed the decision to stand without a hearing. What makes the case of special interest is the number of amicus briefs in support of the right to refuse treatment filed by a wide range of professional, ex-patient, and other organizations when it appeared the Court would review the appellate decision. The arguments in those briefs illuminate the regressive direction in which these organizations would like to take psychiatry. The case is also significant because federal money was used to support the right to refuse treatment. In 1987 California's federally funded Protection and Advocacy system had accepted patient Eleanor Riese as a client, and its attorneys from then on served as co-counsel on the case.

The briefs filed by ex-patient groups and members of the mental health bar were predictable. A coalition of patient groups, including the National Mental Health Consumers' Association (then led by Joseph Rogers) quoted from the latter organization's charter supporting "the inherent autonomy and competency to choose of all who have been 'labeled' mental patients" and affirming the right to refuse all potentially "life threatening, disabling and painful procedures such as ECT, lobotomies, psychotropic drugs and other forms of so-called treatment."[50]

Judges reading the coalition's brief would find no suggestion that the drugs had any benefits whatever.

More remarkable, the briefs filed by *professional associations* were as hostile to treatment as those filed by legal advocacy and ex-patient groups. The amicus brief filed by the American Orthopsychiatric Association, founded by psychiatrists in 1924 and including a substantial number in its membership, declared that almost 50% of patients fell in a category where medication is not effective at all, where they improve without it, or where it actually exacerbates their symptoms.[51] While it is true that there is a sizable (between 10%–20%) treatment-refractory patient population, these are wildly exaggerated figures, not backed up by research. Nor is there any evidence that patients who refuse treatment are those who are refractory to medication.

Similarly, the brief pays only lip service to the positive effects of medication, while exaggerating the side effects: these are portrayed as causing large numbers of deaths from neuroleptic malignant syndrome and disfiguring a million people each year through tardive dyskinesia.[52] It is interesting that an almost uniform feature of these briefs is that along with a terrifying portrait of the damage purportedly wrought by the drugs is an insistence that medication refusal is rare: Advocates argue that medications are life-threatening, brain-damaging, and inef-fective—in which case presumably large numbers of patients would be quite right to refuse to take them. But they allege that the right to refuse will make little practical difference because few patients will exercise it. The reason for the anomaly is that anti-psychiatric advocates want to avoid frightening judges who may anticipate the breakdown of the judicial system in the face of enormous numbers of right to refuse cases if they mandate judicial review.

But perhaps the most remarkable brief of all was that filed by the American Psychological Association. Like the other intervenors, the APA describes anti-psychotic drugs as "high risk treatment," intrusive, risky, powerful in their "mind altering effect." The brief admits the drugs do not lead to "thought control" in the sense of indoctrination; it argues they nonetheless have First Amendment implications because they in-trude on the ability to form and communicate ideas.[53] In other words, the American Psychological Association calls for the preservation of psychotic delusions and hallucinations as a right protected by the First Amendment.

Even more extraordinary are the treatment alternatives the brief suggests. Indeed, they are worth quoting in some detail:

Hospitalization is a form of treatment in itself; the limits, controls, and structure provided to the patient through hospitalization have considerable therapeutic benefit. And mental health professionals have available many alternative treatments to stabilize patients with acute conditions. *Seclusion or restraint with cold, wet sheet packs can provide an effective means of managing some acute episodes of psychosis.* These options are often more humane than forced medication; patients treated in this way often, upon recovery, state that the seclusion or restraint ameliorated their anxieties by restoring a sense of safety and control to their environment. Psychotherapy is also an option that is effective in the treatment of psychosis.[54] [Emphasis added.]

What the American Psychological Association is recommending is nothing less than a return to the "treatments" prevalent in state mental hospitals in the dreadful days described by Deutsch in *The Shame of the States;* what was mainly offered were four walls, straitjackets, and isolation cells ("seclusion or restraint" in the brief), immersion in freezing water (the brief's "cold, wet packs"), and talk (psychotherapy).

Similarly, the Mental Health Association of California in its brief declares that it is an "absurdly narrow" definition of treatment that ignores the most therapeutic aspect of involuntary hospitalization: the provision of a secure, stable environment and caring for needs for food, clothing, and shelter.[55] The four walls theory of psychiatric treatment had returned with a vengeance in the anti-scientific, anti-psychiatric campaign against treatments that worked.

Are Anti-Psychotic Drugs Dangerous?

In producing side effects, psychoactive drugs are no different from all other drugs. *Newsweek* in 1989 reported that 10,000 people die each year from the side effects of nonsteroidal anti-inflammatory drugs like aspirin.[56] Drugs used to treat hypertension have side effects ranging from liver disease to gastrointestinal disturbances.

Are the side effects of psychoactive drugs worse than the side effects of drugs given in other chronic diseases? Dr. Edward King, an internist who has served for over twenty years as the medical doctor for Gracie Square Hospital, a private psychiatric hospital in Manhattan, believes that this is true in the sense that the frequency of permanent side effects with psychoactive drugs is higher.[57]

Most of the side effects are reversible, continuing only so long as the drug is taken, and can be controlled by taking additional drugs to offset them.[58] The most important side effects of the neuroleptic drugs (used for schizophrenia) are akathisia, a motor restlessness making it impossible to sit still, and pseudo-parkinsonism, producing rigidity and tremor, a shuffling gait, and sometimes a mask-like visage.[59] Individuals on high doses of neuroleptics often complain of feeling draggy, or, as one person put it, wrapped in cotton wool.

Because in many cases it is irreversible, tardive dyskinesia (TD) is one of the most serious side effects of the neuroleptics. It is characterized by involuntary irregular movements, particularly of the mouth and face: rapid blinking of the eyes, chewing and smacking movements of the lips with darting out of the tongue (called flycatcher's tongue); there may also be writhing of the limbs and trunk. Older patients are more likely to be afflicted than younger ones, and, some studies suggest, women more than men.

While the *prevalence* is relatively high among patients who take high doses of the drugs for long periods, fortunately, in most cases the disorder takes a mild form.[60] Dr. William Glazer, an expert on the disorder, estimates that the rate of tardive dyskinesia among psychiatric outpatients (the rate is higher among long-term inpatients of state hospitals) is between 20% and 30% but that of these less than 5% (that is, just over 1% of outpatients overall) have a serious form of the disorder.[61]

Dr. Glazer says of his program at the Connecticut Mental Health Center in New Haven: "We have the largest tardive dyskinesia clinic in the solar system here. We've diagnosed over 1,000 cases. We get referrals from Connecticut, New York, New Jersey—this area of the Northeast. I'm likely to have access to the most severe cases and I can tell you that you do not see a lot of what I would call severe cases." Moreover in many cases, particularly among young people, Dr. Glazer says, the disorder is reversible while in other cases there is appreciable improvement.[62]

Although very rare, there are worse side effects of the drugs. In tardive dystonia, muscles contract without any synergy. The head may be bent backward or the body twisted; the patient may be unable to change position. While patients with tardive dyskinesia may be unconscious of the disorder, patients with tardive dystonia are in severe pain. Another rare, but serious side effect, neuroleptic malignant syndrome, most often occurs very early in treatment or upon change from one drug to another. The patient's muscles become rigid; he develops very high fever, and often has difficulty speaking or swallowing. Untreated, the syndrome can be fatal.

Dr. Glazer emphasizes that the risks of psychotic illness must be balanced against the side effects. "The drugs have risks and the drugs

have benefits. And this is where Dr. Breggin is careless and manipulative, distorting facts. He is distorting the data when he tries to say how
bad these drugs are. He is absolutely overlooking the benefit side of
these medications."[63] In fact, the benefit side is so important that clinics
like those of Dr. Glazer that try to relieve tardive dyskinesia find their
main problem is that many patients taken off the drug (or put on much
reduced dosages) experience a return of psychiatric symptoms; they
then have to go back on one of the neuroleptics.

Prescribing dosages as low as possible is a viable strategy, but drug
holidays, once considered a promising way to minimize side effects,
above all tardive dyskinesia, are losing favor.[64] There is no evidence that
they prevent tardive dyskinesia, and there are discouraging indications
that patients require a *higher* maintenance dose when they go back on
the drugs.[65]

Mental illness is a painful, even deadly disease. It has been said that
mental disorders in themselves are as destructive as a malignant growth
and cause far more suffering. A study of patients who had experienced
severe depression and also, at some other time, had a serious physical
injury found that they would rather repeat the experience of physical
injury than that of depression.[66] Dr. Samuel Keith, head of schizophrenia
research at NIMH, points out that the suicide rate in schizophrenia, at
10%, is almost as high as that for affective disorders.[67]

Moreover, as NIMH's Dr. Richard Wyatt points out: "Not only is
schizophrenia injurious to the patient; it can be injurious to those
around him." He reported on a study of a group of patients stabilized on
medication following an acute episode of illness. Some were maintained on medication, while others were given no further treatment.
The study found that within eighteen months those not treated made
three times as many serious suicide attempts and were responsible for
six times as many incidents of antisocial behavior, including arson and
battery.[68]

The Promise of Better Treatments

While for anti-psychiatric activists tardive dyskinesia is merely
another excuse for eliminating treatment, in reality, it should warrant far
more energetic research on drugs with a different profile (all the
neuroleptics block dopamine receptors and thus have the potential for
causing tardive dyskinesia) and use of alternatives, especially ECT.
Tardive dyskinesia, according to Dr. Glazer, is particularly likely to occur

in severe form in patients who suffer from psychotic depression and are given neuroleptics. He says:

> I saw a patient last night who is depressed as well as psychotic and therefore requires the neuroleptics. His depression is coming back and the movements are coming back. He is slated for a course of ECT. And I am delighted they are choosing ECT over restarting neuroleptics. We wouldn't have said that five or ten years ago. But in some cases I feel ECT is a preferable treatment because the benefits are there and the risks are less than they are with neuroleptics.[69]

Dr. Glazer calls clozapine (discovered in the late 1960s but only now coming into use in this country) "the most significant finding as far as treatment for schizophrenia goes since 1952 [when chlorpromazine was discovered]." Trials in a number of state hospitals show a remarkable response among patients resistant to existing drugs, with approximately half of the patients who fail to respond to them improving with clozapine. Moreover, clozapine (marketed under the trade name Clozaril in the United States) does not appear to cause tardive dyskinesia, and so also provides an alternative for treatment-responsive patients who develop TD on neuroleptics. Unfortunately, however, clozapine suppresses bone marrow cell formation in between 1%–2% of patients. If not promptly halted in such cases, the drug becomes deadly.

As a result, Sandoz Pharmaceuticals, makers of Clozaril, will only make the drug available in the United States in a package-combination with its own blood-monitoring system at a cost of just under $9,000 a year. At this writing, only fifteen state Medicaid programs will pay for the drug. Making the drug available to all those who could benefit from it— estimated at between 70,000 to 300,000 persons—could cost Medicaid billions of dollars annually, with the cost of treating patients in some states exceeding the entire current mental-health budget.[70] Moreover, the drug does not cure; the patient's improvement continues only so long as it is taken, so that the cost continues indefinitely.

And while clozapine is the first drug that seems to affect the so-called "negative symptoms" of schizophrenia (apathy, lack of ambition, withdrawal), as in the case of the neuroleptics, some patients improve markedly, others only marginally. Yet those who improve most would be in greatest jeopardy even if Medicaid paid its costs; once they obtained jobs, they would no longer be eligible for government benefits, yet could not afford the cost of the drug that enabled them to work. Because of the difficulty and expense of monitoring the drug in this country, clozapine's most important contribution may be in leading researchers to look for other drugs with a similar profile that will not have its effect on bone marrow.

The answer to the problems associated with treatments for psychosis, as in chemotherapy used against cancer, is not to throw out treatments that work (as insulin coma therapy was too hastily discarded), but to use a greater variety, tailored more carefully to the individual needs and responses of patients. British psychologist and filmmaker David Cohen reports talking to Sukdeb Mukerjhee, an Indian doctor at Long Island's Creedmoor Hospital. Mukerjhee laments that "patients tend to get the same treatment, month in, month out. For most patients, there is no thought out therapeutic strategy, no attempt to change treatment if it is not producing results."[71]

More research also needs to be done to identify subgroups of patients who might respond to specialized treatments. Psychiatrists now talk of the schizophrenias as a group of diseases with similar symptoms but different causes. But because these diseases cannot yet be differentiated, in testing the efficacy of treatments psychiatrists must operate on the hypothesis that everyone is suffering from the *same* disease.

Carol North is a practicing psychiatrist in St. Louis who as a college undergraduate suffered from severe psychotic episodes, was diagnosed as schizophrenic, and was repeatedly hospitalized. She wrote a compelling book, *Welcome Silence,* about her experiences and about her dramatic cure through dialysis. She is convinced there is a small subgroup of patients that would respond, as she did, to this treatment. North says:

> I probably have what is technically correct to call a dialysis-responsive psychosis, which may or may not be part of some kind of schizophrenic spectrum of diseases. I think that there is a very small subgroup of schizophrenics that have whatever biochemical error it is that would respond to dialysis. And I think the studies that have been done had to be small and because of the small sample you can't reach statistical significance. If one person out of sixteen you dialyze gets well, that could be within random error.[72]

Since there is currently no way to identify this small subset, psychiatrists have little choice but to dismiss the treatment altogether.

Today's treatments are far from ideal: they can have serious side effects, and they often do not restore patients to a fully normal life. But the untreated multitudes of mentally ill on the streets bear testimony to the reality that deinstitutionalization cannot work without treatment.

There cannot even be a humane system of hospitalization without treatment. In its annual report for the year 1880, Willard State Hospital in upstate New York noted that 42 men required 532 baths and destroyed 2,996 pieces of clothing in one week.[73] Seventy years later, in *Shame of the States,* Alfred Deutsch painted a terrible and unforgettable scene of naked men herded together in Byberry Hospital; this reflected a more overcrowded and poorly staffed hospital's response to the disordered behavior Willard, a model in its day, coped with more humanely. As psychiatrist Silvano Arieti points out, it is thanks to anti-psychotic medications that wards of incontinent, naked, screaming patients are a thing of the past.[74]

Without treatment there is no way to prevent a return to the conditions of 1880, if not those of 1948. The American Psychological Association in effect condemns patients to no less with its call for a return to "wet packs," "isolation cells," and "restraints."

The chief victims of the war against treatment are the mentally ill, whose needs are being sacrificed to a fraudulent anti-psychiatric ideology. But there are other victims, above all, families who, helpless to aid those they love, disintegrate in the process of trying to do so. The general population falls victim also, as public places become open air institutions for those in desperate need of treatment they are exhorted to avoid.

Tax Dollars Fund Anti-Psychiatry

Nor does the war against treatment show any sign of abating. Earlier we mentioned that NIMH Community Service Program funds began to be funneled to anti-psychiatric groups in the 1980s. Beginning in 1986, millions of federal dollars have been channeled annually into the war through state Protection and Advocacy programs (P&As), whose funds are also administered by the National Institute of Mental Health.

Congress established these programs following hearings by then Senator Lowell Weicker on abuses of mental patients both in hospitals and in community settings.[75] The chief lobbyist for the legislation was the National Alliance for the Mentally Ill (NAMI). Both Congress and NAMI saw the role of the programs to be investigating specific complaints of abuse and neglect in facilities providing care and treatment to a highly vulnerable mentally ill population.

But NAMI (and Congress) had inadvertently created a Frankenstein—and an expensive one at that. As in the case of legal services projects focusing on the mentally ill, P&As in a number of states have become playgrounds for anti-psychiatric activists. Natalie Reatig, responsible for administering the program at NIMH, explained to us the program's direction.

> The reason for P&A is that the constituent client, where they are otherwise unempowered, should have a voice . . . and what the P&A people say is that they are not the judge of the situation; they are simply giving a voice to persons incapable of speaking on their own behalf, and it is as representative of those persons that I think the P&A is rightly and justly taking action independently of what they may personally feel or perhaps contrary to what they may be advocating for systemically.[76]

It is hard to see what this has to do with investigating cases of abuse and neglect. The purpose of the P&A system was to provide independent advocates to determine if mistreatment had in fact occurred, and to act if their investigation showed that it had. Neither NAMI nor Congress had any idea that the program would turn into an advocacy and litigation arm for the "expressed wishes" of mental patients, no matter how deranged these might be even in the opinion of the advocates!

In practice, P&As have been quite selective in deciding which "expressed wishes" of clients they will actively pursue. Some P&As hired ex-patient militants, along with activists from the mental health bar. Members of groups with a strong anti-psychiatric bias far outnumber representatives of family groups on advisory boards. Renée Bostick, an ex-patient who heads a division of Michigan's Protection and Advocacy program admits that the P&A legislation says it is to deal only with "abuse and neglect." However, Bostick says: "Abuse and neglect is what some individuals would call treatment in the mental health system." From this, Bostick deduces that everything that goes on in the mental health system falls in the purview of the Protection and Advocacy system.[77]

Given a perspective equating treatment with abuse, it is not surprising that the National Association of Protection and Advocacy Systems and each of the fifty state Protection and Advocacy programs have endorsed Marilyn Rice's Committee for Truth in Psychiatry's campaign against reclassification of ECT devices. This has almost certainly had an impact upon the Food and Drug Administration in making it seem that political opposition to reclassification of ECT devices goes considerably beyond the ex-patient groups. In a 1988 letter to members of her anti-ECT group, Rice herself writes that the support of the Protection and Advocacy Systems "was a wonderful plus for us . . . I am sure they [the FDA] were impressed at our being supported by an organization substantial enough to be holding a 5-day conference in one of Washington's swankiest hotels."[78]

Around the country, a number of Protection and Advocacy systems work to reinforce the existing pattern of neglect of the mentally ill by imposing obstacles to commitment and treatment. In Hawaii, Kentucky, Oregon, Rhode Island, West Virginia, and California, P&A agencies have labored to prevent legislative reforms of commitment laws to make it possible to treat severely ill patients before they become actively "dangerous." The right to refuse treatment has become a priority issue for a number of these agencies. California's Protection and Advocacy agency, as we have seen, funded Riese v. St. Mary's in the appeal stages. In New York, the attorney who had already won a major right to refuse treatment case (Rivers v. Katz) was promptly hired by the state P&A. In Wisconsin the P&A submitted an amicus brief in yet another right to refuse treatment case.[79] The mental health bar's David Ferleger, an avowed opponent of involuntary commitment and all involuntary treatment, has been assigned to produce a litigation source book for the Protection and Advocacy system.[80]

Many Protection and Advocacy programs are also indoctrinating their staff in anti-psychiatric ideology. They have been sponsoring, organizing, funding, and sending their staff to the annual meetings of the radically anti-psychiatric National Association for Rights Protection and Advocacy (NARPA). A private organization established in 1980 to bring together members of the mental health bar and other advocates, NARPA became even more radical as the most militant sector of the ex-patient movement joined the organization and demanded (and won) a leadership role. At NARPA's 1987 conference in Detroit, planned and largely funded by Michigan's Protection and Advocacy Service, several hundred attendees heard Peter Breggin speak about "Taking on Psychiatry" and radical feminist (and ex-patient) Kate Millett warn of the danger that Protection and Advocacy systems could become a "figleaf for the system."[81] Presumably, conferences like this one were to stave off such danger; Millett insisted on using the terms "abuse" and "forced incarceration," not euphemisms like "treatment."

Indeed, NARPA was so extreme that, prior to its 1988 conference, Joseph Rogers wrote to Protection and Advocacy divisions around the country asking them *not* to participate, noting that NARPA "has aligned itself with the most radical fringe elements of our movement," is "one-sided," "abolitionist," and "completely negativistic."[82]

Nonetheless, in 1988 Oregon's Protection and Advocacy agency formally co-sponsored NARPA's conference. Most of the money for the conference came from federal P&A funds, and many state P&As and departments of mental health sent staff members. The speakers included most of the stars of the anti-psychiatric firmament including Thomas Szasz, Peter Breggin, Leonard Frank, and Jeffrey Masson (whose *Against Therapy* treated psychotherapy as a menace ranking with ECT and drugs).

In one talk, Breggin went so far as call Dr. E. Fuller Torrey "another Mengele."[83] Mengele was the Nazi doctor infamous for performing brutal "experiments" on twins in the German death camps. Dr. Torrey is one of the most admirable and versatile figures in American psychiatry, whose compassion for the mentally ill has led him to donate his time to care for the mentally ill in Washington, D.C.'s shelters. The outrageous comparison presumably arose from Torrey's ongoing study of identical twins *not* concordant for schizophrenia under the auspices of the National Institute for Mental Health.

Even the anti-psychiatric patient publication *Dendron* was satisfied that government funding had not affected the conference's content: "[I]f there were strings attached to this money, organizer and electroshock survivor Lynda Wright seemed very deft at slicing and dicing those strings. It was proudly radical."[84]

NARPA's 1989 conference in St. Paul, Minnesota was no less so. Once again, Breggin was the major attraction, making three speeches. In one, entitled "Psychiatry and the Homeless," Breggin announced: "The homeless are psychiatry's source of power and they have always been." In another talk, "Psychiatric Abuse of Children," Breggin explained:

> Psychiatry is the most abusive institution in the United States today. . . . So you combine the most abusive institution, the most potentially abused individuals, you have a disastrous combination.[85]

Psychiatric "survivor" Huey Freeman was interrupted by loud applause when he proclaimed: "Psychiatry is a bitter joke on humanity. It's like Nazism or Communism. It's an artificial ideology. It's a series of invented ideas that don't work."[86]

The effect on P&A and state mental health staff present was summed up by a social worker from Kentucky's P&A division after the 1988 conference.

> I felt that the NARPA Conference was the most enlightening, informative and educational conference I have attended. . . . The psychiatric industry and the "mental health" system are powerful entities and systemic change will only be won by an equally powerful coalition of ex-inmates

and "radical others," that is, those who believe the system is oppressive and needs to be radically altered whether they've been labeled by that system or not.[87]

At both the 1988 and 1989 conferences, plans were outlined to use government funds to attack psychiatric drugs through the courts. Leaders in the ex-patient movement—including its more moderate wing—had for some time seen this as the next step. Jay Centifanti, the ex-patient who has written amicus briefs for the National Mental Health Consumers' Association, and now serves as a director of Pennsylvania's P&A program, told us:

> I've said for the last few years the right to refuse cases are beside the point. All they did was prove the drugs were dangerous. They raise societal consciousness about the damage the drugs were doing. But the real critical piece was the damage cases. That'll do more to change people's behavior than anything. That's the way our country works. Where dollars are involved people get real serious.[88]

Both in Oregon and Minnesota, NARPA's focus was on suits demanding damages for patients who developed tardive dyskinesia. Suits in this area are recent and thus far have been successful only against psychiatrists and hospitals charged with negligently prescribing or monitoring neuroleptics.[89] But at the 1988 NARPA conference, Breggin spoke of a billion dollar class action suit he had "engineered" against Smith, Kline and French (the makers of Thorazine), and said the lesson was "sue, sue, sue."[90]

Plans were unveiled for one of the state Protection and Advocacy agencies to bring a class action lawsuit on behalf of all mentally retarded persons who had been given neuroleptics,[91] and then use that money as a war chest to bring individual actions on behalf of mentally ill persons with tardive dyskinesia. Ralph Pittle, a Seattle lawyer organizing a major tardive dyskinesia suit against the drug companies, argued against class action suits when it came to the mentally ill.

> Every case has individual factors. . . . Maybe that means there should be thousands or hundreds of thousands of cases if it came to that. And if it puts the manufacturers and all of them out of business so be it.[92]

That this strategem could sentence vast numbers to permanent psychosis does not of course concern anti-treatment activists.

Pittle and others at the NARPA conferences realized that the transformation of liability law has opened up enormous thus far untapped possibilities for litigation in the area of psychiatric drugs.[93] In *Liability: the Legal Revolution and its Consequences,* Peter Huber describes how in the course of the last twenty years a totally new legal environment has been created, in which an $80 billion a year "tort tax" (equalling the total profits of the country's top 200 corporations) has been imposed through free-for-all liability litigation.[94] It is scarcely surprising that Pittle came to the mental health arena fresh from victories in the litigation that eliminated the Dalkon shield and drove the A. H. Robins company to bankruptcy.[95] He reported that he was setting up a special group within the American Trial Lawyers Association on tardive dyskinesia litigation. By 1989, the president of the Tardive Dyskinesia–Tardive Dystonia Association was not a patient, but an attorney whose practice was limited to personal injury cases.[96] (It is such a liability climate that accounts for clozapine being available in Europe—where Sandoz permits the patient's doctor to administer the blood test—at a cost of between $20 to $32 a week, while it costs three to four times as much in the United States, where Sandoz feels impelled to protect itself by providing its own stringent testing system.)

The National Institute of Mental Health, part of whose mission is to find a cure for the major mental illnesses, administers the funds being misused by Protection and Advocacy systems to promote the war on treatment. Angered by Breggin's ad hominem slanders at NARPA's 1988 conference, Dr. E. Fuller Torrey wrote a letter of protest to Lewis Judd, the director of NIMH, posing trenchant objections to the role NIMH has been playing.

> If this were the first time that federal funds administered by NIMH had been used to underwrite antipsychiatry in the United States, I would not be as concerned. It is, however part of an increasingly common pattern. . . .
>
> Is it appropriate for major support for antipsychiatry to be coming from the National Institute of Mental Health? Is it appropriate to use NIMH-administered funds to publicize positions directly antithetical to NIMH's professed interest in improving services and research for the seriously mentally ill? I doubt that most psychiatric professionals in the United States, nor families of the mentally ill, nor taxpayers, nor members of Congress, would say that it is.[97]

Indeed, so widespread is the misuse of P&A funds that Peter Breggin actually sees the *purpose* of P&As as engaging in the war against treatment. At the 1989 NARPA Conference he declared that the mentally disabled "need a little more help . . . being protected from psychiatry, which is why we have the P&A system, hopefully."[98]

In fueling the campaign to deny the very existence of the illnesses it is mandated to cure, NIMH violates the congressional intent that P&A funds be used to counter abuse and neglect of the mentally ill. As Ted Hutchinson points out, the mentally ill need protection from the ravages of disease and advocacy to *secure* treatment (not be deprived of it) as a key to admission to housing and rehabilitation programs. In so far as Protection and Advocacy programs obstruct and deny access to treatment, they exacerbate abuse and neglect of an already abandoned population.

PART V

Families as Mental Institutions

Chapter 12

The Right to Be Crazy

For the families of the mentally ill, the biggest shock of all is to discover that the law supports the inalienable right of their family members to be crazy. If a son or daughter becomes ill as a teenager, and is covered by a parent's insurance, in the initial phase of the illness he or she will in all probability be treated. But as the illness recurs, families feel the impact of the deranged legal system established by the mental health bar. They discover that unless an individual is "dangerous," he cannot be treated against his will. The Catch-22 is that the diseased organ is the brain, with the result that a very high proportion of the mentally ill do not recognize there is anything wrong with them. Their delusions are convincing and real to them, offering an explanation for their distorted perceptions of reality.

If the individual *is* judged to be dangerous, and is treated, he will in all probability be released from the hospital in a matter of days. Most demoralizing of all, even if someone is willing to enter a hospital voluntarily, most public hospitals will only accept him if they believe he satisfies the requirements for being admitted *against* his will, that is, meets the dangerousness standard.

Phyllis Vine decided to write her book, *Families in Pain,* when her cousin Joanna was discharged from the hospital after three days. Vine could not understand how someone who had been receiving messages from radios the previous week and living on the streets could be "well" enough to leave the hospital. She warned the psychiatrist that Joanna would not return for outpatient treatment. He only shrugged; "She is stabilized now." Vine explains that she wanted to find out about a mental

249

health system that permitted someone like Joanna to return to the streets as unprotected from the winter snow as she was from herself.[1]

Television producer Dan Weisburd describes taking his son David for an outpatient appointment with a psychiatrist who said: "Please, take David across the street and check him in. I've called and they have a bed for him." Weisburd says it is very difficult to talk his son into going into the hospital but David agreed this time, and was duly checked in. No sooner had Weisburd driven the long distance to his home when he had a call from David.

> "I'm on the corner of Westwood. The doctor on the floor said I had no business being there and checked me out." So I drove back to find this kid, he could have been sucking his thumb, like Linus. He had a blanket and a suitcase. One doctor is saying he has to be hospitalized, an acute hospitalization. The other is putting him out on the street.

Weisburd says such experiences are typical for families of the mentally ill and all those he knows have had similar ones.[2]

The Family Becomes the Institution

Today the family *is* the institution. It is estimated that 800,000 individuals suffering from schizophrenia and manic-depressive illness now live with their families, mostly their parents.[3] As psychiatrist John Talbott observes, families have become the doctors, the nurses, and the social workers.[4] But if the family has become, as one article put it bluntly, "the replacement for the ward staff,"[5] it is a staff without shifts, without backup, without the ability to enforce daily routines or medication compliance, without techniques of rehabilitation.

Don Richardson, former president of the family organization, the National Alliance for the Mentally Ill, has summed up the plight of many families: "You feel like you are the jailer and you feel you are also in jail."[6] When we interviewed them, Don and Peggy Richardson had been coping with the mental illness of one son for twenty years, of a second for almost eighteen. Says Don Richardson: "It seems like a hundred years." According to Dan Weisburd, who heads California's Alliance for the Mentally Ill: "Most of the families are destroyed. If you look at the divorce figures I'm sure they're much higher than in the population at large."[7]

Dan and Elaine Weisburd brought their brilliant and musically gifted son David—who had planned to become a psychiatrist—home from Harvard when he became ill. Home was a handsome contemporary house with a pool, a stone's throw from James Garner and Bob Hope in the elegant enclave of Toluca Lake in northern Los Angeles. Dan Weisburd describes what happened:

> We experienced every manner of disruption in our lives from violence to all sorts of things.... This place was becoming an asylum. It was a snakepit. It was impossible.... One night the lights go on. It's two in the morning. My wife rolls over, she's a deeper sleeper than I am. There's my son standing there with an eight-inch butcher knife. And he's trembling. "Dad, if you love me, speak to the police. I've got them on the other phone. I'm barricading myself in the bathroom. They're coming to kill me."
>
> I get on the phone with the police. They say, "Sir, are you aware that we get a dozen calls a day from this number, saying that his father is a PCP freak, he's going to kill him, he's mutilating the family?" And I said, well, *I'm* the PCP freak; my son is a mental patient. He's been in and out of hospitals and he's been having a bad night. I think maybe you should come out here and take him to the hospital because I'm scared for him and I'm scared for us.

Weisburd reports the police arrived—eight of them—and he came out of the house with David ten yards behind him. David insisted on bringing his knife. Weisburd continued:

> Two of the policemen had their service revolvers out, pointed at him, and all the lights were shining on him. The sergeant said, "Put down the knife, son, put down the knife." And he had the good judgment to put the knife down.... The sergeant took him and comforted him and came to me and said, "Sir, I can't take him to the hospital because he's fine now." And David said, "It's okay, Dad, they're not coming to kill me," and he came back to the house, snuggled up in a fetal position by his mom and went to sleep.

Weisburd concludes: "We have experienced things that are so bizarre that night was almost like just another one. What's coming tomorrow?"[8]

Even when day-to-day existence is not punctuated by police sirens shrieking to the door in the middle of the night, life with the chronically mentally ill can be almost unendurable. Randolph James, a dignified black career civil servant in Washington, D.C., shares his home with his paranoid schizophrenic daughter Alice. Alice had lived with her mother after the divorce of her parents, until her mother reached the breaking point and called the police to evict her daughter. James explains his decision to invite Alice to live with him: "At this particular time, I did not realize the seriousness of her illness and the extent of it. I thought that love would turn the whole thing around."

But as James soon discovered, in mental illness, love is not enough. He says: "I tried love, compassion, understanding." But Alice refused to take her medication.

> Alice will not do anything that she doesn't want to do. I'm the subject of constant verbal abuse, cursed out. In fact, I feel as if she doesn't live with me, I live with her. And it's an intimidating situation because of the fact it's a constant challenge to your patience.

There is no refuge in sleep; the strain of maintaining self-control goes on around the clock.

> What bothers me now is that one day I may lose my patience because if I say you can't do something and she does it—it's two o'clock in the morning and the radio is blasting and I say turn it down and she says no, it's your fault if you can't sleep and I say, I have to go to work, and she says, you can go late.

Urged by friends to end the painful chaos of his daily life by turning out his daughter, James cannot bring himself to act.

> I've picked up the phone so many times to call [the police], but then I get this mental picture of the homeless sitting out in front of these shelters. I see the people wandering the streets and I see her in that group, and I say well, maybe I can tolerate it a little longer.[9]

Testifying Against a Family Member

When families, desperate to obtain treatment, reluctantly initiate court hearings where they must testify against their children, they often obtain no help; they may even find they have made the situation worse. In 1986 James finally obtained a hearing on his daughter's mental state from the local Commission on Mental Health. There was an appointed lawyer for his daughter Alice (none for him) and two psychiatrists from St. Elizabeth's Hospital. Alice refused to participate voluntarily and two U.S. marshals had to handcuff her. At the hearing, James had the impression they were going to recommend some form of mandatory treatment for his daughter (whether in the hospital or outside it).

But two weeks later he received a notice that his petition for commitment had been dismissed on the ground that Alice was not dangerous. When she saw that, her father reports, she said triumphantly: "They didn't recommend anything—as *I* thought they would—so I'm not going to do a damn thing."[10]

Now in his early eighties, Edward Holder is a retired army officer who subsequently became the psychologist for a small college. He and his wife Ellen have repeatedly sought to commit their middle-aged schizophrenic sons, both of whom have lived on the streets of Washington, D.C. The Holders' son Arnold, a brigade commander in Korea, had almost finished his Ph.D in physics when he became ill and the younger son, Frank, was in law school when his illness began. The Holders never take a vacation in case they might be needed, never visit their two married daughters in California although they would love to see their grandchildren.

Holder described one of his efforts to commit Arnold:

> His shoes were worn off, he hadn't changed his clothing in years. And the [court] psychiatrist said, "I can't help that, he wanted to go [free]." And I said, "At least you could have told him to take the medication." And he said, "I don't believe in medication: I'm a psychoanalyst." That is what you get into with these hearings. I've been through fifteen of them. This doctor was assigned; they have a roster of them at the courthouse. Here's a guy who doesn't believe in medication and won't put people in the hospital and is working as a courtroom psychiatrist![11]

Subsequently, Edward Holder rented an apartment for Arnold as he had numerous times before. It didn't last. Arnold wasn't eating or even going to the bathroom; he was barely able to walk. In yet another commitment hearing, the petition was denied because Arnold wasn't "dangerous" and he returned to the streets, his preferred abode. "I'd like to bring suit someday," his father says bitterly. "He was unable to take care of himself."

Families discover to their initial incredulity that, under the current system, the authorities are not interested in how ill or in need of treatment their family member may be. At a 1988 workshop on how involuntary commitment worked in Philadelphia, the representative of the county mental health department admitted:

> One of the most difficult things to explain [to the family] is that someone being up all night and walking around all night and talking to a television set in response to voices coming out of the set obviously is in need of treatment. Unfortunately, they can do this for a month on end and they will not be committed because it is not committable behavior under the act. . . . And that the court does not want to hear [about such behavior] is

inexplicable to them. I have to tell the family unless you can tell me he tried to hurt somebody the court isn't going to want to hear it.

Another official of the department explained:

Even if what the person did was to say I'm going to kill you, ranting and raving at the top of his lungs, although it's a horrible thing for a family to go through, can the state come in and say you are not allowed to do that to the extent that we are going to put you into a hospital? . . . Because there are a lot of people who threaten to do things and never carry out the threat.

Rita Levine, the court-appointed attorney representing the patients at these hearings (and who was killed shortly afterward in a 1988 terrorist attack on an Israeli bus) affirmed at the workshop:

As much as I may say to myself this person really needs treatment, if he doesn't want to stay in a hospital, it's my job to do all I can to accomplish the end the person wants, even if the reason why they don't want to stay is that the voice of their dead grandmother is telling them they shouldn't go because they will be killed there. . . . My function there is to try and accomplish what this person wants.[12]

But families find there is no court-appointed attorney to represent *their* interests and *their* rights. Even if the individual meets the law's stringent criteria, the family may find he is released because the psychiatrist at the hearing is not prepared and becomes confused or angry when challenged by the patient's court-appointed attorney.[13]

The family discovers that need for treatment is legally irrelevant: only dangerousness counts.[14] Yet as we saw earlier, while psychiatrists can determine the presence of mental illness, they are not necessarily good prophets of dangerous behavior. Attorney and chairman of the Maryland Alliance for the Mentally Ill Penny Kostritsky points out the anomalies.

I was struck by articles in the Baltimore *Sun* recently. There's a Patuxent Institute here in the Department of Corrections that has been involved in rehabilitation. The newspaper said court testimony from psychiatrists about the status of these prisoners was very difficult because psychiatrists are unable to make a determination whether people are dangerous or not. And I thought isn't that interesting. That determination has to be made all the time in order to get treatment for people. On the one hand, you say you can't predict if the prisoner released on furlough is going to be dangerous but the threshold issue for getting treatment to someone is whether he is an imminent danger to self or others. It's just crazy; it's just so awful.[15]

Even Bruce Ennis, more responsible than any other single person for making dangerousness the sole standard, would not wholly disagree. He told us: "I've long been an advocate for the dangerousness standard for commitment, even though I think it's stupid—as a tactical device to limit the number of people who are involuntarily brought into the system...."[16]

Even if an individual passes the dangerousness standard, like Don Richardson's son Bill, he is likely to be whisked out of hospital so quickly that the patient has little benefit—and the family little relief. Bill Richardson was hospitalized twenty-six times in seven years in California. Says Don Richardson:

> The list of admissions to this place and that place has become two single-spaced typewritten pages.... Sometimes the period between discharge from hospital and readmission is only a few days, sometimes two or three weeks. Anyone looking at this list can see that something is wrong, unacceptably wrong.[17]

Joy Doyle reports that her daughter, also in California, was hospitalized six times in one six-month period in 1987, never long enough to become stable.[18]

In some states the family may find that involuntary commitment is an illusory option, no matter how severely ill their family member may be. Penny Kostritsky says that in Maryland very few people ever go through hearings because, on being taken to the hospital, the mentally ill person is told he can become a voluntary patient, retaining greater rights and avoiding locked wards. Most patients choose to become voluntary—and as voluntary patients they are then free to leave.

But this does not mean that voluntary patients are free to *stay*. The chronically ill who seek hospital care are routinely turned away, sometimes with tragic results. Angus McFarlane, after Western State Hospital in the state of Washington denied his request for admission, murdered an elderly couple living in his neighborhood. In New York City, Steven Smith, a black man living in shelters, murdered Dr. Kathleen Hinnant, newly married and pregnant, in her office at Bellevue. The summer before, he had vainly sought admission to the same hospital's psychiatric ward.[19]

Perils in Proving "Grave Disability"

Most states permit involuntary commitment in cases where an individual is dangerous to himself because he is unable to provide for his own most basic needs. But families who believe the manifest helplessness of the person they care for is warrant for treatment under the law find themselves at yet another dead end. Under the law in most states, as long as the family takes care of the individual, he is not gravely disabled, for his needs for food and shelter are being met. Even if the family cannot meet those needs because the individual starves himself, the road to treatment is not necessarily opened. Within a few weeks David Weisburd's weight sank from 155 to 119 lbs. Voices had told him that the life force is on the surface of food—and if he ate the life force, the world would perish. To save the world, he took only bread and water. Often a mentally ill person will stop eating because of paranoid fears of being poisoned.

At the Philadelphia workshop on commitment, the representative of the county mental health department explained:

> The way the law reads now, the doctor has to testify that if the behavior continues for a period of thirty days serious debilitation or death will result. That's a difficult thing to show. Even if someone has lost forty-five pounds in the last month, my first question is what did he weigh before.[20]

Even if the family, in its desperation, puts the person out on the street, he will probably not be eligible for treatment. The person who can survive on the streets is not disabled. The only way to prove grave disability conclusively is to die there.[21]

From Steam Grate to Harvard: The Case of "Billy Boggs"

Perhaps the most celebrated illustration of the patient liberation bar's use of the dangerousness standard to block treatment for the gravely disabled is the case of Joyce Brown, who became better known as "Billy Boggs," the name she called herself after a local television talk show host with whom she had become obsessed.

A secretary with the Human Rights Commission in New Jersey for ten years, Joyce Brown had lost her job as a result of mental illness compounded by drug addiction. Joyce was fortunate in that she came from a religious, middle-class cohesive black family. Her four sisters, each of them with responsible jobs and comfortable homes, took her in on a rotating basis after her disordered behavior led to her eviction from the shelter to which she had been discharged after a fifteen-day stay as a psychiatric patient in East Orange General Hospital.

Her sisters experienced the difficulties typical of life with the mentally ill. One of them told us: "It was like she owned your house. You weren't going to tell her what to do. . . . You were the boarder and she was the owner."[22] In the middle of the night she would come into her sister's bedroom in a rage, "arguing and yelling and swearing at an imaginary person."[23]

Her sister says:

> There was always the possibility of violence. . . . My daughter went down to iron a blouse and she stumbled. And Joyce started to scream and curse her and my daughter wasn't going to let her scream and curse her. Everyone was screaming and I knew if I hadn't been here somebody would have got hurt real bad.

It was in the aftermath of one of these chaotic eruptions that Joyce Brown disappeared.

> I let her stay here until one day my other sister just happened to stop by and I was glad because Joyce was all worked up in a frenzy, cursing and screaming and it was really wild. And my other sister said, if she really felt the way she appeared to about me, because she was really carrying on, I was this and that, "Well, why do you stay here if you feel that way?" And she grabbed her bags and left.

Deeply concerned when Joyce ceased coming for her Social Security checks, her sisters reported her missing to the police. In July 1987, one of the sisters received an abusive collect phone call from Joyce and with that as their sole lead, they went to every city shelter, as well as to Bellevue Hospital.[24] They were unaware that Joyce had taken up residence at 65th Street and Second Avenue, in front of Swensen's ice cream shop and restaurant.

There, Brown remained for nearly a year and a half, in front of a hot air vent built into the wall, clad at times only in a cotton blouse and skirt with socks on her feet and a sheet wrapped around her body.[25] She would urinate against the white brick wall of the Chemical Bank building on the corner and defecate on the street around the corner on the 65th Street side of the same building. She would rip up the money she panhandled, run into traffic, suddenly become agitated and explosive. Brown became particularly excited if a black man tried to help her. She would turn and lift her skirt, exposing her bare buttocks and shake them at the man, screaming "Kiss my black ass, you motherf . . . nigger, come kiss my black ass!"[26]

Project HELP, the city's outreach program to the mentally ill, tried to hospitalize Brown at least five times, but Metropolitan Hospital each time released her on the grounds she was psychotic but not "dangerous." After Mayor Koch decided the city would interpret "gravely disabled" more broadly, so that it was not necessary to be near death before intervention was possible, Brown became the first person to be picked up by Project HELP. Her identity was not known until her sisters saw her on television.

Joyce Brown became the test case the New York Civil Liberties Union had been looking for since 1985 when Mayor Koch, in its view, had first violated the civil liberties of the mentally ill by permitting them to be taken off the street on nights when the temperature dropped below freezing. The NYCLU's Robert Levy told us he considered mental health law his specialty and had taken on Bruce Ennis's former role in the organization.[27]

Along with the NYCLU's Norman Siegel, Levy sued for Brown's release, portraying her way of life in the court hearing as a rational, if deviant lifestyle. Did she urinate on the sidewalk? So did cabdrivers. Did she often tear up or burn the money she had begged? This was a symbolic gesture, akin to the burning of draft cards by anti-Vietnam war protesters. Had Project HELP on a number of occasions found fecal matter in the sheets with which she covered herself? There was no evidence this posed any danger to her well-being.[28] Similarly, Dr. Robert Gould, a psychiatrist called in by the NYCLU, testified that Brown's abusive language to passersby was not unlike that heard in the movies. As for the burning of money, Gould said coyly, "I put a lot of money in the stock market, and I hope Ms. Boggs doesn't think I was crazy for getting a burn there."[29]

Joyce Brown's sisters were horrified to discover what countless other families have learned: judges were not interested in their testimony, although they alone knew the history of Joyce's mental illness, which psychiatrists agree is crucial to an evaluation of the patient's present condition.

> The judge really didn't want to entertain anything I had to say. He said my knowledge of her was almost remote, although he didn't use that word remote; that she had been gone for a length of time so what I had to say was not really valid. . . . I was able to identify her but beyond that he didn't want to hear anything.

In a decision that columnist George Will described as impossible to caricature, Judge Lippmann ruled that Brown should be released to her steam grate. He accepted Joyce Brown's characterization of herself as "an experienced street professional." A former legal aid attorney, Lippmann, like her NYCLU attorneys, seemed to regard Brown as an abstraction through which to make political points. According to Lippmann: "Society, not Brown, was sick: the blame and shame must attach to us." He offered his hope that "the sight of her may improve us. By being an offense to aesthetic senses, she may spur the community to action."[30] Joyce's sisters were furious at this casual dismissal of Joyce as a human being. "If the judge's own wife or mother were on the streets, he would not stand for it. The streets are good enough for her, not for him or his kind."

The city appealed and in a split 3-2 decision, the appellate court overruled Judge Lippmann, permitting Brown's continued hospitalization.[31] Bruce Ennis was indignant.

> I personally had as much role in drafting the relevant portions of the mental hygiene law that was involved in that case as anyone in the country. I was on the New York State Commission to revise the mental hygiene law and I took a particular personal interest in those emergency commitment provisions and wrote them out myself and argued about them and negotiated with others on the committee and there were some changes and I can say from personal knowledge that it was not within the contemplation of those who wrote the mental hygiene law to apply it to people like Brown in her circumstances.[32]

Judge Lippmann's decision to release Brown, then, may have been technically "correct." But, if so, it demonstrates the irresponsibility of the state legislature in turning over to the patient liberation bar the drafting of legislation that determines the fate of the mentally ill.

If, on appeal, the commitment law did not achieve Ennis's purpose in this case, Joyce Brown nonetheless owed her release to the mental health bar. As we saw in Chapter 7, New York's highest court, the Court of Appeals, had followed the pattern of Massachusetts in the Richard Roe case, ruling (in Rivers v. Katz) that a patient had a right to refuse treatment unless found incompetent in a judicial proceeding. Because of that ruling, since Brown refused all medication, the hospital had to take her to court before it could treat her.

The judge ordered an independent evaluation and psychiatrist Francine Cournos recommended against involuntary treatment. She told us that, although she agreed Brown suffered from serious mental illness, she felt Brown had "an unusual degree of capacity."[33] Indeed, Brown was "competent" in the sense that she was articulate and coherent in the courtroom and able to state the benefits and side effects of medications.

As a result, whatever Cournos had recommended, under the law the judge had little choice but to rule Brown could not be treated against her will. Bellevue's spokesman declared that if the hospital could not treat her, there was no point in keeping her. The New York Court of Appeals, to which the NYCLU had appealed the case on the grounds that hospitalizing Joyce Brown violated state commitment statutes, dismissed it as moot.[34]

Calling herself a political prisoner, Brown went on to brief celebrity on national television and, an extraordinary spectacle, to lecture on "The Homeless Crisis" at a Harvard law school forum. Its solution, she said, was to build low-income public housing.[35] But although she now had a room at the Travelers', a single-room occupancy hotel for mentally ill women near the Port Authority bus terminal, her underlying illness had not been affected. Untreated, she was soon back on the streets, screaming and panhandling. She even returned briefly to Swensen's in January 1989. Her sister saw her on TV: "There was a shot of her . . . on the street corner outside of Swensen's yelling, screaming, cursing, and patting her behind. If you see a shot of her at Harvard and then see that you won't believe it's the same person."[36]

The NYCLU, most homeless advocates, and of course Joyce Brown herself insisted that her plight simply illustrated the absence of housing for the poor. However, her sisters point out that Joyce received monthly Social Security disability checks she had not picked up.

> She could have stayed at a motel or hotel or a room or something and she chose to stay on the street? With the cold and the snow? And the rain and the heat? No one in their right mind behaves like that—who has an option. And she had options.[37]

Because she now had a room at the Travelers', Joyce Brown benefited from Mayor Koch's program of taking some of the seriously mentally ill off the streets. Ironically, her lawyers took credit for her improved living conditions.[38]

Live Free—And Die

The consequences of Szaszian ideology-become-law for the mentally ill and their families is poignantly illustrated by the story of Sheila

Broughel, an early tragic victim of the changing standards of commitment. An Irish beauty, with blue eyes and long dark hair, Sheila was one of six children of a Connecticut claims supervisor, and grew up in a bustling, lively household. At Vassar she was a friend of one of the authors of this book (Virginia Armat). Upon graduation, complete with Phi Beta Kappa key, Sheila landed a coveted job at *The New Yorker*.

Gradually, her family recognized there was something wrong. In the summer of 1968, she complained to her brother that her New York apartment, a sunny walkup in the West Village, was bugged. One of her four sisters noticed "her personality changing. . . . There was also talk about poison, someone doing something to the water." One of her sisters told us: "My father was very upset at this time. He said 'Lala [her nickname], why don't you come home,' and she did."[39]

There began what her brother describes as "a long agonizing four years." Within three months, Sheila was very ill. Her mother insisted Sheila needed psychiatric care, but her father could not accept it. Mrs. Broughel says: "His beautiful, brilliant daughter. She was all right." And her sister explains:

> Our whole life growing up, he and Sheila would just intellectualize. . . . They would have wonderful conversations. I would never have dates—they would come to the house and end up talking with Dad and Sheila. The Civil War or the history of making pancakes. Everything you could possibly think of. . . . And Sheila was part of that. And I think that's what was shattering for my father. That circle was lost. Then of course having to put up with her as she was, which was like science fiction.

At one point Sheila locked her father out of the house, claiming he was not really her father.

In despair, refusing to admit his daughter was crazy, Sheila's father moved out of the house to live with his sisters. One of his daughters says: "I went over to see him and his eyes . . . my father used to have the twinkliest eyes. He was very funny, witty, just such a live wire, and it was like looking at a dead person. He was so affectionate and he wasn't affectionate. Just destroyed."

When he came back, says Sheila's older sister Brenda, "he was in a lot of pain emotionally," and he began to fall apart.

> The scene was always my father sitting silent in the rocking chair, and Sheila would be sitting on the couch in her sunglasses giggling and her hair in a knot. . . . It was a pathetic scene because we had a very social house and we always had lots of people in and out and all of a sudden it

stopped. No one wanted to have anyone at the house and it was a very morbid existence.

Sheila's sister says there was constant friction. "My mother would say 'Jim, look, this is not right, she's sick.'" She knew from experience with her schizophrenic brother what was wrong. Finally, in 1971, Sheila's father came around, and the family began encounters with a legal system as crazed as their daughter.

Over the next two years Sheila was in and out of mental hospitals. She was repeatedly released within a couple of days through the action of attorneys who insisted she was not dangerous. Twice she was represented (without pay) by the firm of Michael Avery in Connecticut (then in the news because it was defending the Black Panthers), on other occasions by the federally funded Hudson Valley Legal Services and by Cambridge-Somerville Legal Services. Her sister explained: "Sheila was always very resourceful. She had her intellectual faculties intact; it was just that everything else was out of kilter."

Nor was it only Sheila's family—and ultimately Sheila herself— who fell victim to these champions of "civil rights." Sheila's second admission to Norwich State Hospital was an emergency. Home for the summer, she developed a strong attachment to the family poodle and when the dog died, insisted it be buried in the backyard, which state health regulations did not permit. After a warden had taken away the dog, Sheila headed off in a cab to halt the scheduled cremation. The police had to stop her; she became violent; and Sheila's parents appealed to the family doctor, whose children had grown up with their children, to sign commitment papers.

But seeking to help Sheila obtain the treatment she needed proved costly for this family friend. Technically he was in violation of the law because he had not examined Sheila within the past forty-eight hours. Sheila summoned her attorney from the Avery firm upon her admission to the hospital and to the horror of her family, the attorney sued their doctor, freezing all his assets. The malpractice suit Sheila's attorney filed against him was still pending at the time of her death.

From then on, Sheila spent part of the time at home, part, as her mother put it, "just roaming." She refused all anti-psychotic medication on the grounds that "they were trying to poison her." At home, says Sheila's sister: "She always wore white, white sneakers, white pants. She wore her white linen dress and her sunglasses and sat in the living room staring most of the time." Then she would take off; her mother describes how night after night she would wonder where Sheila was and what was happening to her. The anxiety she felt for her severely ill, vulnerable, recalcitrant daughter was terrible. The day of her funeral, Sheila's sister remembers that her mother took both her hands and said: "At least we know where she is tonight."

In her wanderings Sheila would periodically be hospitalized, once after being arrested at the New Haven YWCA. Disruptive behavior led to hospitalizations when she went to Vassar and on another occasion to Cambridge (where she created a commotion in a restaurant). At Vassar she called Richard Rovere, a writer for *The New Yorker* who lived nearby, demanding that he agree Vassar was evil and ought to be blown up right away. She would go into the hospital with long lists of phone numbers, and be out in a few days. Her sister Brenda, blond, but otherwise strikingly like Sheila, says:

> We knew deep in our gut the outcome was going to be tragic. It was a situation where she was outwitting whoever was trying to help her at every turn. And that was it. Her rights as a sick person were such that she was able to be prevented from getting the help she needed. . . . What the system did was that it reinforced her paranoia instead of reinforcing the positive things that would come out of a methodical program to help her get back on her feet.

Sheila's mother summed up her own experience of those dreadful years: "Under the laws no one can help anyone else."[40]

Finally, in February 1973, Brenda, who was living outside Washington, D.C., received a call from her sister at Union Station to come and get her. Brenda called her mother and a psychiatrist in Connecticut who told her not to bring Sheila to her house, that she would not be able to handle her, and to put her on a plane home. She picked Sheila up, but when she could not persuade her to board a plane, installed her at the Marriott Hotel, near the airport, telling her she would pick her up after work the following day. Once home, Brenda called her minister who promised to help her put Sheila into a hospital if she could not be persuaded to enter the car when Brenda came for her.

When Brenda arrived home from the school where she taught late in the afternoon of the following day, two detectives were waiting for her with pictures of Sheila's mutilated corpse. The police had found Brenda through the key to the hotel room they found buried in Sheila's clothes—all imported, so that they initially thought she was a foreigner. Sheila had not stayed at the Marriott but returned to Union Station. There she apparently met the man—never apprehended—who raped and murdered her. Her body was found in a garage a few blocks away. Brenda had to identify the body. "I recognized it by the teeth. It was the only thing I could recognize. She had forty stab wounds in her head and chest. For about five years I woke up every night, seeing that."

It is not clear how long Sheila was at Union Station. Brenda is certain she called soon after her arrival and was there for no more than a day. A subsequent article in the *Washington Post* claimed she had been there a week, "spending most of her time standing outside by the entrance, in the same spot, even at night and in the rain."[41] Brenda did not know then that on the eve of her sister's death she had been taken to St. Elizabeth's Hospital—but released.

Only hours before her death, Paul Hodge, a *Washington Post* reporter who was at the station to interview travelers stranded by a Penn Central railroad strike, took her to St. Elizabeth's Hospital. (According to Hodge, a police officer at the station told him she was "crazy," but there was nothing he could do because she was not dangerous.) There she was interviewed by Dr. Llewellyn Bigelow, who asked her to sign herself in voluntarily. But Sheila wanted to go "home" to Union Station. Because she was not "dangerous," Dr. Bigelow was therefore unable to detain her and the reporter took her back to Union Station, which she called "home."[42]

Even after Sheila's murder, the family's ordeal was not over. Reporters camped out at Brenda's home and school; the funeral in Connecticut had to be held secretly while the reporters were having lunch. Equally cruel, Paul Hodge wrote extensively and erroneously in the *Washington Post* about Sheila, portraying her as the victim of parents who were "cold and impersonal and didn't like her."[43] In fact, of course, the deep love of her parents, her brother, and her sisters could not save Sheila from her untreated disease and an insane legal system that blocked any hope for her recovery.

And what of the attorneys who had repeatedly "freed" Sheila? Like Bruce Ennis after the death of Catherine Henley, they were self-righteous. Michael Avery said that lawyers in his firm

> discussed this in the office here . . . how would we feel if something like this happened. Suppose she ends up in an alley we said. . . . Still, I think we made the right decision in working to keep her out of hospitals. She was not dangerous and she passionately wanted to be free. That's what it means to have a free society, not to lock people up all the time.[44]

But Sheila was not free. Freedom entails the capacity for rational choice. Without that capacity, the freedom physically to move about—which is how the patient liberation bar defines freedom—is meaningless. The public recognizes this in the case of the severely retarded and the victims of Alzheimer's disease, whose freedom to wander as impulse takes them is not (yet) enshrined as a sacred civil liberty. Sheila's only possibility of freedom lay in treatment, and this was denied her by the attorneys who took her out of its reach before it had a chance to be effective.

Joy Doyle, whose efforts to obtain treatment for her daughter have failed repeatedly, argues passionately:

> Can you imagine an ambulance driver or a policeman responding to a heart attack emergency looking down at the victim, shaking his head, and saying, "Well, there is nothing we can do. It's no crime to have a heart attack, you know. This person has smoked too much, is overweight, has not exercised, and there is nothing I can do. If he wants treatment, he will have to voluntarily agree to go to the hospital. Because he is unconscious, we cannot provide any assistance."[45]

Moreover, unless we want to live in a Szaszian world in which the "solution" is for families to repudiate and cast out members who most need their care, the rights of family members too must weigh in the balance. Looking back, Sheila Broughel's brother says: "What we had was a four-year ordeal that totally drained the family, killed my father ultimately." Brenda sums up the family's sense of betrayal: "The people who are living a normal life . . . I mean in our family there were five other children and two adults. Their lives should have been worth something. But they weren't."

The Growth of NAMI

In the years of Sheila's illness, as her mother says: "There was nowhere to go at that time to find out what to do in such a situation." Many thousands of other families were going through similar experiences, as hospitals that had once kept patients for years, released them in a matter of days—if, under the new laws, they were committed at all. In despair, families banded together. They were prepared to face the public stigma of mental illness as the price of obtaining mutual support and securing a voice in public policy.

In September 1979, just under 300 relatives, mostly parents, formed the National Alliance for the Mentally Ill at a meeting in Madison, Wisconsin. Since, NAMI has become one of the fastest-growing organizations in the country; within a decade it has expanded to include over a thousand local affiliates in all fifty states and the District of Columbia, and over 80,000 members. In its role as a support to families, NAMI has been of tremendous benefit. As Penny Kostritsky puts it:

> Everyone is devastated when this happens to a family member. I simply withdrew from the world; don't talk to me about it; I would break into tears if anyone asked me about my son. . . . The wonderful thing was to go to the first AMI meeting and realize, there are lots and lots and lots of people, perfectly normal people. Don't forget we came at the family-bashing period. It was our fault. And you went through agony. What did I do to cause this? Wait a minute. You're wrong. We didn't do it. That's the greatest relief that can ever come to people. We didn't do it.[46]

The family groups are not only comforting but energizing. Don Richardson explains:

> By linking up and talking to each other the similarities are astounding and pretty soon you wind up saying there must be a better way, there just has to be a better way.[47]

But NAMI has made little progress in changing the system that maintained Sheila Broughel's "rights" at the price of her life. At NAMI's 1987 national conference, flyers were handed out, written by individual families describing their plight in trying to help sons and daughters whose situation had in no way improved in the fourteen years since Sheila Broughel died. As one flyer put it, "Families cannot stand the stress without help!" In it a mother described her son:

> He has been brutalized by the police in North Carolina; picked up unconscious and his life saved by the police in Texas and later in Nevada; hit on the head with baseball bats by local people in Virginia; put in jail for sleeping on the beach in Massachusetts and then released from the hospital on the condition that he leave the state; wandered through Nevada, Utah, and California without money; lived for months in summer and then winter rains on the streets in Washington state; starved in Florida and also in hospital . . . (he does not eat when he is off meds).

Yet another flyer described a young woman whose fate was different from Sheila's only in the absence of publicity.

> After reporting my daughter missing to all of the private and public organizations for the mentally ill and also after contacting many police and missing persons offices, a friend of mine did her own investigating. Within one day she had discovered that my daughter had been brutally murdered and her body laid in a ditch for two months. Dental x-rays

identified that the body was my daughter's in May 1985. . . . I heard of her death in January 1986.

There have been occasional victories. At NAMI's 1988 conference Bill Ryan, a young Kansas attorney, described how, in cooperation with family groups, he had drafted legislation to expand commitment criteria, which the state legislature passed in 1986. The new law made commitment possible when severe mental illness, coupled with substantial incapacity for self-care, created a likelihood of harm.[48]

Prior to the law's passage, in Kansas, as in most other states, the family's only hope for obtaining treatment for their relative was to go through the ordeal of standing up in open court and in the presence of the vulnerable person who depended on them for survival declare they were going to put him on the street. (As one parent put it: "The attorney tells you, that's what you have to say.") One father described his relief after the law was changed. When his son, who lived at home, began to deteriorate, with the cooperation of the local mental health center he and his wife presented testimony to demonstrate this. Under the new law, he could rise in court and tell his son that he would be welcome to come home, after treatment.

The Kansas law survived the familiar array of opponents. No expert on anti-psychiatry, Ryan nonetheless accurately grasped that the opposition to his bill was based on what he termed three fundamental issues.

> There are many opponents who do not believe mental illness exists. . . . They feel severe mental disorder is a myth; it's been made up; therefore they have to rely on violence. There are also those who feel treatment is somehow equated with punishment and that incarceration and treatment are one and the same so only the violent deserve incarceration. And there are those who think having someone make a decision for you is always wrong. That's the bottom line.[49]

Of course opponents did not raise these ideological objections in their effort to defeat the bill. In the workshop, Ryan recounted the kind of arguments that almost defeated it: "This law will allow parents to commit their unpopular or underachieving adult children. You laugh. That was real."

Laws like the one passed by the Kansas legislature, relaxing commitment standards without sacrificing due process protections, have been introduced elsewhere, but for the most part they have been defeated by the familiar alliance of ex-patient groups, civil libertarian attorneys, and various organizations of mental health professionals. In some states, the family groups have themselves been ambivalent, fearing that easier commitment standards will increase hospital costs and make provisions for the mentally ill in the community, in most places already scandalously inadequate, even worse.

Did NAMI Create a Frankenstein? The P&A System

In 1986 NAMI supported legislation that makes it substantially *less* likely the mentally ill will receive the treatment they urgently need, whether in hospitals or in the community. NAMI took the decisive role in lobbying for federal creation of Protection and Advocacy (P&A) systems for the mentally ill (the program already existed for the developmentally disabled). Unfortunately, as seen in Chapter 11, P&As for the mentally ill, staffed largely by the mental health bar, militant ex-patients, and anti-psychiatric patient advocates, in many states operate on precisely the set of assumptions that Bill Ryan identified as underlying the opposition to changing the commitment law in Kansas. Indeed, families have found that in most states, as Penny Kostritsky laments, the P&A "isn't accessible to families."[50] Moreover they have found that many of the P&A staff see treatment itself as an abuse from which the patient needs protection.

Carmen Johnson, the president of Texas AMI, and in 1988 the only family member on the advisory committee of the Texas Protection and Advocacy agency, described to us how the new program, in which families had invested so much hope, was being misused in Texas.

> One reason I was appointed was that our then [AMI] president made a huge brouhaha. P&A did not want a family member on the advisory board. This was in 1987. They had already created a large board of twenty-seven or thirty people, most of them recovering mentally ill people. . . . I immediately asked all the wrong questions. I'll never forget the first meeting when lawyers were holding forth at great length . . . and I said is the purpose of this agency to advocate for the best interests of the mentally ill? And the civil rights lawyer who was the most prominent civil rights lawyer in our state turned on me with great righteous anger and said "No, we advocate for the *current interests* of the mentally ill."[51]

Johnson notes that according to the Texas P&A board *the right to refuse treatment is the chief "current interest" of the mentally ill.*

Often, P&As pursue ideological preferences of their staff members, advocating for the "expressed" wishes of selected clients—often in direct opposition to the best interests of those clients. Johnson holds her state's P&A directly responsible for one young woman's death.

Their hands are red with blood. A mother called the P&A agency and said her daughter was threatening suicide and wanted to get out of the state hospital. The P&A agency is hostile to families so a staff person went over to the San Antonio state hospital, spoke to that girl, ascertained that she really did wish to leave, represented her current wishes, got her out of the hospital, and to the mother's horror, the girl went out and committed suicide. And that was reported at our advisory committee, before they realized who I was, as a successfully closed case. My mouth dropped open.[52]

The anti-ECT stand taken by every single P&A is another example of ideological preferences of anti-psychiatric activists subverting the needs of the mentally ill for effective treatment. As Carmen Johnson points out: "As families, if you recognize mental illness as a pathological condition of the brain, then in fact a whole different level of rights come into play, foremost among them the right to treatment."[53]

Thus, the very P&A agencies NAMI believed would help families navigate are pushing them even deeper into the labyrinth.

Chapter 13

The Specter of Violence

I N addition to the chaos that is a normal feature of life with the chronically mentally ill, some families must also endure a constant fear of violence. Most mentally ill persons are not violent; rather they are withdrawn, isolated, fearful, easy marks for brutal strangers. But there is a segment of the mentally ill—particularly when untreated—at risk of committing violent acts against themselves or others, often both.

For the National Alliance for the Mentally Ill, the issue of violence presents a painful dilemma. Serving as alternative institutions, families are far and away the most frequent targets of violence by a mentally ill member. Yet one of the goals of the organization is to combat the very high stigma that attaches to mental illness.[1] Insofar as the public thinks of the mentally ill as berserk killers—images fostered by films like *Psycho,* and the steady stream of newspaper articles on murder sprees by "former mental patients"—stigma is increased.

Moreover, that stigma has important practical consequences. NAMI seeks increased community services for the mentally ill, including group homes and outpatient programs. The kinds of safe, stable neighborhoods where families would like their mentally ill members to live offer stiff resistance to such programs. Since the fear of violence largely animates that resistance, NAMI understandably wishes to deny that there is a genuine basis for that fear.

Don Richardson, with two mentally ill sons who have been imprisoned for violent assaults—one with a knife against a stranger, the other with a hammer against his mother—feels this is a mistake.

To say the mentally ill are no more dangerous than the general population is a statement all of us family members have been parroting for years

270

because we try hard to break the stigma. . . . But I think in our intensity to reduce stigma the Alliance for the Mentally Ill is also losing a lot of credibility. . . . Out of the mentally ill population there is no question that there is a segment that is much more violent and to deny that is just reducing the credibility of our movement.[2]

For Richardson, the reasons lie in the nature of the illness, which impairs, or as he puts it "deters" judgment. Richardson notes that when you add alcohol and drug addiction—each of which also impairs judgment—a person is even more susceptible to homicidal actions. Large numbers of the mentally ill suffer from these combined impediments to judgment, for a third or more have a "dual diagnosis," also abusing alcohol or drugs. In part this represents an effort at "self-medication." Jay Centifanti, the brilliant attorney who nearly murdered his wife on a Philadelphia train, drank heavily and used street drugs in an effort to control his mood swings. "I took drugs which made it worse. . . . I think it opened some doorways in my mind that would better have been left closed."[3]

Mental Illness and Violence—What the Statistics Show

In minimizing the importance of violence, NAMI has cited a substantial number of studies showing lower arrest rates for mentally ill persons than for the general population. Indeed, *all* studies conducted *in the first half of this century* show that mental hospital patients were then less likely to commit violent acts than the general population as measured by either arrest or conviction rates. However, these studies date from the period when most of the mentally ill were sequestered in state hospitals, where they could scarcely commit crimes in the community. (On the other hand, violence was extremely common on the wards prior to anti-psychotic medications. The more the right to refuse treatment is recognized, even in hospital settings, the more such Bedlamite violence can be expected to increase.)

But studies in the era of deinstitutionalization provide a different picture, *showing consistently higher arrest rates for mental patients, and higher rates for violent crime.* And while individual studies can be, and have been, faulted, the pattern of findings is too consistent for serious challenge. One California study compared arrest rates for ex-patients for several years before and after the Lanterman-Petris-Short Act went into effect in 1969, drastically cutting down the number of long-term patients in state hospitals. The number of ex-patients arrested for nonviolent crimes tripled and for violent offenses more than tripled in the post LPS period. Overall, ex-patients were arrested for violent crimes at nine times the countywide rate. Arrest rates of women patients exceeded that of the female population thirteen fold.[4]

Across the country, in New York, a study of arrest rates in Bellevue Hospital's catchment area found the arrest rates of ex-patients higher than those of the general population in the same area as well as the general population in 4,600 U.S. cities.[5]

Moreover, the studies bear out Richardson's commonsense perception: mental patients disproportionately commit acts revealing lack of judgment or self-control. A 1977 Wyoming study found arrest rates for male mental patients were only modestly larger than those for males generally, except for violent crime, where the patient rate was three times higher.[6] A 1978 New York study found that for a group of patients released in 1973 the arrest rate for murder, manslaughter, and assault was 12.03 per 1000, compared to a non-patient rate of 3.62.[7] A four-year follow-up of over 1,100 patients released from twelve VA psychiatric hospitals found their arrest rate exceeded that of the general population for homicide, aggravated assault, and robbery (but was below that of the general population for burglary, auto theft, larceny, and rape.)[8]

When alcohol and drug abuse coexist with mental illness, impairment of judgment is even greater—and so is the rate of violent crime. In the Bellevue catchment area study the authors found that alcohol and drug-dependent mental patients were twice as likely to be arrested as the other patients.[9]

Authors of a study of psychiatric admissions to four New Jersey state hospitals argue that *arrest records underestimate the prevalence of violence*. The study found that in 36% of admissions, some form of violent behavior had precipitated hospitalization. Yet if only arrest rates were used, the incidence of violence would have appeared only one-fortieth as great, since only three patients in the sample had been arrested.[10] Of course, given the dangerousness standard for commitment, the patient's violence might well have been exaggerated to secure admission. Moreover, the chronically ill who are not violent—and therefore less likely to be admitted to hospitals—are underrepresented in such a study. Recognizing these limitations, the authors nonetheless felt justified in calling their study: "Fear of the Mentally Ill: Empirical Support for the Common Man's Response."

Living with the Fear of Violence

While the public worries about the relatively rare spectacular incident where there are random victims—the Laurie Dann who shoots six children in an elementary school class in a wealthy Illinois community, or the Sylvia Seegrist who opens fire in a suburban Philadelphia shopping mall—for families of the mentally ill, fear of violence can be a grinding undertone of daily life.

A standing-room-only workshop on violence at the 1987 NAMI conference thus offered a series of practical ways to cope with violence and the threat of violence in the home. Panelists suggested ways to avoid or terminate arguments, while acknowledging that sometimes a mentally ill person makes unreasonable demands that make conflict unavoidable. (One common pattern is to make constant demands for excessive amounts of money.) When a potentially violent family member had to be gainsaid, a panelist advised: "Remember to always keep your back to the door—so you have an exit in case you are threatened by your loved one." While the advice sounded low key and practical in the framework of a workshop, it is hard to imagine a worse prospect than having to remember to keep your back to the door in the sanctuary of your own home.

There are usually portents of violence, but the law, with its insistence on overt dangerous acts, often forces the family to wait until it is too late. Don Richardson says:

> When you've lived with this as long as most of us have you can see the signs begin to come up just like red lights flashing and the way the commitment laws are, there's not a thing you can do about it if they won't voluntarily get the help. You just have to watch them disintegrate and fall deeper and deeper into the pit until they crash and it's only at that time that you can get some help for them. We've often thought of it like a runaway train going down the track and there's not a thing that anyone can do until it crashes.[11]

Joy Doyle describes her life after her daughter threatened to kill her.

> I had to cease all contact with her. I now have an answering machine at home and a restraining order. This leaves her without any contact, and it leaves me feeling grief, sorrow, anger, and frustration. I love my daughter but I have no way to help her through those difficult times when she is not well enough to control herself but not sick enough to fall under the guidelines of the current statutes. She has been repeatedly beaten and raped when she has been out of control. . . . Under the SYSTEM, I am powerless to intervene.[12]

In practice, the dangerousness standard does little to protect the family from a member they know is becoming dangerous. Penny Kostritsky told us of the plight of a Maryland family who had become the foster family for a Vietnamese boy who subsequently became mentally ill.

> This young man had been threatening by vicious telephone calls to the point the family had actually moved out of the house and moved into a motel and she [the foster mother] signed for an emergency evaluation on December 5. He was picked up, taken to the hospital, and that same night when she called the hospital she was told he was going to be released. And that family goes back into terror again.[13]

Calling herself Jane Doe, the sister of a mentally ill man wrote in to the *New York Times* concerning her "daily fear of the telephone call that will tell me my 47-year-old brother has killed my 84-year-old father, himself or some bystander." She describes the hospitalizations of her brother (whom she calls Jason) followed by almost immediate release.

> Jason lived with my father, a widower, until recently. In his last several attacks—all following his refusal to take his medication—he physically assaulted my father and destroyed his furnishings.
>
> Several months ago, my father obtained a court order enabling him to commit my brother to a hospital. My father told the hospital officials that Jason could not return to live with him. However, after five days the hospital advised Jason to go to a clinic for medication (which he refused to do) and released him.
>
> He managed to find an apartment near my father's. Three weeks ago, Jason was arrested after neighbors called the police because he had gone into a rage and smashed a window in his apartment. The police released him the next morning. He lost control again, and this time the police sent him to the "crisis center" at a local hospital which released him less than 24 hours later. . . .
>
> So my brother is once again at large, enraged at my father, terrorizing the neighbors. He is a sick, violent individual, filled with hatred, not the kind, thoughtful, intelligent brother I once knew and loved. One day, he will harm himself or others. My father, heartbroken over the fate of his only son is Jason's chief "enemy." I am probably next on his list, as are the neighbors who call the police in self-defense.[14]

Jane Doe describes an all too familiar pattern. Her brother responds to medication, and once he is hospitalized and medicated is no longer tormented by his delusions and regains self-control. No sooner is he released than he stops taking medication, and the cycle is repeated. Those around Jason live in growing fear as they watch him sink deeper into psychosis—the "red lights flashing" of Don Richardson's metaphor—but can do nothing until the next crash, which may take any one of them with him.

Twenty-five-year-old Sylvia Seegrist took ten people with her when she crashed. Clad in military fatigues, seeing herself as a heroine who would save the world's energy supply, Sylvia opened fire with a rifle in the Springfield shopping mall blocks from her parents' home in suburban Philadelphia. Three of those she shot died.

Hospitalized twelve times over a nine-year period, Sylvia had given ample prior evidence that she was dangerous. Testimony during her trial showed that in the previous four years Sylvia was quoted hundreds of times in medical records saying "she felt like getting a gun and killing people." She had called the crisis center repeatedly with similar warnings. Indeed, her mother had found a small, loaded, .25 caliber automatic pistol in Sylvia's apartment during one of her hospitalizations, which police discovered she had bought at a pawn shop.[15] When, after her release from the hospital, her mother asked her why she kept the loaded gun, the unemotional reply was: "I bought it because I thought about suicide and about killing you and Dad."

Although Sylvia failed to carry out that idea, three of her last hospitalizations followed violence against her mother. On one occasion she almost strangled her mother on the parking lot of an auto-tag agency in Springfield. That earned Sylvia twenty-one days in the hospital. The longest of her twelve hospitalizations followed the stabbing of a young woman psychologist. Once released, Sylvia was free to do as she pleased, and it rarely pleased her to take the medications that controlled her symptoms. There was one effort to place her in a residential program; she was told to leave within a month because she repeatedly threatened another resident.

According to Mrs. Seegrist, the week before her murderous rampage, Sylvia

> was completely out of touch with reality—continuously agitated, vitriolic, restless, unable to concentrate or even comprehend questions directed to her. "You," she would screech, pointing an accusing finger at me, eyes ablaze with scorching anger, "you gave me birth. . . . You will be lucky if someday you don't die by my hand."[16]

The very day of the shooting, Sylvia called her mother who told her she needed "a rest and supervised medication." Sylvia's reply was to shout, "You bitch, don't you ever mention medication or hospitalization to me again. . . . I am an adult and independent. You have no right to interfere with my life."

As her mother summed up:

> Except for brief periods, Sylvia had the right to decide on her own treatment, or choose no treatment at all. We saw our daughter's illness progress, but were defenseless. It seemed to us that she had all rights except one. Because she denied her illness, and resisted treatment, Sylvia did not have the right to get well.[17]

The Right to Be Crazy Though Proven Dangerous

In prison, Sylvia Seegrist now takes her medication willingly; once Mrs. Seegrist told us that when a young doctor wanted to reduce the dose, Sylvia even called her in panic to protest.[18] Yet incredibly, as Don and Peggy Richardson have discovered, in many states the right to refuse treatment continues in the prison setting.

The Richardson's youngest son Bill had already been hospitalized over thirty times when Don Richardson was elected president of NAMI. Richardson had gone East to be installed in his new post and Peggy was to join him there. Bill, living in a board and care home at the time, was scheduled to move to an independent apartment and start on a work program. Don Richardson recalls that his wife said: "He's doing so well and we're going to be gone for awhile, why don't I invite him and his friend over to have dinner."

What the Richardsons did not know was that Bill had stopped taking medication six weeks before. Earlier that year they had finally succeeded in arranging for Bill to have injections of the anti-psychotic drug, Prolixin, rather than depending on the pills, which, as Don Richardson says, "he'd take when he felt like it and go off when he felt like it." But without telling them, the young doctor who was taking care of Bill had acceded to his request to return to pills—and predictably, he had ceased to take them.

Peggy Richardson describes what happened:

> I was fixing dinner and the boys were out in back smoking because I don't like smoke, and then I was cleaning up, doing the dishes and going to drive them back down to where they lived. . . . Anyway I woke up that night at midnight in the hospital. I didn't ever hear, see, or know that he had struck me but I had three skull fractures and a broken rib, a tooth knocked out.

Bill had gone out to the garage, taken a hammer, and bludgeoned her from behind as she was doing dishes. Luckily, Bill's friend came, saw what was happening and phoned for an ambulance.

As for Bill, Peggy Richardson reports he told her he had rescued her:

> "When I finally realized what was happening, I saved your life. I gave you mouth to mouth resuscitation. . . . " He said it was voices—command hallucinations is what the doctor called it. It's really incredible. He sat on the lawn and called out to the neighbors "I tried to kill my mom." As if that was something to brag about.

Don Richardson recalls being summoned home and being pulled aside by the doctor who told him: "Now Mr. Richardson, we really do not expect your wife to live through the night." Peggy Richardson survived, but now has a metal plate in the back of her head.

The Richardsons' subsequent experiences have been almost as bizarre as the events of that night:

> The public defender who was assigned to Bill said he would absolutely not let him plead "not guilty by reason of insanity," which would immediately have put him in the hospital. Why? Because he could be in the hospital for the rest of his life. It [the length of hospital stay] is determined by the wellness of the person. And we said, "Well isn't that what we want? We want him to get well and not be out where he can hurt Peggy or somebody else." And he said that's not my job. I'm here to defend him.

In the end the attorneys plea bargained and instead of attempted murder the charge was assault with a deadly weapon. Bill was sentenced to six years in prison.

But of course Bill didn't belong in prison; he belonged in a mental hospital. The Richardsons had lobbied for several years for a bill to allow a mentally ill person to be moved from the forensic unit of the jail system into a hospital. Don Richardson says: "Little did we know it would be our son who would benefit." Yet while they are pleased with the care Bill receives, they have discovered that even now the mental health bar ensures their son's right to psychotic thought. Despite his attempt to murder his mother, Bill has the right to refuse medication. Don Richardson recounts their frustration: "When he is stable he's just the most lovable guy anyone will ever know, and then he'll take himself off the meds and he becomes a monster."

In the periods when he refuses medication, which he will do, for example, to "punish" them if they go on a trip, "he'll call and threaten again. He'll say 'I may not have killed you last time but wait until I get out of here.'" Yet once back on medication, says Richardson, "when we go there, there's so much love and affection and you see this and you remember what happened and the jigsaw puzzle just doesn't fit together and that is what this illness is."

For all their sense of humor (in recounting their experiences they can laugh at the absurdity of some of the most painful of them), the Richardsons are, as they put it, "very apprehensive." They cannot see that their son is any better. He still has not accepted his illness or his need for medication. Yet when we talked to the Richardsons two years of their son's sentence were up, and he was seeking to be transferred back from the hospital to the jail, because his sentence could then be cut in half for good behavior. They faced the possibility that Bill could be out within a year. Don Richardson told us: "I've said more than once that when he is released we're going to just disappear. We're going to get into a fortress somewhere."[19]

Richardson believes families, for their own and others' protection—as well as to protect the mentally ill from themselves—should not gloss over violent incidents that fall short of constituting a felony. Richardson says: "I've been preaching, which has not made me too popular, and encouraging families to make a police report, don't go ahead and try and protect your son or daughter." Richardson notes:

> There's a tremendous denial. Few of these acts of violence are ever really reported. When Bill pushed my sister, who is crippled, a couple of times down in anger, when a friend of ours in Boston, their son pushed her down the stairs, two flights of stairs, they're never reported as violence, they're reported as a symptom of the illness, so the whole record of violence is so skewed you really wonder are we getting the picture. . . . You pull a person's hair and kick him in the groin and pinch him and punch him, to me those are violent acts because they are so frightening. . . . One mother said her daughter got one of those squeezers for garlic and broke her finger, but that was not an act of violence for the police because she did not make a police report on it.

Richardson believes it is important for families to report these things so that if the violence escalates, there will be a record that will prevent subsequent serious acts of violence from being treated too lightly by the courts. His own son, says Richardson, was given the minimum sentence first because he admitted the crime and second because he had no prior record of violence. "We thought through why did we not report these things. If we had made a police report, that would have been part of the record and would perhaps have influenced the court that would have seen this [action] was not just spur of the moment." Another member of the NAMI board, says Richardson, recently had an experience similar to his own: his son came into his parents' bedroom and stabbed his father three times, almost killing him. He received a very small sentence.[20]

The Richardsons were fortunate in that Peggy survived. There are families who live in terror of the violent mentally ill person they care for, and have their worst fears fulfilled. At thirty-seven, Nick Gavrilou dominated his parents in the confines of their apartment in the Flatbush section of Brooklyn, not even permitting his mother, disabled following a stroke, to use the telephone. Suffering from schizophrenia for seven years, he had attacked his parents many times. After each incident police took him to a psychiatric hospital which released him a day or two later. In November 1987 a special team of police officers had to be called in, and finally subdued him with an electric shock gun and pressurized water. This episode earned Gavrilou three weeks in the hospital.

A few months later, on February 26, 1988, neighbors heard a commotion and found Gavrilou's father sitting on the floor in the hallway while his son tugged on his arm trying to pull him back into the apartment. "He's trying to kill me," the elderly Greek immigrant and former shoemaker cried to neighbors, begging them to call for help. The son, wielding a kitchen knife, yanked his father back into the apartment. Before police could arrive, as the horrified neighbors listened to the screams through locked doors, Nick Gavrilou slit his father's throat and stabbed his mother through the heart. Two weeks before the murders he had been released yet again, this time from a jammed psychiatric emergency room at King's County Hospital after only one night. Cowed by her son, the mother had not revealed his violent history to hospital doctors. Investigators learned later that Gavrilou had not been taking his medication.[21]

Taking Out Restraining Orders for Self-Protection

Stymied in their effort to obtain treatment for potentially violent family members,[22] families may obtain restraining orders barring them from the house. Earlier in Bill's illness, Don Richardson had taken out such an order after his son had been phoning and threatening him. When Bill came to the house the next night, the Richardsons explain: "It was lucky we had it because then if you call the police they will come and take him to the hospital instead of to jail if you have the paper. They don't have to see a crime committed because it's a violation of the restraining order." But of course, such orders are no substitute for treatment. Further, they add to the bitterness of the mentally ill person who is arrested if he goes to his own home and to the pain and frustration of the family.

Moreover, the orders run out and may not be enforced. In Philadelphia, Marie Piscitelli took out a restraining order after the repeated failure of her attempts to secure treatment for her mentally ill and drug-addicted son. He spent time in prison for violating the order, but after his release in 1989 he returned to drugs, refused treatment, and—in defiance of the order—returned, said his mother, ten, twelve times a day, to beg for money. When she called the parole officer she was told jail overcrowding prevented his rearrest. "So all day long," says Mrs. Piscitelli, who lives with her daughter Cathy (whom her son nearly killed years earlier, plunging a gold-handled stiletto in her chest), "we have to watch for a face at the window."[23]

In the end, feeling insufficiently protected by restraining orders—or unwilling to use them against their child—families may flee their homes. Also in Philadelphia, Maggie Phillips and her disabled husband fled the violent rages of their mentally ill son who refused all treatment. They moved into Maggie's parents' small apartment, leaving their three-bedroom row house to their son. He set fires on the lawn, put up obscene posters, removed most of the doors, bashed in the gas range, and stripped the house of all its wallpaper.

Maggie brought food to her son, replaced the windows he broke, and vainly continued to seek treatment for him. But even when she found scab-encrusted wounds on his wrists and ankles, she was told a commitment petition would be rejected unless she had actually *seen* him cut himself. In May 1985, police were called to the house by neighbors. Maggie's son had smashed the front door and downstairs windows of the house, breaking not only the glass, but even the sashes. Taken to the mental health center by police, he was at first not committed, this time because no one had *witnessed* him ravage the house! He would have been sent away, were it not that he got into an argument and struck at the glass door of the mental health center. This behavior earned him a brief period of treatment, but Maggie and her husband never returned to their battered home.[24]

Penalties of Covering Up the Issue of Violence

How widespread is the problem of violence against family members? There are no figures, but the problem is clearly a serious one. According to Don Richardson, "Since we've been so open with this incident I don't know how many hundreds of families have said, 'Since you're willing to be so open, let me tell you our story.'" Richardson wants NAMI to cooperate with NIMH in making a survey of members to obtain data on the extent of the problem. He feels that confronting the problem will lead to *greater* acceptance of the mentally ill in the community:

> If acting out mentally ill persons go untreated in the community, all mentally ill persons suffer rejection, blame, and stigma; all, even the most timid and gentle among them are tarred with the same brush; and all are thought of as unpredictable, dangerous, and undesirable. Thus, they are forced to bear another stigma simply because they are unlucky enough to suffer mental illness.

Moreover, this very issue could help family members to make the public understand why it is the right to treatment, not the right to "be different," that the mentally ill require.

Far more common among the mentally ill than lethal violence against others is lethal violence against oneself. Suicide rates in schizophrenia are almost as high as they are in depression, where they are estimated to run between 10% and 15%. Author William Styron, who has suffered from depression, describes the overwhelming sense of malaise that can precipitate this form of violence. He writes:

> [A] vague spooky restlessness had gained gradual momentum until my nights were without sleep and my days were pervaded by a gray drizzle of unrelenting horror. This horror is virtually indescribable since it bears no relation to normal experience.[25]

Sometimes schizophrenics are responding to command voices. Only the arrival of a night janitor kept Carol North from leaping to her death at the urging of voices that told her she would thereby attain the "Pure Perception" of "Other Worlds" and do well on her medical school exams.[26]

Research by British psychiatrist Dr. Martin Weller shows that the suicide rate is seventeen times higher among schizophrenics than in the population as a whole, and even higher among recently discharged patients. Weller notes that the numbers are skewed downward by the reluctance of coroners to record a verdict of suicide. When one of Weller's patients jumped to his death from a tall building, for example, it was listed as "a misadventure."[27]

Yet even if the individual threatens to kill himself—although this is known to be a very serious sign in both schizophrenia and affective disorders—the family often cannot get help until the individual has taken action. And so families live in fear that threats of suicide will be successfully carried out before help can be obtained. Alice Russell's severely ill son talked constantly of suicide and she reports: "I taught Head Start and remember coming home and looking over the house when Johnnie was with us and not knowing whether he was dead or alive."

Prisons of the Mind

Pretending that mental illness is a civil rights issue does enormous disservice not just to families but to the mentally ill themselves. Penny Kostritsky, herself an attorney, says: "All of the principles taken from the criminal law are simply inapplicable when you're talking about a person who is ill and in need of medicine."[28] At the legislative hearings prompted by her daughter's action, Mrs. Seegrist argued:

> Just as it was cruel and unjust to indiscriminately lock up the mentally ill years ago, so it is unjust and irresponsible to allow the severely ill with established records of violent behavior to fend for themselves. . . . In doing this you have not given the severely ill greater civil liberty. You have merely given them the right to be slaves to their own devastating and debilitating brain disease.[29]

The impact on those who harm can be almost as devastating as on those who are harmed. Untreated, young Stan Norman became a parricide. He killed his father under the delusion he formed, while starving on the streets in California, that his father, faraway in Vermont, was causing his weight loss. Yet he responded so well to medication, finally administered to him after his arrest, that during the trial the psychiatrist withdrew his original assessment that the boy was mentally ill and psychotic! Sentenced to twenty-five years in prison as an ordinary criminal, Norman endures the burden of intense guilt and shame for what he did, as well as fear of being preyed upon like Billy, in the NBC documentary, by prison inmates. (Jay Centifanti says of his former fellow forensic patients at Norristown State Hospital: "Putting them in with the general prison population would be like sacrificing them to a wild angry mob.")

Jonathan Miller, the remarkable physician, actor, opera director, and producer of the famed BBC television series on the mind, calls our treatment of the mentally ill "one of the more dehumanizing effects of the late twentieth century though it comes from what purported to be humanists."[30] Perhaps no one sums it up better than psychiatrist Darold Treffert:

> What kind of "freedom" is it to be wandering the streets severely mentally ill, deteriorating, and getting warmth from a steel grate or food from a garbage can? That's not freedom; that's abandonment.
>
> And what kind of "liberty" is it to be jailed for disorderly conduct, crazed and delusional, because that is all the law will allow, instead of being hospitalized, treated, and released? That's not liberty; that's imprisonment for the crime of being sick.
>
> And what kind of twisted "right" is it to stab or shoot to death yourself or some innocent bystander while in a psychotic frenzy, directed by terrifying voices from a disordered and disabled mind? . . .
>
> Enough of the helpless have been made homeless, enough of the bystanders have died, enough family members have been exhausted in a fruitless effort to help, and enough patients have *died with their rights on.*[31] [Italics added.]

PART VI

*The Mentally Ill
in the Community*

Chapter 14

Winging It with Pilot Programs in the Community

A VACUUM of aftercare followed the collapse of the mental hospital as a place offering asylum for the severely and chronically mentally ill. President Kennedy had promised to replace "the cold mercy of custodial isolation" with the "open warmth of community concern and capability." But this rhetoric reflected what Kathleen Jones, professor of social administration at the University of York in England, calls "remarkably romantic ideas about the nature of 'the community.'"[1] In fact, "the community" was neither warm, concerned nor capable, when it came to the mentally ill.

As expert on deinstitutionalization Leona Bachrach points out: "Nobody had ever actually proved that community-based care was either more humane, more therapeutic, or less expensive than state hospital care."[2] The enormous shift from institution to community occurred without elementary forethought. Bachrach admits: "As deinstitutionalization was getting started, we also should have anticipated—but we didn't—that the community would now have to provide an extensive array of services for chronic mental patients."[3] A South Carolina father told writer Mary Ellen Walsh: "The schizophrenic is left to drift like a piece of flotsam once the hospital throws him back in the world."[4]

As we have seen, in practice, "the community" has meant above all the family, chiefly parents. But as parents died, or families broke under the stress of caring for untreated patients, or the mentally ill restlessly wandered off, rooming houses, single-room occupancy hotels (SROs), streets, and jails increasingly supplemented the family as alternatives to mental hospitals.

Often the mentally ill moved from one to another. In a 1986 article, Mona Wasow reports that her twenty-eight-year-old son lived "in the community" in fifteen different settings over a twelve-year period: three times with relatives, four times in a room by himself, twice at the YMCA, in two different group homes, once in jail awaiting placement (his only "crime" was having no place to live), once in a room with a roommate, once in an unlocked facility for the mentally ill and mentally retarded; as she wrote, he was once again in a single room. "Moves are stressful even for people in good health," Wasow observes. "Imagine what all that moving does to a frightened, fragile, mentally ill person."[5]

While the *New York Times* now calls for building new SROs as the solution for the problem of the mentally disabled "homeless" population,[6] those living in the SROs that remain are often only marginally better off than those on the street. Mona Wasow describes her son, living by himself in a single room.

> He is filthy and very skinny; he has boils on his body and is essentially mute. There was no toilet paper in his room, no food, no sheets on the mattress; the chaos in the room was congruent with the chaos in his poor sick mind.[7]

The Failure of Anti-Psychiatry Becomes Obvious

Because nursing homes (in the case of the elderly), families, and SROs took in most of those turned out of institutions in the late 1960s and early 1970s, the problem of the untreated mentally ill in the community long remained hidden from public view. Also, at first, mentally ill street people blended with hippies and countercultural mavericks. Dane County, Wisconsin's mental health administrator David LeCount points out that in the anti-establishment 1960s, it wasn't always clear who suffered from mental illness and who had an "alternative life style."[8] Mark Vonnegut, who recovered from severe mental illness to become a psychiatrist, describes in *Eden Express* how his use of psychedelic drugs and nonconformist way of life masked his actual psychoses much of the time.

Today, the mentally ill lack such camouflage, and the devastation wrought by anti-psychiatry is visible to all. "Liberating" patients from asylums did not free them from their brain disease. The public has become acutely aware of this "new generation of untouchables," lice-infested, hallucinatory, uncared for, and ignored.[9]

Given the reality of mental illness, shifting severely ill people from asylum to community merely alters the location in which patients need not only treatment, but most of the services the hospital had provided. A series of imaginative programs serving the mentally ill, which were established singly, in ad hoc fashion, in different parts of the country, have discovered this, often reluctantly, for their founders sometimes held anti-psychiatric assumptions, believing that former mental patients needed only a short-term "rehabilitation" program, which would prepare them to resume normal life in the larger community. They learned they were wrong.

These model programs serve only a small proportion of the mentally ill in the community, and are not suited for everyone. But they deserve attention, both for what they have achieved and for what they reveal concerning the needs of the mentally ill living in the community.

Fountain House: The Clubhouse Model

In the mid-1940s, a group of ex-patients at Rockland State Hospital in New York began meeting on the steps of the New York Public Library. They called their group WANA—We Are Not Alone. By 1948 they had raised money to buy a brownstone on Manhattan's West 47th Street, still the address of Fountain House.

What was at first a low-key social club came into its own when John Beard, who had formerly worked at Wayne State Hospital in Detroit, became director in 1955. James Schmidt, now executive director, who had come to the program a year before Beard's arrival, remembers being excited by Beard's ideas on ways to enhance the dignity and self-respect of the mentally ill. Before Beard assumed command, Schmidt recalls, it was an evening program. Patients slept during the day. The only tool, says Schmidt, was to talk to people about their problems: "It didn't work."[10]

Believing that work "is a deeply generative and reintegrative force in the life of every human being," Beard insisted that it "underlic, pervade, and inform all of the activities that make up the lifeblood of the clubhouse."[11] At the clubhouse, members are expected to work in one or another part of the program: preparing and serving food to other members, cleaning and maintenance, clerical work, in the club's Thrift Shop, guiding the many visitors.

Beginning in 1960, through its pioneering transitional employment program, Fountain House promised all its members the opportunity to work in commerce and industry at regular wages in nonsubsidized jobs. Its first outside placement, at an advertising agency, has been handed down from member to member for thirty years. At the beginning of a placement, a staff person accompanies the member to train and assist him. Later, if a member cannot go to work one day, staff will stand in for him. A substantial proportion of members who stick with the program—many who drop out return to try again—go on to find jobs of their own.[12]

Membership in Fountain House is lifelong. Providing the mentally ill with a place to go, where they will always feel safe and valued, from which they will never be "evicted," has been an important innovation in community care. Moreover, members are not treated as patients being "rehabilitated" by staff, but as individuals whose participation in the club on a daily basis is expected, wanted, and needed. Staff work alongside members at the same tasks to reinforce member dignity and equality. One member explains:

> Working together, staff and members become engaged in a process where a different concept of disability begins to develop. Staff grow more aware of the social and vocational potential and capabilities of a member, and the member gradually discovers abilities and talents which enhance his or her social relations and make it possible to work more productively.[13]

One staffer told us that when a Fountain House member stopped vacuuming to listen to his voices, she said, "I don't care if you are hallucinating, go on vacuuming." The member did. As one fan puts it, at Fountain House "the emphasis is on what the client can do *best,* not what he does worst or can't do at all."

Because of its stress on "empowerment," Fountain House has generally avoided providing medication at the clubhouse, fearing it would keep members in a patient role. Most members receive it through a community mental health center, and the club relies primarily on peer pressure to persuade individuals who are deteriorating off medication to resume it.

Fairweather Lodge: Forming a Business Commune

In the late 1940s, Dr. George Fairweather, a psychologist at the VA hospital in Dansville, Illinois, was disturbed by the rapid rate of return of mental patients who had supposedly been cured. With colleagues, Fairweather developed the idea of forming groups of patients who might help one another in the hospital and then move together into the community. He hoped that they would care for each other, fostering better adjustmènt outside of the hospital.[14]

For the next twenty years, Fairweather experimented in forming such small groups in a hospital setting. He found that while patient morale improved in the hospital, the return rate remained the same as that for patients in the control group. (Fairweather was unusual, not only for his imaginative work in social rehabilitation, but for his scrupulous use of control groups to test the value of his ideas.) He and his colleagues also discovered, however, that the notion behind the experiment was sound; success in staying out of the hospital correlated highly with the amount of support the individual had in the community. This gave Fairweather the idea for the social invention that has become identified with his name: the Fairweather Lodge. The hospital small group—by this time Fairweather was working in a VA hospital in Palo Alto, California—would become an autonomous society in the community, in which staff would serve only as consultants.[15]

In the hospital, staff prepared patients by focusing on skills for daily living, from managing money and doing chores to socially acceptable behavior. Then the ward group moved out together into a common residence in the community, where they set up a governing body to establish rules for their small society, and created a janitorial and gardening service.[16] This time, the comparison with a control group showed dramatic results: the lodge members had a much lower rate of return to the hospital over a four-year span, and a much higher employment rate. In fact, the lodge became self-supporting. Fairweather reported with justifiable pride: "By any outcome criteria one wished to use this was a successful treatment program."[17]

The PACT Program

PACT, the Program for Assertive Community Treatment, like the Fairweather Lodge, began as a pilot project of a publicly funded mental hospital—in this case the Mendota Mental Health Institute in Madison, Wisconsin. In the early 1970s psychiatrist Leonard Stein and psychologist Mary Ann Test, along with Dr. Arnold Marx, were staff members at Mendota. Like Fairweather, they were disheartened by the numerous readmissions. They began to experiment with sending staff from an in-hospital unit into the community to help patients adjust there. They found that, under these conditions, even patients who had made minimal progress in the hospital, and whom they "prematurely" discharged, did well outside. Independently, they came to Fairweather's conclusion: what was crucial was the amount and kind of support the individual found in the community.[18]

To test further this conclusion, Stein and Test, with a "hospital improvement grant" from NIMH, in 1972 began a program called "Training in Community Living" to serve as an *alternative* to hospitalization. Incoming patients to Mendota were randomly assigned to the hospital and to the model community program, in which a retrained hospital ward staff, working in shifts so as to be available seven days a week, twenty-four hours a day, helped with everything.

> [S]taff members, "on the spot" in patients' homes and neighborhoods, teach and assist them in such daily living activities as laundry upkeep, shopping, cooking, restaurant utilization, grooming, budgeting, and use of transportation. Additionally, patients are given sustained and intensive assistance in finding a job or sheltered workshop placement.... Furthermore patients are aided in the constructive use of leisure time and the development of effective social skills.[19]

The patients in the Training in Community Living program did better than those in the control group, who had been hospitalized and given routine community aftercare, on almost all outcome measures over the following year.[20] However, the program was not cheap: indeed, it cost 10% more than the hospital-based program.[21] Training for Community Living eventually became the Program for Assertive Community Treatment (PACT), whose funding derives partly from NIMH and Dane County, but chiefly from the state. PACT now treats around 120 chronically mentally ill outpatients.

Saint Francis: A "Voluntary" Provider

Appalled at the wholesale abandonment of very sick people, private citizens have also stepped in to create support systems for the mentally ill.

Two Franciscans, Fathers John McVean and John Felice, wanted to start a senior citizens club at a church on 31st Street in Manhattan and went around the neighborhood to hand out flyers. Father McVean entered the Aberdeen, a nearby hotel, and found "the place was full of deinstitutionalized chronic schizophrenics."

We started by just hanging out with people to see what they needed. We began as a mental health program, and we went into it without any preconceived notions. This was back in 1971 and 1972. We call it deinstitutionalization now, but it didn't have a name back then. Back then, homelessness was not the perceived social issue. Back then, in the mental health field it was called the revolving door syndrome, and it still is.[22]

Thus, the Aberdeen project, providing needed support services to the mentally ill in the neighborhood, was born by accident.

Father Felice, who was superior of the monastery in which Father McVean lived, became involved full time in 1979 after the Aberdeen, like so many other SRO hotels in that period, was sold to developers. Father McVean lamented that these people would wind up on the streets. Father Felice recalls: "I said, you'll have to start your own hotel because no hotel is going to welcome you with a bunch of schizophrenics." Together, they decided to take over a former single-room occupancy hotel, the Beechwood, just off Lexington Avenue on 24th Street and convert it into a dormitory for "their people."

Early on, we realized what these people needed was what social workers call activities of daily living: help in managing money, taking their medications. Those we saw were not great in terms of their nutritional needs. We were sent the most fragile of the population by the mental hospitals. A lot of our folks didn't qualify for day programs. We realized we had to provide our own activities on site.[23]

Renovated and cheerful, the Beechwood has ninety-nine rooms. It is a private, nonprofit corporation, separate from the church. In 1982, a second St. Francis residence opened up on West 22nd Street, and in 1988 a third, only a few blocks away. Most tenants have their own rooms and make breakfast and lunch at the hotel with some supervision from staff. Staff accompany residents to the laundromat and organize activities, art classes, movies, or other social outings during the day. Psychiatric care is available on the premises. The daily cost in 1988 was an incredibly low $12.35 a person.

Always concentrating on the most impaired among the chronically mentally ill, the St. Francis residences increasingly serve a vagrant population. Of the ninety-two new residents in 1987, 80% had been homeless. (They were first stabilized on medication; St. Francis does not take people directly from the street.[24]) Stan, age thirty, had lived under a bridge, nearly buried in many layers of clothing when he was discovered by a city outreach worker. He refused to leave his burrow for six months; more months passed before he would see a psychiatrist. Once on medication, according to his doctor, "he shed those layers of clothing like he was shedding his psychosis."[25]

Father McVean says he will not hesitate to hospitalize someone when necessary, even against the person's will. Nor does he have any problem with a policy of taking severely mentally ill people off the street to the hospital for treatment. Says Father McVean:

> Because then they can lead relatively dignified lives, become human beings again. I'm liberal in a lot of areas but there are a few where I'm not and, on those lines . . . I personally think the ACLU is off the wall on this issue, just off the wall.[26]

The Hybrid Model: Thresholds–The Bridge

Some pilot programs eclectically combine elements of existing models to create something distinctive. In 1965 Jerry Dincin, who had worked under John Beard for five years at Fountain House, came to Thresholds, a small clubhouse started by the National Council of Jewish Women in 1959. Energetic, restless, and creative, Dincin is always ready to try "anything that works."[27]

Like Fountain House, Thresholds focuses on jobs, social skills, and giving members a sense of "empowerment." But Thresholds has branched out, incorporating PACT principles as well. In 1978, Dincin obtained funds from NIMH for a special project for fifty clients who did not respond well to the structured clubhouse, and who had been hospitalized at least five times, three times in the previous year. In the Bridge program of "assertive case management," staff visited patients daily, and attended to each of their problems.[28] Says Dincin: "Ours is a total team approach. We stole the idea from the Wisconsin [PACT] program. We stole it, lifted it, and then put our own spin on the ball."[29] The Bridge was able to cut down hospital days for this group of people by 2,000 days in one year; Dincin claims that even including the program's cost, the state saved $150,000.[30]

Dincin offered to take over one unit of the state hospital, apply his methods as patients were released, and compare the results with those of patients released from the rest of the hospital. What he discovered, Dincin says, is that hospitalizations often occurred because of crises precipitated by the "nitty gritty details of everyday life," above all, failure to manage money properly. Most chronically mentally ill are on SSI, which in Chicago in 1989 paid $368 a month. As Dincin notes, "with the

best of money management it's not hard to blow that kind of money."
When people who are not well integrated psychologically get their
checks, says Dincin,

> what they do, they spend it and fast, and what they do after that, they go to
> the state hospital and they say the magic words, which are "I'm afraid I'm
> going to hurt myself" and they get taken into the state hospital until their
> next check comes.[31]

Those patients on the hospital unit covered by the Bridge used 59%
fewer hospital days the first year.

Thresholds–The Bridge now runs Chicago's major citywide program for "homeless outreach." Bridge team staff find the mentally ill
where they are, on the street, or in temporary housing, and help with
medical, financial, social, and vocational needs. As a result of its far-
ranging activities, Thresholds has become a very large program, much
bigger than Fountain House, which has hewed closely to its clubhouse
format. There are seventy full-time staff who do nothing but visit chronically mentally ill in their own home. The Bridge also acts as payee for
300 people, doling out money to them, sometimes on a weekly basis,
and where necessary, daily. In 1989, with a $10.5 million budget,
Thresholds–The Bridge, employed a staff of 255 to serve 2,000 people.[32]

The Core Program Elements

The model programs thus discovered, independently, that the
mentally ill in the community had a wide range of needs. They needed
what the hospital (at least before the days of peonage suits) used to
provide: work—as well as treatment, housing, and social interaction.

Above all, the programs discovered that, for most of the chronically
ill, medication was the key to community tenure. Fountain House executive director James Schmidt told us that over 90% of members are on
medication and "the environment at Fountain House is fully supportive
of medication." According to Thresholds' Jerry Dincin, after medication
concerns are taken care of "then you can do the rehabilitation, which
consists of the social and psychological part." Dincin stresses that "the
majority of people who go back to the hospital do so because they don't
comply with their medication. We've done research studies and we
know that to be true."[33] As a result, Thresholds incorporates medication
compliance into its program. Says Dincin: "We have medication educa-

tion groups, medication compliance groups, our own psychiatrist who comes and prescribes, psychiatrists who make home visits."[34]

George Fairweather is as emphatic as Dincin in underscoring the importance of medication in the Lodge program: "any social subsystem for chronically disturbed people must establish an appropriate mechanism for handling medication."[35]

The PACT program also puts major emphasis on medication. Susan Estroff, an anthropologist who did a participant-observer study of PACT published under the title *Making It Crazy,* noted that patients were given their medications at the PACT house, and staff made strenuous efforts to ensure compliance. "Nurses sometimes gave shots to clients while in the back seat of the state vehicles driven by staff, or they sometimes took to the streets with syringe and injection in hand to deliver meds."[36] Although personally sympathetic to patients who rejected drugs—she has since emerged as one of those who challenge their use—Estroff admitted the heavy costs of refusal:

> The momentary satisfaction of refusal usually resulted in despair, regret, or life problems when the seemingly inevitable escalation of psychotic thoughts and feelings occurred, attended by severe losses associated with eviction, termination at work, or hospitalization.[37]

At St. Francis, Father McVean considers medication, along with housing, basic to community care.

> We ... feel very strongly about the importance of medication—unlike some groups. We are painfully aware as everyone is of the potentially serious side effects of these drugs. But over the years, observing the people we get to know, it is very painful for the staff to see someone decide he won't take his medication any more ... The painful part is to see someone slowly decompensate to the point where they become like another person.[38]

On rare occasions when someone from St. Francis is hospitalized and refuses medication, Father McVean reports; "I've gone over to testify against the person. I've said I can't handle this person in an unstructured setting, which we are, if he is not medicated."[39]

Except for St. Francis, which caters to the most impaired population, all the model programs make work the centerpiece of their rehabilitation efforts. Fairweather Lodges are of course organized as business cooperatives, and John Beard made the transitional employment program the focal point of Fountain House. Dincin is tireless in his efforts to expand work opportunities for Threshold members:

We're kind of innovative. We went to a firm that does microfilming—hospital records and legal records. We asked "What could we do that would encourage you to hire our members?" And the guy said "I need a couple more cameras. I can get the business, but I don't have the cash to get the cameras." So we went to the state vocational rehabilitation agency. We said: "Give us $50,000 to buy two cameras we will own and put on the premises of this business. In that way . . . we will have jobs for members, and the VR system will have what it wants, which is people working. . . . And it worked out exactly as planned.[40]

The morning of our interview he had driven half a dozen members to Chicago's Brookfield Zoo, where Thresholds operates two concession stands.

At PACT too, Estroff noted:

It would be difficult to overestimate the emphasis placed by both staff and clients . . . on securing and maintaining employment. Clients often greeted each other not with "Hello, how are you?" but with "You working?" or "Got a job yet?"[41]

Housing is the third basic need that all the model programs have been forced to address. Father McVean is emphatic:

Philosophically, we have come up with a couple of very strong positions. One is that for this population you need permanent residence. To get someone stabilized and keep him stabilized, people have to know they don't have to move on to get a sense of security.[42]

Although their initial focus was on social interaction and work, clubhouse programs have also been forced by member need to go into the housing business. Fountain House now owns, operates or leases apartments and group residences all over New York City. By 1989, Thresholds operated twenty-two residences with varying degrees of supervision. The Bridge program, says Dincin, meets patients with "nowhere to go" at the door of the hospital.

We take them physically from the exit door of the hospital to a place to live. We [provide] . . . all the things that I described about the Bridge, and that prevents homelessness of the mentally ill. We don't deal with it after the fact, but as it occurs.[43]

Finally, all the programs discovered that the chronically ill in the community needed not only the services the hospital had once provided, but a whole range of new services as well, from income maintenance to money management to education in shopping and nutrition. Moreover, they discovered that for many of the chronically ill, the need was *ongoing*. At first, Stein and Test report:

> We made strong efforts with all our patients to integrate them into the fabric of the community. Initially we had the hope that they would succeed sufficiently to disappear among the rest of us and no longer need to see themselves or be seen by others as patients. Indeed, this did happen in a few cases. The majority, however, continue to require a wide variety of services, including psychiatric services, social welfare service, housing, financial aid, sheltered employment, recreational and the like.[44]

Says Leonard Stein: "Psychosis is a lifelong problem so the mental health system should support people in life, not prepare them for it."[45]

Mental Health Bar Undercuts Principles of Community Care

Strikingly, the discoveries of all the community programs contradict the premises of the anti-psychiatric legal activists. The eighteenth-century pioneers of moral treatment had understood the therapeutic value of work. As psychiatrist Ranjit Chacko points out, hospitals valued such therapy long before it was "rediscovered in the community support program models and the lodge programs of the 1970s":

> Only 25 years ago, two out of every three hours of labor in mental hospitals were performed by unpaid patients. These chronic mental patients operated food services, housekeeping, laundry services, worked on paint crews, and maintained the grounds of state hospitals with minimal supervision for many years.[46]

Many state hospitals operated large farms with patient labor, providing most of the institution's food.

To be sure, this made the hospitals cheaper to operate, but so does patient labor make the clubhouses less expensive to run. Yet legal advocates have succeeded in branding patient labor in hospitals "peonage," unless it is paid at the minimum wage or can be proven to be "therapeutic" to the individual patient. Given the difficulties of providing such proof, state hospitals have taken the easy way out, institutionalizing idleness. Community programs thus far have evaded accusations of peonage by calling their work details "therapy"; they are nonetheless vulnerable to legal challenge.

Community programs rely on medication for the vast majority of patients. Yet advocates have successfully established in law a right to refuse medication, which applies even to those disabled or dangerous enough to be involuntarily committed under the stringent statutes they have secured.

Finally, community programs have come to understand the importance of being able to intervene promptly, *before* the patient's condition deteriorates sharply. Leonard Stein and Mary Ann Test write: "One aspect of our program that cannot be overemphasized is our commitment to monitoring all our patients so that intervention can be instituted at the first sign of trouble."[47] Yet the mental health bar has so deformed the law as to prevent intervention until the patient is on the verge of killing himself or someone else, or is so gravely disabled as to be on the point of death, for example, because of starvation.

Model Programs Replicated

At first slowly, then in the late 1970s (with NIMH funding) more rapidly, the pilot programs were replicated. Fountain House led to Horizon House in Philadelphia in 1953, Council House in Pittsburgh in 1957, Thresholds in 1958, and the Center Club in Boston in 1959. By 1989 there were 230 clubhouses in thirty-nine states modeled after Fountain House (as well as twenty abroad, chiefly in Canada and Sweden). Many were day programs of community mental health centers, which were reorganized to follow the principles laid down by John Beard.

Although Fairweather's efforts to persuade San Francisco's VA hospital to expand the Lodge program foundered on bureaucratic dedication to business-as-usual, he found early disciples in Arkansas, then in other states. Most followed the pattern of the pioneering lodge, originating as small groups on state hospital wards and moving as a unit to the community. Like the original lodge, most established a cleaning and janitorial service, but some operate other businesses, including landscaping, catering, car wash, car repair, duplicating, and furniture repair. There are now approximately one hundred Fairweather Lodges in sixteen states, the majority in Texas and Michigan.[48]

PACT served as model for the famous Dane County mental health system, of which it remains an independent component. Like PACT, Dane County also has a Mobile Community Treatment Unit that gives a team responsibility for a group of patients: the team follows the patients into the community. Leonard Stein and Mary Ann Test explain:

> If someone does not show up for his appointment or for his job . . . we will go out and find the person. We have to go to his home; we may drive along the street we know he frequents. When we find the client, we don't hit him (or her) over the head, shanghai him, and haul him back; . . . but we do stop him, talk to him, and try to convince him that we would really like to get reinvolved with him.[49]

Dane County also provides round-the-clock crisis intervention service. Hospitalization has been kept to a minimum as a result, so that 76% of Dane County's 1989 budget went for outpatient services.[50] (In many parts of the country the proportions are reversed.) Principles developed by PACT underpin successful community programs from Boulder, Colorado to Kent County, Rhode Island.

Finding What Works—And for Whom

Such limited outcome studies as exist suggest all the pilot programs are effective. In 1982, the Texas Department of Mental Health and Retardation compared several kinds of community support programs, using the criteria of need for rehospitalization, employment, and quality of life. Those enrolled in *any* of the programs did far better than a control group. Most dramatic was the drop in need for hospitalization: 19% overall for those in the model programs compared to 86% for the control group.[51]

The Fairweather Lodge emerged as the most effective. Those in the lodges had the lowest recidivism rate,[52] not surprising because the lodge combines a high degree of social support—members both live and work together—with maximum autonomy. As Barbara Shaw, the executive director of Sunshine Projects in Hartford, Connecticut, one of the handful of lodges in the Northeast, put it:

> Our members live together without staff; they have self-governing bodies; they have their own businesses, individual for-profit legal partnerships; they fund themselves; they work; they earn money; they make their own decisions.

The Fairweather Lodge scored particularly well on employment; its 92% rate was by far the highest. Again, given the episodic nature of the crises that mark chronic mental illness, this is not surprising. In the period of transitional employment, a Fountain House can provide a substitute for the worker, but it cannot step in once he has found permanent employment. Studies of psychosocial rehabilitation programs show that employment of members increases after involvement in the program but then drops off within a year or so.[53] Reentering the job market after each failure becomes more difficult. A major strength of the Fairweather Lodge model is that it can always substitute workers, restoring a member to work as he recovers from an episode of illness.

Thus far, the lodges have served primarily an older male population with an extensive history of hospitalization. In Texas, 68% of members are male, and their mean age is forty-two. The average age is declining but this has created problems for the stability of lodges. Older members have tended to have greater commitment to the lodge, while younger members are more likely to look at it as an interim stopping place. Also younger members are more likely to be addicted to drugs or alcohol, a further cause of disruption to the Lodge society.[54]

This is not to say that young members and women may not flourish in the Fairweather program. Appleton, Wisconsin, for example, started a lodge in 1976 for seven women. According to a staff member:

> The difference in these women is absolutely unbelievable. We know how sick they were when we got them; we know what they are now. If the world could know—if we could educate the public—we would have lodges everywhere. . . . One of them is doing all the book work; another goes out as a coordinator to be sure that the work is done well.[55]

On the other hand, for the most part, the Lodges have not proven to be fully self-supporting, as Fairweather originally hoped they would be. A study of the Anchorage, Alaska lodge found that disability payments (SSI and SSDI) accounted for 64% of income and janitorial contracts for 31%. A study of the lodge program in Texas found the cost (to government programs) per client averaged around $10 a day.[56] Nor have the lodges been able to dispense wholly with staff, as originally hoped, although the staff need not be mental health professionals.[57] Still, compared with any other model, the lodges are highly cost effective.

Clubhouses have tended to attract a younger population than lodges: Jerry Dincin, for example, says the average age of Thresholds members is twenty-six.[58] PACT also serves young people from eighteen to thirty. Such differences underscore Leona Bachrach's assertion that no model can serve all patients. Bachrach points out that it is tempting to think replication of one successful model is *the* answer to community-based treatment, but this is not so.[59]

For many patients, clubhouses and lodges alike, with their emphasis upon employment and social interaction, make demands which they cannot meet. The lower demands of a St. Francis residence, or the outreach services of a program like the Bridge, may be more suitable for them. Other patients, especially those highly educated before they became ill, are impatient with the entry-level jobs offered by clubhouses, and dismiss the programs as "baby-sitting." Nonetheless, there is scope for a substantial increase in the number both of Fairweather Lodges and clubhouses. Clearly, for example, if Texas has forty lodges, and New York (and many other states) none, many more chronically mentally ill throughout the country could benefit from the lodge program.[60]

Models That Failed—Soteria

Given the anti-psychiatric ferment of the 1960s, it was inevitable that community services based on anti-psychiatric ideology would surface. One that deserves mention, if only because its loss is often mistakenly lamented, is Soteria House, which operated in California from 1971 to 1983.

In 1968, Dr. Loren Mosher, a disciple of Laing, was appointed to a key position as Chief of NIMH's Center for the Study of Schizophrenia. Under his controversial watch, Mary Ellen Walsh points out acerbically, parent-blaming was "institutionalized, supported by the tax money of the four million American parents that are the targets of the barrage."[61]

Mosher reports his enthusiasm when a proposal came across his desk from a group at Agnews State Hospital in California for creating a house modeled on Laing's Kingsley Hall, with Laing himself as one of its heads. Although that proposal, which lacked provision for any control group, could not be funded, Mosher became committed to the idea and eventually assumed overall responsibility for the design of the Soteria House project.[62]

A six-bed residence, Soteria (with its twin Emanon House) adhered to the Laingian notion of psychosis as a psychological growth experience. The program was limited to unmarried persons, between sixteen and thirty years old, diagnosed as schizophrenic, and with no previous hospitalizations (one brief hospital stay was permissible). Soteria avoided anti-psychotic medications: Mosher set out to demonstrate that "there were viable paradigms for understanding and being with madness besides the medical disease one."[63]

The problem with the Soteria model was that although the side effects of medication were avoided, patients were left with the *primary* effects of their illness. The average patient remained in the house 166 days while his "experience of acute psychosis," in Mosher's words, became "an important subject of interpersonal communication."[64] Mosher presents the following staffer's report as typical of Soteria's approach.

> I had had three hours of sleep, and even that had been broken sleep. Sleeping with and guarding Sara is not especially conducive to good resting. I was sleeping on the floor by the door so that I would waken if she tried to leave. . . . [At six] I got up and started to fix her breakfast. She was sitting at the table waiting more impatiently; she then urinated on the bench she was sitting on. . . . I was tired, I was sad—it was Sara's 16th birthday, "Sweet 16." It was Sara's special day to celebrate, and there sat Sara in Soteria, soiling herself, terrified of dying, of being alone, or being with people, of spiders, of noises, of being loved, of being unloved. Happy Birthday, Sara—it was so goddamned sad.[65]

The staff member describes this incident (in which Sara goes on to suck at her keeper's breast) as "the kind of incident that makes our house a special and more-than-good place." But Sara could more accurately be regarded as a victim of Laing's fantastical theories of mental illness, implemented by Mosher with taxpayer money. Medicated, Sara might well have spent her sixteenth birthday with her family, delivered from the terrors she was sentenced to endure by her ideological warders.

Mosher was deposed at NIMH in 1980,[66] and by 1983 both Soteria and Emanon had lost their funding. Mosher claims that Crossing Place in Washington, D.C. continues the Soteria model because of its "informality, earthiness, honesty, and lack of professional jargon."[67] But 96% of patients at Crossing Place receive anti-psychotic drugs upon admission. Not surprisingly the average length of stay at Crossing Place is less than a fifth what it was at Soteria.[68]

There are now many crisis houses which serve as a cheaper alternative to hospitalization; in this sense Soteria has been replicated. What the mental health system has fortunately *not* implemented further—although as we shall see, Vermont may change that—is its core conception that mental illness can be made into a growth experience through "interpersonal communication."

NIMH's Community Support Program

By the mid-1970s NIMH bureaucrats could no longer avoid the recognition that their prized social invention, the community mental health center, had failed to address adequately the needs of the chronically mentally ill. A 1972 NIMH study had asked CMHC directors to rank in order ten goals: 175 responded, and reducing state hospital utilization ranked next to last. Two years later, an internal NIMH study revealed that only 3.8% of referrals to CMHCs were from public mental hospitals, which accounted for fewer referrals than any other source except clergy.[69]

In 1974, under Dr. Lucy Ozarin's direction, an internal ad hoc group began to examine the unmet needs of the chronically ill in a community-based system of care.[70] Three years later, then NIMH director Dr. Bertram Brown authorized the Community Support Program (CSP), providing $3.5 million annually for three years for pilot demonstration projects in nineteen states.

CSP was eclectic. Its money went to train mental health providers to use the model programs we have described, and to replicate and adapt them in other parts of the country. Money also went to militant ex-patient groups for consciousness-raising, as well as for patient-run "drop-in centers." Such leaders of the movement as Sally Zinman, who started one in Berkeley, see them as a first step in obtaining total control of services by "consumers."[71] The drop-in center, which provides a social haven without the demands typical of more structured programs, has been more successful than other models in attracting a homeless, hard-to-reach population and, often professionally staffed, is increasingly a feature of mental health systems.

But the Community Support Program—its funding up to $16 million a year in 1989—has become most identified with the concept of the "case manager," who is supposed to make sure that the chronically mentally ill person does not get lost in the bureaucratic maze. Case management, however, has its limitations, one of them being the extremely high dropout rate of case managers themselves. (PACT's team approach counteracts this problem.) Nor can case managers coordinate or deliver services that do not exist: if there are no places available in supervised residences, for example, the case manager cannot provide one.

So when caseloads are heavy and available services thin, the case manager becomes merely another costly bureaucratic layer. Although Pennsylvania boasts of its system of "intensive case management," some months before she was strangled by her case-managed son Fred, Jean Pisano wrote to state Deputy Welfare Secretary Martha Knisley to complain: "I am the one doing case management. He [Fred's case manager] just has the title and is receiving the paycheck. . . . When do I get my check?"[72]

With the passage of the Mental Health Systems Act in 1980, NIMH's Community Support Program, like the Community Mental Health Centers almost twenty years earlier, seemed destined to become the basis of a major federal program.[73] Following Ronald Reagan's election, however, block grants, with states funding their own programs, made the Act a dead letter. And despite CSP's emphasis on services to the chronically ill, this is probably just as well. As Henry Foley and Steven Sharfstein (who headed the CSP program at NIMH for some years) point out in *Madness and Government,* the Mental Health Systems Act would have mired programs in a swamp of requirements—"paper, paper, paper."[74]

Moreover, the Act incorporated the contradictory perspectives of special interest groups—including militant anti-psychiatric patients—consulted in the hearings of the Carter-appointed President's Commission on Mental Health. On the one hand, it stressed aggressive follow-up of released patients, on the other the mental patient's right to freedom from interference, including a patients' Bill of Rights.[75] Finally, the Act resuscitated the discredited notion of "preventing" mental illness, which had helped derail community mental health centers from treating the chronically ill, actually calling for an Office of Prevention within NIMH.[76]

Block Grants Promote Focus on Chronically Ill

Fuller Torrey points out that the Community Support Program's role in helping states innovate and plan comprehensive services should not obscure its goal of correcting the deficiencies in the original $3 billion dollar CMHC program. The shift to block grants in the Reagan administration, by giving states control of funds for CMHCs, has enabled them to force community mental health centers to treat more of the chronically ill. Moreover, with states funding both CMHCs and state hospitals, coordination between them has necessarily improved.

On studying seventy-one community mental health centers in fifteen states in 1983 and 1984, researchers Jeanette Jerrell and Judith Larsen reported that the mentally ill "are benefiting from the shift of policy and funding responsibility to state mental health authorities."

> Services for the chronically mentally ill are being increased in all states. . . . This increased emphasis is a direct result of state directives assigning priority to these target groups, along with continued levels of

funding for local programs serving these clients.... Furthermore, in most states, state policy and funding guidelines emphasize service to clients with severe acute mental disorders.[77]

The range of services had also increased.

> Emergency services, structured partial care programs with a psychoso-cial or vocational rehabilitation focus, community residential alterna-tives, and case management services ... are being developed at a faster pace than was previously true, primarily due to the policy and funding support of state mental health authorities. Thus, a more comprehensive system of care is evolving for the chronically mentally ill patient.[78]

Nonetheless, they caution that resources have not kept pace with need, and that young chronic patients who became ill in the era of the "dangerousness" standard, with little or no history of hospitalization, may not be eligible for services.

A Private Foundation Seeks to Reshape the Service System

In another, positive development, private foundations are finally beginning to commit energy and funds to improving services for chronic patients. Although the Robert Wood Johnson Foundation, estab-lished by the head of the Johnson & Johnson company, is this country's second largest foundation and the largest devoted to health care, it had traditionally ignored mental illness. Martin Cohen, now deputy director of its program for the homeless mentally ill, is frank: "The foundation wanted to stay away from mental health—viewed it as a black hole."[79]

Then, despite itself, the Johnson foundation became involved in mental illness through its program to provide medical care to those in shelters. With the United Hospital Fund and the Pew Memorial Trust, it funded a program called Health Care for the Homeless in a number of cities. Those staffing the program, mostly nurse practitioners, says Cohen, reported back:

> We can deal with the TB; we can deal with the substance abuse; we can deal with the illness and disease; but the thing we are having a hard time dealing with is the mental health component. We are having a hard time accessing services.... We go to the state and they say it's a county prob-lem; we go to the county and they say it's a community mental health centers problem; we go to the community mental health centers and they say no, not this catchment area.[80]

The foundation concluded that the greatest need was to unify the fragmented nonsystem of care. The best program models would avail little as long as each authority could point the finger at another and disclaim responsibility. The foundation put together a $100 million dollar package (part of it from HUD), inviting the sixty largest cities in the United States to compete for a share by submitting proposals for improving the organization and financing of care for the chronically mentally ill. Even to compete—and all but four cities did so—those involved in any aspect of care had to cooperate, often for the first time. Eight cities were selected, three of them in Ohio, in recognition of that state's strong push to reorganize services.[81]

Denver, one of the cities selected, established a Mental Health Corporation to provide a single source of clinical, administrative, and financial responsibility. The state cooperated by agreeing to send the funds, which had gone to disparate agencies—including four mental health centers that according to Cohen, "did not speak to one another," to the new corporation. Like Dane County's Mental Health Board, the Denver Mental Health Corporation now contracts out all the mental health services for the area.

Whatever the outcome of the Robert Wood Johnson foundation's multipronged effort—it is also encouraging mental health agencies to develop new housing, and not simply, as before, hunt up existing housing, it has already made a major contribution. Its involvement means that mental illness from now on is likely to engage other private groups and organizations. Simply by introducing a spirit of competition among state and local mental health systems, it performs a valuable service.

Fuller Torrey and Sidney Wolfe of the Public Citizen Health Research Group, created by Ralph Nader, initiated the rating of state programs for the seriously mentally ill in 1986. Whatever its flaws, the rating has had a similar salutary effect: for example, legislators in Hawaii, stung by its last-place ranking, demanded hearings on why theirs was the worst system in the nation, and how it could be improved.

The involvement of the Robert Wood Johnson Foundation is owing, of course, to the mentally ill homeless, which have drawn attention to mental illness as nothing since Albert Deutsch and Mike Gorman's fierce exposés of state hospitals. While the current degradation of the mentally ill on the streets cries out for major crucial change, it must not be forgotten that previous reform efforts often preceded even worse neglect of the mentally ill.

Anti-psychiatric fictions about the nature of mental illness conditioned the disastrous course of deinstitutionalization. Now there is danger that misconceptions rooted in the same ideology will sabotage community programs. Those who pioneered the successful models we have described all recognized that in most cases rehabilitation depends on medical treatment of the underlying illness. But within community psychiatry today, there is a segment that views *services as a substitute for treatment.* Policies based on this anti-psychiatric fallacy can only undermine public support for community psychiatry and destroy the chance for creating a system that protects the interests of both the mentally ill and the broader society.

Chapter 15

Community Services Are Not Enough

THAT more community programs are needed has become a truism. By late 1989, lawsuits were in progress, or had recently resulted in court orders, in twenty-one states demanding that state governments provide more services for the mentally disabled.[1] Even militant anti-psychiatric patient groups do not disagree on the need for services: on the contrary, they would like funds for such programs turned over entirely to them, to operate drop-in centers, patient-run housing, and so on.

That services need to be better integrated, in a comprehensive mental health *system,* the assumption underlying the Robert Wood Johnson program, is also generally recognized. Seriously mentally ill people cannot be expected to negotiate a bureaucratic maze to obtain unconnected, scattered services from disparate authorities, none of which takes any overall responsibility for their welfare.

But this accord obscures disagreement on fundamental issues. For example, many of those active in the drive for more services, including anti-psychiatric ideologues and members of the mental health bar, assume that an entirely *voluntary* system of community services will suffice. The burden is on the provider, in this view, to offer services attractive enough to engage the chronically ill. As psychiatrists Robert Drake and David Adler observe, "when patients' refusal of services is cited, caregivers are sometimes severely rebuked for suggesting that anyone would decline services offered in a dignified manner."[2]

In addition, many of those agitating for services argue that they can substitute for state hospitals, not merely cut down on their use. As we shall see, the evidence is strong that a purely voluntary system of community care for the mentally ill cannot be sustained at acceptable financial and social cost. In fact, in a voluntary system, even vastly increased expenditures for services are often wasted because they can bypass—and indeed adversely affect—many of the most severely ill.

Refusing Treatment: The Problem of Compliance

We have seen that the model programs consider medication the bedrock of community programs: echoing Jerry Dincin, Richard Adelman, a clinical specialist with the Dane County (Wisconsin) Mobile Community Treatment team, told us: "If you were to list our priorities for the things we do, keeping clients on medication might be our number one priority, because without that, you can't do very much else of anything."[3] The problem becomes: How can the chronically ill in the community, so long as they are completely free to choose or avoid medication, be persuaded to accept it? How indeed can the chronically ill be persuaded to accept treatment or services of any kind?

Psychiatrist Darold Treffert emphasizes that making programs attractive is not a sufficient answer.

> You can have the zenith of community programs and can have a patient who doesn't care to have treatment, or see the need for it, or is convinced mental health centers are all communist organizations . . . so you can invite and plead and bribe and make it nice and glitzy—and a person will not want any part of it. . . . It's preposterous to think if you make the services acceptable, everyone will take advantage of them.[4]

Fuller Torrey and Sidney Wolfe agree:

> The state can make the psychiatric services as attractive and convenient as possible, as recommended by civil liberties lawyers, but there will still remain a sizeable hard core of individuals who refuse treatment because they believe that nothing is wrong with them. . . . The part of their brain which allows a normal person to check beliefs against reality is damaged and the only way they will ever be treated is involuntarily.[5]

Involuntary Community Treatment in Dane County

Dane County's integrated system of community care has led the way for the rest of the country. Largely because of it, Wisconsin ranked first in Torrey and Wolfe's rating of state programs for care of the seriously ill in 1986 and second in 1988—despite the fact that its per capita spending on mental health of $27.80 puts it thirty-first in the nation.[6]

What is glossed over is the extent to which Dane County's mental health system depends for its success on its ability to coerce, as necessary, patients living in the community to take the treatment prescribed for them. Dane County has concentrated on a minority of revolving-door patients who elsewhere take up a great many hospital days. Such people, typically stabilized on medication in the hospital, stop taking it when they leave, and wind up back in the hospital or in jail.

Wisconsin, the home of the 1972 Lessard decision, which, as we saw in Chapter 6, imposed on civil commitment most of the procedural requirements of criminal law, has one of the most stringent commitment laws based on dangerousness in the country. So Dane County looked to another section of the law: "Chapter 55: Protective Services or Placement," which had been primarily intended to serve mentally retarded and disabled old people. Using these statutes, Dane County's Richard Adelman explains:

> With clients who go off meds and get committed again and again, we try to get a limited guardianship, a guardianship for treatment and medications. In that case the client has a court hearing, an investigation done by social services, and if the judge finds the client incompetent in regard to their need for medication, then a guardian will be assigned for that purpose.[7]

Recently, there was a successful legal challenge in Milwaukee to the practice of keeping patients indefinitely on protective services or placement; it is too early to tell whether this will have much practical impact.[8]

Dianne Greenley of Wisconsin's Coalition for Advocacy (the state's Protection and Advocacy agency) describes what she calls the "creative process" by which protective placement was adapted to obtain medication compliance.

> We have long had a protective services system which allows for court-ordered protective services in the community. Those can range from in-home services and housekeeping to living in an adult family home. Several years ago in Dane County they started reading this particular law and saying "Ha! I wonder if we can call medication a protective service and order it." You appoint a guardian and the guardianship is limited to consenting to or refusing medication. . . . In Dane County this has been going on for five or six years at least. The [state] statute was revised only last year to make it clear that this could be done.[9]

The chronically mentally ill are now the largest proportion—more than the aged or retarded—under guardianship and protective placement. Mary Hein, a clinical specialist in the protective services program, is enthusiastic about its impact:

> The law never said anything about limited guardianships, but we would see people who were competent in all areas of their life except that area where they would decide whether they should take ongoing psychiatric medication or not. We had one man, a competent computer programmer here in town who when he was unmedicated was very dangerous, but when medicated functioned quite well; or a person might set fires, but when medicated is able to get along. We'll get a limited guardianship to ensure they get ongoing medication. That's the only right taken away from these people.[10]

David LeCount informed us that in 1989, 350 of Dane County's roughly 1,500 chronically mentally ill population—almost 25%—were under some variety of compulsory medication court order in the community.[11] In addition to the 200 under protective placement, there were an additional 150 who were mandated to accept treatment for a six-month period under the regular civil commitment statutes or had entered into ninety-day "settlement agreements."[12]

Failure to abide by court orders to accept treatment is contempt of court. LeCount describes how this works in practice:

> [One patient] had a history of many psychotic decompensations and long hospitalizations. He had been stable for the last three years, working full-time as a dishwasher, living in his own apartment, and owning his own car. He had been taking medications on his own, although he does have a limited guardian, who has the legal power to force him to take medications if it becomes necessary. Several weeks ago, David broke off contact with his parents, started to become suspicious and angry and began to have trouble at work. . . . As David became more paranoid, he refused first to take an increased amount of medication, then to take any medication at all. . . . David's guardian obtained a court order requiring the police to bring David to the mental health center for a Prolixin Deconate injection. After the first injection, David agreed to take oral medication with daily staff supervision.[13]

Because the laws have teeth, LeCount observes that few people refuse to comply, and it rarely happens more than once.

LeCount reports that Dane County's use of medication orders, together with its outreach and crisis intervention, has resulted in a drop in inpatient days from a peak of over 10,000 a decade ago to around 2,600 in 1988.[14] Mary Hein observes: "Very few people have to be involuntarily committed [to the hospital] while they are under our system. I think it's enlightening to know how small that number is."[15] And although Wisconsin is unique in its use of protective placement statutes to obtain medication compliance, Dianne Greenley estimates that half the states have similar statutes which could be adapted to the needs of the chronically mentally ill.

Interestingly, a 1967 law review article elaborated suggestions for developing intermediate legal statuses for some mental patients between the total confinement of the mental hospital and the complete freedom of community living—this before commitment laws had been rewritten to scrap the need for treatment in favor of a pure dangerousness standard. The author quotes California law, which then permitted commitment for someone "of such mental condition that he is in need of supervision, treatment, care or restraint." In what would turn out to be a prophetic suggestion, the author proposed guardianship as a means for exerting necessary control over patients' lives, from making sure they had homes to imposing treatment.[16]

Other Forms of Outpatient Commitment

Both Wisconsin's protective placement and guardianship statutes and its civil commitment laws are being used to effect essentially "outpatient commitment," i.e., the patient is "committed" for treatment, while continuing to live in the community. In California, "conservatorship" has to a large extent replaced civil commitment as a method for securing long-term treatment in both hospital and community. Mental health authorities in other states have looked at other forms of outpatient commitment to slow the revolving door. While only twenty-six states and the District of Columbia *explicitly* provide for outpatient commitment, the statutes of every state except for New York, which equates involuntary commitment with hospitalization, could be interpreted to permit its use.[17]

So long as outpatient commitment is used for patients who would otherwise be committed as inpatients under the dangerousness standard, and only continued for the period they would otherwise have been hospitalized, it is not controversial. For the mental health bar, outpatient commitment has appeal as a "least restrictive alternative," particularly because it typically lacks enforcement. (Wisconsin is an exception. Elsewhere, mental health authorities seeking to enforce court-ordered outpatient treatment come up against the strict standard: the noncomplying individual must be seen as imminently dangerous before any action can be taken.) It is when outpatient commitment is used to prevent the *need* for hospitalization that it comes under challenge.

North Carolina: A Different Standard for Outpatient Commitment

In 1984, North Carolina became the first state to provide a lower standard for outpatient than for inpatient commitment. Louise Galloway, who currently directs a community mental health center in Asheboro, North Carolina and was involved in writing the law, explains: "The criterion is that the person is mentally ill, capable of surviving safely in the community with supervision, but on the basis of his treatment history needs treatment to prevent a situation that would predictably result in dangerousness."[18] Such an individual can be court-ordered to take medication in the community.

Galloway reports that the impetus came from Dr. Robert Fincher, a psychiatrist at the community mental health center she headed earlier, in High Point, North Carolina.

> He believed there had to be a way that the commitment laws could be written so that we could do something about the clients who were noncompliant and who were decompensating and we had to wait until they were full-fledged dangerous before we could do anything. . . . He had a great deal of compassion and concern and didn't want to see people falling apart before clinicians' eyes, before family members' eyes, before you could do something.[19]

By 1989 mental health workers in North Carolina were convinced the law worked well and reduced hospital use. The number of patients under outpatient commitment had quadrupled to over 1,200 within a few years. Encouraged by the success of those using the program, more community mental health centers were participating each year.[20] A major factor in making the law work was that the state defrayed its cost through a special fund, allowing centers to hire case managers to follow up patients on the program. Says Galloway:

> I'd like to say, in terms of this law, it's my belief it's absolutely essential that outpatient commitment go hand in hand with a very solid case management outreach program. . . . Outpatient commitment does not work well unless there is follow-through.[21]

There is, however, a major problem with North Carolina's law. Fearful of legal challenge by the patient liberation bar, legislators put no teeth in it. Elaine Purpel, the founder of North Carolina's Alliance for the Mentally Ill, works under Louise Galloway as supervisor of the Asheboro Center's intensive case management program. She admits:

> This is really where the law breaks down. . . . Basically the law works and is successful to the extent that patients can be persuaded by the threat of something, by the judge saying "Thou shalt." If the patient really challenges it and pushes it to the limit they soon find out they can noncomply as much as they like and nothing is going to happen.[22]

This legislative strategy has been effective in that the law has thus far suffered only verbal assault; it was denounced as "preventive commitment" in the pages of the *Mental and Physical Disability Law Reporter*. But those attacking it have a legitimate point when they argue that outpatient commitment under present circumstances is a form of judicial intimidation. It works only if the respondent mistakenly assumes the judge's order must be obeyed.[23]

Psychiatrist Jeffrey Geller, who believes outpatient commitment can be extremely useful, agrees on this point, saying that because in most states outpatient commitment is not enforceable, its successful use leaves the psychiatrist feeling he has duped the patient, who has been told he is "committed," but not what it means. He urges that either careful statutes with clear standards and sanctions should be enacted, or there should be no outpatient commitment.[24]

Restoring the Need-for-Treatment Standard

Psychiatrist Darold Treffert has for years argued for a return to *parens patriae* concerns in mental health law (where the state acts in behalf of citizens unable to act in their own best interests), instead of relying solely on the police powers of the state. He has called for the addition of a "Fourth Standard" (in addition to dangerousness to self, dangerousness to others, and gravely disabled), that would permit involuntary treatment for those who *have a severe mental disorder and lack the capacity, because of that disorder, to make an informed decision regarding treatment.*[25] Making treatment for mental illness depend purely on "dangerousness," as Charles Krauthammer has said, "is not just unfeeling; it is uncivilized."

Most of the problems with outpatient commitment would disappear if there were a need-for-treatment standard, with appropriate legal safeguards. Attorney Penny Kostritsky emphasizes the need for a single enforceable standard:

> A treating therapist has got to be free to make the decision on whether a person needs to be an inpatient or whether that person can survive as an outpatient. . . . Then you can have an outpatient commitment that makes sense because the two are dovetailed. . . . If someone meets the standard and is in need of treatment, then the treating psychiatrist makes a determination of whether to try that person on an outpatient [basis]; if it doesn't work, he has the ability to move that patient into an in-patient setting and then can move them again into an outpatient.[26]

No state legislature has taken the pioneering step of reintroducing a need-for-treatment standard and making outpatient commitment the preferred method for securing that treatment. To do so would require legislatures to brave the patient liberation bar.

It would also require a new climate in the courts, which for three decades have steadily expanded the patient's right to be crazy at the expense of the patient's ability to function in the community. Yet, with hospitalization typically so brief, patients are discharged "with their most obvious, threatening, and troublesome symptoms reduced, but with their mental/emotional state still severely compromised."[27] Outpatient commitment becomes all the more important for this disturbed and dysfunctional segment of the mentally ill.

Even if a need-for-treatment standard were combined with outpatient commitment, it would not work in the absence of good follow-up. If the patient can "disappear" in the community, legal provisions are worthless. One of the two states (the other is Georgia) to follow in North Carolina's footsteps is Hawaii, whose bottom-ranked mental health system lacks the services to back it up. Evidently Hawaiian legislators see outpatient commitment as a quick fix.

State Hospitals: Backing Up Community Services

All the model programs described earlier have discovered that hospitals play a necessary role in treating mental illness. The PACT program, originally conceived as an alternative to hospitalization, found that 18% of those initially enrolled in the program had to be hospitalized, if only for brief periods. Leonard Stein and Mary Ann Test concluded that the hospital would always have to be available for homicidal, suicidal, or very severely psychotic patients.[28] (It is true that, in principle, the hospitals need not be state hospitals; private hospitals would do equally well or better, *if* they functioned as state hospitals do, in taking the most severely disturbed patients and putting no time limit on their stay.)

Nonetheless, anti-psychiatric activists won mainstream adherents for their view that state hospitals are the reason deinstitutionalization has failed. Their answer was to close down more—some said all—state hospitals. For example, anti-psychiatry sympathizer and community psychiatry proponent Loren Mosher wrote:

> [M]ental health money must be gotten out of hospitals, particularly large ones. Until this happens community programs will get only leftovers. This does not mean that clients should be forced out of institutions. Rather, large institutions (state hospitals) should not be allowed to admit anyone. In a few years they'll disappear by attrition.[29]

California Alliance for the Mentally Ill's Ted Hutchinson warns against this false dichotomy.

> The anti-psychiatric strategy is to frame the question as "*which* needs support—community care and rehabilitation, *or* involuntary treatment?" Of course, the truth is that the episodic nature of mental illness requires *both* for success. The proper question is: "How can short-term involuntary treatment *best be coordinated with* community care, treatment and rehabilitation?"[30]

Addressing a NAMI workshop, Elaine Purpel was even more emphatic.

> Don't get caught up in rhetoric that there's only so much money so we have to choose where to put our resources. Baloney. It's a continuum. The hospital is part of it.[31]

The Need for Hospitals: The Case of Northampton

Perhaps the best evidence of the need for the state hospital comes from Western Massachusetts, where Steven Schwartz, a member of the mental health bar, won a consent decree from the state in 1978 calling for all but eliminating the state hospital, and creating community-based services instead. A similar consent decree was signed in Washington, D.C. in 1980, but what makes Northampton a much more compelling experiment is that in this case funds were provided for community services to make the plan work. As psychiatrist Jeffrey Geller, who has studied the Northampton experience closely, observes:

[T]his is arguably the first instance where the fiscal supports were actually allocated to create the entire range of requisite community services necessary to support and sustain a population of the chronic mentally ill in the community. Whatever successes and failures have resulted from the effort are not ascribable to inadequate monetary support. The cry heard so often in the era of deinstitutionalization, "if only we had more money," is not applicable here.[32]

Brewster v. Dukakis was brought on behalf of a group of patients at Northampton State Hospital on the grounds they were being denied treatment in the least restrictive alternative because community services were not available. The case had all the hallmarks of a "sweetheart" suit, where opposing sides, formally at loggerheads, are actually in agreement.

Elizabeth Jones, now with the Mental Health Law Project, pivot of the mental health bar, was working for the state of Massachusetts when the suit was brought. She says:

There was a remarkable closeness in values and goals between the defendants and plaintiffs in Western Mass. In fact as the defendants there, we were often accused by our bosses in Boston and other people in other parts of the state of being too closely allied with the plaintiffs. There was an enormous amount of interaction about planning and problem solving. I guess I could confess now that I don't work there that we used to meet before every court meeting and go over problems, share information back and forth.[33]

The similarity in views on opposite sides of the case was not surprising. Robert Okin, a strong advocate of community treatment, had become the state's commissioner of mental health in 1975, the year before Schwartz brought suit. The consent decree stipulated that the census of Northampton Hospital would be brought down from 450 to 50 patients in a three-year period. The planned 90% reduction reflected the conclusion of a study the state had embarked on in 1972. Okin reports:

The results of this assessment process were really quite striking. Of all the people still living in the state hospitals in Massachusetts, the vast majority, almost 90% in fact, although quite disabled, were determined to be capable of living in the community *if* the community mental health system were expanded and organized to help them do so.[34]

The study was purely theoretical: no effort was made to take a sample of patients, move them into the community, and evaluate the results.

Okin was eager to reallocate funds on a large scale from the state hospital to the community mental health system, and the Schwartz suit offered him the opportunity he sought. The desire of the Massachusetts mental health commissioner to do precisely what the consent decree mandated helps to explain why funds were made available and the mental health department staff cooperated to implement the decree.

Anti-Psychiatric Premises in the Consent Decree

Although the consent decree called for appropriate community placement—it was not a program for dumping patients—many of the anti-psychiatric premises endemic to the mental health bar were implicit in it. Geller notes, for example, that the decree only called for "three quarters of a psychiatrist" for each of five catchment areas to serve the large numbers of patients going into the community.

> There was a very naive assumption that if you put people in the community they would be better because they suffered from all these terrible horrors [because of] being in the institution.[35]

Anti-psychiatric conceptions similarly underlay projections of future needs. Says Geller:

> One thing completely ignored in the model was the incidence of mental illness. They acted as if there would be nobody new, because in part their argument was if we didn't institutionalize people, they wouldn't have the same needs as the poor souls we'd institutionalized. It ignored the fact that what we were talking about was chronic mental illness that has the panoply of awful symptoms itself.[36]

A third flawed premise underlay the consent decree. The assumption was that patients would gradually improve, and graduate through a series of residences (there were no less than twelve grades) with progressively fewer staff, to independent living. There is some dispute as to the extent to which this has occurred. A study of the decree's impact by a team led by Geller and funded by the state department of mental health found that "fewer than 5% of the clients in the sample had 'graduated' from a more restrictive setting." Instead of the projected movement of patients toward independence, the study reported:

> Life for some patients appears to have become decompensation in the residential setting, stabilization in the hospital, return to the residential setting, decompensation again, and the cycle repeats.[37]

Elaine Kirsten, the department of mental health's area director for the region including the city of Northampton, disputes these findings. She says that in her area there is substantial movement *within* the system, and some movement out of it, as patients go on to independent living under intensive case management.[38] But there is no dispute that not enough people move on. The result is that too few new patients can enter.

And so, even though by 1986 the state had created 510 community beds, 25% more than the 406 placements the consent decree stipulated,[39] it proved impossible to reduce the hospital population to the stipulated 50 patients by 1981. The average daily census at Northampton hospital decreased by half, remaining at around 125. (Part of that reduction is illusory, since Geller observes that the newly created crisis respite facilities in the community actually operate like hospitals.[40]) Moreover, while per capita expenditures for *outpatient* services in Western Massachusetts are almost two and a half times that of the rest of the state, expenses for inpatient services are only a fifth less.[41]

In part, the difficulty in lowering the hospital census arises from the inability to obtain medication compliance in the community. Massachusetts has no outpatient commitment statutes, but does have "Rogers orders," after the famous right to refuse treatment case described in Chapter 7. If a court rules a patient is incompetent to make treatment decisions, and determines, using "substituted judgment," that he would have taken medication were he competent, it can order him to take it. But, says Elaine Kirsten:

> A lot of people in the really intensive end of the residential program will go back in [the hospital] because everything's voluntary, and if people refuse to take their medication, the Rogers thing we have here really doesn't work. We have them [Rogers orders] but they're useless. They have no teeth. None whatsoever.[42]

Patients sign an agreement to follow a treatment plan, says Kirsten, but they cannot be held to it. "If they're not compliant you can't blame the victim. . . . If people refuse, the burden is ours. If people refuse, it is something we've done." Kirsten, who accepts the validity of this notion, admits that the resulting problem of assaultive behavior "is constant, ongoing, and real. . . . The staff gets bopped. People punch out walls and hit other residents. It always happens when people go off their meds." Kirsten says that when patients deteriorate sufficiently, "we put them back in the hospital . . . and that's one of the cores of recidivism, is the failure to follow up on medication."[43]

Dr. Jeffrey Geller has also called attention to what he calls "communicative arson," by which he means primarily fires set by patients as a way of expressing their desire to change the location of their care. While fire-setting accounts for only a small percentage of admissions to Northampton Hospital, the potential consequences make this behavior of serious concern.[44]

All this helps to drive up the cost of the Northampton system: when someone is hospitalized, both the expensive residential bed, which is held open, and the even more expensive hospital bed, must be paid for. Compared with Dane County, the costs of the Western Massachusetts system, with its emphasis on management over treatment, are very high. In 1989, Dane County, which has a population of 336,000, spent $10.3 million, *including* hospital care, for the mentally ill (both adults and children). In 1989, Western Massachusetts, with a little more than double the population of Dane County, spent just under $63 million, *six times as much* as Dane County.[45]

Patients Not Covered by Decree Lack Services

For many of the mentally ill not covered by the consent decree, the situation in Western Massachusetts worsened after 1978. Northampton Hospital was allowed to deteriorate. Elizabeth Jones now acknowledges this was a mistake: "It was believed if you neglected it, it would become such a horrible place that it would help to force the placement of people in the community."[46] Moreover, admission to the hospital became extremely difficult. Ruth Stein, a founder of the Western Massachusetts Alliance for the Mentally Ill told us: "In order to get into the state hospital you have to be practically cutting your throat. . . . The main concern seems to be keeping the census low."[47]

The hospital of course was trying to meet the consent decree's requirement that there be no more than fifty patients. But it was also trying to avoid creating another person eligible for the class of patient covered by the decree—for whom a costly residential placement would have to be found. Covered were those who had spent six consecutive months as patients at Northampton State Hospital. Those who spent less time in the hospital—even if they had been in other hospitals for years—were not covered. Their families often found such patients (including individuals falling ill for the first time) barred from *both* hospital and community residences.

One mother (who asked that her name be withheld) described to us how her son had finally been admitted to Northampton Hospital in the spring of 1989. The hospital rapidly discharged him, still actively psychotic, and too soon to make him eligible for a community placement. Residences with minimal supervision are available to those not covered by the consent decree. But, the mother explains, the mental health authorities say her son needs a higher level of supervision: "They're right but he can't get in."[48]

The lesson of Northampton, then, is that even with high quality residential programs, as these are generally conceded to be, and enormous tax-dollar investment, the role of the hospital continues to be crucial. As a result of pressure from the strong Alliance for the Mentally Ill chapter in Western Massachusetts, which has been monitoring the hospital, Northampton Hospital has improved. Despite the consent decree, AMI now hopes to see a new 120-bed facility built within the decrepit framework of the old.

Anti-Psychiatric Ideology Drives Policy

At least in Northampton, community programs were developed for those eligible under terms of the consent decree. In Washington, D.C., where in 1980 the Mental Health Law Project in Dixon *v.* Weinberger won a similar consent decree,[49] calling for a drastic reduction in the population of St. Elizabeth's Hospital, the required community-based system of care never got off the ground. The money apparently became sandbagged in the city's scandal-ridden municipal agencies. (The District of Columbia, which spends almost $200 per capita on mental health services, far more than any other jurisdiction, has been described as dollar for dollar the worst system in the country.) Yet anti-psychiatric ideologues continue their drive against the city's only public mental hospital, regardless of the consequences for the mentally ill and their families.

In 1988, the Dixon Implementation Monitoring Committee (so-named after the original plaintiff in the case) reported on the abandonment suffered by members of the "Dixon class." The monitoring committee found there were between 2,000 and 3,000 mentally ill living on the streets or in shelters, many of whom had been residents of St. Elizabeth's at the time of the consent decree and entitled to community-based care under its terms.

Most of the members of the "Dixon class" who were housed at all were in board and care homes. The committee reported it "did not see a single residence that met the definition of 'small and homelike' established in the 1980 Dixon plan."[50] It described one large board and care establishment in which a staff member reported an intolerable stench in the air, with piles of dirty clothing on the floor of the residents' living quarters, while patients urinated and defecated on themselves and slept in their own filth.[51]

In the meantime, St. Elizabeth's Hospital declined. In 1989 Hannah Schussheim, who heads Friends of St. Elizabeth's, castigated the Dixon plan:

> At the crux of [Norman] Rosenberg's argument for deinstitutionalization is that dollars should be taken out of the hospital and put in the community. His enforcement of the Dixon decree by the Mental Health Law Project (which he directs) has done just that.
>
> Where there was one psychiatrist to 30 patients [at St. Elizabeth's], there is now one to 70 or 80 patients.
>
> Where there were escorts and buses to take patients needing supervision for walks or to the parks, these patients now sit day after day in locked wards with nothing to do.
>
> Where there were a variety of programs for supervised and un-supervised patients, many of the patients no longer have access to thera-peutic and rehabilitative services. . . . The library has been reduced from 45 hours a week to 16. Magazines and periodicals were cut off in October 1987. Rosenberg is trying to shut down St. Elizabeth's Hospital. The result of his efforts is a deteriorated life for patients.

Schussheim pleads for recognition that "the District's mental health system must integrate hospital services into mental health planning. Dismantling the hospital has been a bad policy."[52]

Yet the Mental Health Law Project presses relentlessly forward with the very policies whose failure it admits. The Project's Elizabeth Jones, who heads the Dixon implementation committee, declared in 1988: "I would say that the mental health system is on the brink of disaster."[53] Still, in June 1989, the Dixon Committee secured yet another agreement with the District's mayor Marion Barry to move 400 more patients out of St. Elizabeth's into "small homelike facilities for six or fewer patients."[54] This despite the Dixon Committee's report of the previous year that, after eight years of the consent decree, *not one* such facility existed!

Whither Vermont?

Originally hoping to close down its state hospital altogether, Vermont has settled on the more modest goal of sharply reducing its census. After June 1990 there are to be no more than twenty-four acute and long-term beds, with an additional twenty forensic and thirty-six nursing home beds, for a maximum hospital population of eighty-six.[55] The state is geographically small, with comparatively high per capita spending on mental health, well-developed community programs, and only an estimated 3,000 chronically mentally ill. Vermont has also avoided the traditional mistake of forcing patients out of the hospital *before* putting community programs in place. Aided by a $600,000 grant from the Robert Wood Johnson Foundation, Vermont was able initially to "double-fund" hospital and community placements. Boding less well for its deinstitutionalization plan, Vermont is a hotbed of anti-psychiatric ideology.

As in the case of Northampton, there seems to be little awareness that large numbers of *new* cases of mental illness must be factored in. Roch Thibodeau, who heads the Vermont Alliance for the Mentally Ill and is sympathetic to the state's effort, says: "They're only concerned with the immediate population that they identify. They're not anticipating that from this day on anyone else is going to have mental illness."[56]

Moreover, those involved in this latest round of deinstitutionalization seem to have little comprehension of the need for involuntary commitment or some mechanism for ensuring seriously ill patients take medication in the community. On the contrary, the Division of Mental Health appointed a task force of University of Vermont professors (among whom anti-psychiatric sentiment was strong) which in 1987 proposed a system of "safe houses" where individuals could "work through" their "crises" for up to six months without medication.[57] Replacing state mental hospitals with residences on the Laingian-style Soteria model is a prescription for disaster.

Vermont has a militant, anti-psychiatric ex-patient group, the Vermont Liberation Organization, which receives grants from NIMH's Community Support Program.[58] The VLO hands out buttons summarizing its program: "Ban shock. Ban forced drugging. Abolish psychiatric institutions." Nonetheless, its leaders are accepted as representative of patient interests by the state's mental health officials and they take an active role in shaping the new system. Roch Thibodeau observes:

> There's never a group that's convened, a task force or subcommittee, that doesn't have a parent or an ex-patient on the panel, and it gets to be basically Paul Dorfner [head of the Vermont Liberation Organization] and me. . . . One of the things I try to get the department of health or the university or whoever it is that is inviting me or other family members to be on their task forces is to say hey, why don't we have consumers who are not VLO members.[59]

Thibodeau believes the reason for the reliance on the Vermont Liberation Organization is precisely that its leaders are so unrepresentative of the severely mentally ill.

> It's easy to bring in Paul. He's well educated and very knowledgeable. He's very knowledgeable politically. He's very knowledgeable about his agenda, so it makes it easier if you're looking for a performance type of response—to make out a white paper or do something. You're going to get the goods right there.

Vermont's emerging system is permeated by the inaccurate assumption that a major problem with mental illness—that many most severely afflicted deny or cannot recognize they are sick—can be overcome by good services. A small number of additional beds in general hospitals are planned, but none of them will take involuntary patients.[60]

Abolishing Hospitals: The Italian Experience

One country in particular provides the most instructive lesson on the perils of carrying anti-psychiatry to its logical conclusion. In 1978, Italy passed Law 180, which banned new admissions to public asylums and converted all existing inmates to voluntary status. In place of state hospitals, diagnosis and care units, consisting of 15 beds for every 150,000 population, were to be established in general hospitals. (In the United States, even in the era of deinstitutionalization, there are 130 psychiatric beds in public and private hospitals combined, for every 100,000 population.) Involuntary admission, even to those units, required the signature of the town's mayor and would be limited to forty-eight hours, with judicial approval needed for a seven-day renewal.[61]

Law 180 was the handiwork of Franco Basaglia, the most politically successful of the anti-psychiatric psychiatrists of the 1960s. Basaglia, who in 1961 became head of a mental hospital at Gorizia (near the Yugoslavia border) and in 1972 of San Giovanni hospital in Trieste, was able to rally the radical student groups of the period and Italy's influential Communist Party behind his Psichiatria Democratica, the movement he founded in 1974 to close down mental hospitals. Like conservative Republicans in the United States who failed to stand up to the mental health bar, right-wing Christian Democrats welcomed Law 180 as a money-saving measure.

Basaglia's appeal for the Left lay in his merging of anti-psychiatry and Marxism: like Laing's books, his abstruse tracts became bestsellers.

The decision to label someone mentally ill, according to Basaglia, was a political decision. Medicine was simply a cover concealing "the fundamental contradiction between the separation of the productive and the unproductive, which then becomes opposition between 'sane' and 'sick.'"[62] Under capitalism, those who worked were sane and those who did not were viewed as a danger to the system, "a mere germ, a source of infection and an agent of contagion to be identified, isolated and sterilized within the social vacuum of the asylum."[63] For Basaglia, the community mental health center movement in the United States was another capitalist conspiracy "to justify more forms of surveillance and regulation of 'problem' populations in the ghetto."[64]

A professor of psychiatry at the Institute of Clinical Psychiatry at the University of Pisa summed up the results of Law 180: "There has actually been a very severe decline in the quality of psychiatric care, with very unfortunate consequences for patients, their families and society in general."[65] Approximately 35,000 of the estimated 55,000 patients who were in mental hospitals at the time Law 180 was passed have remained there. The difference is that now they are called "guests," rather than patients, and are virtually without care.

English social policy expert Kathleen Jones and researcher Alison Poletti toured Italy twice to study the impact of the new law. Particularly in the south, Kathleen Jones told us:

> Conditions are generally appalling—buildings falling down, few staff, no administration, few drugs or other treatments. . . . I have been visiting mental hospitals in many countries for years, and these are the worst I have seen anywhere.[66]

In a number of hospitals Jones and Poletti found wards of sixty to eighty "guests" attended only by two untrained nurses. There were not even any cleaning people or porters, so the nurses had all the work of cleaning the wards as well as attending to patients. The buildings were allowed to decay; officially "closed," there was no money to maintain them. Surprised to find "guests" in straitjackets in locked wards, they learned that in order to stay, guests signed a voluntary form which included agreement to be locked up or put in restraints, as necessary.[67]

Since work was forbidden as "exploitative," "guests" were kept in total idleness. At the hospital at Maggiano, where patients used to tend olive groves and vineyards, the fields and terraces are choked with weeds. Nor did other activities take the place of productive work. There were no classes, no ward activities, often not even television or radio. Jones and Poletti write: "It was hard to escape the conclusion that patients and staff alike had been written off by an ideological movement which preferred to ignore their existence."[68]

On the other hand, private nursing homes have mushroomed to fill the vacuum of care. Although the government often pays for patients to stay in them, there is no system of inspection. Jones and Poletti saw one home with 800 patients, most in a very deteriorated state. There were no activities and some patients were on locked wards—contrary to Law 180.

In the community, except for some pockets where the Communist Party was strong, Jones and Poletti found that support services were meager: in the south, they were virtually nonexistent. Kathleen Jones told us:

> Rehabilitation is disapproved of because it involves structured and planned activity for the patient. The essence of the reform movement is that mentally ill people are not "patients" but "users." They decide what they want to do; nobody else can plan for them.[69]

Trieste is considered a model, one of the few places with good community support services. Indeed, at three mental health centers one of us (Virginia Armat) visited in that city, patients come often, for lunch or to chat; relations with doctors and staff are warm and informal; there is a lot of kissing and hugging. Nonetheless, at the San Vito Mental Health Center in downtown Trieste, which Basaglia had once directed, queried as to how things were going, a psychiatrist who had been there since 1971 shook his head and sighed: "We need better medications, much better." A surprising response indeed, coming from a disciple of Basaglia, in a mecca of anti-psychiatry.

Paradoxically, Basaglia's anti-psychiatric crusade has produced a system where in most cases the *only* treatment is drugs. ECT has declined dramatically in the country where it originated. Psychiatric nursing was abandoned as a specialty in 1975. Occupational therapists are few and far between. Group therapy is considered "manipulative," and psychoanalysis "bourgeois."[70] According to Jones and Poletti: "What we have seen in Italy is a violent step along the path to deinstitutionalization . . . with nothing in the way of planned community services to mitigate its effects."[71] Where exposés used to refer to the 'abbandonati' in Italian hospitals, now it is the patients in the community who are called 'abbandonati.'"[72]

The burden on many families has become intolerable, especially when they have to deal with individuals who are violent and refuse treatment. Dangerousness is not specified as cause for commitment, and the entire thrust of Law 180 is to curtail the possibilities for involuntary confinement and treatment. One Italian noblewoman we interviewed was unable to have her schizophrenic son committed despite her many connections among politicians and doctors and her son's repeated threats to her and her husband. While she was out buying the newspaper one morning, her son stabbed his father to death. Although he had been treated as a sane adult in the community, his particular crime entitled him to be considered as insane. Thus he is deemed only a third as responsible as a normal individual. Accordingly, his ten-year prison term for a crime committed while he was still legally a sane adult is a third the normal length! In 1988, in the sixth year of his term, he vowed to commit matricide too as soon as he was released. His despairing mother, a princess in her sixties, is in the same situation as Don and Peggy Richardson in California: she has no idea what she will do when he gets out.

Luigi di Marchi, a psychologist and father of a mentally ill daughter, who with his wife, Maria Luisa Zardini, founded the families' lobby group, the Association for the Reform of Psychiatric Assistance, told us he expects the law will be changed, but not quickly.[73] (While only the Communist Party remains opposed to changing it, there is much disagreement on how to restructure the system.) Meantime, the chaos continues. The only time their daughter, who has schizophrenia, ever received any care at all was when she ended up on the streets of London and was committed for several years to the Maudsley Clinic. In Italy, her mother told us, since she refuses treatment, she can get no care. We heard the same story from many Italian families.

Italy—A False Model for Community Psychiatry

The failure of Law 180 warrants emphasis because Italy is being held up as a model by a number of community psychiatrists both in England and the United States. Loren Mosher's 1988 book, *Community Mental Health,* written with Dr. Lorenzo Burti of the South Verona Mental Health Center, devotes several chapters to a glowing account of the Italian experience; one is called, incredibly, "Utopia at Work." As we noted earlier, Mosher urges the United States to follow Italy's example and bar all further admissions to state hospitals.

Kathleen Jones asks, "Why has the myth of the success of the 'Italian experience' . . . persisted in the face of overwhelming evidence to the contrary?" She answers that "many of us suffer from tunnel vision when we look at events in other countries."[74] What Jones leaves out is that vision in this case is impaired by anti-psychiatric ideology, which is alive and well in many corners of community psychiatry.

Tensions over anti-psychiatry have been growing in IAPSRS, the International Association of Psycho-Social Rehabilitation Services, an organization of community mental health workers formed in 1975. Many speakers at its 1988 conference denounced "the medical model" in psychiatry. We mentioned in Chapter 11 Peter Breggin's workshop on psychoactive medication where no psychiatrists were invited to participate who could have challenged his highly distorted presentation.

The conference was hosted and organized by Horizon House, one of the first clubhouses, and the views of its director, Jerome Gardner, who bestowed an award on Thomas Szasz, presumably do much to explain its tenor. Like Szasz, Gardner brooks no interference with the "choices" of those called mentally ill, including suicide.

> We must stop being "parents," and let our "children" go. The dignity of risk [of suicide] far outweighs the humanity of treatment for one's own good.[75]

For Gardner, both ECT and psychoactive drugs are "adverse strategies"; he believes the chief problems of mental illness, used to justify hospitalization, are in fact "caused by the treatment."[76] Gardner's view that rehabilitation is "in conflict" with the medical model of mental illness may explain Breggin's presence. But it does not account for the latter's enthusiastic reception, the standing-room-only audiences and the absence of challenges in question periods.

Only a small minority of community mental health workers—as indeed a small minority of attorneys—may hold anti-psychiatric views. What makes that minority significant is that the majority is unwilling to confront it on major issues, preferring to gloss over differences. Without unity, it is difficult for a mental health lobby to obtain funds from state legislatures. The price of unity becomes the inability to achieve constructive change.

The Keys to Community Living for the Mentally Ill

The chronically mentally ill people who do thrive in the community are invisible because they are doing well. Others, who are doing badly, barely surviving on the streets or housed miserably, could also thrive, if the mental health system adapted to the realities of the illness. What then *are* the keys to maintaining patients decently in the community?

1. *The mentally ill need appropriate treatment for their disease.*
Existing treatments need to be used more aggressively and intelligently. Poor medical practice abounds in public psychiatry.

Perhaps the most famous modern mental patient is Sylvia Frumkin (a pseudonym), whose many years in and out of hospitals, group residences, and her parents' home, were chronicled in *The New Yorker* by Susan Sheehan and later published as the book *Is There No Place On Earth for Me?* One psychopharmacologist whom Sheehan asked to review Frumkin's dismal history, declared:

> No treatment she received over a period of thirteen years bore any logical relation to a previous treatment. You get the impression that the psychiatrists pulled a drug out of a hat and gave her too little of whatever they pulled out, or that they dumped the contents of the hat out on a tray and gave her too little of several drugs.[77]

When properly medicated, she did respond. Yet any therapeutic dose was lowered the instant she showed any sign of improvement. She would soon relapse. Many psychiatrists, said the expert, fail to study the case histories of their patients.[78]

ECT has virtually disappeared as a treatment for individuals with schizophrenia who are suffering their first acute psychotic episode; yet, as we noted in Chapter 10, there is evidence that, precisely at that point in the illness, it may be the most effective of all available treatments.

For better and more vigorous treatment to replace the often slipshod and inadequate psychiatric care given the chronically ill, public attitudes will have to change. That will require education by and of the media, which for decades, with rare exceptions, has portrayed ECT, for example, as a barbaric relic.

2. *Hospitalization must be available as needed, and for some on a long-term basis.*
Hospitals are a key to maintaining the mentally ill in the community. Many mentally ill individuals, including some who take medication as prescribed, suffer periodic exacerbations of their illness, and require hospitalization and treatment when this happens.

Barring better therapies, there will also be patients who require long-term institutional care, whether in a state hospital or functional equivalent, because their severe illness does not respond to existing treatments. Louise Broderick, of the Michigan community program Places for People, declares that everyone is aware of the need for more community services. In addition, she says:

[T]here needs to be an awareness, an acknowledgment that . . . some people are going to need long-term care, probably in a state hospital. Because the private facilities don't have to take them, and if they become too much of a behavior problem, they put them out and they end up on the street. There should be a place where these people can go, that has to take them.[79]

3. *Legal statuses intermediate between the confinement of the institution and total freedom in the community must be created for a group of patients who cannot otherwise sustain a satisfactory life in the community.*

An all-voluntary system cannot be maintained at acceptable costs in both human and financial terms. There is no getting away from the reality that *judgment is impaired in mental illness.*

Forms of guardianship or outpatient commitment can keep a certain type of patient in the community: this is someone who does well on medication but consistently stops taking it, leading to rapid deterioration. Such people often become revolving-door patients in hospitals at high and unnecessary costs to themselves, their families, and society. Or they may join the ranks of grate-dwellers.

For some, as Dane County has discovered, only medication compliance need be required. Others, who have great difficulty exercising self-control even with medication, need to be placed in highly structured residential settings intermediate between hospitals and the open-door of the typical board and care or group residence.

Not all forms of coercion involve treatment. For those who rapidly squander benefit checks, a designated payee can mean remaining off the streets and out of the hospital. Money management can also be integrated with medication compliance. In Dane County a number of chronically ill for whom the county acts as payee receive their money and medications together.

4. *Community services, including supported residential and rehabilitation programs must be provided in one, integrated system.*

The model programs all more or less independently discovered what ingredients enable the chronically mentally ill to function in the community: now, finally, mental health authorities must fix responsibility and organize service delivery to meet patients' needs. As Fuller Torrey emphasizes, responsibility for the mentally ill must be fixed at a single level of government, along with the financial resources to carry out those responsibilities.

Admittedly, it is not easy to put the Humpty Dumpty of hospital services together again in the community. Service providers must be prepared to follow patients, not wait in offices for patients to come to them. Thus, the Robert Wood Johnson Foundation gave the caseworkers in its demonstration program, instead of offices, cellular telephones.

Outpatient commitment is not a substitute for services, and indeed will not work without them.

5. *The need for treatment must be restored as a basis both for involuntary commitment and treatment in the community.*

Even in Wisconsin, with its limited guardianship and outpatient commitment, David LeCount says:

> There are people we would love to place in inpatient settings and get them stabilized. But we don't have dangerousness. We're constantly in that bind—we're waiting for dangerousness.[80]

Elimination of the need-for-treatment standard, as we have seen, has resulted in preventing *voluntary* as well as involuntary patients from obtaining needed care. Unless patients meet the dangerousness standard, public hospitals for the most part will not accept them. Yet as Hannah Schussheim of Friends of St. Elizabeth's says:

> They've set up this criterion of people having to prove themselves harmful to themselves or others whereas they may just be terribly, terribly sick . . . and I find that very inappropriate. In any other illness, you have a right to go to a doctor or a hospital. But somehow in this illness it's only if it's life-threatening you have a right to be admitted to a hospital.[81]

If the seriously mentally ill on our streets are to be rescued from degradation, a need-for-treatment standard—with appropriate safeguards—must be restored.[82]

6. *Responsibility for treating the mentally ill must rest with the medical profession.*

The shift in power from psychiatrists to attorneys has been calamitous, leading to the obstruction and denial of needed treatment. The lawyers responsible for the shift must recognize that, as has been said, they are practicing medicine with the wrong graduate degree.

Money, in short supply for the care of patients, has been siphoned off to pay for legal minuets either wholly without value or absurdly incommensurate with their costs. While no one has estimated the proportion of the mental health dollar that goes to lawyers, or lawyer-mandated procedures, it is clearly sizable and growing. In 1989, after the California Supreme Court allowed the Court of Appeals decision in Riese v. St. Mary's to stand, a psychiatrist wrote in to the Ventura County *Star-Free Press:*

> [W]e are now forced to keep our patients unmedicated for about an extra week to wait until the Court can see the patient. . . . As every day in the hospital costs some $500 . . . it will cost Ventura County quite a bundle over a year's time to hold these patients for this extra time. It . . . also . . . seriously further clogs our already overcrowded facility.[83]

Contrary to their avowed purpose of securing treatment in the least restrictive alternative, in state after state, through their "right to refuse treatment" suits, legal advocates have imposed *a system of non-care in the most restrictive alternative.*

Disabled or Labeled?

The radical patient movement cannot have it both ways. Its members see nothing illogical in accepting $6.5 billion in mental health benefits as *disabled,* while claiming they are falsely *labeled.* If they demand SSI, SSDI, Medicaid, subsidized housing, and vocational and rehabilitation services, they cannot at the same time declare mental illness does not exist and treatment for it is superfluous. Either mental illness exists and deserves special dispensation from society, or it doesn't. How can advocates demand funds for Protection and Advocacy systems for those diagnosed as mentally ill believing that the diagnosis has no validity? Even Szasz told an audience of radical activists that such a pursuit was fundamentally dishonest.[84]

Moreover, the public will not pay indefinitely for costly community services without visible results. The experience of Philadelphia is instructive. In the early 1980s, a strong patient lobby was a factor in leading that city to develop a comprehensive program for the homeless. In 1989 the city announced plans to halve those funds. The *New York Times* noted that the cuts reflected decreasing public support, especially by business, for expensive programs that had failed to clear the streets of beggars and mentally ill people.[85] The failure of Philadelphia's programs to have a major impact on the disorder in the streets should come as no surprise: Philadelphia ranks as one of the most difficult cities in the country in which to treat an individual against his will.

A rational system of care for the mentally ill in the community can be constructed. But community care cannot work without treatment, and enthusiasts for rehabilitation who oppose what they call "the medical model" in fact undercut the basis for maintaining the mentally ill in the community. For, as has been aptly said, in a democracy, objectionable behavior will be voted out. Unless a way is found to provide needed treatment, sooner or later, there will be a public outcry for reinstitutionalizing the mentally ill—including those who could live a dignified life in the community with appropriate care and support.

Conclusion
Forging a New Bipartisan Consensus

THIRTY years after "the myth of mental illness" first gained currency, its grave consequences have become apparent. As Paul Appelbaum observes:

> The idea that mental illness might really not exist . . . made it a lot easier for massive deinstitutionalization to occur. It made it easier for funding not to be provided for adequate community services, for in the back of everyone's mind was the gnawing question, "Does mental illness really exist?" If it doesn't, what are we paying for? It had an enormous pernicious effect on public policy.[1]

Not even the tragedy of the mentally ill abandoned on our streets has wholly dispelled the myth. Precisely a year before his July 1990 suicide, homeless advocate and guest speaker Mitch Snyder told a National Alliance for the Mentally Ill conference:

> The problem is not those people who live in different realities, but the people who make up the majority who determine what normalcy will be and determines anyone who lives outside those parameters to be either disabled or persona non grata or outcasts. . . . We have to speak to a nation that is no more anxious to hear the truth about mental disability than it is about homelessness—that there is no mental disability, there is no mental illness except perhaps in those places where people are trying to figure out how to destroy the planet or how to destroy the human race.[2]

Thus do advocates sow confusion. Those who deny mental illness pretend to champion the victims of their own policies. Groups like the ACLU become self-righteous spokesmen for the very people they have "liberated" to the shame of the streets. The real torment of their victims is buried under the cant of "homelessness" with its hypocritical indictment of the political system for mistreating the poor.

As we have seen, a bipartisan consensus formed around a lie. A new one must now form around the truth—that mental illness is a tragic reality requiring protective social intervention. For if the hoax that mental illness was a myth won adherents at both ends of the political spectrum, it is now obvious that the consequences of the hoax corrode central values of conservatives and liberals alike.

Conservatives react to the adverse consequences for the social order of the anarchy in our public places. Even libertarian Thomas Szasz refuses to grant that the homeless have the right to defecate and urinate in our streets. Columnist George Will points out that the homeless "present a spectacle of disorder and decay that becomes a contagion."[3] Writing in *Time,* Charles Krauthammer compared the danger posed by the homeless to the "broken window" described by political scientist James Q. Wilson, which advertises a neighborhood where care is not taken. This, in turn, encourages vandalism, crime, and culminates in total social disintegration. The homeless, wrote Krauthammer, are a kind of broken social window announcing that suffering and chaos will be tolerated.[4]

More fundamental, those who lie on our streets challenge the very legitimacy of our political and economic system. Attorney Frances Werner reports that at the 1982 House subcommittee hearings on homelessness

> Each speaker, whether a soup kitchen worker, a Salvation Army or church group member, or a government agency employee, implicitly or explicitly questioned the worth of a society that allows its members to sleep on the streets for want of homes.[5]

Liberals have of course traditionally sought government solutions to aid the helpless and prevent human degradation. And while social order, as a value, may concern them less, they too must feel compassion for the suffering of the mentally ill and their families. Surely they cannot ignore the plea of Alicia González, a Bolivian divorcée living in the United States for fifteen years, for help for her mentally ill daughter, whose symptoms respond dramatically to anti-psychotic drugs, which she refuses to take:

> The worst thing is—it's not the illness—it's this country with this stupid idea of freedom for the mentally ill. I tell you that's the cause of the agony. Because if you have a pain, I take you to the hospital. You have a heart attack, you're treated immediately. They don't let you die there in front of me while I watch, until you tell them "Please give me the digitalis, so my heart can start pumping."[6]

Equally, liberals can share the indignation of Norma Wanucha, mother of two mentally ill children, who works with mentally ill vagrants in Lucas County, Ohio.

> It's the biggest tragedy I've ever encountered. How we can get to the point where we can allow people who are so ill to just wander, wander, wander, all under the guise of supposed freedom is beyond me.[7]

Conservatives and liberals alike must heed Charles Krauthammer's observation that "the city, with its army of grate-dwellers, is a school for callousness."[8] When one's natural instinct to help the homeless is thwarted every day, it gives way to indifference. As the homeless make our cities American Calcuttas the *Washington Post*'s Juan Williams notes, "Their presence becomes a background noise—to be ignored as easily as the sound of passing cars."[9]

A fundamental change in policy demands more than recognition that mental illness "is not some palpable falsehood propagated among the populace by power-mad psychiatrists, but a cruel and bitter reality that has been with the human race since antiquity."[10] It is also necessary to recognize how important precepts of our legal system have been distorted to enshrine the right of the mentally ill to self-destruct. One precept is the right to individual self-determination, now used to block civil commitment of the mentally ill unless and until they pose an *imminent* danger to themselves or others. The other is the right of the individual to informed consent to medical treatment, used now to *prevent* treatment—even after an individual is committed *for the purpose of treatment.*

Liberal individualism that makes autonomy the premier social value is today rightly under attack. A number of social philosophers have emphasized the atomism this breeds, and are calling for a morality that recognizes individual rights and social obligations as interdependent.[11] But *even in the context of liberal individualism as defined by those who shaped the philosophy,* there is no implied right to self-fulfillment in madness. John Stuart Mill's words in *On Liberty* are erroneously cited by exponents of this alleged right:

> [T]he only purpose for which power can rightfully be exercised over any member of a civilized community, against his will, is to prevent harm to others. His own good, either physical or moral, is not a sufficient warrant. . . . The only part of the conduct of anyone for which he is amenable to society is that which concerns others. In the part which merely

concerns himself, his independence is, of right, absolute. Over himself, over his own body and mind, the individual is sovereign.[12]

What those who cite Mill to defend freedom from intrusion by society never mention is what comes *immediately after* these words.

It is, perhaps, hardly necessary to say that this doctrine is meant to apply only to human beings in the maturity of their faculties. We are not speaking of children or of young persons below the age which the law may fix as that of manhood or womanhood. Those who are still in a state to require being taken care of by others must be protected against their own actions as well as against external injury.[13]

Mill clearly had in mind more than those below a certain age. Indeed, he specifically exempted entire societies, "in which the race itself may be considered as in its nonage." Despotism, says Mill "is a legitimate mode of government in dealing with barbarians, provided the end be their improvement." The reason, Mill explains, is that liberty has no application to any state of things where man is not capable "of being improved by free and equal discussion."[14]

In other words, Mill's concept of liberty depends on man's being a civilized, rational creature: he asserts that his principles apply to those who "have attained the capacity of being guided to their own improvement by conviction or persuasion." Later in *On Liberty,* Mill returns to circumstances that warrant interference with liberty: for example, when a person crosses a bridge known to be unsafe and there is no time to warn him of his danger. However, if the person has been warned, and nonetheless decides to cross the dangerous bridge, he is free to do so— unless, Mill reiterates, "he is a child, or delirious, or in some state of excitement or absorption incompatible with the full use of the reflecting faculty."[15]

Although Mill does not specifically mention the mentally ill, there can be no doubt that he would be horrified to be cited as a source for the doctrine that society has no right to intervene on their behalf. *For it is precisely the reflecting faculty that is diseased in the mentally ill.* Try "free and equal discussion" with the individual convinced aliens from outer space are radioing to him from under the living room sofa, or "conviction or persuasion" with someone suffering from schizophrenia and declaiming in a jabberwocky that no one else can understand. (Except for Laing, who, as noted in Chapter 1, conjured up translations for this speech that psychiatrists call "schizophrenic salad.")

Furthermore, legal advocates who hold up Mill as authority for the right of the mad to behave as their illness impels them, ignore his entire statement that an individual's actions can be deterred if they are "calculated to produce evil to some one else." In the case of the mentally ill, the individual's untrammeled "freedom" is immensely costly above all to family members, who lose much of *their* freedom. Earlier we quoted Sheila Broughel's sister on Sheila's successful battle to be free (at the cost of her life): "I mean in our family there were five other children and two adults. Their lives should have been worth something. But they weren't." What of the rights of the elderly, ill parents of Nick Gavrilou? Even before he murdered them, Nick had imposed a reign of terror upon the household. In repeatedly releasing Nick into their care following violent episodes, with no more than a few days' treatment, society placed his right to be mad and free over their right to freedom from justifiable fear.

Contemporary rights language upholds the point of view of the "victim." In the case of mental illness, the "victim" is assumed to be the person who has the illness. But the "victim" could equally well be defined as the family members forced to care for those they cannot treat. When the mentally ill attack family members—or, less commonly, a random member of the public—the victim is *better* defined as the target of mentally disordered behavior. Even the shopkeeper who loses customers because a mentally ill person has taken up residence in his doorway is a victim of the mentally ill.

Although the law may intend to enforce the unfettered self-interest of the mentally ill "victim," its end result is to undermine his interests. Thus, In the Matter of Guardianship of Richard Roe III, the Massachusetts Supreme Judicial Court assigned supreme value to the expressed wishes of Richard Roe. However, as Larry Churchill and Jose Siman point out in *The Hastings Center Report,* a journal devoted to bioethics, rights are not freestanding absolutes, "but are organically related to the larger body of duties and obligations which they incur."[16] The court disdained this, treating Richard's rights as entailing no reciprocal obligation to respect the rights of other family members. In the short run, this might seem to benefit Richard, whose selfish interests were treated as primary. But in the longer run, the family disintegrated under the stress, depriving Richard of the support of which he, more than any other member of the family, had need.

So long as rights are treated as "truncheons," it is the mentally ill who will ultimately feel most of their weight. There is no room for the dependent severely impaired—the mentally ill among them—in a society where it is permissible for others always to behave in a narrowly self-interested way, always to prefer self-serving actions at the expense of communal bonds.[17] Courts cannot have it both ways. If the selfish wishes of Richard Roe are sacrosanct, why should not the selfish desires of each of his family members be accorded equal weight?

Sooner or later, many families, for self-protection, must reluctantly conclude that their own interest precludes any ongoing effort to care for the individual who owes no responsibility to them. Unable to obtain treatment for his daughter Alice because she is not defined as "dangerous," how much longer can James Randolph be expected to avoid calling the police to secure freedom from the daily torment she makes of his life? So far, as we noted earlier, visions of his daughter as a homeless wanderer have caused him to reject this course. His friends are urging him to act now. At some point, he is likely to join the growing ranks of families with court orders barring a mentally ill son or daughter, husband or wife, from intruding upon their property on pain of arrest.

The *Philadelphia Inquirer* conducted a two-year study in which its reporters reviewed court and hospital records and interviewed almost 300 people. Some families told of fabricating tales of violence in their desperation to obtain treatment for their children; they press criminal charges, hoping that the justice system will force treatment where the mental health system will not. The result is often that their children serve time with real criminals—without receiving any treatment for their mental illness.[18]

If the rights of family members are breached by the emphasis on the rights of mental patients, the interests of a broader public are also affected. The public has a right to expect legitimate standards of behavior in public places. Parks, transportation terminals, libraries, even sidewalks, are public amenities, and the ordinary citizen is entitled to expect that they will maintain a civilized ambience. Both Thomas Szasz and George Will point out that there can be no reasonable right to live on sidewalks. As things stand now, there is little power to enforce community standards of public civility in public places. When attempts are made to do so—as New York Park Commissioner Henry Stern did in 1989 with proposed regulations against begging, lying on benches, and erecting tents in city parks—protests by homeless advocates, or court decisions, often vitiate the rulings.[19] Countering the trends, in 1990 a federal appeals court did uphold the right of New York City's Transit Authority to ban panhandling on the subways.

The second legal principle that has been distorted vis-à-vis the mentally ill is the right to informed consent to medical treatment. While Mill is misquoted as authority for limiting involuntary commitment of the mentally ill to a strict "dangerousness-to-others" standard, a 1914 New York Court of Appeals decision, Schloendorff v. Society of New York Hospital, is misused as a basis for affirming a mental patient's right to refuse treatment even after he is committed. In his opinion, Judge Benjamin Cardozo then wrote: "Every human being of adult years *and sound mind* has a right to determine what shall be done with his own body."[20] (Italics added.)

How could Judge Cardozo's words, specifically exempting the mentally ill, be used as ground for giving them the same right to determine their own treatment as normal individuals? The key has been the legal fiction, enshrined in state laws during the late 1960s and 1970s, that mental patients are competent.

The intention of those who first advocated overturning the traditional assumption that mental patients were incompetent, as we noted earlier, was to *make treatment easier*. As Albert Deutsch pointed out in the Senate's 1961 hearings, "mental hospital commitment in most States automatically strips them *en masse* of specific civil rights—sometimes of all such rights, regardless of their individual capacity."[21] It was argued that the mentally ill and their families were reluctant to seek treatment early in the illness because of the legal consequences that could haunt them later. And so people like psychiatrist Manfred Guttmacher, who termed some of the then minimal procedural protections for involuntarily committed patients "legal obstructionism," nonetheless argued against equating mental illness with incompetency. "The stigma of incompetency should be added to that of insanity only when practical necessity so dictates and never otherwise in my opinion."[22]

Advocates of these desirable and necessary reforms little thought that their efforts would be perverted to mean that patients could no longer be treated for mental illness because they were now "competent" to refuse all treatment. Yet the mental health bar has successfully asserted that since the law assumes mental patients to be competent, they are legally of "sound mind." They thus fall under the purview of the Schloendorff decision—despite the fact it specifically excluded them!

In permitting mentally ill persons who meet the stringent "dangerousness" criteria to refuse treatment even after they have been committed, courts have been so intent on individual autonomy that they have ignored a legitimate state interest that, for the commonweal, ought at times to circumscribe its exercise. As philosophy professor David C.

Blake points out, the state, for example, has an interest in preserving the ethical integrity of medicine.

> The ethical integrity of medicine might not be affected by an individual's unqualified right to refuse the care of medicine altogether. But it does not follow that the profession's integrity can permit an unqualified right of patients to refuse whatever particular treatment they wish *while remaining in the care of medicine.*[23]

While he does not specifically mention mental illness, there is no better illustration of his thesis. Blake identifies three "goods" that health care professionals seek, whose service makes the profession a praiseworthy endeavor: these are human life, the lessening of pain and suffering, and the autonomy of patients, understood as the self-conscious, independent functioning of the human being. The ethical integrity of medicine, says Blake, rests on the balanced and reasonable pursuit of all three of these basic human goods.

Treatment of psychosis not only lessens the pain and suffering of patients, and promotes their independent functioning, but is also often literally lifesaving. When doctors are forced to care for patients they are banned from treating, society undermines its own interest in preserving the integrity of medicine. It is little wonder that psychiatrists in turn are eager to release such patients.

Attorney Joel Klein has a unique perspective as a one-time lawyer for the anti-psychiatric Mental Health Law Project and, more recently, for the American Psychiatric Association. To counter the destructive fiction of patient "competence," Klein would frame the question not as "Is this person legally competent?" but is what "happens in the institution . . . is that related to the legitimate or reasonable purposes for why you are placed there?" In Klein's view:

> [S]omebody put into a state hospital for the purpose of treatment—and indeed I think it is a constitutional essential that there be treatment provided—can be treated since that is the purpose of the original deprivation of liberty. On the other hand, somebody committed to a state hospital cannot have an involuntary abortion or involuntary tonsillectomy. It is not because a tonsillectomy is less intrusive . . . than antipsychotic medication. It is because the purpose of the state's acting in this form (i.e., to commit) which is recognized by the Supreme Court now to be legitimate, is to treat.[24]

Klein describes "the whole competency notion" applied to the decision to treat as a "great red herring." If we can hospitalize people without their consent, says Klein, "it seems to me that legally it is going to follow that we can treat them without their consent if it is appropriate treatment, again subject to review."[25] (The review Klein speaks of is peer review by other qualified doctors, not review of medical treatment by judges.)

California's Alliance for the Mentally Ill has suggested another way to deal with competency and informed consent. California's Lanterman-Petris-Short Act, for all its flaws, provides that each person admitted for treatment be evaluated by a multidisciplinary team. There is no reason why this initial evaluation should not include a determination whether the individual is competent to make treatment decisions. In fact, as noted earlier, a California survey mandated by the legislature indicated that fully 90% *lacked* capacity to make a rational treatment decision. California AMI proposes a substitute decision-maker, preferably a family member, be appointed to discuss the patient's treatment with the psychiatrist when the individual is found to lack the capacity for informed consent.[26] However the problem of informed consent is handled, what is essential is that it not impair patients' ability to obtain needed treatment.

Instituting a humane system of care for the mentally ill will be both financially and politically costly. It is true that the quality of services seems to have little relation to the amounts spent—per capita, Madison, Wisconsin, with one of the best systems of care, spends a small fraction of what Washington, D.C. with one of the worst does. But Dr. Torrey is probably overoptimistic in suggesting that the estimated $17 billion a year (since he wrote the amount has topped $20 billion) already being spent on the mentally ill is sufficient. Torrey believes better allocation, and fixing responsibility—and funds—at a single (state or local) level, would suffice.[27]

There is no question that much money is wasted or misallocated. Community psychiatrist Richard Lamb notes that in Los Angeles an incredible 50% of mental health funds are spent on administration.[28] Because of similar figures elsewhere, Torrey observes that it has been said that public psychiatric services could be improved dramatically in New York and Massachusetts simply by putting administrators to work caring for patients. Moreover, large sums are now going to lawyers and advocates, who work to block needed treatment. (Their activism of course robs patients of clinical care, forcing psychiatrists to spend more and more of their time in court and on tasks associated with the constant legal challenges to treatment.)

But even if funds were better and more efficiently spent, the bill for adequate care of the mentally ill would almost surely rise, at least in the short term. For all their enormous benefits, anti-psychotic drugs have indirectly driven up the costs of caring for the mentally ill. Because the drugs significantly improve the symptoms of most patients, the great majority of mentally ill people can function in the community; however, many, as we have seen, still require in the community all or most of the supports formerly provided by the hospital.[29]

Moreover there are problems in the community that did not arise in state hospital settings. Patients often fail to take their medication, or manage money; and large numbers succumb to the temptations of drugs and alcohol. Providing for the enormous range of needs of chronic patients in the community, who with treatment become better but not well, may not be as costly as state hospital beds, but does not come cheap.

Unfortunately, because the drugs do not work well on 10% to 20% of patients, hospitals providing long-term care (in practice, state or county hospitals) continue to be necessary. These hospitals are extremely expensive and it is hard to see how the costs can be significantly brought down now that peonage suits have outlawed patient labor. Indeed, state hospitals—in inflation-corrected dollars—cost almost as much today as they did in 1955 when they harbored almost five times as many patients. Initially, an expansion in the number of beds will be necessary. New York City, in its modest program to take some of the most severely ill homeless off the streets, has found that stabilizing them often requires many months of hospital care. Alas, once stabilized, they may wind up in shelters without follow-up or supervision, because community residences for them do not exist.

If enough programs were created in the community, including highly structured ones (in essence mini-institutions), the need for hospital beds would decline. But while that would cut hospital costs eventually, in the short run *both* would have to be available. Dumping patients in the community on the theory that alternatives *will* be created is a well-tested recipe for chaos.[30] And while additional expenditures on mental illness may be a daunting prospect, in figuring current expenses, one must consider alternative costs not ordinarily chalked up to mental health that would be much reduced if appropriate community programs existed: shelters, the burden on public facilities, added police costs, the costs to merchants, and the psychic costs to everyone of turning public places into open air mental wards. For example, removing one mentally ill man poised to jump from the catwalk of a tower above New York harbor required twenty police officers and supervisors, six emergency vehicles, several highway units, and a helicopter.[31]

Precisely because of the staggering costs to society of mental illness (and we have not figured in the hidden toll of hundreds of thousands of young people unable to participate in the work force), research becomes an essential investment. Says Paul Appelbaum:

> The real advances will come from the laboratory in Bethesda or San Diego or New York. Someone in a lab somewhere will find a receptor that when properly stimulated clears thought disorders and stops auditory hallucinations, or they'll find a virus. . . . It's that solution that can solve the public policy problems. . . . If you've got a good treatment, society, given the magnitude of the disorder, is going to let you use it. And the rest of us are just trying to hold the fort until those on the science side of things come up with something.[32]

Helping those advances come sooner could be our best mental health bargain. The amount of money spent annually on research on mental illness—NIMH, for example, spent $90.2 million on research directly targeted to major mental illness—has gone up substantially in the last few years. But this amount is still proportionately much lower than that spent for other major (and minor) diseases, ranging from cancer and heart disease to muscular dystrophy. Yet schizophrenia, in its lengthy duration, is a far worse scourge than most other diseases that strike later in life. As Dr. Ben Lambiotte of the South Mountain Restoration Center near Gettysburg, Pennsylvania points out, "Schizophrenia takes away the entire life of the person. . . . [It] destroys the mind, it destroys the soul of a youth."[33]

If public funds have been scant, private funds for research on major mental illness have been negligible. Private money underwrites half of the rest of biomedical research, whereas government pays for 85% of research on mental illness.[34] In an attempt to redress this imbalance the National Alliance for the Mentally Ill, along with the National Mental Health Association, the Schizophrenia Foundation, and the National Depressive and Manic-Depressive Association, created NARSAD (the National Alliance for Research on Schizophrenia and Depression). But private sector funds are still pitifully small.

Clearly, more private and public funds are necessary—those active in research on schizophrenia, for example, say five to six times the amount now being spent is needed. But money must be spent productively, meaning in research on the *biological* basis of major mental illness. In the past, a substantial proportion of the meager funds allotted to research was squandered on explorations of family interaction and a mishmash of sociological studies. The danger today is of investment less in this type of research than in intensive study of trendy rehabilitation programs in the community.

Certainly, any programs that attempt to enhance the life of chronic mental patients should build in a way of measuring outcome, but all such programs are at best palliative; they will not cure. Research should focus on areas with promise of substantially improved treatment or cure. Scientific developments from genetics to brain imaging augur well for major advances in understanding—and treating—major mental illness.

Reforming the mental health system will be politically costly as well. That is because until the cure, or even the "insulin" for these diseases is found, mental patients must be cared for, many of them, at least initially, against their will. The virtually voluntary system of mental health care we have tried to implement over the last thirty years is a proven failure. As we have seen, it has failed the voluntary patient as much as the patient unwilling or unable to recognize there is anything wrong with him. *All* chronic patients become hostage to the dangerousness standard, which denies hospitalization to those who do not conform to it. In practice, this standard does not even contain the dangerous effectively. As psychiatrist Steven Zavodnick puts it: "You've got to grab the patient between the time [he] fires the gun and the bullet hits the victim—and just hope he's not a good shot."[35]

Housing, including specialized group residences, and social and vocational programs are sorely lacking for this population; but the most seriously ill will evade—or be evicted from—even the best programs if controls cannot be exercised. A telling example of how untreated mental illness destroys an individual's ability to remain in housing is Joyce Brown. ACLU attorneys described her repeatedly as a victim of inadequate government housing policies. This was simply not true.

In Brown's case, the inability to keep a home preceded her inability to hold a job. According to her sisters, while she was working as a secretary, Joyce "wanted to spend her money on what she wanted to spend her money, and housing was not one of those things." Repeatedly evicted for failure to pay rent, she was taken in by her sisters who obtained yet another apartment for her, put up the rent deposit, and installed her: she again refused to pay rent and was evicted. Even after she was hospitalized in New Jersey and released to a shelter, the same pattern continued: She was ejected when she refused to make any contribution to the shelter from her welfare check. Her sisters observe:

"We've been through this with her. We know she doesn't pay rent. She gets money but will not pay rent. She was kicked out of every place."[36] There was thus considerable irony in Brown's solemn words to a Harvard audience: "My problems were not that I was mentally ill, my problems were that I did not have a place to live."[37]

Community psychiatrist Richard Lamb is blunt: "We need to come to terms with the fact that we can't maintain all the severely ill in the community, at least not freely in the community."[38] Controls like guardianship and outpatient commitment can make community living viable for many of the most severely ill, ensuring a structured living situation and treatment for their illness.

Despite these incontestable facts, a large coalition of interest groups continues to view mental disease as a civil right, making reform much more difficult than in the 1960s. Then Left and Right rallied around the "mental illness is a myth" doctrine to dismantle the existing mental health system. Now, there are civil libertarian lawyers and assorted advocates like those in the National Association of Rights Protection and Advocacy (NARPA). There are the politically active patient or consumer groups. A number of state mental health associations, like the parent National Mental Health Association, have also lent support to the radical patient movement, and can be expected to follow its lead. There are the federally funded Protection and Advocacy organizations in each state—for which an ingenuous family movement lobbied. There are professional organizations like the American Psychological Association, seeing an opportunity to aggrandize the status of its members at the expense of psychiatrists.

In addition, there are interest groups protecting jobs. The only forceful opposition to the changes of the 1960s and 1970s came from those whose jobs were threatened: state hospital employees. Today, community mental health workers could be a formidable lobbying force in their turn. Such workers may fear that laws making commitment easier will mean fatter budgets for state hospitals, and squeeze community programs. (In fact, in a humane system of care, while there will have to be more state hospital beds, the major expansion will be in community programs.)

In *Nowhere to Go,* Fuller Torrey hails the combined efforts of NAMI and the National Mental Health Consumers Association as offering a promising avenue for change.[39] On the contrary, regarding the core issues of commitment and treatment, such a coalition guarantees legislative gridlock. Basically what both organizations agree on is more community services, and while these are necessary, as we have seen, they will never in themselves suffice. Indeed, in striking alliances with radical patient groups, NAMI is in danger of being neutralized as a force for solving the very problems that spurred its founding.

Responsible leaders of both political parties, backed by a concerned public, will have to demand reform. But they will do so only when they come to realize that a cruel travesty of civil rights cloaks abuse and neglect of the mentally ill. As Paul Appelbaum suggests, for the mentally ill, the apparent conflict between coercive treatment and autonomy may be an illusory one, since such treatment can increase their capacity to make autonomous choices. Says Appelbaum:

> Meaningful autonomy does not consist merely in the ability to make choices for oneself. Witness the psychotic ex-patients on the streets, who withdraw into rarely used doorways, rigidly still for hours at a time, hoping, like chameleons on the forest floor, that immobility will help them fade into the grimy urban background. . . . Can the choices they make, limited as they are to the selection of a doorway for the day, be called a significant embodiment of human autonomy?[40]

In the Saikewicz case, which served as the basis for the Richard Roe decision, the Massachusetts Supreme Court stated explicitly that the value of life is in "free choice and self-determination."[41] Under its own guidelines then, logically it should have endorsed the treatment that could make Richard Roe capable of *rational* choice. As Charles Krauthammer observes, "What does freedom mean for a paranoid schizophrenic who is ruled by voices commanded by his persecutors and rattling around in his head?"[42]

Earlier we pointed out that individuals who have experienced both severe mental illness and physical trauma because of an accident rank the pain of mental illness as far greater. In intervening to alleviate that pain society acts in the best interests of the mentally ill.

For the human dignity of the mentally ill—and for our own—it is time to end "the myth of mental illness," and the shameful era spawned by this great lie.

Notes

Introduction.   *The Shame of the Streets*

1. Psychiatrist Robert Reich is quoted in Steven Rachlin, "The Case Against Closing of State Hospitals," in Paul Ahmed and Stanley Plog, eds., *State Mental Hospitals* (New York: Plenum, 1976), p. 38.

2. Albert Deutsch, *The Mentally Ill in America* (New York: Columbia University Press, 1949), p. 90.

3. *New York Times,* September 4, 1987.

4. Interview, Robert Levy, New York Civil Liberties Union, August 11, 1988.

5. *New York Times,* December 25, 1988.

6. Leona Bachrach, "The Homeless Mentally Ill and Mental Health Services: An Analytical Review of the Literature," in H. Richard Lamb, ed., *The Homeless Mentally Ill* (Washington, D.C.: American Psychiatric Association, 1984), p. 14.

7. *U.S. News and World Report,* March 20, 1989, p. 28. Journalist Tom Bethell, speaking at the Heritage Foundation, reminds us that Aristotle pointed out that defining groups by the absence of a characteristic is confusing; these are not real groups: a false homogeneity is attributed to a large number of people who may have little in common except that they lack something. His remarks are published in *Rethinking Policy on Homelessness,* a Conference Sponsored by the Heritage Foundation and *The American Spectator* (Washington, D.C.: Heritage Foundation, 1989), p. 2.

8. Mary Ellen Hombs and Mitch Snyder, *Homelessness in America: A Forced March to Nowhere* (Washington, D.C.: Community for Creative Non-Violence, 1982), p. 20.

9. Quoted in Thomas Main, "What We Know About the Homeless," *Commentary,* May 1988, p. 31.

10. Robert Hayes, "Thoughts," in Mary Ellen Hombs and Mitch Snyder, op. cit., p. 31.

11. "Homelessness: Experts Differ on Root Causes," *Science,* May 2, 1986, p. 570.

12. *Rethinking Policy on Homelessness,* op. cit., p. 28.

13. Written testimony by Mitch Snyder, Joint Hearing on HUD Report on Homelessness, House Banking and Government Operations Committees, May 24, 1984, p. 32. Department of Agriculture official Anna Kondratas points out that Snyder first came up with the three million figure in 1982 and even though advocates and mayors have since said the numbers are rapidly increasing, we still have the figure of three million homeless. The number was pulled out of the air and, as Kondratas observes, it "has no relationship to reality, and neither Mitch Snyder nor anyone else has ever produced a shred of evidence to support it, yet newspaper after newspaper, reporting an otherwise good story on some local problem that really needs addressing, will just pop in these bogus national numbers. This gives the public a completely erroneous perception and makes it very difficult for Congress to act." *Rethinking Policy on Homelessness,* op. cit., p. 58.

14. Thomas Main, op. cit., p. 27.

15. Ibid.

16. *Homeless Mentally Ill: Problems and Options in Estimating Numbers and Trends,* U.S. General Accounting Office Report to the Chairman, Committee on Labor and Human Resources, U.S. Senate, August 1988, p. 30.

17. Peter H. Rossi et al., "The Urban Homeless: Estimating Composition and Size," *Science,* March 13, 1987, p. 1341.

18. Thomas Main, op. cit., p. 27.

19. Martha Burt at Heritage conference. *Rethinking Policy on Homelessness,* op. cit., p. 17.

20. S. Robert Lichter, "Media's Typical Homeless Are Anything But," *Wall Street Journal,* December 14, 1989.

21. In a study of media coverage of the homeless from 1986 to 1989, media analysts Robert and Linda Lichter report that overall the media portrayed "an image of the deserving poor who differ from other Americans mainly in their lack of housing, not in any social, psychological, or behavioral deficiency." See "The Visible Poor: Media Coverage of the Homeless 1986–1989," *Media Monitor,* Center for Media and Public Affairs, Washington, D.C., March 1989, p. 6. Those trying to minimize pathology among the homeless often emphasize the number of families in this population, writing of them as the "fastest growing" element, some even going so far as to claim the homeless are "mostly families." The most detailed study on this issue comes from the national survey by the Urban Institute for the Food and Nutrition Service of the U.S. Department of Agriculture, which examined those using shelters, those using shelters and soup kitchens, and those using soup kitchens alone (almost half of whom lived on the streets). The authors found a relatively low proportion of families: "[O]nly 10 percent of service-using homeless are families (defined as a multiperson household with at least one child present), whereas 83 percent are single-person households. This finding contrasts sharply with popular reports that as high as one-third of the homeless are families." They explain one source of the confusion. Families were overrepresented in the shelter-using, as against the street population. Furthermore, "A provider, looking at who occupies the available beds on any given night, makes an estimate that more than half of the shelter's beds are occupied by members of families, including children. However, family households are larger than single-person households, so a count of *households* will result in a lower proportion of families." Even if children are included in the total count, only 23% of homeless persons are members of homeless families. "Of these, two thirds are children (15 percent of the 23 percent.)" See Martha R. Burt and Barbara E. Cohen, "A Sociodemographic Profile of the Service-Using Homeless: Findings from a National Survey," in Jamshid A. Momeni, ed., *Homelessness in the United States—Data and Issues* (New York: Praeger, 1990), p. 20. The study found those who did not use any services were more disabled, on virtually every measure, and 89% were male (p. 33).

22. For reports on a range of studies in the early 1980s see Anthony Arce and Michael Vergare, "Identifying and Characterizing the Mentally Ill among the Homeless," and Leona Bachrach, "The Homeless Mentally Ill and Mental Health Services: An Analytical Review of the Literature," both in H. Richard Lamb, ed., op. cit., pp. 75–90 and 11–54.

23. Joseph P. Morrissey and Deborah Dennis, *NIMH-Funded Research Concerning Homeless Mentally Ill Persons: Implications for Policy and Practice,* U.S. Department of Health and Human Services, December 1, 1986, p. 15. Even in New York City, an *additional* 15% have some symptoms or a history of mental illness (*New York Times,*

April 2, 1990). The reason a relatively low proportion of New York's homeless are mentally ill is presumably related to the city's housing policies. In his 1990 book *The Excluded Americans* (Regnery-Gateway), journalist William Tucker asserts that 27% of the variation in rate among cities derives from rent control, which results in the abandonment and lack of availability of low-rent housing stock. Certainly in New York City, which has one of the strictest and longest-standing systems of rent controls in the country, and one affecting the largest proportion of units, the impact of rent control in reducing housing availability is significant.

24. Joseph P. Morrissey and Deborah Dennis, op. cit., p. 15.

25. William R. Breakey et al., "Health and Mental Health Problems of Homeless Men and Woman in Baltimore," *Journal of the American Medical Association,* September 9, 1989, p. 1355.

26. Irene S. Levine, "Service Programs for the Homeless Mentally Ill," in H. Richard Lamb, ed., op. cit., p. 178.

27. E. Fuller Torrey, Sidney M. Wolfe, and Laurie M. Flynn, *Care of the Seriously Mentally Ill: A Rating of State Programs,* 2nd edition (Washington, D.C.: Public Citizen Health Research Group and National Alliance for the Mentally Ill, 1988), p. 7.

28. See *A Report to the Secretary on the Homeless and Emergency Shelters,* U.S. Department of Housing and Urban Development, April 23, 1984, pp. 16–17 and *Homeless Mentally Ill,* GAO study, op. cit., p. 28. The HUD figures in this case are poor, extrapolating national figures from only three cities, Phoenix, Pittsburgh, and Boston. The proportion of shelter- to street-dwellers, of course, changes with the seasons, especially in the northern part of the country. In Chicago, for example, the Rossi team found 59% of the homeless on the streets and in other public places in the fall, but only 27% in the winter (GAO study, p. 28).

29. *A Report on the 1988 National Survey of Shelters for the Homeless,* U.S. Department of Housing and Urban Development, March 1989, p. 15. The rise is not surprising, since the mentally ill are least able to obtain and remain in permanent housing. New mentally ill people come into the system, while the earlier population does not leave. HUD's study found that while about 70% of the clients in shelters serving primarily families with children had been homeless for less than three months, 38% of clients in shelters serving predominantly men had been homeless *for more than three years* (ibid.).

30. William Breakey et al., op. cit., p. 1355. This figure is low compared to some other studies. A Rand Corporation study of three California counties and the Los Angeles skid row area, *Review of California's Program for the Homeless Mentally Disabled* (Santa Monica: February 1988), found that between 54% and 93% of the mentally ill homeless had a history of substance abuse (p. vi). The *New York Times* of April 2, 1990 reported a rapidly rising use of crack cocaine among the homeless mentally ill. According to Dr. Luis Marcos, vice president for mental hygiene of the Health and Hospitals Corporation in New York City, visits by homeless people to psychiatric emergency rooms of city hospitals had risen steadily, with those tied to crack going from 11% in 1987 to 45% in 1989.

The Urban Institute national study found one out of four of the homeless had served state or federal prison time, indicating a fairly serious degree of criminal behavior. See *Rethinking Policy on Homelessness,* op. cit., p. 21.

31. Interview, Dr. E. Fuller Torrey, August 3, 1987.

32. Robert E. Drake and David Adler, "Shelter Is Not Enough: Clinical Work with the Homeless Mentally Ill," in H. Richard Lamb, ed., op. cit., p. 143.

33. Ibid.

34. Interview, Dr. E. Fuller Torrey, August 3, 1987.

35. E. Fuller Torrey, *Nowhere to Go: The Tragic Odyssey of the Homeless Mentally Ill* (New York: Harper & Row, 1988), pp. 9, 13.

36. *Rethinking Policy on Homelessness,* op. cit., pp. 10–11.

37. John R. Belcher, "Defining the Service Needs of Homeless Mentally Ill Persons," *Hospital and Community Psychiatry,* November 1988, p. 1204. Ohio ranked seventh among the fifty states in E. Fuller Torrey, Sidney M. Wolfe, and Laurie Flynn, op. cit.

38. *New York Times,* August 17, 1986.

39. Ibid., November 16, 1989.

40. Ibid., February 22, 1988.

41. Rand Corporation, *Review of California's Program for the Homeless Mentally Disabled,* op. cit., p. 323.

42. Ellen Baxter and Kim Hopper, "Shelter and Housing for the Homeless Mentally Ill," in H. Richard Lamb, ed., op. cit., p. 114.

43. Interview, Merion Kane, May 6, 1988.

44. E. Fuller Torrey, *Nowhere to Go,* op. cit., p. 10.

45. Ellen Baxter and Kim Hopper, op. cit., p. 127.

46. Kathleen Jones, *Lunacy, Law, and Conscience, 1744–1845* (London: Routledge and Kegan Paul, 1955), pp. 15–16.

47. "Giving Mental Illness Its Research Due," *Science,* May 30, 1986, p. 1085.

48. Ibid., p. 1084.

49. In New York City the number of SROs went from 50,000 in 1975 to 19,619 in 1981, a loss of 61%. Other cities experienced similar sharp declines. However, the widely quoted number of a million SROs lost in the 1970s, like the alleged three million homeless, is another figure apparently plucked out of the air. See Randall Filer and Marjorie Honig, *Policy Issues in Homelessness: Current Understanding and Directions for Research,* The Manhattan Institute, New York City, March 1990.

50. Interview, James and Carol Howe, September 30, 1988.

51. Agnes Hatfield, Elizabeth Farrell, and Shirley Starr, "The Family's Perspective on the Homeless," in H. Richard Lamb, ed., op. cit., p. 297.

52. Elizabeth Hilton, "Networks to Help Homeless and Missing Mentally Ill," Workshop at National Alliance for the Mentally Ill Conference, Boulder, Colo., July 3–4, 1988.

53. Interview, June Wild, February 19, 1988.

54. *New York Times,* January 31, 1982.

55. Interview, Edward Holder (pseudonym), May 7, 1988.

56. Interview, Jean Holt (pseudonym), April 1, 1989.

57. Interview, Dr. Jerome Klein, May 18, 1988.

58. Interview, Robert Hayes, September 21, 1988.

59. *New York Times,* July 10, 1986.

60. Ibid., September 9, 1988, September 23, 1988.

61. Ibid., November 29, 1987.

62. Daniel Patrick Moynihan, "The Homeless," Letter to New York, March 10, 1988.

63. Charles Krauthammer, "How to Save the Homeless Mentally Ill," *The New Republic,* February 8, 1988, p. 24.

64. Ellen Baxter and Kim Hopper, "Shelter and Housing for the Homeless Mentally Ill," in H. Richard Lamb, ed., op. cit., p. 114.

65. *Homelessness in New York State: A Report to the Governor and the Legislature,* Part III, Department of Social Services, October 1984, p. 32.

66. Even *U.S. News and World Report* (March 20, 1989), in an essay ostensibly devoted to "Shattering Myths about the Homeless," propagates the myth that deinstitutionalization "did little to create the homelessness problem of the 1980s." The article assumes that because one study found that only 5% had been in mental institutions *immediately* prior to becoming homeless, deinstitutionalization was not an important factor.

67. P. J. O'Rourke, "Put Us in Mental Institutions, Please!" *The American Spectator,* December 1989, p. 17.

68. Susan Blank, "The Homeless: ACLU Responds to the Emergency," *Civil Liberties,* Winter 1986, p. 3.

69. *New York Times,* May 22, 1989.

70. Myron Magnet, "Homeless: Craziness, Dope and Danger," *New York Times,* January 26, 1990.

71. Paul Appelbaum, "Fear of Psychiatry: Legacy of the Sixties," *The World and I,* July 1989, pp. 577–85.

72. In 1978 Dan White, who had been a city supervisor in San Francisco, successfully used the defense that junk food had made him violent in his trial for the murder of both San Francisco Mayor George Moscone and another city supervisor, Harvey Milk, whom he killed in a job-related dispute. See Carol Gallo, "The Insanity of the Insanity Defense," *Human Events,* September 26, 1981, p. 12.

73. Eugene Bardach, *The Skill Factor in Politics: Repealing the Mental Commitment Laws in California* (Berkeley: University of California Press, 1972), p. 140.

74. E. Fuller Torrey, "Fiscal Shell Game Cheats Mentally Ill," *Wall Street Journal,* November 3, 1987.

Chapter 1.   The Origins of Anti-Psychiatry

1. Charles Krauthammer, *Cutting Edges* (New York: Random House, 1983), p. 69.

2. Martin Roth and Jerome Kroll, *The Reality of Mental Illness* (Cambridge: Cambridge University Press, 1986), p. 75.

3. David J. Rothman, *The Discovery of the Asylum* (Boston: Little, Brown, 1971), p. 110.

4. Albert Deutsch, *The Mentally Ill in America* (New York: Columbia University Press, 1949), pp. 229, 506.

5. Ibid., p. 229. Part of the reason for the enormous growth in the size of mental hospitals was that they were used to house, among others, alcoholics, the mentally retarded, and the demented aged.

6. *New York Times* (letter to the editor), May 22, 1989.

7. *Action for Mental Health: Final Report of the Joint Commission on Mental Illness and Health* (New York: Basic Books, 1961), p. 39. The report notes: "Unquestionably, the drugs have delivered the greatest blow for patient freedom, in terms of nonrestraint, since Pinel struck off the chains of the lunatics in the Paris asylum 168 years ago."

8. Aldous Huxley, *The Doors of Perception* (New York: Harper & Row, 1963), p. 23.

9. Martin Lee and Bruce Shlain, *Acid Dreams: the CIA, LSD and the Sixties Rebellion* (New York: Grove Press, 1985), p. 55.

10. Ibid., p. 69.

11. Ibid., p. 84.

12. Ibid., p. 119.

13. Todd Gitlin, *The Sixties: Years of Hope, Days of Rage* (New York: Bantam, 1987), p. 246.

14. Ken Kesey, *One Flew Over the Cuckoo's Nest* (New York: Viking, 1962), p. 63.

15. Seymour Krim, "The Insanity Bit," in Thomas Szasz, ed., *The Age of Madness* (New York: Doubleday Anchor, 1973), p. 287.

16. Ibid., p. 298.

17. Gregory Bateson, ed., *Perceval's Narrative* (Stanford: Stanford University Press, 1961), p. xiv.

18. Martin Lee and Bruce Shlain, op. cit., p. 166.

19. Herbert Marcuse, *Negations* (Boston: Beacon Press, 1968), p. 251.

20. Herbert Marcuse, "Liberation from the Affluent Society," in David Cooper, ed., *To Free a Generation: The Dialectics of Liberation* (New York: Collier Books, 1969), p. 182.

21. David Ingleby, *Critical Psychiatry: The Politics of Mental Health* (New York: Pantheon, 1980), p. 10.

22. Peter Sedgwick, *Psycho Politics* (New York: Harper & Row, 1982), p. 6.

23. R. D. Laing, *The Politics of Experience* (New York: Ballantine, 1967), pp. 114–15.

24. R. D. Laing, *The Divided Self* (New York: Pantheon, 1969), p. 9.

25. Ibid., p. 31.

26. Ibid., pp. 209, 222.

27. "R. D. Laing: Interview," *Omni,* April 1988, p. 76.

28. Jeff Nuttall, *Bomb Culture* (New York: Delacorte Press, 1968), p. 121.

29. James Gordon, "Who is Mad? Who is Sane? R. D. Laing: In Search of a New Psychiatry," *Atlantic,* January 1971, p. 57.

30. Peter Sedgwick, op. cit., p. 94.

31. Ibid., p. 95.

32. Richard I. Evans, *R. D. Laing: The Man and His Ideas* (New York: E. P. Dutton, 1976), p. xxiii.

33. R. D. Laing, *The Divided Self,* op cit., p. 39.

34. Ibid.

35. R. D. Laing, *The Politics of Experience,* op cit., p. 121.

36. Robert Boyers, ed., *R. D. Laing and Anti-Psychiatry* (New York: Octagon Books, 1974), p. 275.

37. Laing, *The Politics of Experience,* op cit., p. 129.

38. Ibid., p. 28.

39. Ibid., p. 167.

40. Ibid., p. 120.

41. Aldous Huxley, op. cit., p. 56.

42. Ibid., p. 58.

43. Richard I. Evans, op. cit., p. 50.

44. Quoted in Thomas Szasz, *The Therapeutic State* (Buffalo: Prometheus Books, 1984), p. 42.

45. Jeff Nuttall, op. cit., p. 234.

46. David Ingleby, ed., op. cit., p. 56.

47. Peter Sedgwick, op. cit., p. 267.

48. Richard I. Evans, op. cit.; p. xxxviii; Sedgwick, op. cit., p. 108.

49. Peter Sedgwick, op. cit., p. 108.

50. Thomas Szasz, *Schizophenia: The Sacred Symbol of Psychiatry* (New York: Basic Books, 1976), p. 49. Szasz also declared the term anti-psychiatry was "imprecise, misleading and cheaply self-aggrandizing" (p. 48).

51. His chief "proof," as Michael Moore has shown in a careful study, rests on his interpretation of philosopher of language Gilbert Ryle's *The Concept of Mind* (London: Hutchinson & Co., 1949). Ryle popularized the notion of the "category mistake." Szasz considers the term "mental illness" a category mistake—mental illness has improperly been placed in the same category as physical illnesses. Moore analyzes the fallacies in Szasz's use of Ryle's work. See Michael S. Moore, "Some Myths About 'Mental Illness,'" *Archives of General Psychiatry,* December 1975, pp. 1483–97.

52. Thomas Szasz, "The Myth of Mental Illness," in Thomas Scheff, ed., *Mental Illness and Social Processes* (New York: Harper & Row, 1967), p. 254.

53. Interview, Dr. Thomas Szasz, January 24, 1989. The only change in Szasz's views seem to have occurred *prior* to 1960. It is little known that in 1957 Szasz published a book *Pain and Pleasure* (Basic Books) in which he accepted the existence of schizophrenia as a matter of course, referring casually to "overt schizophrenic psychosis," even entitling a chapter "Bodily Feelings in Schizophrenia."

54. R. D. Laing, *The Divided Self,* op cit., p. 39.

55. Richard E. Vatz and Lee S. Weinberg, eds., *Thomas Szasz: Primary Values and Major Contentions* (Buffalo: Prometheus Books, 1983), p. 38.

56. Perhaps not. In our interview with him Szasz said: "Suppose we discovered that someone with so-called schizophrenia had some genetic component. The question is 'How does this affect our behavior toward people we call schizophrenic?'" Szasz would treat them as fully responsible for their actions, brain disease or no.

57. Thomas Szasz, *Schizophrenia,* op. cit., p. 136.

58. Interview, Dr. E. Fuller Torrey, May 3, 1988.

59. Interview, Dr. Thomas Szasz, January 24, 1989.

60. Thomas Szasz, *The Therapeutic State,* op. cit., p. 15.

61. Richard E. Vatz and Lee S. Weinberg, op. cit., p. 199.

62. Thomas Szasz, *Insanity: The Idea and its Consequences,* (New York: John Wiley & Sons, 1987), p. 70. However Szasz covers himself against this eventuality by saying that even if a chemical substance were found in the brain associated with behavior we call schizophrenic, such a discovery would no more establish the chemical etiology of schizophrenia than discovery of adrenaline established the chemical etiology of anger (p. 346).

63. Martin Roth and Jerome Kroll, op. cit., p. 12. As Krauthammer points out, to follow Szasz's logic, demented syphilitics, who accounted for a large number of those in asylums in the nineteenth century, had a fraudulent claim to illness until Wasserman discovered a test for the disease. An historical accident transformed the nondiseased to the status of diseased. (Charles Krauthammer, op. cit., p. 77.)

64. Thomas Szasz, "The Myth of Mental Illness," op. cit., pp. 243–44.

65. Thomas Szasz, *Insanity: The Idea and Its Consequences,* op. cit., p. 157.

66. Ibid., pp. 12, 71.

67. Letter to Rael Jean Isaac from Stanley Robbins, April 26, 1990.

68. Thomas Szasz, *The Manufacture of Madness* (New York: Harper & Row, 1970), p. xv.

69. Thomas Szasz, *Ideology and Insanity* (New York: Doubleday, 1970), p. 113.

70. Thomas Szasz, *The Manufacture of Madness,* op. cit., p. 27.

71. Ibid., p. 138.

72. Thomas Szasz, *Ideology and Insanity,* op. cit., p. 59.

73. *The Berkeley Barb,* March 28–April 3, 1975.

74. Thomas Szasz, *The Therapeutic State,* op. cit., p. 83.

75. Thomas Szasz, "The Therapeutic State," in Sherry Hersch, ed., *Madness Network News Reader* (San Francisco: Glide Publications, 1974), p. 127.

76. Except David Cooper, who argues in *The Grammar of Living* (New York: Pantheon, 1974) that all the institutions to which the individual is exposed from the family to school, university, trade union, profession, and so on induce a "conformism" or "normality" that "represents the arrest or sclerosis of a person and at least the moronization if not the death of personal existence."

77. Thomas Szasz, *Law, Liberty and Psychiatry* (New York: Macmillan, 1963), p. 154.

78. Ibid., pp. 153–54.

79. Ibid., p. 154.

80. Thomas Szasz, *Insanity: The Idea and Its Consequences,* op. cit., p. 365.

81. Thomas Szasz, *Ideology and Insanity,* op. cit., p. 6.

82. Ronald Leifer, *In the Name of Mental Health* (New York: Science House, 1969), pp. 113–14.

83. Ernest Becker, *The Revolution in Psychiatry* (New York: Free Press, 1964).

84. Interview, Dr. Peter Breggin, May 6, 1988.

85. Ibid.

86. Interview, Dr. E. Fuller Torrey, May 3, 1988.

87. E. Fuller Torrey, *The Death of Psychiatry* (Radnor, Pa.: Chilton Book Co., 1974), p. 156.

88. Ibid., p. 89.

89. Michael Fleming and Roger Manvell, *Images of Madness: A Portrayal of Insanity in the Feature Film* (Cranbury, N.J.: Associated Universities Presses, 1985), p. 179.

90. Interview, Dr. Torrey, May 3, 1988.

91. John K. Wing, *Reasoning About Madness* (London: Oxford University Press, 1978), p. 3.

92. Robert Boyers, ed., op. cit., p. 192.

93. John Wing, op. cit., p. 158.

94. Jacqueline Atkinson, *Schizophrenia at Home* (New York: New York University Press, 1986), p. 39. This did not stop psychiatrists from reacting with horror to families of the mentally ill. Lidz takes as corroboration of his theories the reaction of one of his medical students after observing family therapy sessions: "My God, I couldn't live in that family for a week, there is something so malignant." (Interview with Dr. Theodore Lidz in Robert Boyers, op. cit., p. 174.)

95. Peter Sedgwick, op. cit., p. 82.

96. Ibid., pp. 83–84.

97. Murray Bowen, "Theory in the Practice of Psychotherapy," in Philip Gerin, ed., *Family Therapy: Theory and Practice* (New York: Gardner Press, 1976), pp. 77–86.

98. R. D. Laing and Aaron Esterson, *Sanity, Madness and the Family,* (London: Penguin, 1970), p. 14.

99. R. D. Laing, *The Politics of Experience,* op. cit., p. 127.

100. David Cooper, *Psychiatry and Anti-Psychiatry* (London: Tavistock Publications, 1967), p. 24.

101. Robert Boyers, op. cit., p. 275.

102. John Wing, op. cit., p. 83.

103. Thomas Szasz, *Ideology and Insanity*, op. cit., p. 4.

104. Thomas Szasz, *Law, Liberty and Psychiatry*, op. cit., p. 16.

Chapter 2.   Mental Illness as Label

1. Peter Sedgwick, *Psycho Politics* (New York: Harper & Row, 1982), p. 15. In an interesting paper, "Social Discrediting of Psychiatry: The Protasis of Legal Disfranchisement" (*American Journal of Psychiatry*, December 1977, pp. 1356–60), Park Elliott Dietz traces the roots of anti-psychiatry to a number of sociological studies and essays in the 1920s. These portrayed "insanity" as a social situation rather than a personal trait; suggested it is the civilized world that is insane and we have no absolute criteria to differentiate mental illness from genius or vice; and documented ecological variations in the distribution of psychiatric disorders. Dietz points out that only when these ideas reemerged a generation later did they have an impact in discrediting the medical model.

2. Howard S. Becker, *Outsiders: Studies in the Sociology of Deviance* (New York: Free Press, 1963), p. 9.

3. Erving Goffman, *Asylums* (New York: Doubleday Anchor, 1961), p. x.

4. Ibid., pp. 33–35.

5. Erving Goffman, *Interaction Ritual* (New York: Doubleday Anchor, 1967), p. 147.

6. Erving Goffman, *Asylums*, pp. 363–64.

7. Erving Goffman, *Interaction Ritual*, p. 147.

8. Erving Goffman, *Asylums*, pp. 306, 386.

9. Ibid., p. 73.

10. Martin Roth and Jerome Kroll, *The Reality of Mental Illness* (Cambridge: Cambridge University Press, 1986), p. 16.

11. Erving Goffman, *Asylums*, op. cit., p. 384.

12. Ibid., p. 365. On the other hand, when the American Association for the Abolition of Involuntary Hospitalization was formed in 1970, its directors included both Goffman and Szasz. See Jonas Robitscher, "Moving Patients Out of Hospitals," in Paul I. Ahmed and Stanley Plog, eds., *State Mental Hospitals* (New York: Plenum, 1976), p. 142.

13. Daniel Patrick Moynihan, "The Homeless," *Letter to New York*, Washington, D.C., March 10, 1988. There has been debate concerning the extent to which large-scale introduction of the neuroleptic drugs was responsible for deinstitutionalization. Dr. Henry Brill, then Deputy Commissioner of the New York State Department of Mental Hygiene and Robert Patton, its Director of Statistics, in their article in the *American Journal of Psychiatry* in July 1962, "Clinical-Statistical Analysis of Population Changes in New York State Mental Hospitals Since Introduction of Psychotropic Drugs" even then found their role clear. "We still find no other explanation for a change of such magnitude which has involved hospitals across the country and abroad and which, in its larger aspects, began quite abruptly in 1956, the year when psychiatric drug therapy first began to be applied on a large scale. There is no doubt that population reduction may be and has been brought about by many other means. However, the fact is that it was never before accomplished on a scale remotely approaching the national and international level reported since 1956" (p. 33).

14. He has been an editor of *The American Sociological Review, Social Problems, The American Sociologist, Journal of Health and Social Behavior,* and *The American Journal of Sociology.*

15. Thomas Scheff, *Being Mentally Ill* (Chicago: Aldine Publishing Co., 1966), p. 33.

16. The Midtown Manhattan Study on which Scheff relied was absurd, built on nebulous psychoanalytic notions of "mental health." Serious studies of the period offered no evidence for Scheff's assumption. On the contrary, they indicated great reluctance on the part of families to admit the existence of mental illness in a family member. In a classic 1955 study, John A. Clausen and Marian R. Yarrow showed that wives resisted labeling their husband's behavior for a number of years, going to great lengths to normalize or deny it. They were able to avoid the label for an average of two years, until the husband's behavior became so bizarre they had no alternative, and even then it was often not the wife but the police who brought the man in for disturbing the peace. See Allan V. Horwitz, *The Social Control of Mental Illness* (New York: Academic Press, 1982), pp. 35–36.

17. Thomas Scheff, *Being Mentally Ill,* op. cit., p. 54.

18. Ibid., p. 64.

19. Martin Roth and Jerome Kroll, op. cit., p. 40.

20. Thomas Scheff, "Labeling, Emotion, and Individual Change," in Thomas Scheff, ed., *Labeling Madness* (Englewood Cliffs, N.J.: Prentice-Hall, 1975), p. 75.

21. Ibid.

22. Kai T. Erickson, "Notes on the Sociology of Deviance," in Thomas Scheff, ed., *Mental Illness and Social Processes* (New York: Harper & Row, 1967), p. 300.

23. Like Szasz, Scheff has remained intellectually immobile over the years. Although neuroleptics had been in general use for over a decade when Scheff wrote *Being Mentally Ill,* he took no notice of their existence. In the 1984 edition (New York: Aldine) he at last notes the medical advances, only to dismiss their significance. He adopts Szasz's strange notion of medical illness as "lesion" and adds an even more peculiar requirement of "uniform and invariate symptoms." Scheff declares mental illness lacks both and so does not meet the definition of disease (p. 156).

24. Schizophrenics, says Scheff, "would not have the competence or the motivation to napalm civilians, defoliate forests and rice crops, and to push the button that would destroy much of the world that we know" (ibid., pp. 160–61).

25. Ibid.

26. Thomas Scheff, *Being Mentally Ill,* 2nd edition (New York: Aldine, 1984), p. 156.

27. Michel Foucault, *Madness and Civilization: A History of Insanity in the Age of Reason* (New York: Pantheon, 1965), pp. 247, 278.

28. Michael Walzer, "The Politics of Michel Foucault," in David Couzens, ed., *Foucault: A Critical Reader* (London: Basil Blackwell, 1986), p. 61.

29. David Rothman, *The Discovery of the Asylum* (Boston: Little, Brown, 1971), p. xvi.

30. Ibid., p. 294.

31. Ibid., pp. 294–95.

32. Ibid.

33. David Rosenhan, "On Being Sane in Insane Places," *Science,* January 19, 1973, pp. 251, 258.

34. Ibid., p. 251.

35. Ibid., pp. 251–52.

36. Ibid., p. 256.

37. Ibid., p. 252.

38. John Wing, *Reasoning About Madness* (London: Oxford University Press, 1978), pp. 98–99.

39. David Rosenhan, op. cit., p. 257.

40. Ibid., p. 254.

41. Mary Ellen Hombs and Mitch Snyder, *Homelessness in America* (Washington, D.C.: Center for Creative Non-Violence, 1982), pp. 43, 45. The second quotation heading the chapter is from Szasz: "Mental hospitals are the POW camps of our undeclared and inarticulated civil wars" (p. 43).

42. Letter from Hal Breen, *Commentary,* September 1987, p. 16.

43. Thomas Szasz, *Law, Liberty and Psychiatry* (New York: Macmillan, 1963), pp. 231–32.

44. Jerome Agel, ed., *Rough Times* (New York: Ballantine, 1973), p. ix.

45. Ibid., pp. xi, 6.

46. Michael Glenn and Richard Kunnes, *Repression or Revolution? Therapy in the United States Today* (New York: Harper Colophon Books, 1973), p. 166.

47. Phil Brown, *Toward a Marxist Psychology* (New York: Harper Colophon Books, 1974), p. xviii. For Brown psychiatric commitment was "a last line of defense for the ruling class against the working class" (p. 45). Brown would go on to become chairman of the sociology department at Brown University.

48. Peter Sedgwick, op. cit., pp. 211, 283.

49. Jane Kramer, *The Europeans* (New York: Farrar, Straus & Giroux, 1988), p. 126.

50. Ibid.

51. Quoted in Martin Roth and Jerome Kroll, op. cit., p. 23.

52. Judi Chamberlin, *On Our Own: Patient-Controlled Alternatives to the Mental Health System* (New York: Hawthorn Books, 1978), p. 78.

53. Ibid., p. xvi.

54. Ibid., pp. 7, 112.

55. Michael Fleming and Roger Manvell, "Through a Lens, Darkly," *Psychology Today,* July 1987, pp. 29–30.

56. *Berkeley Barb,* March 5–11, 1976.

57. Arnold's case is built on surmise, and it is hard to believe Farmer could have been given the operation without knowing it. Moreover, Walter Freeman does not mention giving Farmer the operation in his memoirs. On the other hand, David Shutts, in *Resort to the Knife* (New York: Van Nostrand Reinhold, 1982, pp. 184–85), claims that Frank Freeman, Walter Freeman's son, wrote to him that not only was it true that Frances Farmer was given a lobotomy by his father, but the photo in Arnold's book showing Freeman performing a transorbital lobotomy was a photo of Farmer being given the operation. She was so fat that even Arnold did not recognize her! The facts of the matter remain unresolved.

58. Phyllis Chesler, *Women and Madness* (New York: Doubleday, 1972), p. 92.

59. Ibid., p. 36.

60. Ibid., p. 56.

61. "Giving Mental Illness Its Research Due," *Science,* May 30, 1986, p. 1084.

62. Michael Fleming and Roger Manvell, *Images of Madness,* op. cit., p. 179.

63. Henry Brill and Robert E. Patton, "Clinical-Statistical Analysis of Population Changes in New York State Mental Hospitals Since Introduction of Psychotropic Drugs," *American Journal of Psychiatry,* July 1962, p. 20.

64. Ibid., p. 35.

65. Fritz A. Freyhan, "The History of Recent Developments in Psychiatry," *Comprehensive Psychiatry,* November/December 1980, p. 408.

Chapter 3.   Community Mental Health Centers:
The Dream

1. Interview, Mort Wagenfeld, June 29, 1989.

2. Mike Gorman, *Every Other Bed* (Cleveland: World Publishing, 1956), p. 9.

3. Albert Deutsch, *The Shame of the States* (New York: Harcourt Brace, 1948), p. 28.

4. Kenneth Appel, "The Present Challenge of Psychiatry," in *New Directions in American Psychiatry 1944–1968: The Presidential Addresses of the American Psychiatric Association Over the Past Twenty-Five Years* (Washington, D.C.: American Psychiatric Association, 1969), p. 131.

5. Mike Gorman, op. cit., p. 28.

6. Gorman created this group as a rival to the National Mental Health Association, which he accused of being conservative and timid. Gorman wrote bitingly of the Association: "Like Calvin Coolidge's minister, who was against sin, I believe the NAMH is against both sin and mental illness, but I have little evidence to go on" (ibid., p. 306).

7. Ibid., p. 15.

8. Harry Solomon, "The American Psychiatric Association in Relation to American Psychiatry," *New Directions,* op. cit., p. 185.

9. Psychiatrist David Musto points out that the battle-fatigue successes were not necessarily of broader significance. Breakdowns under extreme battlefield conditions, although they may appear similar in their expression to civilian neuroses, can apparently be relieved much more easily once the extraordinary specific stress is removed. Thus there was no necessary connection between the wartime successes and the ability to treat more chronic emotional disturbances. See David A. Musto, "Whatever Happened to 'Community Mental Health'?" *The Public Interest,* Spring 1975, p. 59.

10. Musto points out that these huge numbers were probably due to unnecessarily rigid screening for any hint of mental disorder. The U.S. rejection rate for mental problems was six times higher than at British induction centers, although the British rate of discharge for psychological reasons was not higher than the American one. See ibid.

11. These studies used nonmedical interviewers to administer questionnaires on mental health items; the responses were then rated for "symptom formation." In the Midtown Manhattan Study 58.1% were rated as having mild or moderate symptoms, and 20.7% marked or severe ones. English psychiatrist John Wing notes dryly that such figures "fill some theorists with foreboding," but "give no information about the frequency of depressions of various kinds, of schizophrenia, or of anxiety states, and they tell us nothing about the need for medical help." See John Wing, *Reasoning About Madness* (Oxford: Oxford University Press, 1978), p. 83.

12. Maxwell Jones, *The Therapeutic Community: A New Treatment Method in Psychiatry* (New York: Basic Books, 1953), p. 25.

13. Ibid., p. vii.

14. E. Fuller Torrey, *Nowhere to Go: The Tragic Odyssey of the Homeless Mentally Ill* (New York: Harper & Row, 1988), p. 40.

15. In the preface to his 1964 *Principles of Preventive Psychiatry* (New York: Basic Books, 1964), Caplan wrote that Lindemann "has guided, stimulated, and supported me during this eleven year period [at Harvard] and . . . has made fundamental contributions to the development of my ideas" (p. ix).

16. Lindemann engaged in minute studies of family patterns, to discover, as he put it, "a typology of pathological forms of family organization." Caplan's views were equally

conventional. As Caplan saw it, mild regression led to neurosis, severe regression to psychosis. To avoid dealing with his unsolved problem, the patient "just smashes up his personality, as it were. This gives him a psychosis. One of the most typical of these is schizophrenia." (Quoted in E. Fuller Torrey, op. cit., p. 100.)

17. Gerald Caplan, *Principles of Preventive Psychiatry* (New York: Basic Books, 1964), p. 26.

18. Ibid., pp. 31–33.

19. Ibid., pp. 66–67.

20. There was a "central need" to view the primary institutions of society as "key targets for concerned mental health-oriented endeavors." Emory L. Cowan, Elmer A. Gardner, and Melvin Zax, eds., *Emergent Approaches to Mental Health Problems* (New York: Appleton-Century-Crofts, 1967), p. 399.

21. Quoted in Justin Joffe and George Albee, eds., *Prevention Through Political Action and Social Change* (Hanover, N.H.: University Press of New England, 1981), pp. 8–9.

22. Quoted in E. Fuller Torrey, op. cit., p. 124.

23. Ibid., p. 125.

24. Gerald Caplan, op. cit., p. 17.

25. This attitude was already becoming manifest during World War II. In his presidential address to the American Psychiatric Association in 1944 Edward Strecker declared: "We have looked long and searchingly into many human souls. Does not this faithfully served apprenticeship give us the capacity and the right to look into the sick and tortured soul of a world twice within a span of less than a quarter of a century saddened and ravished by the sinister passions of war?" Schizophrenics, declared Strecker, were psychological isolationists. Long experience with their problems qualified psychiatrists "to teach the dangers of national isolationism." (Edward Strecker, "Presidential Address," *New Directions . . . ,* op. cit., pp. 5, 7.)

26. Harold Rome, "Psychiatry and Foreign Affairs: The Expanding Competence of Psychiatry," *The American Journal of Psychiatry,* December 1968, p. 729.

27. Ibid., p. 728.

28. Donald Light, *Becoming Psychiatrists* (New York: W. W. Norton, 1980), p. 332.

29. Mike Gorman, op. cit., p. 43.

30. Ibid., p. 171.

31. Ibid., p. 172.

32. Ibid., pp. 172–74.

33. Ibid., p. 296.

34. Actually Ewalt was not the first chairman, but according to Bertram Brown, was appointed in the second year, after a scandal surrounding the original chairman. See Bertram Brown interview for the Kennedy library in Bertram Brown papers, National Library of Medicine, Bethesda, Md.

35. E. Fuller Torrey, op. cit., p. 91.

36. Ibid., p. 92.

37. Joint Commission on Mental Illness and Health, *Action for Mental Health,* (New York: Basic Books, 1961), p. xx.

38. Ruth B. Caplan, *Psychiatry and the Community in Nineteenth Century America* (New York: Basic Books, 1969), p. 31. Only on such a small scale, it was felt, could the proper conditions for moral treatment be maintained: the courtesies of social life, the comfortable conditions, the liberty and freedom from restraint. In some early institu-

tions implementing moral treatment there were lectures, poetry recitations, music, even monthly cotillion dances for the patients (ibid., pp. 31–35).

39. *Action for Mental Health,* op. cit., p. xvi.

40. Ibid., p. xv.

41. Ibid., pp. 178–79.

42. Ibid., p. 242.

43. Ibid., p. xv.

44. Ibid., p. xx.

45. Gerald Caplan, op. cit., p. 17.

46. Emory L. Cowan, Elmer A. Gardner, and Melvin Zax, op. cit., p. 22.

47. Gerald Caplan, op. cit., p. 8. Caplan wrote that Felix "exerted a more important influence than any other American psychiatrist in providing legislative leaders with a body of professional data and concepts as a basis for their community, preventive approach to mental health and mental disorder" (ibid).

48. Foreword to Caplan, ibid.

49. Quoted in Robert H. Connery et al., *The Politics of Mental Health* (New York: Columbia University Press, 1968), p. 45. In his 1961 presidential address to the American Psychiatric Association, Felix called for a "national decision to eliminate so far as we can the prolonged hospitalization and institutionalization of the mentally ill." (Robert H. Felix, "Psychiatrist, Medicinae Doctor," *New Directions,* op. cit., p. 227).

50. E. Fuller Torrey, op. cit., pp. 68–70. Torrey points out that the hearings that led to the creation of NIMH in 1945 and 1946 emphasized the need for a public health approach to mental illness, and "contained within them the seeds of the community mental health centers that would blossom forth twenty years later."

51. Henry A. Foley and Steven S. Sharfstein, *Madness and Government* (Washington, D.C.: American Psychiatric Press, 1983), p. 47.

52. Ernest M. Gruenberg and Janet Archer, "Abandonment of Responsibility for the Seriously Mentally Ill," *Milbank Memorial Fund Quarterly,* Vol. 57, No. 4, 1979, p. 493.

53. See Letter of Transmittal to the President of the Report "A National Mental Health Program" from Secretary Anthony Celebrezze, Arthur Goldberg, John Gleason, et al., August 1962, Bertram Brown papers, National Library of Medicine, Bethesda, Md.

54. Ibid.

55. "Message from the President of the United States," February 5, 1963, reprinted in Henry A. Foley and Steven S. Sharfstein, op. cit., p. 164.

56. Ibid., p. 166.

57. Ibid.

58. Ibid.

59. Ibid., pp. 168–69.

60. Ibid., p. 165.

61. *Mental Health (Supplemental).* Hearings before a Subcommittee of the Committee on Interstate and Foreign Commerce, House of Representatives, 88th Congress, First Session on S. 1576, July 10 and 11, 1963 (Washington, D.C.: U.S. Government Printing Office, 1963), p. 19.

62. Ibid., pp. 25–26.

63. Ibid., p. 101.

64. Interview, Dr. Saul Feldman, July 24, 1989.

65. *Mental Health,* Hearings, op. cit., p. 26.

66. Ibid., p. 27.

67. *Action for Mental Health,* op. cit., p. xvii.

68. "Report of Task Force on the Status of State Mental Hospitals in the United States," National Institute of Mental Health, March 30, 1962. Bertram Brown papers, National Library of Medicine, Bethesda, Md.

69. "A Proposal for a Comprehensive Mental Health Program to Implement the Findings of the Joint Commission on Mental Illness and Health," 1962, Bertram Brown papers, National Library of Medicine, Bethesda, Md.

70. Interview, Dr. Harry Cain, June 26, 1989.

71. Henry A. Foley and Steven S. Sharfstein, op. cit., p. 101.

72. Interview Dr. Saul Feldman, June 24, 1989.

73. Interview, Dr. Richard Cravens, June 19, 1989.

74. Ibid.

75. Fritz Freyhan, "The History of Recent Developments in Psychiatry," *Comprehensive Psychiatry,* November/December 1980, p. 406.

76. Interview, Dr. Saul Feldman, June 24, 1989.

77. Interview, Dr. Bertram Brown, June 22, 1989.

78. Interview, Dr. Harry Cain, June 26, 1989. Dr. Brown told us that the hospitals were taken care of through the program of hospital improvement and staff development. However Harry Cain felt the existence of the program of grants to state hospitals made the lack of attention to coordination *more* surprising.

79. Interview, Dr. Lucy Ozarin, June 19, 1989.

80. Ibid. Ozarin says that when a CMHC applied for funds it had to produce a letter from the state mental hospital saying they would coordinate. However she admits "it just didn't happen" and feels the CMHCs were generally even more to blame than the hospitals that this was the case.

81. Wing originally developed this theme in "Institutionalism in Mental Hospitals," *British Journal of Social and Clinical Psychology,* February 1962, pp. 38–51.

82. *Action for Mental Health,* op. cit., p. 49.

83. Gerald Caplan, op. cit., p. 116.

84. Interview, Dr. Saul Feldman, July 24, 1989.

85. Interview, Dr. Charles Windle, June 13, 1989.

86. Interview, Dr. Harry Cain, June 26, 1989.

87. It is interesting that NIMH only belatedly recognized the importance of antipsychotic drugs. Mike Gorman describes its initial dismissive attitude (*Every Other Bed,* op. cit., pp. 94, 104).

88. Henry Brill and Robert E. Patton, "Clinical-Statistical Analysis of Population Changes in New York State Mental Hospitals Since Introduction of Psychotropic Drugs," *American Journal of Psychiatry,* July 1962, pp. 21, 33, 35.

89. Interview, Dr. Richard Cravens, June 19, 1989.

Chapter 4.   Community Mental Health Centers:
The Reality

1. George W. Albee, "Relation of Conceptual Models to Manpower Needs," in Emory L. Cowen, Elmer A. Gardner, and Melvin Zax, eds., *Emergent Approaches to Mental Health Problems* (New York: Appleton-Century-Crofts, 1967), p. 70.

2. It became the Lincoln Hospital Community Mental Health Center in 1968 when it received federal funding.

3. The Lincoln Hospital Center was a joint project of the New York City Department of Hospitals and Yeshiva University.

4. Interview, Dr. Anthony Panzetta, April 11, 1989.

5. Ibid.

6. Anthony F. Panzetta, *Community Mental Health: Myth and Reality* (Philadelphia: Lea and Febiger, 1971), p. 31.

7. Seymour R. Kaplan and Melvin Roman, *The Organization and Delivery of Mental Health Services in the Ghetto: The Lincoln Hospital Experience* (New York: Praeger, 1973), pp. 19–20.

8. Ibid., p. 25.

9. Ibid., p. 31.

10. Ibid., p. 43.

11. E. Fuller Torrey, *Nowhere to Go* (New York: Harper & Row, 1988), p. 136.

12. Interview, Dr. William Hetznecker, April 3, 1989.

13. Interview, Dr. Anthony Panzetta, April 11, 1989.

14. Anthony Panzetta, *Community Mental Health,* op. cit., p. xvi.

15. Interview, Dr. Anthony Panzetta, April 11, 1989.

16. Ibid. By this time Panzetta had concluded that the focus on social activism was a mistake, since psychiatrists lacked any special expertise in this area. Kaplan and Roman came to the same conclusion: "It is only too obvious in hindsight that we had neither the expertise nor the resources to both explore innovative clinical services and social action programs at the same time." (Seymour R. Kaplan and Melvin Roman, op. cit., p. 271.)

17. Raymond H. Glasscote et al., *The Community Mental Health Center: An Analysis of Existing Models* (Washington, D.C.: Joint Information Service, 1964).

18. Seymour R. Kaplan and Melvin Roman, op. cit., p. xxviii.

19. This was the big "sin" of the program's leaders from the standpoint of some of those on the "rebel" side. See Robert Shaw and Carol Eagle, "Programmed Failure: The Lincoln Hospital Story," *Community Mental Health Journal,* December 1971, pp. 255–263. The authors argue that the crucial sin of the program's directors was to apply for a CMHC grant! "It is our conviction that a combination of colonialism and racism led to the crucial act that started the crisis of the spring of 1969. This act consisted of submitting an application for a community mental health center staffing grant" (p. 262).

20. Seymour R. Kaplan and Melvin Roman, op. cit., p. x.

21. Stanley S. Robin and Morton O. Wagenfeld, "Community Activism and Community Mental Health: A Chimera of the Sixties, a View from the Eighties," *Journal of Community Psychology,* July 1988, p. 280.

22. Raymond Glasscote et al., *The Community Mental Health Center: An Interim Appraisal* (Washington, D.C., Joint Information Service, 1969), p. 10.

23. Ibid., p. 11.

24. Quoted in David Musto, "Whatever Happened to 'Community Mental Health,'" *The Public Interest,* Spring 1975, p. 66.

25. Alan Levenson, "Staffing," in Henry Grunebaum, ed., *The Practice of Community Mental Health* (Boston: Little, Brown, 1970), p. 552.

26. Quoted in E. Fuller Torrey, *Nowhere to Go,* op. cit., p. 130.

27. Interview, Dr. Saul Feldman, July 24, 1989.

28. Raymond Glasscote et al., *The CMHC: An Interim Appraisal,* op. cit., p. 21.

29. Ibid., pp. 45–46.

30. Ibid., p. 41.

31. Ibid., p. 45.

32. Ibid., p. 49.

33. Ibid., p. 48.

34. Ibid., p. 60.

35. Ibid., p. 60.

36. Ibid., p. 45.

37. Ibid., p. 57.

38. Ibid., pp. 46–47.

39. Ibid., p. 87.

40. Ibid., pp. 12–13.

41. Ibid., p. 2.

42. Interview, Dr. Saul Feldman, July 24, 1989.

43. Interview, Dr. Bertram Brown, June 22, 1989.

44. Anthony Panzetta, *Community Mental Health,* op. cit., p. 114.

45. Stanley Robin and Morton Wagenfeld, "Community Activism," op. cit., p. 281.

46. Donald G. Langsley, "The Community Mental Health Center: Does It Treat Patients?" *Hospital and Community Psychiatry,* December 1980, p. 816.

47. E. Fuller Torrey, *Nowhere to Go,* op. cit., p. 148.

48. Interview, Dr. Saul Feldman, July 24, 1989.

49. E. Fuller Torrey, op. cit., p. 143.

50. Ibid., pp. 145–46. See also David Dowell and James Ciarlo, "Overview of the Community Mental Health Centers Program from an Evaluation Perspective," *Community Mental Health Journal,* Summer 1983, p. 104. Dr. Feldman says that rural centers on the whole did the best job: "In general it would be fair to say the most successful CMHCs we had were rural centers. They were much more connected to state mental hospitals. . . . Their communities were much more accepting and I think they did a much better job." Interview, July 24, 1989.

51. Howard Goldman et al., "Community Mental Health Centers and the Treatment of Severe Mental Disorder," *American Journal of Psychiatry,* January 1980, p. 84.

52. Anthony Panzetta, *Community Mental Health,* op. cit., p. 124.

53. Quoted in David Dowell and James Ciarlo, op. cit., p. 106.

54. Raymond Glasscote et al., *The Community Mental Health Center. An Interim Appraisal,* op. cit., p. 41.

55. Interview, Dr. Charles Windle, June 13, 1989.

56. *New York Times,* March 23, 1990. The information aired at the House Human Resources Subcommittee was gathered under the Freedom of Information Act by the Nader-established Public Citizen and the National Alliance for the Mentally Ill.

57. E. Fuller Torrey, "Community Mental Health Policy—Tennis Anyone?" *The Wall Street Journal,* March 29, 1990. In Michigan, the Battle Creek Adventist Hospital was given $709,988 to construct a new building which was to become a CMHC. It built the building but used it as a private psychiatric hospital. Torrey calls this a "phantom CMHC."

58. David Dowell and James Ciarlo, op. cit., p. 100.

59. Interview, Dr. Anthony Panzetta, April 11, 1989.

60. Interview, Dr. Charles Ray, July 27, 1989.

61. Dr. Bockoven was the author of *Moral Treatment in Community Mental Health* (New York: Springer, 1972) The first edition was published in 1963, the same year as the CMHC legislation.

62. Bockoven wrote: "Growth of understanding in the community that mental illness has to do with the frustrations, disappointments, and injured sentiments which

people unwittingly inflict on each other can lead to recognition that sub-standard living conditions and imprisonment only add injury to the patient's already damaged self-esteem" (ibid., p. 111).

63. Bockoven outlined his ideas for creating a favorable total environment in his book. He sought to transform the attitudes of staff, and emphasize rehabilitation rather than custody.

64. Interview, Dr. Jerome Klein, May 18, 1988.

65. Ibid.

66. E. Fuller Torrey, *Nowhere to Go,* op. cit., p. 149.

67. Judith Clark Turner and Irene Shifren, "Community Support Systems: How Comprehensive?" in Leonard Stein, ed., *Community Support Systems for the Long-Term Patient* (San Francisco: Jossey Bass, 1979), p. 9.

68. Ibid., p. 4.

69. E. Fuller Torrey, *Nowhere to Go,* op. cit., p. 195.

70. Donald Langsley, op. cit., p. 816.

71. Quoted in William Gronfein, "Incentives and Intentions in Mental Health Policy: A Comparison of the Medicaid and Community Mental Health Programs," *Journal of Health and Social Behavior,* September 1985, p. 197.

72. Quoted in Franklin B. Chu and Sharland Trotter, *The Madness Establishment* (New York: Grossman Publishers, 1974), p. 29.

73. Charles Windle and Diana Scully, "Community Mental Health Centers and the Decreasing Use of State Mental Hospitals," *Community Mental Health Journal,* Fall 1976, p. 241.

74. David Musto, op. cit., p. 70.

75. *New York Times,* October 30, 1984.

76. William Gronfein, op. cit., pp. 192–203. Gronfein points out that the greater a state's involvement with Medicaid, the larger the rate of decline in the state's mental hospital population. Patients were transferred from state hospitals to nursing homes in the community to shift the financial burden to the federal government. Gronfein found a *negative* correlation between state hospital decline and the number of inpatient beds, outpatient hours and daycare provided by CMHCs. One possible explanation, wrote Gronfein, "is that the provision of greater resources to the CMHCs meant a relative inattention to the problems of the chronic state hospital population, and a greater reluctance to become involved in providing services for them" (p. 199).

77. Ibid., p. 196.

78. John A. Talbott, "Presidential Address: Our Patients' Future in a Changing World: The Imperative for Psychiatric Involvement in Public Policy," *American Journal of Psychiatry,* September 1985, p. 1003.

79. John A. Talbott, "Deinstitutionalization: Avoiding the Disasters of the Past," Hospital and Community Psychiatry, September 1979, p. 622.

80. Ibid.

81. Interview, Dr. Paul Appelbaum, May 18, 1988.

82. Donald Light, *Becoming Psychiatrists* (New York: W. W. Norton, 1980), p. xi.

83. Fritz Freyhan, "The History of Recent Developments in Psychiatry," *Comprehensive Psychiatry,* Vol. 21, 1980, p. 406.

84. Quoted in Robert H. Connery et al., *The Politics of Mental Health* (New York: Columbia University Press, 1964), p. 478.

85. Raymond Glasscote et al. *The Community Mental Health Center: An Interim Appraisal,* op. cit., p. 54.

86. Interview, Dr. Saul Feldman, July 24, 1989.

87. Saul Feldman, "Out of the Hospital, onto the Streets: The Overselling of Benevolence," *The Hastings Center Report,* June 1983, p. 6.

88. Ibid., p. 7.

89. Fritz Freyhan, op. cit., p. 406.

90. R. Jay Turner and John Cumming, "Theoretical Malaise and Community Mental Health," in Emory L. Elmer A. Cowen, Elmer A. Gardner, and Melvin Zax, eds., *Emergent Approaches to Mental Health Problems* (New York: Appleton-Century-Crofts, 1967), p. 41.

91. Interview, Dr. Bertram Brown, June 22, 1989.

92. Henry A. Foley and Steven S. Sharfstein, *Madness and Government* (Washington, D.C.: American Psychiatric Press, 1983), p. 101.

93. Stuart A. Kirk and Mark E. Therrien, "Community Mental Health Myths and the Fate of Former Hospitalized Patients," *Psychiatry,* August 1975, p. 210.

94. Dr. Bertram Brown, "The Impact of New Federal Mental Health Legislation on the State Mental Health System." Speech to Northeast Governor's Conference, Hartford, Conn., October 22, 1964.

Chapter 5. The Rise of the Mental Health Bar

1. Interview, Bruce Ennis, December 29, 1988.

2. The ACLU's model law provided a dangerousness standard for commitment. But in 1968, the ACLU, on whose board sat Karl Menninger, one of the country's foremost psychiatrists, had no intention of denying the reality of mental illness or the need for the state's intervention to protect society.

3. Bruce Ennis, *Prisoners of Psychiatry* (New York: Harcourt Brace Jovanovich, 1972), p. xvii.

4. Leonard Roy Frank, "An Interview with Bruce Ennis," in *Madness Network News Reader* (San Francisco: Glide Publications, 1974), p. 162.

5. Ibid., p. 165.

6. Interview, Bruce Ennis, December 29, 1988.

7. Bruce Ennis, op cit., p. xvii.

8. Ibid., pp. 82, 230.

9. Leonard Roy Frank, op. cit., p. 163. In Ennis's view, there did not seem to be any sick people in need of treatment in state hospitals. Asked by Frank what the "function" of these hospitals was, Ennis said it was to confine and hold old people, enforce parental control over rebellious young people who smoke marijuana or adopt life styles their parents oppose, and provide custodial welfare to people who "bitch and scream about the welfare system and demand more clothes for their kids or for whatever reason just don't work out well within the system."

10. While there was no organized movement challenging the existence of mental illness prior to the 1960s, there were a few ex-patients in the nineteenth century who are looked upon as forerunners by today's radical ex-patient movement. Elizabeth Stone, hospitalized between 1840 and 1842 at Charlestown McLean Asylum (today suburban Boston's McLean Hospital) claimed "there is no such thing as insanity" and declared "This power of calling people crazy has got to be stamped with God's eternal vengeance." *Madness Network News,* Autumn 1978, provides a synopsis of her writings.

11. Charles Reade, *Hard Cash* (Boston: De Wolfe, Fiske and Co., 1863), p. 12. Responding to indignant asylum superintendents who claimed that legal safeguards made the events described in his novel impossible, Reade insisted in the introduction to the 1863 edition of his book "that under existing arrangements any English man or woman may without much difficulty be incarcerated in a private lunatic asylum when not deprived of reason."

12. Albert Deutsch, *The Mentally Ill in America* (New York: Columbia University Press, 1949), pp. 424–25.

13. Ibid., pp. 426–27.

14. Massachusetts, one of the first states to respond to Mrs. Packard's crusade, now became one of the first states to simplify the process of commitment. In 1909 it enacted legislation for "temporary commitment" which provided that someone believed to be mentally ill could be confined for treatment for a brief period on the signature of a single physician. David Rothman, *Conscience and Convenience* (Boston: Little, Brown, 1980), p. 327.

15. Nicholas N. Kittrie, *The Right to Be Different: Deviance and Enforced Therapy* (Baltimore: Johns Hopkins University Press, 1971), pp. 67–68. Even the criterion of "dangerousness" was interpreted so broadly that it did not serve as a barrier to commitment. In the District of Columbia, for example, instructions given to juries defined injury to others to include "intentional or unintentional acts which result in harm to others or cause trouble or inconvenience to others" (ibid., p. 68).

16. "Projects: Civil Commitment of the Mentally Ill," *UCLA Law Review,* Vol. 14, 1967, p. 829.

17. Bruce J. Ennis and Thomas R. Litwack, "Psychiatry and the Presumption of Expertise: Flipping Coins in the Courtroom," *California Law Review,* Vol. 62, 1974, pp. 737–38. Even psychotherapy did not escape the onslaught. The same issue included an article by Ralph Schwitzgebel that assumed the major form of treatment in state mental hospitals was psychotherapy and attacked its effectiveness. To imagine psychotherapy was the chief form of treatment in state hospitals was itself delusional.

18. Robert Plotkin, "Limiting the Therapeutic Orgy: Mental Patients' Right to Refuse Treatment," *Northwestern University Law Review,* Vol. 72, 1978, p. 478.

19. "Mental Illness: A Suspect Classification?" *Yale Law Journal,* Vol. 83, 1974, pp. 1237–70.

20. Mary L. Durham and John Q. LaFond, "A Search for the Missing Premise of Involuntary Therapeutic Commitment: Effective Treatment of the Mentally Ill," *Rutgers Law Review,* Vol. 40, 1988, pp. 303–68.

21. Interview, Richard Cole, August 19, 1988.

22. Jay Centifanti, "The Right to Refuse Treatment," Workshop, National Mental Health Consumers Association Conference, Philadelphia, June 29, 1988.

23. John Parry, "Civil Commitment: Three Proposals for Change," *Mental and Physical Disability Law Reporter,* September–October 1986, p. 334.

24. Robert H. Bork, *The Tempting of America* (New York: Free Press, 1990), p. 2.

25. Ibid., pp. 42–43.

26. Nathan Glazer, "Towards an Imperial Judiciary?" *The Public Interest,* Fall 1975, p. 118.

27. In uncovering an alleged constitutional right to beg in subways, Judge Leonard Sands engaged in precisely the kind of fallacious reasoning Bork assails in *The Tempting of America.* Courts add to the constitution a principle that had not been there before by saying existing law denies equal protection because people who have done similar

things are treated differently. In his decision, Judge Sands argued that because the U.S. Supreme Court in 1980 found fundraising protected by the First Amendment, begging had to be permitted: there could be no distinction between "sophisticated" alms seekers (charities) and threadbare mendicants (*New York Times,* January 30, 1990). But, as Bork points out, when a judge assumes the power to decide which distinctions are legitimate and which are not, he assumes the power to disapprove of any and all legislation, because all legislation makes distinctions (*The Tempting of America,* op. cit., p. 65). Of course, for two hundred years prior to Judge Sands, no one had realized that state and local ordinances against begging violated the First Amendment.

In May 1990, the U.S. Court of Appeals for the Second Circuit overturned Judge Sands' decision. Judge Frank X. Altimari, writing the majority opinion, chastised the lower court (i.e., Sands) for deferring to the rights of beggars while overlooking the concerns of the system's millions of riders (*New York Times,* May 11, 1990). At this writing, the lawyers for the homeless men who had challenged the ban on begging have not decided whether to appeal to the U.S. Supreme Court.

28. *Constitutional Rights of the Mentally Ill.* Hearings Before the Subcommittee on Constitutional Rights of the Committee on the Judiciary, U.S. Senate, 87th Congress, 1st session. Pt. I, Civil Aspects, March 28, 29 and 30, 1961 (Washington, D.C.: U.S. Government Printing Office, 1961), pp. 9, 11. This is not to say there were no traces of anti-psychiatric influence in the hearings. Nicholas Kittrie, the first lawyer to write a major anti-psychiatric book, *The Right to Be Different* (Baltimore: Johns Hopkins University Press, 1971), took an active role in the hearings as legislative assistant to Senator Alexander Wiley, a member of the committee. Moreover, Thomas Szasz was one of those testifying.

29. Ibid., p. 41.

30. *To Protect the Constitutional Rights of the Mentally Ill.* Hearings Before the Subcommittee on Constitutional rights of the Committee on the Judiciary, U.S. Senate, 88th Congress, 1st session, May 2, 3, and 8, 1963 (Washington, D.C.: U.S. Government Printing Office, 1963), p. 47.

31. Ibid., p. 41.

32. Ibid., p. 61.

33. Ibid., pp. 6–8. The bill was more responsive to the concerns expressed by ACLU representatives than to psychiatric concerns. Psychiatrists wanted to make commitment procedures even more liberal than they were in 1961. The ACLU—in what was to become a familiar theme of the mental health bar—stressed the disparity between the way in which the law treated individuals accused of a crime and those "suspected of mental illness."

34. Interview, Morton Birnbaum, September 28, 1988.

35. Morton Birnbaum, "The Right to Treatment," *American Bar Association Journal,* May 1960, p. 503.

36. Interview, Morton Birnbaum, September 28, 1988.

37. Ibid.

38. Morton Birnbaum, "The Right to Treatment: Some Comments on Its Development" in Frank J. Ayd, Jr., ed., *Medical, Moral and Legal Issues in Mental Health Care* (Baltimore: Williams and Wilkins, 1974), pp. 120–21. The decision was Rouse v. Cameron, 373 F. 2d 451 (D.C. Cir. 1976) and was written by Chief Judge David L. Bazelon. It held that a statutory right to treatment existed under the revised District of Columbia Mental Health Code. Charles Rouse had been arrested in 1962 for carrying a dangerous weapon. On being found not guilty by reason of insanity he was committed to St.

Elizabeth's hospital, where he was confined for three years (although the maximum sentence for the offense was one year). He petitioned for his release, saying he had been given no treatment. Bazelon ruled the purpose of involuntary hospitalization was treatment and if a patient was not receiving it, he could not be held indefinitely for no convicted offense.

39. Morton Birnbaum, "The Right to Treatment," op. cit., pp. 500–1.

40. Ibid., p. 503.

41. Eugene Bardach, *The Skill Factor in Politics: Repealing the Mental Commitment Laws in California* (Berkeley: University of California Press, 1972), pp. 106–7.

42. *The Dilemma of Mental Commitments in California: A Background Document*, Subcommittee on Mental Health Services, California Legislative Assembly Interim Committee on Ways and Means, 1967, p. 71–72.

43. Ibid., p. 74.

44. P. John Mathai and P.S. Gopinath, "Deficits of Schizophrenia in Relation to Long Term Hospitalization," *British Journal of Psychiatry,* Vol. 148, 1985, p. 515. The study was conducted at two mental hospitals in South India. Deficits were least marked in patients with manic-depressive psychosis, regardless of length of hospital stay. This, says the authors, "suggests that hospital care as such does not have a significant bearing on the deficits, otherwise the patients with MDP would have developed as many as did schizophrenics" (p. 515).

45. *The Dilemma of Mental Commitments,* op. cit., p. 105.

46. Eugene Bardach, op. cit., p. 75.

47. Ibid., p. 132.

48. The case was Riese v. St. Mary's Hospital and Medical Center, 196 Cal. App. 3d 1388. The lower (state) court's decision upholding a right to refuse was appealed to the state supreme court, which first agreed to review the decision, but then changed its mind, allowing the lower court decision to stand. Originally, under LPS, a person detained during the seventeen-day period might request a court hearing, but the burden was on him to initiate the procedure. This was changed in 1983 as a result of Doe v. Gallinot which provided that an individual held over three days (for the fourteen-day treatment period) had to be notified of his right to a judicial hearing and if he did not pursue a hearing would in any case receive an administrative hearing within four days. In some areas these hearings are by a judge, in others by a specially selected hearing officer.

49. "Projects: Civil Commitment," *UCLA Law Review,* op. cit., 1967, p. 868.

50. Albert H. Urmer, "An Assessment of California's Mental Health Program," in Calvin T. Frederick, ed., *Dangerous Behavior: A Problem in Law and Mental Health* (Rockville, Md.: U.S. Department of Health, Education and Welfare Publication no. [ADM] 78–563, 1978), p. 143. The resident population in state hospitals dropped 33% during the first two years of LPS. See Eugene Bardach, *The Implementation Game* (Cambridge: MIT Press, 1978), p. 285.

51. Ghettos of mentally ill persons sprang up in areas near state mental hospitals, arousing public concern, and increased mental health funds to communities largely went to previously unserved populations, not to those suffering from major mental illness.

52. Grant H. Morris, "Conservatorship for the 'Gravely Disabled': California's Non-declaration of Nonindependence," *Journal of Law and Psychiatry,* Vol. 1, 1978, p. 400.

53. Ibid., p. 403.

54. Bardach points out that Republican state legislator Frank Lanterman was the first to question the strict libertarianism of the *Dilemma* report as it applied to potentially assaultive and homicidal patients who would be released after a maximum of seventeen days. As a result of his intervention, the certification provision was redrafted to permit detention for an additional ninety days of patients who had "threatened, attempted, or actually inflicted physical harm upon the person of another after having been taken into custody for evaluation and treatment." Bardach, op. cit., pp. 123–24. Persons who remained actively suicidal could be held an additional thirty days after an initial twenty-one day period.

55. Grant Morris, op. cit., p. 405.

56. Ibid., p. 422.

57. For example, a letter dated March 17, 1986 to the California Alliance for the Mentally Ill from Dr. Leo Ingle of the San Luis Obispo County Community Mental Health Services recounted a series of cases in which conservatorship investigators used extremely stringent criteria with disastrous results.

Chapter 6. Hospitalization Under Attack:
The Major Legal Cases

1. Lessard v. Schmidt, 349 F. Supp. 1978, reported in *Clearinghouse Review,* October 1974, p. 451.

2. Alexander D. Brooks, "Notes on Defining the Dangerousness of the Mentally Ill," in Calvin J. Frederick, ed., *Dangerous Behavior,* (Washington, D.C.: Dept, Health, Education and Welfare Publication No. [ADM] 78–563, 1978), p. 47.

3. Robert Miller, Gary Maier, and Michael Kaye, "Miranda Comes to the Hospital: The Right to Remain Silent in Civil Commitment," *American Journal of Psychiatry,* September 1985, pp. 1074–77. They report that Illinois, Massachusetts, and Hawaii also provide a right to remain silent. Their study of the impact of the law at Mendota Mental Health Institute, the state hospital in Dane County, Wisconsin, found that of fifty patients studied in 1984, almost all talked to clinicians. The authors point out that the "right to remain silent" in practice has not fulfilled the expectations of civil libertarian attorneys that it would serve as a covert way to abolish civil commitment. They also observe that no attorney was present during the patient's psychiatric examination and so far no court has required this. If attorneys were present during "questioning" of the patient, the authors note that the outcome would probably be different.

4. Leonard Roy Frank, "An Interview with Bruce Ennis," *Madness Network News Reader* (San Francisco: Glide Publications, 1974), p. 162.

5. Ibid.

6. Philip J. Leaf and Michael Holt, "How *Wyatt* Affected Patients," in Ralph Jones and Richard Parlour, eds., *Wyatt v. Stickney: Retrospect and Prospect* (New York: Grune and Stratton, 1981), p. 55.

7. Stonewall B. Stickney, "The Inception of *Wyatt* and the State's Response," in ibid., p. 15.

8. Interview, Morton Birnbaum, September 28, 1988.

9. The Department of Mental Health even took the initiative in arguing that all involuntary patients "unquestionably have a constitutional right to receive such individual treatment as will give each of them a realistic opportunity to be cured or improve his

or her mental condition." The very words the Department used came from Birnbaum's article. See Philip J. Leaf and Michael Holt, op. cit., p. 56.

10. Stonewall B. Stickney, "Wyatt v. Stickney: Background and Postscript," in Stuart Golann and William J. Fremouw, eds., *The Right to Treatment for Mental Patients* (New York: Irvington Publishers, 1976), pp. 42–43. Stickney wanted the emphasis to be on effectiveness of treatment rather than the "objective" criteria favored by Birnbaum, who simply assumed treatment was effective if staffing ratios were high.

11. The series of decisions in Wyatt v. Stickney (later Wyatt v. Aderholt and then Wyatt v. Hardin) are reprinted in Stuart Golann and William Fremouw, ibid., pp. 129–85. For the specific standards imposed by Judge Johnson see especially pp. 135–39.

12. Morton Birnbaum, "The Right to Treatment: Some Comments on Its Development," in Frank J. Ayd Jr., ed., *Medical, Moral and Legal Issues in Mental Health Care* (Baltimore: Williams and Wilkins, 1974), p. 131.

13. Interview, Morton Birnbaum, September 28, 1988.

14. Morton Birnbaum, "The Right to Treatment," in Frank J. Ayd, op. cit., pp. 134, 138. The case Birnbaum brought was Legion v. Richardson (354 F. Supp. 456, S.D., N.Y. 1973).

15. While Leaf and Holt write that "Wyatt litigation did much to decrease the patient population," they also say that it is not clear how much decline would have occurred without it. They point out that an unfortunate result of the suit was the expenditure of an enormous amount of money on improvements to seriously outmoded buildings which were promptly abandoned as large numbers of patients were released. See Philip J. Leaf and Michael Holt, op. cit., pp. 73, 104.

The case dragged on for many years after Judge Johnson's 1972 decision. Complaining that the state was failing to live up to the mandated standards, the mental health bar succeeded in obtaining a federal court office to monitor state compliance with Wyatt standards. In 1986 a settlement finally abolished that federal office in exchange for a state promise to spend more money and secure accreditation for its hospitals. See Grace Nordhoff, "Keys to the Asylum," *Southern Exposure,* Fall 1989, p. 21.

16. *Madness Network News,* October 1975, p. 1.

17. Kenneth Donaldson, *Insanity Inside Out* (New York: Crown Publishers, 1976), p. 12.

18. Ibid., pp. 190–191, 251. In 1963 Helping Hands Inc., a halfway house in Minnesota for mental patients, wrote Dr. O'Connor asking him to release Donaldson to its care. The request was accompanied by a supporting letter from the Minneapolis Clinic of Psychiatry and Neurology. In addition, on four separate occasions, between 1964 and 1968, John Lembcke, a college classmate of Donaldson and longtime family friend living in Syracuse, New York, asked O'Connor to release Donaldson to his care. Lembcke was a serious and responsible person, willing and able to assume responsibility for Donaldson. See Thomas A. Shannon and Jo Ann Manfra, *Law and Bioethics: Texts with Commentary on Major Court Decisions* (New York: Paulist Press, 1982) p. 222.

19. Kenneth Donaldson, op. cit., pp. 136–37. Donaldson writes "My brief was based on the Right to Treatment (because I was getting no treatment and because I needed no treatment, I was entitled to my freedom) and based on fraud (because the statements on my commitment papers were uniformly untrue)."

20. Ibid., p. 66–67.

21. Ibid., pp. 198–99.

22. Ibid., p. 183.

23. Ibid., p. 216.

24. Ibid., p. 278.

25. Ibid., p. 139.

26. Ibid., p. 279.

27. Ibid., p. 196.

28. Ibid., p. 211. Szasz too was sharply critical of Donaldson's behavior, insisting that he basically chose the nuthouse as a career. Writes Szasz: "For many years, the relationship between O'Connor and Donaldson thus closely resembled that of a married couple seeking a divorce but unable to agree on the terms for it, each insisting on his or her complete innocence and demanding that a judge settle their dispute." Thomas Szasz, *Psychiatric Slavery* (New York: Free Press, 1977), p. 27.

29. Interview, Morton Birnbaum, September 28, 1988. The case, by directly attacking psychiatrists, also abruptly terminated the honeymoon between the American Psychiatric Association and the mental health bar on right to treatment suits. As Louis McGarry points out in "The Holy Legal War Against State-Hospital Psychiatry" (*New England Journal of Medicine,* February 5, 1976, p. 319), these law cases were initially dubbed sweetheart suits.

30. Thomas A. Shannon and Jo Ann Manfra eds., op. cit., p. 223.

31. Donaldson v. O'Connor, U.S. Court of Appeals, Fifth Circuit, April 26, 1974, reprinted in Stuart Golann and William J. Fremouw, eds., op. cit., pp. 191–92. The reason Donaldson was denied occupational therapy, according to his own account, was because Dr. Gumanis feared he would learn touch typing and use the skill to prepare even more habeas corpus petitions. When he was transferred to another doctor within the hospital, he was permitted to take occupational therapy.

32. Philip R. A. May, *Treatment of Schizophrenia: A Comparative Study of Five Treatment Methods* (New York: Science House, 1968), pp. 244–62.

33. Wyatt v. Aderholt, U.S. Court of Appeals, Fifth Circuit, November 8, 1974. Reprinted in Golann and Fremouw, eds., op. cit., p. 173.

34. O'Connor v. Donaldson, Supreme Court of the United States, No. 74-8, June 26, 1975, reprinted in ibid., p. 219.

35. Kenneth Donaldson, op. cit., p. 330.

36. Ibid., p. 330.

37. The Burger decision is reprinted in Golann v. Fremouw, eds., op. cit., pp. 225–36.

38. Alan Stone notes that in the wake of Donaldson, for example, the New York State Commissioner of Mental Health announced he was prepared to convert all chronic patients to voluntary status and let them leave. Stone argues that the bag lady is the symbol of the Donaldson decision; he did not need paternalism but others did. Alan Stone, *Law, Psychiatry and Morality* (Washington, D.C.: American Psychiatric Press, 1984), pp. 116–18.

39. Emil Kraepelin, *A Hundred Years of Psychiatry* (New York: Philosophical Library, 1962), pp. 96–97.

40. The Pennsylvania suit, brought by Ferleger, was Downs v. Pennsylvania Department of Welfare. (See *Clearinghouse Review,* February 1974, p. 625.) The Mental Health Law Project's case was Souder v. Brennan, 367 F. Supp. 808 (D.D.C. 1973).

41. Interview, Jay Centifanti, August 26, 1988. The case was Schinderwolf v. Klein. For a summary, see *Clearinghouse Review,* September 1976, p. 393. Technically, Centifanti was a "law clerk," not an attorney, at the time; his license had been suspended following an incident in which, suffering from manic-depressive psychosis, he had shot his wife on a Philadelphia train.

42. "Living Conditions in New York State Psychiatric Centers Revisited: A Report of Follow Up Visits to Nine Psychiatric Centers, Feb. 1985," New York State Commission on Quality of Care for the Mentally Disabled, Nov. 1985, p. 80.

43. E. Fuller Torrey, *Nowhere to Go* (New York: Harper & Row, 1988), p. 141.

44. Joseph Morrissey, "Deinstitutionalizing the Mentally Ill," in W. R. Gove, ed., *Deviance and Mental Illness* (Beverly Hills: Sage Publications, 1982), p. 151.

45. This right, first recognized by the Washington, D.C. Court of Appeals (Lake v. Cameron, 364 F. 2d 657 D.C. Cir. 1966), was later incorporated into many state commitment statutes and was affirmed in a number of judicial decisions. For a detailed discussion see P. Browning Hoffman and Lawrence L. Faust, "Least Restrictive Treatment of the Mentally Ill: A Doctrine in Search of Its Senses," *San Diego Law Review,* Vol. 14, 1977, pp. 1100ff. One of the major suits to implement this right was brought by the Mental Health Law Project in Washington, D.C. (Dixon v. Weinberger, 405 F. Supp. 974, 1976). The judge ruled that patients at St. Elizabeth's had the right to placement in the least restrictive alternative. While the District was supposed to create a system of community care as a result of the ruling, in fact there was massive dumping of patients on the streets.

46. Patricia M. Wald and Paul R. Friedman, "The Politics of Mental Health Advocacy in the United States," *International Journal of Law and Psychiatry,* Vol. 1, 1978, p. 146.

Chapter 7.   From the Right to Treatment to the Right to Refuse Treatment

1. Leonard Roy Frank, "An Interview with Bruce Ennis," in *Madness Network News Reader* (San Francisco: Glide Publications, 1974), pp. 162, 167.

2. Ibid., p. 163.

3. "Developments in the Law—Civil Commitment of the Mentally Ill," *Harvard Law Review,* Vol. 87, 1974, p. 1344. According to the article: "It would be incongruous if an individual who lacks capacity to make a treatment decision could frustrate the very justification for the state's action by refusing such treatments."

4. See Nason v. Superintendent of Bridgewater State Hospital, 233 N.E. 2d 908 (Mass. 1968), and Whitree v. State, 56 Misc. 2d 693 N.Y.S. 2d 486 (1968).

5. Interview, Dr. Thomas Gutheil, May 17, 1988.

6. The case repeatedly cited by the mental health bar is a 1914 decision by the New York Court of Appeals, Schloendorff v. Society of N.Y. Hospital. Judge Cardozo ruled that "every human being of adult years and sound mind has a right to determine what shall be done with his own body." The mental health bar conveniently overlooked the phrase "and sound mind."

7. *In re* Quinlan, Supreme Court of New Jersey, 1976. Reprinted in Thomas A. Shannon and Jo Ann Manfra, eds., *Law and Bioethics: Texts with Commentary on Major Court Decisions* (New York: Paulist Press, 1982), p 149.

8. Superintendent of Belchertown State School v. Saikewicz, Supreme Judicial Court of Massachusetts, 1977. Reprinted in Ibid., p. 186.

9. In the Matter of Guardianship of Richard Roe III, Supreme Judicial Court of Massachusetts, 421 N.E. Rep. 2d 40, pp. 42–43.

10. Interview, Mark Berson, July 25, 1988. Northampton State was the subject of the consent decree, mentioned earlier, and initial plans were for it to be closed down by

1981 and replaced by community programs. While the plan to close it was abandoned, the hospital has been extremely reluctant to admit and retain patients.

11. In the Matter of Guardianship of Richard Roe III, op. cit., p. 50.

12. Ibid., p. 58.

13. Alan Stone, *Law, Psychiatry and Morality* (Washington, D.C.: American Psychiatric Press, 1984), p. 150. As Stone points out, the Roe case illustrates ludicrous misuse of both public funds and the legal system. Roe was "sinking into psychosis and there was a good chance he could be treated, yet—at enormous legal expense to his family and the taxpayers—the law is seeing to it . . . that he will not get timely or appropriate treatment" (pp. 144–45).

14. In the Matter of Guardianship of Richard Roe III, op. cit., p. 56.

15. The crucial point that medical evidence indicated that the administration of drugs could make Richard Roe competent, thus negating the need for elaborate substituted judgment procedures, was relegated by the Massachusetts Supreme Judicial Court to a footnote, which treated it as merely one, nondecisive factor. As Thomas Gutheil and Paul Appelbaum point out, in the name of protecting the autonomy of the individual, the court denied his opportunity to enhance his autonomy through becoming competent. See "Substituted Judgment: Best Interests in Disguise," *The Hastings Center Report,* June 1983, p. 10.

16. Robert H. Bork, *The Tempting of America* (New York: Free Press, 1990), pp. 248–49.

17. Thomas Gutheil and Paul Appelbaum, op. cit., pp. 9–10.

18. In the Matter of Guardianship of Richard Roe III, pp. 42, 53.

19. Ibid., p. 53.

20. Paul Appelbaum and Thomas Gutheil, "The Boston State Hospital Case: 'Involuntary Mind Control,' the Constitution, and the 'Right to Rot,'" *American Journal of Psychiatry,* June 1980, p. 721. The authors note that psychiatrists do not administer neuroleptics in at attempt to "control minds but to restore them to the patient's control."

21. In the Supreme Court of the United States, October Term, 1980. Mills v. Rogers. Brief for the American College of Neuropsychopharmacology as Amicus Curiae.

22. In the Matter of Guardianship of Richard Roe III, op. cit., p. 53. The judges were seemingly impelled more by their misconceptions concerning anti-psychiatric drugs than by zeal for the principle of substituted judgment, for they wrote in a footnote: "[W]e do not foreclose reconsideration of these issues when and if it can be shown that the character of anti-psychotic drugs have changed" (p. 54).

23. Interview, Mark Berson, July 25, 1988.

24. Rennie v. Klein (481 F. Supp. 552 D.N.J. 1979), on appeal, resulted in a decision that state administrative procedure, instituted during the course of the original trial, was satisfactory. It provided an optional review by an independent psychiatrist when the patient refused treatment.

25. State of Washington et al. v. Walter Harper, Petition for a Writ of Certiorari to the Washington State Supreme Court, In the Supreme Court of the United States, October Term, 1988, p. 4. Brought by the ACLU and Evergreen Legal Services, a member group of the Legal Services Corporation, the original suit against the state of Washington was another example of activism by the mental health bar.

26. Interview, Paul Appelbaum, July 29, 1988. See also Steven Hoge et al., "A Prospective, Multi-Center Study of Patients' Refusal of Antipsychotic Medication," *Archives of General Psychiatry,* in press.

27. Ibid.

28. Francine Cournos, Karen McKinnon, and Carole Adams, "A Comparison of Clinical and Judicial Procedures for Reviewing Requests for Involuntary Medication in New York," *Hospital and Community Psychiatry,* August 1988, pp. 852, 853.

29. Interview, Julie Zito, February 27, 1989. The multi-center study of patients' refusal conducted by Hoge, Appelbaum, and others suggests that Zito's rate, based on the Minnesota experience, with its in-house procedure (making refusal relatively easy) is too high. The multi-center study found a refusal rate for the entire sample of 7.2%, with refusal defined as rejecting drugs for more than twenty-four hours. Even then, the majority of refusing patients refused one week or less. Nonetheless, hospital staff found the effect on both the refusing patients and the ward milieu highly negative, with significant increases in assaultive behavior. See Steven Hoge et al., op. cit.

30. Jim Simon, "Court Must OK Drug Treatment If Patient Balks," *Seattle Times,* reprinted as Appendix C, State of Washington et al. v. Walter Harper, Petition for a Writ of Certiorari to the Washington State Supreme Court, In the Supreme Court of the United States, October Term, 1988.

31. Ibid.

32. Richard W. Cole, "Rogers v. Okin: A Lawsuit to Guarantee Patients' Right to Refuse Anti-Psychotic Medication," *American Journal of Forensic Psychiatry,* July 1979, p. 131.

33. United States of America versus Michael Francis Charters, Jr., United States Court of Appeals for the Fourth Circuit, No. 86-5568, Decided December 9, 1988, p. 15.

34. Ibid. The judges observe that the effect of the two-stage judicial procedure, in putting the burden upon the government to prove the patient's lack of competence is to accord "less rather than more deference to the decisions of institutional professionals than to the conflicting opinions of outside expert witnesses."

35. *New York Times,* February 28, 1990. The Harper case involved a prisoner, limiting its applicability to civil commitment cases. However, Paul Appelbaum believes the analysis would be equally appropriate to a civil setting. Still, until a case involving a civil setting is decided by the Supreme Court, it could be argued that the decision applies only to the narrower prison situation.

In what has become a typical pattern, the American Psychiatric Association and the American Psychological Association submitted briefs on opposite sides, the latter emphasizing the evils of anti-psychiatric drugs.

36. Interview, Paul Appelbaum, March 2, 1990.

37. Julian R. Friedman and Robert W. Daly, "Civil Commitment and the Doctrine of Balance: A Critical Analysis," *Santa Clara Lawyer,* Vol. 13, 1973, pp. 503–4, 509.

38. Joseph M. Livermore, Carl P. Malmquist, and Paul E. Meehl, "On the Justifications for Civil Commitment," *University of Pennsylvania Law Review,* Vol. 117, 1968, p. 84.

39. Bruce Ennis, *Prisoners of Psychiatry* (New York: Harcourt Brace Jovanovich, 1972), p. 227.

40. Tarasoff v. Regents of University of California, Supreme Court of California, In Bank, 1976. Reprinted in Thomas Shannon and Jo Ann Manfra, eds., op. cit., p. 304.

41. Alan Stone, *Law, Psychiatry and Morality* (Washington, D.C.: American Psychiatric Press, 1984), p. 51.

42. Interview, Paul Appelbaum, May 18, 1988.

43. Alan Stone, op. cit., p. 140.

44. Berel Caesar, "Preserving the Family: A Brief for Limited Commitment of Non-Dangerous Mentally Ill Persons," *Journal of Marital and Family Therapy,* July 1980, p. 309. The mental health bar has even sought to revoke the ability of parents to secure treatment for their minor children by interposing the full panoply of procedural rights,

lawyers, and court hearings. James Ellis, an attorney with the Mental Health Law Project, conceded that a family, unable to obtain treatment for a severely ill child, might be unwilling to take him back into their home. He called for "some individual or institution . . . to assume the familial function if the child's right to contest his or her hospitalization is to be meaningful."

Of course, it is hard to imagine a better recipe for disaster than cutting off an untreated psychotic child from his family in order to bestow him upon "some individual or institution." While the mental health bar has had some success in this effort in individual states—responding to a suit brought by David Ferleger, Pennsylvania bestowed the rights of adults on children of fourteen—the Supreme Court in 1979 came down on the side of the family. In a Georgia case it ruled that a child had a right to a "neutral fact finder," but this could be a hospital doctor and there was no need to involve the courts. See James W. Ellis, "Volunteering Children: Parental Commitment of Minors to Mental Institutions," *University of California Law Review,* Vol. 62, 1974, p. 891.

45. Robert L. Sadoff, "Developing Community Mental Health Center-Criminal Justice System Interactions," *International Journal of Law and Psychiatry,* Vol. 1, 1978, p. 429.

46. "They Have Souls Too," NBC News Documentary, June 26, 1987.

47. Alan Stone, op. cit., p. 142.

48. Interview Robert Jackson (pseudonym), March 14, 1988.

49. The psychiatric social worker was Faye Kahn of Philadelphia.

50. Interview Edward and Ellen Holder (pseudonyms), May 7, 1988.

51. Interview, Joel Klein, September 30, 1988.

52. Bruce Ennis, op. cit., p. 180.

53. Ibid., p. 184.

54. Ibid., p. 188.

55. Elizabeth Hilton, "NAMI-Travelers Aid: Joining Networks to Help Homeless and Missing Mentally Ill," Workshop, National Alliance for the Mentally Ill National Conference, Boulder, Colorado, July 1988.

56. Richard Lamb, "Family Advocates for a Change," NAMI Conference, Washington, D.C., September 1987.

57. Berel Caesar, op. cit., p. 315.

Chapter 8.   The Rise of the Ex-Patient Movement

1. *Madness Network News,* November 1972, p. 13.

2. Richard E. Vatz and Lee S. Weinberg, eds. *Thomas Szasz: Primary Values and Major Contentions* (Buffalo: Prometheus Press, 1983), p. 175.

3. There was the same attitude toward electroshock therapy. Psychiatrist Robert Heath reports: "The psychodynamic interpretations, in retrospect, were ludicrous. 'Depressed patients are in need of punishment. The shock provides sufficient expiation to signify forgiveness, and therefore accounts for the patient's improvement.' Of course, it was assumed that the therapeutic result would not last unless the patient's hidden motivation for wanting punishment was magically resolved on the analyst's couch." Robert G. Heath, "Commentary: Does Electroconvulsive Therapy Cause Brain Damage," *The Behavioral and Brain Sciences,* Vol. 7, 1984, p. 27.

4. Interview, Dr. Terence Early, May 31, 1988.

5. Ibid.

6. Richard Suddath, George Christison, E. Fuller Torrey, Manuel Casanova, and Daniel Weinberger, "Anatomical Abnormalities in the Brains of Monozygotic Twins Discordant for Schizophrenia," *The New England Journal of Medicine,* March 22, 1990, p. 792. See also *New York Times,* March 22, 1990.

7. *New York Times,* March 22, 1990. There was of course the strong possibility that both schizophrenia and manic-depressive illness were in fact groups of diseases with similar symptoms, but different causation.

8. *New York Times,* November 7, 1989.

9. *Madness Network News,* Fall 1980, p. 14.

10. Interview, Ted Chabasinski, July 6, 1988.

11. Ibid.

12. Interview, Leonard Frank, July 5, 1988. Frank obtained and published his psychiatric records in *Madness Network News,* December 1974, pp. 12–17.

13. Interview, Leonard Frank, July 5, 1988.

14. *Madness Network News,* Winter 1978, p. 17.

15. Jeffrey M. Masson, *Against Therapy* (New York: Atheneum, 1988), p. 135.

16. *Madness Network News,* Summer 1983, p. 4.

17. Ibid., Winter 1978, p. 1.

18. Ibid.

19. Ibid., Summer 1983, p. 4.

20. Wade Hudson, "Strike Another Match," in *Madness Network News Reader* (San Francisco: Glide Publications, 1974), pp. 53–55.

21. Interview, Sally Zinman, May 3, 1988.

22. Leonard Frank, *The History of Shock Treatment* (San Francisco, 1978), p. x.

23. Interview, Sally Zinman, May 3, 1988.

24. From Laing came an emphasis on the spiritual character of the experience others called mental illness.

25. *Madness Network News,* Spring 1983, p. 15.

26. Ibid., October 1975, p. 7.

27. Ibid., p. 18.

28. Ibid. Spring 1983, p. 39. Richman presumably chose the name "Dr. Caligari" to refer to the 1919 German expressionist horror film *The Cabinet of Dr. Caligari,* in which a showman manipulates a somnambulist to commit murder. The horror builds as the audience discovers the showman is actually the director of a lunatic asylum. In the end the entire story turns out to be the dream of a madman. In evoking the film, Richman may have intended to convey the idea that madness itself is an unreal dream in the minds of a "sane" audience.

29. Ibid., Summer/Fall 1979, p. 1.

30. Ibid., December 1974, p. 29.

31. Ibid., 1974 (n.d.), Vol. 2, No. 1, p. 1.

32. Ibid., 1976 (n.d.), Vol. 3, No. 9. What was called mental illness was really political dissidence. People's feelings of rage and frustration were seen "as symptoms of a disease rather than being seen for what they really are—natural reactions to living in an exploitative and unjust society where profits are put before basic human needs" (ibid., Fall 1980, p. 1). Ironically, in the "socialist" society of the Soviet Union, psychiatry was indeed being used to coerce political dissidents into conformity—but such inconvenient facts were ignored by the psychiatry-as-capitalist-plot groups.

33. Ibid., February 1974, p. 21.

34. Ibid, December 1975, p. 3.

35. Ibid., Winter 1985, p. 6.

36. Ibid., Winter 1978, p. 21.

37. Ibid., Spring 1983, p. 19. Ted Chabasinski thinks the movement's refusal to countenance the possibility that mental illness had a medical basis was a mistake. "We had this party line. If you would come into the movement and say 'Gee, I think drugs helped me,' you'd be attacked, 'you sellout, you pig, you dirty dog.' And naturally 99% of the people who put their toe in the water and would be denounced because they didn't have the proper party line would leave. The groups were all very small, but they were ideologically pure" (interview, July 6, 1988).

38. *Madness Network News,* Late Summer 1978, p. 1.

39. Ibid., Fall/Winter 1982–83, p. 1.

40. Ibid., Winter 1983–84, p. 3.

41. Ibid., October 1976, p. 1. Demonstrators also chanted a standard litany of the movement: "One, two, three, four, We won't take your drugs no more. Five, six, seven, eight, Smash the therapeutic state."

42. Ibid., p. 2.

43. Ibid., October 1975, p. 4.

44. Ibid., December 1975, p. 9.

45. Ibid., Winter 1981, p. 1.

46. Ibid., p. 5.

47. Radical Caucus of the American Psychiatric Association, Annual Newsletter, 1987.

48. *Madness Network News,* Winter 1981, p. 5.

49. Ibid., p. 3.

50. Ibid., October 1975, p. 21.

51. Jeffrey M. Masson, op. cit., passim.

52. *Madness Network News,* 1974 (n.d.), Vol. 2, No. 1, p. 12.

53. *Dendron,* December 1988, pp. 3–4.

54. For a study of the debased behavior of psychiatrists in Nazi Germany see German geneticist Benno Muller-Hill's *Murderous Science: Elimination by Scientific Selection of Jews, Gypsies and Others, Germany 1933–45,* trans. by George R. Fraser (New York: Oxford University Press, 1988). Hitler introduced the policy of mass murder of mental patients in 1939—before the policy was applied to Jews. At least 75,000 were killed, many by poison gas, marking its first use for extermination purposes.

55. *The Rights Tenet,* Newsletter of the National Association for Rights Protection and Advocacy, January 1988, p. 2.

56. Interview, Dr. Peter Breggin, May 6, 1988.

57. Peter Breggin, Oprah Winfrey show, April 2, 1987.

58. Breggin, Oprah Winfrey show, August 17, 1987.

59. George Walden, "Our Moralistic Media," *Encounter,* February 1988, p. 18.

Chapter 9. Psychosurgery: *The First Domino*

1. Thomas Ballantine, "A Critical Assessment of Psychiatric Surgery: Past, Present and Future," in Silvano Arieti and Keith Brodie, eds., *American Handbook of Psychiatry,* Vol. 7 (New York: Basic Books, 1981), p. 1031.

2. David Shutts, *Lobotomy: Resort to the Knife* (New York: Van Nostrand Reinhold, 1982), p. 70.

3. Paul De Kruif, *A Man Against Insanity* (New York: Harcourt Brace, 1957), p. 100. The new procedure could be performed in minutes rather than the hours required for the earlier operation.

4. David Shutts, op. cit., p. 146.

5. *Appendix: Psychosurgery,* The National Commission for the Protection of Human Subjects of Biomedical and Behavioral Research, U.S. Department of Health, Education and Welfare, Publ. No. Os 77-0003 (Washington, D.C.: U.S. Government Printing Office, 1977), p. I-6.

6. Paul De Kruif, op. cit., p. 103.

7. David Shutts, op. cit., p. 60.

8. Ibid., p. 245. Indomitable to the end, Freeman visited Mexico shortly before his death. Seventy-six years old, suffering from advanced cancer, he traveled 500 miles to Yucatán with two former students, Zigmond Lebensohn and Manuel Suárez, then governor of the Mexican state of Chiapas, and climbed the sheer and difficult steps of a Mayan temple. In Lebensohn's words: "A triumph of will over infirmity, this was a fitting gesture to close the life of a remarkable man whose like we shall never see again" (ibid., p. 249).

9. Ibid., p. 259.

10. Interview, Dr. Desmond Kelly, October 5, 1988. The most famous "tombstone" of the negative effects of surgery was President John Kennedy's sister Rosemary. Mildly retarded, she became mentally ill when she was twenty-one. She suffered from wild moods and tantrums, wandered the streets at night, and became physically abusive. Dr. Freeman had begun performing lobotomies several years earlier, and in 1941 the Kennedys decided to give Rosemary the operation. The result in her case was disastrous. One member of the family claimed the operation "made her go from being mildly retarded to very retarded." Since 1941 Rosemary has been confined to a nursing convent in Wisconsin. See E. Fuller Torrey, *Nowhere to Go* (New York: Harper & Row, 1988), pp. 104–6.

On the other hand, Dr. Paul Bridges, also an English psychiatrist who is an expert on psychosurgery, points out that the Department of Health, in an English study of 10,000 crude operations carried out from 1940 to 1945, "showed that 20%, one fifth of the patients, could be discharged from the hospital after the operation. That's really astonishingly good." Interview, Dr. Bridges, October 13, 1988. Similarly, a series of studies in the United States, including the California-Greystone projects and studies at Boston Psychopathic Hospital, found that lobotomy performed on patients who had failed to respond to other available treatments permitted hospital discharge at a rate substantially exceeding what could otherwise be expected, especially since the patients selected for surgery were often chronic institutionalized schizophrenics. Moreover, the studies found that despite the occurrence of major untoward effects on personality in some cases, there was little or no evidence of intellectual deterioration following surgery. See Herbert G. Vaughan, Jr., "Psychosurgery and Brain Stimulation in Historical Perspective," in Willard M. Gaylin, Josel Meister, and Robert Neville, eds., *Operating on the Mind: The Psychosurgery Conflict* (New York: Basic Books, 1975), p. 41.

11. Stewart A. Shevitz, "Psychosurgery: Some Current Observations," *American Journal of Psychiatry,* March 1976, p. 267.

12. Thomas Ballantine, "A Critical Assessment," op. cit., p. 1037. The device was a modification of one invented at the turn of the century for use in animal neurophysiology research.

13. Desmond Kelly, *Anxiety and Emotions* (Springfield, Ill.: Charles C. Thomas, 1980), p. 210.

14. *Report and Recommendations: Psychosurgery.* National Commission for the Protection of Human Subjects of Biomedical and Behavioral Research, U.S. Dept. of Health, Education and Welfare Publ. No. OS 77-0001. (Washington, D.C.: U.S. Government Printing Office, 1977), p. 53.

15. Jesse Yap, "Psychosurgery: Its Definition," *American Journal of Forensic Psychiatry,* July 1979, p. 93.

16. Testimony, neurosurgeon Dr. Charles Fager, to National Commission for the Protection of Human Subjects of Biomedical and Behavioral Research, July 19, 1976. Although psychosurgery was originally used extensively in schizophrenia, as early as 1936 it was apparent to Egas Moniz that agitated depression responded best, while cases of chronic schizophrenia showed little improvement. See Paul Bridges and John Bartlett, "Psychosurgery Yesterday and Today, *British Journal of Psychiatry,* Vol. 131, 1977, p. 249.

17. Interview, Dr. Peter Breggin, May 6, 1988.

18. Ibid. One of Breggin's methods of eliciting information has been described by neurosurgeon Thomas Ballantine. Dr. Ballantine writes: "On April 14, 1971 I received a short letter dated April 12, 1972. It said:

Dear Dr. Ballantine:

I read with great interest about the international psychosurgery conference.

I would appreciate any reprints you may have concerning your work in this area as well as any other material which you feel might be of interest to a psychiatrist in general practice.

Thanks very much.

Sincerely,
Peter R. Breggin, M.D."

Ballantine reports receiving two more letters from Breggin, in which he said he was completing "a review of the literature and a historical study," and requesting Dr. Ballantine's "impressions on the field," the number of cases he had treated with psychosurgery since 1965, his estimate of how many other surgeons were involved in psychosurgery and the techniques used and illustrative material, photograph or diagram, illustrating his technique. The correspondence was cut short when Dr. Ballantine saw a copy of an article by Nicholas von Hoffman in *The Washington Post* of July 16, 1971 entitled "Brain Maim" quoting Breggin as saying that women had "their brains smooshed twice as often as men" by husbands and doctors who wanted to "put an end to their nagging, whining helplessness." He reports sending Breggin a last note: "Is this the article which caused you to request information and reprints from me? Or, have you published an article in a scientific journal on the subject—or, have you prepared such an article for publication?"

Ballantine originally included a detailed account of the correspondence in a chapter on psychosurgery he prepared for *The American Handbook of Psychiatry,* but, in his words, "succumbed to their agonized entreaties and agreed to have all references to Breggin deleted from the published chapter." Unpublished section of manuscript and letter from Dr. Thomas Ballantine to Rael Jean Isaac, November 30, 1989.

19. *Quality of Health Care—Human Experimentation,* 1973 Hearings Before the Subcommittee on Health of the Committee on Labor and Public Welfare, U.S. Senate, 93 Congress, 1st Session, Feb. 23 and March 6, 1973 (Washington, D.C.: U.S. Government Printing Office, 1973), p. 358.

20. Ibid., p. 374.

21. Peter Breggin, "The Return of Lobotomy and Psychosurgery," *Congressional Record,* February 24, 1972, p. 5575.

22. Interview, Dr. Desmond Kelly, October 5, 1988.

23. Interview, Dr. Paul Bridges, October 13, 1988.

24. Vernon H. Mark, "A Psychosurgeon's Case *for* Psychosurgery," *Psychology Today,* July 1974, p. 28. Mark and Robert Neville are also quoted to this effect in Elliot S. Valenstein, ed., *The Psychosurgery Debate: Scientific, Legal and Ethical Perspectives* (San Francisco: W. H. Freeman, 1980), p. 94.

25. Interview, Dr. Peter Breggin, May 6, 1988.

26. Stephan L. Chorover, "The Psychosurgery Evaluation Studies and Their Impact on the Commission's Report," in Elliot S. Valenstein, ed., op. cit., p. 247.

27. Ibid., p. 248.

28. Samuel I. Shuman, "The Emotional, Medical and Legal Reasons for the Special Concern about Psychosurgery" in Frank Ayd, Jr., ed., *Medical, Moral and Legal Issues in Mental Health Care* (Baltimore: Williams and Wilkins, 1974), p. 72. An exception to this pattern of herd rejection of the treatment was Eugene Methvin's article "Should We Halt the Brain-Probers?" in *Reader's Digest,* February 1979.

29. Interview Dr. Peter Breggin, May 6, 1988.

30. *Madness Network News,* Center Section, Summer 1977, p. 8. See also ibid., Fall 1977, p. 2.

31. Interview, Dr. Peter Breggin, May 6, 1988.

32. Accounts of the Church of Scientologist's beliefs and activities can be found in *Newsweek,* Dec. 6, 1982; *Time,* April 5, 1976; *Reader's Digest,* May 1980 and September 1981 (both by Eugene Methvin); *Clinical Psychiatry News,* March, 1981; and *Cult Awareness Network News,* November 1988. Its tactics are illustrated by the letter its Citizens Commission on Human Rights sent to psychiatrists in 1975 offering "amnesty to any psychiatrist or technician who will come forward to confess his or her crimes against humanity." See *News,* Southern California Psychiatric Society, June 1975, p. 10. In 1986 the same gimmick was being used by the Citizens Commission on Human Rights, now formally independent of Scientology, which again produced a flyer offering "Amnesty" to "all psychiatrists, psychologists and psychiatric technicians who truthfully and fully confess their crimes against humanity."

33. Barry Stavro, "Psychosurgery Resurgent," *Politics Today,* January/February 1980, p. 49.

34. Gabe Kaimowitz, "The Case Against Psychosurgery," in Elliot Valenstein, ed., op. cit., pp. 514–15. Kaimowitz was already engaged in a pioneering right-to-refuse anti-psychotic medication case when he brought his case against psychosurgery.

35. Jonas Robitscher, "Psychosurgery and Other Somatic Means of Altering Behavior," *Bulletin of the American Academy on Psychiatry and the Law,* 1974, p. 23.

36. Jonas Robitscher, *The Powers of Psychiatry* (Boston: Houghton Mifflin, 1980), p. 289.

37. Interview, Dr. Peter Breggin, May 6, 1988.

38. S. I. Shuman, "The Emotional, Medical and Legal Reasons," op. cit., pp. 65–66. Shuman (p. 67) notes the problem is exacerbated by the fact that scientists unwilling to

be politicians about their science almost universally will not come forward to participate even as scientists in the decisional process. As a result the decision-maker suffers from a double blindness. He receives relevant scientific material filtered through a political screen and is left ignorant of material which is not so filtered.

39. Interview, Dr. Peter Breggin, May 6, 1988.

40. David Wexler, "Mental Health Law and the Movement Toward Voluntary Treatment," *California Law Review,* Vol. 62, 1974, p. 681.

41. Jonas Robitscher, *The Powers of Psychiatry,* op. cit., p. 289.

42. Interview, Dr. Peter Breggin, May 6, 1988.

43. Francis C. Pizzuli, "Psychosurgery Legislation and Case Law," in Elliot Valenstein, ed., op. cit., pp. 374–75. Also Stephen Morse, "Regulation of Psychosurgery," in ibid., p. 435.

44. Interview, Dr. Donald Becker, March 31, 1989.

45. Jonas Robitscher, "Psychosurgery and Other Somatic Means," op. cit., p. 25.

46. Interview, Dr. Donald Becker, March 31, 1989.

47. Jonas Robitscher, "Psychosurgery and Other Somatic Means," op. cit., p. 24.

48. Interview, Dr. Donald Becker, March 31, 1989.

49. Jonas Robitscher, "Psychosurgery and Other Somatic Means," op. cit., p. 25.

50. H. Thomas Ballantine Jr., Anthony J. Bouckoms, Elizabeth K. Thomas, and Ida Giriunas, "Treatment of Psychiatric Illness by Stereotactic Cingulotomy," *Journal of Biological Psychiatry,* Vol. 22, 1987, pp. 812–13.

51. Interview, Paula Perlstein, December 10, 1988.

52. Interview, Dr. Desmond Kelly, October 5, 1988.

53. H. Thomas Ballantine, Jr. "A Critical Assessment of Psychiatric Surgery," op. cit., p. 1043. Ballantine writes that his team has been reluctant to perform limbic leucotomies because of the slight but definite risk of undesirable alterations of personality. Ballantine notes: "In Great Britain this risk is apparently acceptable in view of the potential benefit. In the United States it might not be tolerated at this time." As far as the risks from his own operation are concerned, Dr. Ballantine reports that as of November 1989, 752 cingulotomies had been performed at Massachusetts General Hospital, and there have been only two serious complications: strokes resulting from laceration of a blood vessel during passage of the needle electrodes to the cingulum bundle that is the target of surgery. (Letter to Rael Jean Isaac, November 30, 1989.)

In terms of benefits, Dr. Kelly, studying the postoperative status of 148 patients who underwent stereotactic limbic leucotomy, has found that results have been best in those with obsessional neurosis (84% improved), while good results were obtained with only 60% of patients with a primary diagnosis of anxiety and/or depression. Kelly also found surprisingly good results with the relatively small number (19) of schizophrenic patients in the group, 63% of whom improved. These were selected patients with very distressing psychotic symptoms or high levels of anxiety, depression or obsessions accompanying their illness.

Ballantine's 1975 study of the postoperative status of 154 patients who had undergone cingulotomy for severe affective disorders found 17% to be "well" and an additional 58% "significantly improved." For a discussion of the risk-benefit equation on these operations see Ballantine, "A Critical Assessment of Psychiatric Surgery," op. cit., pp. 1041–42; and John Bartlett, Paul Bridges and Desmond Kelly, "Contemporary Indications for Psychosurgery," *British Journal of Psychiatry,* Vol. 138, 1981, pp. 507–11. Bartlett, Bridges, and Kelly sum up: "As present day stereotactic operations produce so few side-effects they can be regarded as acceptable forms of treatment for certain intractable psychiatric illnesses, especially when the associated mental anguish, the possibility of death by suicide and the personality deterioration that accompanies these chronic incapacitating conditions is taken into account."

54. *Appendix: Psychosurgery.* National Commission for the Protection of Human Subjects, op. cit., p. I-35.

55. Interview, Dr. H. Thomas Ballantine, Jr., January 12, 1989.

56. Interview, Dr. Charles Fager, January 26, 1989.

57. Interview, Dr. Paul Bridges, October 13, 1988.

58. Interview, Dr. H. Thomas Ballantine, Jr., January 12, 1989.

59. Interview, Dr. Peter Breggin, May 6, 1988.

Chapter 10.   Electroconvulsive Therapy:
The Second Domino

1. T. George Bidder, "Peer Commentary," on Richard D. Weiner, "Does Electroconvulsive Therapy Cause Brain Damage?" *The Behavioral and Brain Sciences,* Vol. 7, 1984, p. 23. Similarly, psychiatrist Trevor R. P. Price calls ECT "one of the most dramatically effective and safest treatments in psychiatry, if not all of medicine" (ibid., pp. 31–32).

2. Richard Abrams, *Electroconvulsive Therapy* (Oxford: Oxford University Press, 1988), pp. 3, 5.

3. Interview, Dr. Steven Potkin, July 7, 1988.

4. Richard Abrams, "Out of the Blue: The Rehabilitation of Electroconvulsive Therapy," *The Sciences,* New York Academy of Sciences, November/December 1989, p. 28. It is often said that Cerletti obtained the idea for ECT from the Rome slaughterhouse, where electric shocks were given to pigs prior to slaughter. In fact, even after Bini overcame the obstacles posed by the mouth-anus placement of electrodes, Cerletti was reluctant to use the technique on humans because he heard that pigs were being killed by electric shocks to the head. A visit to the slaughterhouse dispelled his fears. Electricity was passed through the pigs' heads but only to render them unconscious, and Cerletti discovered each pig displayed an epileptic seizure before becoming unconscious. Cerletti was now ready to try the procedure on people (Abrams, ibid.).

5. See Ugo Cerletti, "Old and New Information about Electroshock," *American Journal of Psychiatry,* August 1950, p. 90, and Ferdinando Accornero, "An Eyewitness Account of the Discovery of Electroshock," *Convulsive Therapy,* Vol. 4, 1988, p. 48.

6. Richard Abrams, "Interview with Lothar Kalinowsky, M. D., October 8, 1987," in *Convulsive Therapy,* Vol. 4, 1988, p. 28.

7. It is often said that insulin shock was never shown to be effective, and the impression is thus left that it was *ineffective.* It is technically correct that insulin shock was never shown to be effective, but only because rigorous scientific double-blind studies using the treatment were never conducted. It was abandoned, as a result of the advent of psychotropic drugs, the expense of the treatment, and a small but significant mortality rate associated with it before its effectiveness was determined. On the other hand, Dr. Kalinowsky, whose clinical experience with both treatments is unrivaled, told us that he had found insulin coma treatments to be more effective than ECT in the treatment of schizophrenia (interview, August 13, 1987).

8. Richard Abrams, "Interview with Lothar Kalinowsky M.D.," op. cit., p. 26.

9. Interview, Lothar Kalinowsky, August 13, 1987.

10. James Roy Morrison, *Your Brother's Keeper* (Chicago: Nelson Hall, 1981), p. 230.

11. Lothar Kalinowsky and Paul Hoch, *Somatic Treatments in Psychiatry* (New York: Grune and Stratton, 1961), p. 125. They explain that the metrazol patient does not lose consciousness in the interval between injection and convulsion and has the feeling of impending death and sudden annihilation; he subsequently remembers his feeling of deadly fear.

12. Joshua Logan, *Josh* (New York: Dell, 1976), pp. 333–34.

13. Ugo Cerletti, op cit., p. 90.

14. Richard Abrams, "Interview with Lothar Kalinowsky," op. cit., p. 30.

15. Quoted in Leonard Roy Frank, *The History of Shock Treatment* (San Francisco: L. R. Frank, 1978), p. 88. W. T. Liberson writes: "During very mild convulsions, the patient may conserve a partial insight.... At times this 'dissociation' of the total electric shock pattern results only in an incomplete retrograde amnesia for the stimulating period. This is never described as painful, but definitely unpleasant. The patient feels that he is being lifted in the air, is seeing lights, or hearing the nurse's voice ('ready, doctor'). These 'dissociations' should be very carefully avoided, as they increase fearfulness and make the patient resistive to the treatment. It seems such dissociation is increased by the use of very brief stimuli—00.3 millisecond or below" ("Current Evaluation of Electric Convulsive Therapy," *Research Publication—Association for Research in Nervous and Mental Disease,* Vol. 31, 1953, p. 217). Such incomplete or partial seizures could be avoided by using household current waveform at suprathreshold current levels.

Psychiatrists nonetheless sometimes gave such ultra-brief stimuli in an attempt to minimize confusion, fractures, and memory loss. See Jaclav Hyman et al., "ECT: The Search for the Perfect Stimulus," *Biological Psychiatry,* Vol. 20, 1985, pp. 634–45. "In 1938, Cerletti used modified household current....[T]he search for better stimuli began....[C]urrents and waveforms that could produce the seizures with minimal energy were sought."

16. Ferris N. Pitts, "Medical Physiology of ECT," in Abrams and Essman, eds., *Electroconvulsive Therapy: Biological and Clinical Applications* (New York: Spectrum, 1987), pp. 68–69.

17. Interview, Dr. Sidney Brandon, October 12, 1988.

18. Quoted from a 1967 study by A. E. Schwartzman and P. E. Termanseen in Peter R. Breggin, *Electroshock: Its Brain-Disabling Effects* (New York: Springer, 1979), p. 84. Actually it was Lucio Bini, co-developer with Cerletti of ECT, who first suggested giving some patients ECT many times on the same day, which he aptly described as "annihilation" therapy. (Ugo Cerletti, "Old and New Information," op. cit., p. 93).

19. Richard Abrams, "Out of the Blue," op. cit., p. 27. Abrams notes that the method was discredited and abandoned, but not before it contributed mightily to ECT's negative public image.

20. The term electroconvulsive therapy gradually replaced "electroshock," used by Cerletti. Abrams notes it is more accurate, since the person is asleep, does not experience the electrical stimulus and there is no cardiovascular collapse, the other association with the term "shock" in medicine. (Interview, December 4, 1989.)

21. Jennifer Hughes, B. M. Barraclough, and W. Rieve, "Are Patients Shocked by ECT?" *Journal of the Royal Society of Medicine,* Vol. 74, April 1981, pp. 283–84. Also C. P. L. Freeman and R. E. Kendell, "Patients' Experience of and Attitude to ECT," *British Journal of Psychiatry,* Vol. 137, 1980, pp. 8–16.

22. Psychologist Larry Squire has done a great many studies in this area. See for example his "ECT and Memory Loss," *American Journal of Psychiatry,* September 1977,

pp. 997–1001; Larry Squire and Pamela C. Slater, "Electroconvulsive Therapy and Complaints of Memory Dysfunction: A Prospective Three Year Follow-up Study," *British Journal of Psychiatry,* Vol. 142, 1983, pp. 1–8; Larry Squire, "Memory Functions as Affected by Electroconvulsive Therapy," *Annals of the New York Academy of Science,* Vol. 462, 1986, pp. 307–14. See also Richard Weiner, "Does Electroconvulsive Therapy Cause Brain Damage?" op. cit., pp. 9–16.

23. Interview, Dr. Lothar Kalinowksky, August 13, 1987.

24. A 1976 survey showed 75% of psychiatrists used only bilateral ECT, and only 10% of patients receiving ECT had unilateral placement. A 1978 survey in New York City found 83% of psychiatrists used bilateral only. In England the findings are similar. Richard Abrams, *Electroconvulsive Therapy,* op. cit., p. 1.

25. "Interview Max Fink, M.D.: Update on ECT," *Psychiatric Annals,* Vol. 17, January 1987, p. 52. Dr. Abrams agrees, although he points out that many studies show "much greater improvement with bilateral than right-unilateral ECT." Richard Abrams, *Electroconvulsive Therapy,* op. cit., pp. 122, 128.

There are indications the effectiveness of unilateral ECT can be enhanced by attention to electrode placement and stimulus intensity. In "Unilateral ECT in the Treatment of Manic Episodes" (*Convulsive Therapy,* Vol. 4, No. 1, 1988, pp. 74–80), Sukdeb Mukherjee, Harold Sackeim, and Carl Lee point out that the therapeutic advantage of bilateral ECT is reduced when unilateral ECT is administered with longer inter-electrode distance. They also observe that unilateral ECT may be therapeutically less effective when treatments are administered with stimulus intensities close to threshold.

26. The original ECT apparatus designed by Lucio Bini delivered a kind of electricity known as sine-wave current, which fluctuates in a smooth pattern. There is another type, known as brief-pulse, or square-wave, current, that ascends abruptly to its high point, drops to its low point and repeats the cycle. Brief-pulse current, not widely used in ECT until the 1980s, minimized the total dosage of current necessary, reducing memory loss. See Richard Abrams, "Out of the Blue," op. cit., p. 30.

27. *Madness Network News,* December 1974, p. 32.

28. See *Point by Point Analysis of the American Psychiatric Association Task Force Report on Electroconvulsive Therapy,* The Citizens Commission on Human Rights, Los Angeles, Calif., n.d. There are three doctors on the eight-man "national advisory board," Friedberg, Coleman, and a Dr. Ray Reynolds. Breggin, to his credit, after an initial period of cooperation with the Scientologists, cut his ties to them.

29. Nothing better typifies the changing attitudes to ECT than the contrast in portrayal of ECT in this film and in *The Snake Pit,* which in 1948 also brought an Academy Award to its star, Olivia DeHavilland. In *The Snake Pit,* ECT is portrayed as a valuable tool, which restores the heroine to a state of sufficient reason so that the wise Freudian psychiatrist can uncover the "real" roots of her problem in her infant jealousy of her father's attentions to her mother. This reflected a then prevalent wrong-headed view of the nature of mental illness, but what is relevant here is that ECT is *not* shown as a horrible procedure, even though the film was made before anesthesia, oxygenation, and muscle relaxation had been added to ECT. The film could have shown the body of the heroine pinned down by orderlies, racked by convulsions. Instead, it shows a typewriter recording the dates of a succession of treatments.

30. *Madness Network News,* October 1975, p. 21.

31. John Friedberg, "Electroshock Therapy: Let's Stop Blasting the Brain," *Psychology Today,* August 1975, p. 98.

32. John Friedberg, "Shock Treatment, Brain Damage, and Memory Loss: A Neurological Perspective," *American Journal of Psychiatry,* September 1977, p. 1010.

33. Fred H. Frankel, "Current Perspectives on ECT: A Discussion," *American Journal of Psychiatry,* September 1977, pp. 1016–17. Frankel chides Friedberg, for example, for misusing studies on epilepsy by Brian S. Meldrum and associates. Friedberg quotes Meldrum's suggestion that "the overexcited neuron by itself may be an important factor in seizure damage," without explaining that the "overexcited neuron" in Meldrum's paper referred to the neuron after seizure activity lasting from three to seven hours, scarcely comparable to neuronal activity associated with a single session of ECT.

34. Peter Breggin, *Electroshock: Its Brain-Disabling Effects,* op. cit., p. 184.

35. Ibid., p. 182.

36. Ibid., p. 169.

37. Richard Weiner, "Author's Response" in "Does Electroconvulsive Therapy Cause Brain Damage?" op. cit., p. 42.

38. *Madness Network News,* June 1974, p. 19; September 1974, p. 8; December 1975, p. 17. Richard Abrams (*Electroconvulsive Therapy,* op. cit., p. 169) identifies the bill's drafter as a junior at the University of Massachusetts, who wrote the bill as part of a special study project at the University of California. *Madness Network News* identifies her as Darlene Doban.

39. *Madness Network News,* February 1975, p. 9. This issue also carries a summary of the bill's provisions, pp. 30–31.

40. Francis Pizzuli, "Psychosurgery Legislation and Case Law," in Elliot Valenstein, ed., *The Psychosurgery Debate* (San Francisco: W. H. Freeman, 1980), pp. 377–78.

41. The individual capable of giving informed consent must pay for a second medical opinion to confirm capacity to consent before he can be given the treatment. The 3% figure of those unable to give informed consent suggests a radical underuse of ECT. Even if we just consider patients suffering from depression, approximately a third have psychotic symptoms, calling in question their ability to give informed consent. Yet those suffering from delusional depression should be *overrepresented* among those receiving ECT since they respond best to the treatment. See Peter Roy-Byrne and Robert H. Gerner, "Legal Restrictions on the Use of ECT in California: Clinical Impact on the Incompetent Patient," *Clinical Psychiatry,* Vol. 41, August 1981, pp. 300–303.

42. Ibid., p. 301. The statute requires that the hearing be held within three judicial days after a petition is filed; however, there is no way to enforce the three-day limit. Often a temporary conservatorship is required to extend the involuntary treatment time limit. There are no exceptions for life-threatening emergencies, including suicide attempts and self-starvation.

43. Ibid. Evidence that bureaucratic bungling was also involved in the death of this young woman comes from a letter published in *The American Journal of Psychiatry* in August 1987 by a Dr. Barbara Parry, who describes herself as a "concerned first year psychiatric resident." She explains that in trying to obtain legal approval to treat the patient with ECT she encountered both legal and bureaucratic difficulties entailed by "the confusion, disagreements and uncertainty at all administrative levels over the proper procedure for obtaining such requests [for administering ECT]." The young woman's unnecessary death seems especially tragic in that the letter writer points out that when she was not manic she was a good student, held a job, and was an accomplished flutist. She was loved by her family, friends, and the hospital staff.

44. Interview, Dr. Glen Peterson, January 19, 1989.

45. Standard 9 of Federal Judge Johnson's 1972 court order established the right of psychiatric inmates in state hospitals not to be subjected to lobotomy, ECT, or other "unusual treatments" without the patient's express and informed consent after consultation with counsel or an interested party of the patient's choice. There was no provision for administering ECT to those incapable of giving informed consent, although it was from this population the state hospital would have chosen candidates for the treatment. A few patients were in fact given ECT after the order, and the psychiatrists responsible were charged with criminal contempt for their pains. See *Madness Network News,* Spring 1977, p. 4.

46. Sheila Taub, "Electroconvulsive Therapy, Malpractice and Informed Consent," *The Journal of Psychiatry and Law,* Spring 1987, pp. 30–32.

47. Barry Alan Kramer, "Use of ECT in California, 1977–1983," *American Journal of Psychiatry,* October 1985, p. 1191.

48. Ibid. ECT was given twice as much in psychiatrists' offices as in state and VA hospitals combined!

49. "Electroconvulsive Therapy Today: An Interview with Max Fink, M.D.," *Currents in Affective Illness,* October 1986, p. 5.

50. James W. Thompson and Jack D. Blaine, "Use of ECT in the United States in 1975 and 1980," *American Journal of Psychiatry,* May 1987, p. 557. There has been dispute over the accuracy of these figures because the APA task force survey in 1976 came out with higher estimates. However the APA survey assumed nonrespondents used ECT to the same extent as respondents, and Thompson and Blaine suggest this is probably not the case. The lower figures receive additional support from figures for New York State quoted by Breggin in his anti-ECT book. The New York State Department of Mental Health found a 50% decline in the number of ECT treatments in the state from 1972 to 1977. Breggin calculates that this means approximately 2,700 patients in New York received ECT, and extrapolating this to the country would mean 32,000 people received ECT in 1977, very close to the Thompson and Blaine figures. See Breggin, op. cit., pp. 3,5.

51. James W. Thompson and Jack D. Blaine, op. cit., p. 558. These figures concealed an enormous range in the use of ECT in private hospitals. For example in 1973–74, reports submitted by private hospitals to the Massachusetts department of mental health showed that while some private hospitals gave ECT to less than 1% of their patients, at others it was given to as many as 70% of patients. See Leonard Frank, *The History of Shock Treatment,* op. cit., p. 101.

52. James W. Thompson and Jack D. Blaine, op. cit., p. 558.

53. Ibid., p. 557.

54. Ibid. p. 559. Contrast this with 1942, when a study showed ECT was used in 93.8% of state hospitals sampled and 79.4% of federal facilities—private facilities brought up the rear with 74% using ECT. Breggin, op. cit., p. 152.

55. The letter, originally published in *The American Journal of Psychiatry* in June 1974, is reprinted in Leonard Frank, op. cit., p. 101.

56. Interview, Kathleen O'Brien (pseudonym), April 10, 1989.

57. The recommendation was allegedly based on "hearings" held by a subcommittee of the council. The manipulation of the material actually presented to the subcommittee in its report was too much for the Department of Mental Health, which in 1981 was not yet as fearful of taking positions at odds with the ex-patient movement as it would become under the subsequent tenure of Dr. Michael O'Connor. The Department responded sharply that the report did not accurately summarize the testimony received

and rejected the call for a moratorium on ECT as "an irresponsible denial of an effective treatment to individuals needing and desiring it." California Department of Mental Health letter to Ruth Ann Terry of Citizens Advisory Council, dated December 22, 1981.

58. *Madness Network News,* Spring 1983, p. 4.

59. These figures have remained fairly stable since the Department of Mental Health began collecting statistics on ECT in 1977. In 1987 only 42 blacks and 84 Hispanics received ECT as against 2,418 whites. Tabulations of the use of ECT by treating facility, county by county, and including figures on age, sex, and ethnicity are available from the Patients Rights Office of the Department of Mental Health, 1600 Ninth Street, Sacramento, CA 95814.

60. *Mental and Physical Disability Law Reporter,* May-June 1986, p. 173.

61. *Madness Network News,* Summer 1985, p. 12. The Vermont Liberation Organization did not give up its efforts. The patient-activist paper *Dendron* (January 11, 1990) reported that the VLO had been "lobbying progressives in the city government of Burlington, Vermont against electroshock" and VLO leader Paul Dorfner said he had "good reason to believe the socialist mayor, Paul Cravelle, will help get electroshock banned from the local University Medical Center."

62. The case, brought by attorney and ex-patient activist Carla McKague, concerned a Mrs. T., who had been hospitalized for severe depression. Her psychiatrist, following Ontario law, appealed to a medical review board after she refused ECT and the board ruled it should be administered. McKague argued ECT was a brain damaging treatment and as such a form of psychosurgery; since Ontario law provided the board could not approve psychosurgery for an unwilling patient, she claimed it could not approve ECT either.

63. "ECT and Brain Damage: The Ontario Supreme Court Hearing of the Evidence," *Canadian Journal of Psychiatry,* June 1986, p. 385.

64. Carla McKague, "The Anti-Electroshock Campaign," Workshop, Conference of the National Association for Rights Protection and Advocacy, Portland, Oregon, October 26–29, 1988. An Electro-Convulsive Therapy Review Committee was set up following the court case (McKague was one of the members) and while (with the exception of McKague) it recommended continuing to make the treatment available, it called for further procedural restrictions. See *Report of the Electro-Convulsive Therapy Review Committee,* December 1985, available from the Ministry of Health in Toronto. The legislature went beyond even the Review Committee's recommendations.

65. Interview, Joseph Sheehan, Regulations Desk, Center for Devices and Radiological Health, March 6, 1989.

66. Berton Roueché, "As Empty as Eve," *New Yorker,* September 9, 1974, p. 96.

67. "Patient Information about ECT," submitted by Committee for Truth in Psychiatry to FDA, petition 84P-0430. Rice's group also petitioned the FDA to make CAT scan studies of the brains of individuals (and animals) given ECT. However, there have been CAT scan studies, and they do not indicate the presence of structural damage. Particularly interesting was a study of twelve patients who had received a large number of unilateral treatments. An asymmetrical excess of atrophy or ventricular enlargement was as often on the side receiving the electrodes as on the side opposite. See B. Kendell and R. T. C. Pratt, "Brain Damage and ECT," *British Journal of Psychiatry,* Vol. 143, 1983, pp. 99–100. Even more significant, a team led by C. Edward Coffey at Duke University used the more sensitive magnetic resonance imaging to examine the brains of patients before and after ECT and found no changes in brain structure according to blind raters' assessments of pre- and post-ECT studies. See C. Edward Coffey et al., "Effects of ECT on

Brain Structure: A Pilot Prospective Magnetic Resonance Imaging Study," *American Journal of Psychiatry,* June 1988, pp. 701–6.

68. Cited by Peter Breggin, *Electroshock: Its Brain-Disabling Effects,* op. cit., p. 15.

69. A Practising Psychiatrist, "An Experience of Electroconvulsive Therapy," *British Journal of Psychiatry,* Vol. 111, 1965, p. 365. It is noteworthy that the psychiatrist felt it necessary to publish his experience anonymously.

70. For a brief history of the organization see Gary C. Aden, "The International Psychiatric Association for the Advancement of Electrotherapy: A Brief History," *The American Journal of Social Psychiatry,* Fall 1984, pp. 9–10.

71. *Electroconvulsive Therapy,* Task Force Report 14, American Psychiatric Association, September 1978, pp. 2–4. While only 2% of the psychiatrists polled were "totally opposed" to the use of ECT, 23% were generally opposed (but willing to see it used as a last resort), and an additional 8% were more opposed than favorable. And while 54% were "generally favorable for appropriate patients," only 7% were "decidedly favorable to its use."

72. Richard Weiner, "Does Electroconvulsive Therapy Cause Brain Damage?" op. cit., p. 5.

73. Ibid., pp. 20–21.

74. Ibid., p. 21.

75. Max Fink, "ECT—Verdict: Not Guilty," in "Peer Commentary," ibid., p. 26.

76. Steven F. Zornetzer, "ECT: Out of the Shadows and into the Light," "Peer Commentary," ibid., p. 41.

77. *IEEE Spectrum,* November 1985, p. 24. By the mid 1980s the amount had risen to between $400,000 to $500,000 a year. NIMH's first paper on ECT was by Steven M. Paul et al., "Use of ECT with Treatment-Resistant Depressed Patients at the National Institute of Mental Health," *American Journal of Psychiatry,* April 1981, pp. 486–489. This article reported use of ECT on nine patients over an eight-year period on an NIMH research ward for depressed patients. "All patients showed substantial and usually dramatic improvement with ECT in contrast to their previous failure to respond to medications." Of the nine patients seven were followed for seven to nine years and remained free of depression (five were kept prophylactically on anti-depressants). The authors point out: "It is likely that the high morbidity and mortality associated with affective illness could be reduced by early treatment with ECT in selected patients, rather than turning to it as a last resort" (p. 488). Max Fink notes sharply that anti-ECT bias is obvious "when a major educational and research center finds so few cases for this treatment, a treatment which was more successful than a wide range of prior therapies" (*Psychopharmacology Bulletin,* Vol. 18, 1982, p. 114).

78. Breggin reports Rubenstein's role in arranging these matters, Interview, Dr. Peter Breggin, May 6, 1988.

79. "Statement of the Consensus Development Panel," reprinted in *Psychopharmacology Bulletin,* Vol. 22, 1986, p. 452.

80. Interview, Dr. Peter Breggin, May 6, 1988.

81. Max Fink, "American Psychiatric Association, May 1987," *Convulsive Therapy,* Vol. 3, No. 3, 1987, p. 240.

82. Norman Endler, *Holiday of Darkness* (New York: John Wiley & Sons, 1982), pp. 45, 83, 165.

83. Ibid., p. 87.

84. From 1943 to 1950 Windle's group developed techniques for fixation and staining of brain tissue (perfusion fixation) far superior to the method then in use

(immersion fixation). Perfusion fixation simultaneously kills the animal and starts preservation of brain tissue, using the beating heart to circulate fixative solution through the brain. Windle's group was able to show that in immersion fixation, natural decomposition starts before the formaldehyde can soak into an immersed block of brain. Windle's group exposed five healthy monkeys to electroshock at clinical intervals (three times a week) for from thirteen to nineteen shocks. Three animals were killed twenty-four hours, and two forty-eight hours subsequent to the last convulsion. There were no differences between brain tissue specimens of control and of electroshocked animals. Windle's group reviewed the 1942–1949 animal studies attributing brain damage to electroshock and concluded: "Failure to recognize postmortem artifacts may explain much of the cytopathologic alteration reported by other investigators who have attributed their observations to electric shock." See Robert G. Siekert, S. Culver Williams, and William F. Windle, "Histologic Study of the Brains of Monkeys after Experimental Electric Shock," *Archives of Neurology and Psychiatry,* Vol. 63, 1950, pp. 79–86.

85. By 1955 Windle was Chief, Laboratory of Neuroanatomical Sciences, National Institute of Neurological Diseases and Blindness, of the National Institutes of Health, but it was 1972 before Cammermeyer, Chief of the Laboratory Section on Experimental Neuropathology, wrote " . . . perfusion is now becoming the accepted procedure and tissue free of artifactitious changes is the ambitious aim of most investigators." Yet the few notices of Windle's work by psychiatrists ignore his critique of the 1942–1949 studies attributing changes in brain tissue to electroshock. Only R. Michael Allen ("Electroconvulsive Therapy: Old Question, New Answers," *Psychiatric Annals,* Vol. 8, May 1978) even refers to the superiority of Windle's techniques.

86. In addition to the report in the *Archives of Neurology and Psychiatry* already cited, see William F. Windle, Wendell S. Krieg, and Alex J. Arieff, "Failure to Detect Structural Changes in the Brain after Electrical Shock," *Quarterly Bulletin,* Northwestern University Medical School, Vol 29, October 1945, pp. 181–88.

87. A. G. Chapman, Brian S. Meldrum, and Bo K. Siesjo, "Cerebral Metabolic Changes During Prolonged Epileptic Seizures in Rats," *Journal of Neurochemistry,* Vol. 28, 1977, pp. 1025–35, cited in letter from Ted Hutchinson to Delmar Gregory, M.D., May 15, 1984.

88. In his letter to Delmar Gregory, Hutchinson cites Jan Corsellis and Brian S. Meldrum, "Epilepsy," Chapter 17 in Blackwood and Corsellis, eds., *Greenfield's Neuropathology,* 3rd edition, 1976, p. 790.

89. Selected Staff, University of Louisville School of Medicine, "1,250 Electroconvulsive Treatments without Evidence of Brain Injury," *British Journal of Psychiatry,* Vol. 147, 1985, pp. 203–4.

90. Interview, Ted Hutchinson, April 2, 1989.

91. Hutchinson discovered this from the Annual Report of the Patients' Rights Office to the California Legislature which summarizes all ECT use in the state. The 1977 report revealed that Stanford University Medical Center had given no ECT during the year, and the 1978 report noted that it had been "discontinued as a treatment modality" at Stanford. Lorrin Koran, M.D. ("Electroconvulsive Therapy: Risks and Benefits," *Stanford Medicine,* Spring 1986, p. 89) says that Stanford began offering ECT again in 1986 but when Hutchinson subsequently talked to Koran, it transpired that the hospital had no one on its staff able to give the treatment.

92. Letter from Dr. Richard Weiner to Ted Hutchinson, August 8, 1984.

93. "Report of the NIMH-NIH Consensus Development Conference on Electroconvulsive Therapy," *Psychopharmacology Bulletin,* Vol. 22, No. 2, 1986, p. 449. This issue of

the *Bulletin* contains the Statement of the Consensus Development Panel and abstracts of presentations to the panel and conference (pp. 445–502).

94. Letter from Michael O'Connor, Director, Department of Mental Health, to Ted Hutchinson, July 1, 1985.

95. See "In re: Department of Mental Health, Decision of Disapproval of Regulatory Action" Office of Administration Law (California) File No. 87-1120-03, December 28, 1987, which quoted Hutchinson's objections to the regulations in rejecting them as unclear and inconsistent with statutory law.

To be sure, Hutchinson did not win all the bureaucratic battles. In 1985, the Department of Mental Health, in a regulation defining excessive ECT, limited the number of ECT treatments that could be given and ruled that subconvulsive seizures had to be counted as treatments. Alerted by Hutchinson in advance, thirty leading California psychiatrists, including the chairman of the American Psychiatric Association's Task Force on ECT, wrote to the Department of Mental Health in 1984 to point out the counterproductive nature of the regulations, which would lead to psychiatrists using higher levels of electricity (thereby causing more memory loss). It made no difference. Intent on winning favor with the ex-patient activists, Department of Mental Health director Dr. Michael O'Connor, himself a psychiatrist, responded that unless non-therapeutic seizures were counted, the psychiatrist might perform an unlimited number of treatments. This assumed that psychiatrists would pass electricity into people's bodies merely to satisfy their sadistic impulses.

96. Interview, Ted Hutchinson, January 20, 1989.

97. Interview, Taylor Neff, (pseudonym) February 24, 1989.

98. Interview, Lorraine Richter of the National Depressive and Manic-Depressive Association, March 27, 1989.

99. E. Fuller Torrey, *Surviving Schizophrenia* (New York: Harper & Row, 1988) pp. 224–25. Torrey suggests a great variety of drugs and drug combinations (pp. 218–19) for treatment-resistant patients, but never suggests a trial of ECT even for the 10% of patients he estimates to be "truly treatment resistant," i.e., will not respond to any of the suggested drug combinations.

100. Richard Abrams, *Electroconvulsive Therapy,* op. cit., p. 168, cites the figure of 50,000 to 100,000; in "Out of the Blue," *The Sciences,* New York Academy of Science, November/December 1989, p. 27, Dr. Abrams offers the 30,000 figure.

101. "Interview, Max Fink, M.D.: Update on ECT," *Psychiatric Annals,* Vol. 17, No. 1, January 1987, p. 47.

102. Richard Abrams, *Electroconvulsive Therapy,* op. cit, p. 14. The extent to which ECT has been neglected, even in depression, is suggested by a 1989 book published by the American Psychiatric Association Press, *Treatment of Tricyclic Resistant Depression* by Dr. Irl Extein. The chapter on ECT is subtitled "The forgotten option in the treatment of therapy-resistant depression."

103. Interview, Dr. Steven Potkin, July 7, 1988.

104. Richard Abrams, *Electroconvulsive Therapy,* op. cit., pp. 15–16.

105. Philip R. A. May, *Treatment of Schizophrenia: A Comparative Study of Five Treatment Methods* (New York: Science House, 1968), p. 267. The most important single result of the May study was to discredit psychotherapy as a treatment for schizophrenia. In his introduction, Milton Greenblatt, then Commissioner of the Department of Mental Health in Massachusetts, accurately foretold its impact: "[T]his study has dealt the use of psychotherapy, as an essential modality of treatment for hospitalized schizophrenics, a

hard blow. It may even turn out to be a mortal blow ... " (p. 26). May summed up the study's findings: "From the evidence in this project we can dismiss as a fairy tale the story that ataraxic [neuroleptic] drugs should be avoided because they interfere with the *psychotherapy* of the hospitalized schizophrenic patient. ... The difference between drugs alone and psychotherapy and drugs is not impressive or statistically significant" (pp. 262–63).

106. Ibid., p. 267.

107. Ibid.

108. Philip R. A. May, A. Hussain Tuma, and Wilfrid J. Dixon, "Schizophrenia: A Follow-up Study of the Results of Five Forms of Treatment," *Archives of General Psychiatry,* July 1981, p. 783.

109. Ibid., p. 778.

110. Interview, Dr. Pamela Taylor, October 6, 1988.

111. Interview, Dr. Sydney Brandon, October 12, 1988.

112. Interview, Dr. Jeffrey Geller, March 22, 1989.

113. *Clinical Psychiatry News,* Vol. 17, No. 7, July 1989, p. 5.

114. Richard Ries, Lawrence Wilson, et al., "ECT in Medication Resistant Schizoaffective Disorder," *Comprehensive Psychiatry,* Vol. 22, 1981, pp. 167–71; G. Michael Dempsey et al., "Treatment of Schizo-Affective Disorder," *Comprehensive Psychiatry,* Vol. 16, 1975, pp. 55–59.

115. Interview, Dr. Sydney Brandon, October 12, 1988.

Chapter 11. Psychoactive Drugs:
The Last Domino

1. Max Fink, "Introduction," in Milton Greenblatt and Ernest Hartman, eds., *Seminars in Psychiatry,* Vol. IV, No. 1, February 1972.

2. Cited in *Madness Network News,* October 1976, p. 14.

3. Peter Breggin, *Psychiatric Drugs: Hazards to the Brain* (New York: Springer, 1983), pp. 2,4.

4. Jarvis v. Levine (Minn. 1988) 418 N.W. 2d 139.

5. State of Washington v. Walter Harper, Petition for a Writ of Certiorari, In the Supreme Court of the United States, October Term, 1988, p. A-5.

6. Interview, Dr. Paul Appelbaum, May 18, 1988.

7. Interview, Joseph Rogers, March 14, 1988. According to Rogers the National Alliance of Mental Patients consisted of no more than twenty leaders with forty or fifty active followers around the country.

8. The radical ex-patients had a point in their criticism of the word "consumer." Its use resulted in such anomalous terms as "institutionalized consumer." See California Citizens Advisory Council, "Report of the Year of the Consumer Steering Committee," 1982, p. 6.

9. Interview, Joseph Rogers, March 14, 1988.

10. *Counterpoint* (Burlington, Vermont), Holidays 1988.

11. *Philadelphia Inquirer,* June 30, 1988.

12. *Madness Network News,* Summer 1985, p. 11.

13. *Dendron* (Eugene, Oregon), May 1988, p. 4.

14. See amicus brief of the Coalition for the Fundamental Rights and Equality of Ex-Patients in Eleanor Riese et al. v. St. Mary's Hospital and Medical Center, No. S004002, p.

4. Rogers' position fluctuates confusingly. Debating the National Alliance of Mental Patients' (now National Association of Psychiatric Survivors) Judi Chamberlin, who opposes commitment under any circumstances, Rogers said: "I want intervention based on rights and respect. . . . But there are times when interventions are necessary. Because otherwise the realities are . . . they end up in jail, or on the streets or they end up dead." (Oprah Winfrey show, August 17, 1987.)

15. *Dendron,* May 1988, p. 4.

16. Ibid., p. 3.

17. Jay Centifanti, Right to Refuse Treatment Workshop, Conference of National Mental Health Consumers' Association, June 29, 1988.

18. Ibid.

19. Leonard Roy Frank, *The History of Shock Treatment* (San Francisco: L. R. Frank, 1978), p. xiii.

20. Eugene Bardach, *The Skill Factor in Politics: Repealing the Mental Commitment Laws in California* (Berkeley: University of California Press, 1972), p. 75.

21. Dr. Peter Breggin, Workshop on Medications at IAPSRS Conference, Philadelphia, June 1, 1988.

22. Jay Mahler, Workshop on Right to Refuse Treatment, National Mental Health Consumers' Association, Philadelphia, June 29, 1988.

23. Ted Hutchinson, "Events Generating California Network of Mental Health Clients and Ever Expanding Role for Patients' Rights Advocates," January 9, 1987, mimeographed.

24. *Madness Network News,* Fall/Winter 1982–1983, pp. 20–21.

25. Interview, Ted Chabasinski, July 6, 1988.

26. *Madness Network News,* Winter 1985, p. 6.

27. Ibid., Summer 1985, p. 19.

28. Peter Breggin, *Psychiatric Drugs,* op. cit., p. 2.

29. Ibid., p. 3.

30. Ibid., p. 4.

31. Ibid., p. 62.

32. Leo Hollister, "Psychopharmacology," in John C. Shershow, ed., *Schizophrenia: Science and Practice* (Cambridge: Harvard University Press, 1978), p. 154.

33. Peter Breggin, *Psychiatric Drugs,* op. cit., p. 57.

34. Ibid., p. 66.

35. Ibid., p. 110.

36. Ibid., p. 246.

37. Interview, Dr. Peter Breggin, May 6, 1988.

38. Peter Breggin, *Psychiatric Drugs,* op. cit., p. 68.

39. Ibid., p. 254.

40. Interview, Dr. Peter Breggin, May 6, 1988.

41. Chapter 2 of the LPS Act beginning with Section 5150 is entitled "Involuntary Treatment," indicating that the legislature fully intended that hospitals treat those involuntarily committed. Moreover Section 5152 mandates that the individual "receive such treatment and care as his or her condition requires for the full period of the involuntary hold."

42. See Petitioner's Brief on the Merits in Riese v. St. Mary's Hospital, S004002 (Supreme Court of the State of California), pp. 16–17.

43. This point is hammered upon in all the amicus briefs submitted on behalf of Riese's "right to refuse" psychoactive drugs.

44. In 1972 in Cobbs v. Grant (8 Cal. 3d, 229), the California Supreme Court affirmed the right to informed consent to medical treatment was a constitutional right which could only be denied if the patient was incompetent, in which case the patient's "authority to consent is transferred to a guardian or the closest available relative."

45. The earlier case, Jamison v. Farabee, brought in 1978, ended in a consent decree in May 1983. No one was satisfied with the result. While the suit had sought "to prohibit treatment with antipsychotic medications except with the informed consent of the patient," the ex-patients complained that refusals could easily be overridden: the decree merely made "it somewhat harder for psychiatrists to drug inmates—more paperwork, more procedures to follow" (*Madness Network News,* Winter 1983–1984, p. 13).

From the standpoint of administrators of the mental health system, the second opinions mandated by the decree cost an additional $300,000 (not including time diverted for paperwork) in one year for a single hospital and in only thirty cases (1.1% of the total) did the review result in denial of medication. (Half of those patients then deteriorated.) Costs for implementing the program at other state hospitals for a single year were estimated at $1.5 million. The only people who benefited were a few psychiatrists, for whom it was a financial windfall. See William A. Hargreaves et al., "Effect of the Jamison-Farabee Consent Decree," *American Journal of Psychiatry,* February 1977.

46. For a description of the specifics concerning Eleanor Riese see the Brief of the California Psychiatric Association as Amicus Curiae, In the Supreme Court of the State of California, No. S004002, p. 11.

47. If the evaluation leads to the person's certification for up to fourteen days of intensive treatment, he or she must receive an independent administrative certification review at which the patient, entitled to counsel and accompanied by a patients' rights advocate, may confront and question witnesses. The patient is also informed of his or her right to petition the court for a judicial hearing. (Upon request, staff of the facility must assist in preparation and filing of the petition.) The administrative hearing must occur within seven days of the initial detention.

The existence of this hearing is the result of another line of attack on the LPS Act by the mental health bar. In 1980, in Doe v. Gallinot (486 F. Supp. 983) the mental health bar obtained a federal court ruling that a hearing is needed to determine whether there is probable cause that a person certified for up to fourteen additional days after the seventy-two hour hold is either dangerous or gravely disabled as a result of mental disorder. But this too was not the victory the militants were seeking, because the court ruled due process was satisfied by an independent administrative hearing, leaving open to the patient an option to petition for a judicial hearing. Less than 10% go to court.

48. *Report to the Legislature: California Conference of Local Mental Health Directors,* June 1988. The report, by an outside consulting firm, examines the effect that expanding the definition of the term "gravely disabled" would have on the number of commitments in California. In the course of the report, it is noted (p. 12) that the proportion of those judged *not* to lack capacity to give informed consent at the time of certification hearings (after the three-day hold) was 10%. In other words, 90% *lacked* that capacity.

49. Hutchinson's amicus brief, arguing for the use of administrative procedures already in place, was filed by the California Alliance for the Mentally Ill in Riese v. St. Mary's Hospital, S004002, in the Supreme Court of California. In it he points out that evaluation of each involuntary patient's capacity to consent would ensure equal protection for all detainees, not just for the (supposedly few) objectors to medication. If family

members were appointed as substitute decision-makers this would have the further advantage of ensuring that the treating psychiatrist knew the patient's history of treatment response, an invaluable aid in instituting intelligent treatment.

50. Amicus Brief of the Coalition for the Fundamental Rights and Equality of Ex-Patients in Riese v. St. Mary's Hospital, No. S004002, in the Supreme Court of the State of California, 1988, p. 3.

51. Amicus Brief filed by the American Orthopsychiatric Association, Riese v. St. Mary's Hospital, p. 3.

52. Ibid., p. 12.

53. Amicus Brief filed by the American Psychological Association and the California Psychological Association in Riese v. St. Mary's Hospital, pp. 2–3, 18–19.

54. Ibid., p. 20.

55. Amicus Brief filed by the Mental Health Association of California in Riese v. St. Mary's Hospital, p. 13.

56. *Newsweek,* March 20, 1989, pp. 65–66.

57. Interview, Dr. Edward King, January 12, 1988.

58. Cogentin and Artane are two of the drugs most often used to counter the most common side effects. For a discussion of the most common side effects, their relative importance, and drugs used to control them see E. Fuller Torrey, *Surviving Schizophrenia* (New York: Harper & Row, 1988), pp. 194–201. For an excellent layman's overview, see Jean K. Bouricius, *Psychoactive Drugs and Their Effects on Mentally Ill Persons,* National Alliance for the Mentally Ill Publication No. 3, 1989.

59. Other possible side effects include dry mouth, constipation, urinary retention, blurred vision, rapid heart beat, and high blood pressure. High potency drugs like Haldol, Navane, and Prolixin tend to produce these anticholinergic side effects *less* than the lower potency drugs like Mellaril and Thorazine. See Jean Bouricius, op. cit., p. 18.

60. Some research suggests tardive dyskinesia is related more to the sensitivity of the patient than to the duration or amount of exposure to neuroleptics. In some cases the medication used against the side effects of the neuroleptics may exacerbate tardive dyskinesia and withdrawal of those drugs will greatly reduce the symptoms. One study found large doses of vitamin E markedly improved the symptoms of TD, and research continues in this area (Jean Bouricius, op. cit., pp. 22–23).

61. Interview, Dr. William Glazer, January 12, 1988. Interestingly, patients with schizophrenia seem to be *less* likely to develop severe TD than patients with affective disorders (Jean Bouricius, op. cit., p. 22).

62. Interview, Dr. William Glazer, January 12, 1988. If the medication can be stopped, studies indicate TD will disappear in about one-third of cases (Jean Bouricius, op. cit. p. 21).

63. Interview, Dr. William Glazer, January 12, 1988.

64. Keeping dosages as low as possible is in any case a desirable strategy since it minimizes unpleasant side effects generally, thus reducing patients' resistance to taking the drugs. It is generally agreed the object should be to find the lowest dose on which the patient can be maintained without a recurrence of symptoms (Jean Bouricius, op. cit. p. 14).

65. *Clinical Psychiatry News,* July 1989, p. 5.

66. "Panel Discussion" in Ralph Jones and Richard Parlour, eds., *Wyatt v. Stickney: Retrospect and Prospect* (New York: Grune and Stratton, 1981), p. 199.

67. Interview, Dr. Samuel Keith, May 2, 1988.

68. *Clinical Psychiatry News,* Vol. 17, No. 7, July 1989, p. 5.

69. Interview, Dr. William Glazer, January 12, 1988.

70. *The Wall Street Journal,* May 14, 1990. For the risk/benefits of clozapine, see Stephen Marder and Theodore Von Putten, "Who Should Receive Clozapine," *Archives of General Psychiatry,* September 1988, pp. 865–67.

71. David Cohen, *Forgotten Millions* (London: Paladin-Grafton, 1988), p. 108.

72. Interview, Carol North, May 27, 1988.

73. Ellen Dwyer, *Homes for the Mad: Life Inside Two Nineteenth Century Asylums* (New Brunswick, N.J.: Rutgers University Press, 1987), p. 140.

74. Silvano Arieti, *Understanding and Helping the Schizophrenic* (New York: Basic Books, 1979), p. 133.

75. *Care of Institutionalized Mentally Disabled Persons,* Joint Hearings before the Subcommittee on the Handicapped of the Committee on Labor and Human Resources and the Subcommittee on Labor, Health and Human Services of the Committee on Appropriations, U.S. Senate, 99th Congress, 1st session, April 1–3, 1985.

76. Interview, Natalie Reatig, May 2, 1988.

77. Interview, Renée Bostick, April 12, 1989.

78. Marilyn Rice, "Message to CTIP [Committee for Truth in Psychiatry] Members and Supporters," June 18, 1988.

79. The case was Jones v. Gerhardstein. Fiscal 1987 "Report of Activities under Protection and Advocacy for Mentally Ill Individuals Act," available from Community Support and Advocacy Branch, National Institute for Mental Health, Rockville, Md. Susan Curran of the Florida P&A lamented to us that the right to refuse treatment only extended to somatic therapies; they were considering bringing a case to establish a right to refuse behavior modification treatment (interview, June 4, 1989). Back to the four walls indeed!

80. Fiscal 1987 "Report of Activities under Protection and Advocacy for Mentally Ill Individuals Act," op. cit.

81. For the key role taken by Michigan Protection and Advocacy in organizing the conference, see *The Rights Tenet* (Newsletter of National Association for Rights Protection and Advocacy), January 1988, p. 1. In addition, Michigan's P&A contributed $25,000 to the conference, Michigan's Department of Mental Health gave $8,000, and Ohio Legal Rights Service $6,500. NIMH and individual P&As as well as state mental health departments contributed funds for ex-patients to attend.

82. *Dendron,* October 1988, pp. 6–7. *Dendron's* editor David Oaks was indignant, accusing Rogers of "irresponsible tactics."

83. Breggin made this remark in the question and answer period following his presentation entitled "The Myth of Schizophrenia and Genetics," NARPA Conference, Portland, Oregon, October 26–29, 1988. Tapes are available from Dennis Nestor, 4510 East Willow Avenue, Phoenix, AZ 45032.

84. *Dendron,* December 1988, p. 3.

85. Breggin described the psychiatric profession as "street-sweepers" of poor people beginning with the Industrial Revolution. According to Breggin, "The whole concept of psychiatry is rooted in the giant lockup of the homeless." Peter Breggin's lectures "Psychiatry and the Homeless" and "Psychiatric Abuse of Children" (National Association for Rights, Protection and Advocacy Annual Conference, St. Paul, Minnesota, September 27–30, 1989) are also available from Dennis Nestor.

86. Huey Freeman, "What Really Works," 1989 NARPA Conference, September 27–30, 1989. Freeman continued: "People are put away purely for profit, and for the convenience of family members who are incompetent to deal with them, often incom-

petent to deal with the problems they've caused. Why do you think they form family organizations?" It is interesting that the radical ex-patients, so critical of psychiatry, should revive discredited psychiatric theories of family causation.

87. *Dendron,* December 1988, p. 4.

88. Interview, Jay Centifanti, August 26, 1988.

89. The largest award to date was in Larry Hadeen v. U.S. Veterans Administration. Hadeen received $2.2 million, despite the evidence of much contributory negligence on his part. See Curtis Carlson "Medical Lapses: Tardive Dyskinesia: Hadeen vs. U.S. Veterans Administration," *American Journal of Forensic Psychiatry,* Vol. VII, No. 4, 1986, pp. 49–56. Other large awards include Clites v. Iowa in 1980 ($760,000) and Sibley v. Board of Supervisors of Louisiana State University in 1985 ($500,000).

90. Peter Breggin, "Tardive Dyskinesia Lawsuits," Workshop, NARPA Conference, Portland, Oregon, October 26–29, 1988. At the 1989 conference the potential for suits based on failure to obtain informed consent prior to treatment with anti-psychotic drugs was also emphasized by attorneys Steven Schwartz and Pam Clay.

91. Ralph Pittle, "Tardive Dyskinesia Lawsuits," ibid. The suit would be based on the argument that since neuroleptic drugs do not "cure" retardation, it is always malpractice to give these drugs to retarded persons. But as in nursing homes, the drugs are given to control disruptive behavior. They can be—and often are—overused, but their use is not in and of itself inappropriate and can obviate the need for physical restraints.

92. Ibid. Bringing more anti-ECT suits was also discussed at a workshop at the 1988 NARPA conference. Breggin spoke of his encouragement that more of these suits were now proving successful. The first suit (for $110 million) against the *manufacturers* of ECT devices is being brought by a young woman named Linda André, who is also suing New York's Payne Whitney Clinic, where she received ECT. As the consumer journal *Counterpoint* (Summer 1987) observed, this is the first case to charge that the use of ECT under any circumstances constitutes medical malpractice.

93. At the 1989 NARPA conference attorney Steven Schwartz pointed out that between 1946 and 1961 there were only 18 reported damage decisions in the United States for persons with disabilities; from 1961 to 1977, there were 372; and from 1977 to 1989 there were over 1,700 cases. These were only cases that ended in judicial decisions or jury trials. A much higher number had been settled out of court.

94. Peter W. Huber, *Liability: The Legal Revolution and Its Consequences* (New York: Basic Books, 1988), p. 4.

95. The result of all the litigation against makers of contraceptives has been to put the U.S. "Decades Behind Europe in Contraceptives" as a *New York Times* headline of February 15, 1990 put it. A panel of experts convened by the National Academy of Sciences reported that companies were unwilling even to try to market already researched methods. Until the 1980s seventeen major companies in the United States were carrying on contraceptive development, but the number had dropped to one. The committee recommended new laws to shield companies from lawsuits. Similarly, the litigation planned by patient liberation lawyers (much of it with taxpayer money!) predictably will substantially drive up the costs of psychoactive medication (which will have to include a "liability tax"), and prevent research and dissemination of new and better drugs for fear they will spark more litigation.

96. The attorney was Thomas Graham. Attorney Pam Clay, who had brought tardive dyskinesia suits in Kentucky, reported at the 1989 NARPA conference that a personal injury attorney there, recognizing the untapped potential in these suits, had said there was a "gold mine" (for attorneys) in the state hospitals.

97. Letter from Dr. E. Fuller Torrey to Dr. Lewis Judd, Director, National Institute of Mental Health, April 10, 1989.

98. Peter Breggin, "Psychiatry and the Homeless," NARPA 1989 conference, op. cit.

Chapter 12.   The Right to Be Crazy

1. Phyllis Vine, *Families in Pain: Children, Siblings, Spouses and Parents of the Mentally Ill Speak Out* (New York: Pantheon, 1982), p. 7.

2. Interview, Dan Weisburd, July 9, 1988.

3. The proportion of severely disabled mentally ill living with relatives (not in institutions, nursing homes, group homes, independently, etc.) in California is just over 50%, and it is estimated that in states with less in-migration the proportion is as high as two-thirds. See *A Family Affair: Helping Families Cope with Mental Illness* (New York: Brunner/Mazel, 1986), p. xi.

4. *New York Times,* March 17, 1986.

5. Agnes Hatfield and Harriet Lefley, *Families of the Mentally Ill: Coping and Adaptation* (New York: Guilford Press, 1987), p. 8.

6. Don Richardson, Speech to California Alliance for the Mentally Ill, Redding, Calif., October 29, 1983.

7. Interview, Dan Weisburd, July 9, 1988.

8. Ibid.

9. Interview, Randolph James (pseudonym), May 6, 1988.

10. Ibid.

11. Interview, Edward Holder (pseudonym), May 7, 1988.

12. "Involuntary Commitments: The Rights of the Individual and the Rights of the Community," Workshop, International Association of Psychosocial Rehabilitation Services (IAPSRS), Philadelphia, June 30, 1988.

13. Ibid.

14. As an article in the *Philadelphia Inquirer* (September 12, 1989) noted: "A mentally ill person may break up the furniture in his parents' house and run outside naked, but those acts alone aren't enough to assure an involuntary commitment under the law. Even if the child threatens to kill his parents, and even if he has a history of violence, he still may not be committed. He must actually do something. Then often, it is too late: somebody has been hurt."

15. Interview, Penny Kostritsky, December 27, 1988.

16. Interview, Bruce Ennis, December 29, 1988.

17. Don Richardson, Speech to California AMI, Redding, Calif., October 29, 1983.

18. Letter to Rita Schwartz from Joy Doyle, May 22, 1989.

19. *Daily News* (New York), January 11, 1989.

20. "Involuntary Commitments," op. cit., IAPSRS Conference, June 30, 1988.

21. In a letter to the California Alliance for the Mentally Ill dated March 17, 1986, Leo Ingle, a psychiatrist at San Luis Obispo County Community Mental Health Services, reported the case of a handsome, blond mentally ill man in his twenties who had become a homeless wanderer. At one point he was buried when the earthen cave he lived in along the coast collapsed, but was rescued. He lived in a large culvert for a year. On his return home his father sought to have him declared gravely disabled so he could be treated, but the conservatorship investigator decided as long as the father provided

food and shelter he could not be called gravely disabled. A month later he was found dead of exposure near the Salinas River bed.

22. Interview, Joyce Brown's sisters, February 25, 1989. The following section is from our interview with the sisters, unless otherwise indicated.

23. Jeanie Kasindorf, "The Real Story of Billie Boggs," *New York* Magazine, May 2, 1988, p. 39.

24. *New York Times,* November 7, 1987.

25. Ibid., May 2, 1988.

26. Jeanie Kasindorf, op. cit., p. 39.

27. Interview, Robert Levy, August 11, 1988. Levy says he originally came to the New York Civil Liberties Union to head the New York office for the Washington-based Mental Health Law Project started by Ennis. After the funding for the New York mental health law project was lost, he still saw mental health law as his specialty.

28. The mental health bar does not even find *eating* feces a cause for concern. At a commitment hearing for a schizophrenic man in Wisconsin, mute, refusing all food and eating feces, the public defender cross-examined the psychiatrist. "Doctor, would the eating of fecal material on one occasion by an individual pose a serious risk of harm to that person?" The judge ruled the man was not imminently dangerous and released him. Darold A. Treffert, "The Obviously Ill Patient in Need of Treatment: A Fourth Standard for Civil Commitment," *Hospital and Community Psychiatry,* March 1985, p. 264.

At the same time as the Billy Boggs case, another case was brought to court, involving a homeless man also brought in by Project Help. He lived on the southern end of Central Park in a plastic bag surrounded by rats and rat excrement. The lawyer appointed for the man argued there was no evidence he had been bitten by rats or endangered by them.

29. Jeanie Kasindorf, op. cit., p. 42.

30. *New York Times,* November 13, 1987. The judge did not seem interested in information about Joyce's history of psychiatric illness. When, in the courtroom, Levy objected that testimony about Joyce's prior mental condition was not relevant (!), the judge upheld his objection. Interview, Joyce Brown's sisters, February 25, 1989.

31. *New York Times,* December 19, 1987. There were two dissenting judges who echoed Judge Lippmann. They wrote in their dissent: "She [Brown] derives a unique sense of success and accomplishment in her street life," and has "obvious pride in her ability to survive on her own." They also declared that while defecating in one's clothes "may be unpleasant [to those] around her," there was no proof "that it is dangerous."

32. Interview, Bruce Ennis, December 29, 1988.

33. Interview, Francine Cournos, January 18, 1989.

34. *New York Times,* February 5, 1988.

35. Thomas Main, "What We Know About the Homeless," *Commentary,* May 1988, p. 26.

36. Interview, Joyce Brown's sisters, February 25, 1989.

37. Ibid.

38. Levy told us Brown was dissatisfied with the Travelers'. "She comes from a background where she . . . she's a little snooty; she'd like to live on the upper East Side and I think it really hurts her to live in a place like that." Levy seemed to find no contradiction between Brown's middle-class background, which gave her expectations of superior housing and her "choice" of life on the streets. Probed as to why Brown, if her mental condition was as good as he posited, could not work, Levy was evasive. He explained her failure to continue her brief stint as receptionist at the NYCLU on the

grounds that "she's on the phone and people call up and start talking about Joyce Brown" (interview, Robert Levy, August 11, 1988).

39. Interview, Sheila Broughel's family, September 23, 1988. The following is based on the interview with the family except where the *Washington Post* (as indicated) is the source.

40. *Washington Post,* March 19, 1973.

41. Ibid.

42. Ibid.

43. Ibid.

44. Ibid.

45. Letter to Rael Jean Isaac from Joy Doyle, May 25, 1989.

46. Interview, Penny Kostritsky, December 27, 1988.

47. Interview, Don and Peggy Richardson, July 9, 1988.

48. Bill Ryan, "Kansas Changes Its Commitment Law," NAMI conference, Boulder, Colorado, July 1988.

49. Ibid. Ryan described his distress when the bill was excoriated in the pages of his own law school journal for its supposed indifference to civil liberty.

50. Interview, Penny Kostritsky, December 27, 1988.

51. Interview, Carmen Johnson, July 4, 1988.

52. Ibid.

53. Ibid.

Chapter 13.   The Specter of Violence

1. A 1970 public opinion study of attitudes toward twenty-one disabled groups revealed that the mentally ill were the *least* preferred, and J. Nunnally's 1961 research determined that fear of unpredictable behavior, especially violence, was a key element in shaping public attitudes toward the mentally ill. Phil Brown, *The Transfer of Care: Psychiatric Deinstitutionalization and Its Aftermath* (London, Boston: Routledge and Kegan Paul, 1985), p. 131.

2. Interview, Don and Peggy Richardson, July 9, 1988.

3. Interview, Jay Centifanti, August 26, 1988.

4. Phil Brown, *The Transfer of Care,* op. cit., p. 134.

5. Arthur Zitrin et al. "Crime and Violence Among Mental Patients," *American Journal of Psychiatry,* February 1976, pp. 144–46.

6. Phil Brown, op. cit., p. 135.

7. Ibid.

8. Ibid., p. 133. Six investigators using eight different patient samples have found higher arrest (and/or conviction) rates for the crimes of homicide and assault among patients than in control groups. No studies have reported contrary findings. See Judith G. Rabkin and Arthur Zitrin, "Antisocial Behavior and Discharged Mental Patients," in Bernard Bloom and Shirley Asher, eds., *Psychiatric Patients Rights and Patient Advocacy* (New York: Human Sciences Press, 1982), p. 161.

9. Arthur Zitrin et al., op. cit., p. 144.

10. John M. Lagos, Kenneth Perlmutter, and Herbert Saexinger, "Fear of the Mentally Ill: Empirical Support for the Common Man's Response," *American Journal of Psychiatry,* October 1977, p. 1136.

11. Interview, Don Richardson, July 9, 1988.

12. Letter of Joy Doyle to Senate Committee on Human Services (California) dated August 1, 1987. Doyle writes that mental health professionals evaluate the existence of a "crisis" on "whether or not the client is able to determine the day, the president, and other very simple facts. My daughter was a brilliant woman when she became ill, and she rarely ever progresses to a condition where she loses the ability to tend to mundane issues. However, we know when she is moving 'over the edge' because she believes she is in charge of the 'lake of fire' and will decide who lives and who goes into the lake. . . . Families have access to the client's history, but the 'professionals' continue to use absurd criteria as a basis for evaluating the crisis" (letter from Joy Doyle to Rael Jean Isaac, May 25, 1989).

13. Interview, Penny Kostritsky, December 27, 1988.

14. *New York Times,* May 6, 1987.

15. Ruth Seegrist, "A Danger to Others," *Philadelphia Inquirer Magazine,* August 24, 1986, p. 22. Outraged, Ruth Seegist demanded to know from the police how someone like Sylvia could buy a handgun. She reports the sergeant told her anyone who does not have a record with the local police can buy a handgun and police don't have mental health records. They're confidential. Next time, Sylvia bought a rifle.

16. Ibid., p. 34.

17. Ibid., p. 13. A similar incident was reported in the *New York Times* of April 26, 1990. A day after his release from a state mental hospital in Atlanta, James Calvin Brady shot five people in a shopping mall north of the city. The *Times* reported that Georgians were puzzled that Brady had been released despite a clinic worker's report, found in his pocket, that he had "homicidal and suicidal tendencies." For those with any familiarity with civil commitment laws, there was no mystery about the hospital's actions. Under Georgia law, a person can be held involuntarily for a maximum of ten days, exactly the time Brady was kept. After that, a formal proceeding involving the courts (including time, trouble, and paperwork for hospital staff) is necessary. Furthermore, Brady—his real name was Reginald Mooreman—was technically a voluntary patient.

18. Interview, Ruth Seegrist, May 9, 1988.

19. Interview, Don and Peggy Richardson, July 9, 1988. Of course, it is not only families who are forced to live in fear of their lives because of inappropriate release of dangerous psychotic patients. In June 1989 the plight of actress Theresa Saldana drew widespread attention. Seven years earlier she had nearly been butchered by Arthur Jackson, a middle-aged fan with a long history of mental illness, whose diaries revealed that he thought he was on a "divine mission" and could win the actress by "sending her into eternity."

In 1982 he entered the United States illegally from Scotland to hunt her down, attacking her outside her apartment and stabbing her ten times. Miss Saldana said in 1984: "I will never forget the searing, ghastly pain, the grotesque and devastating experience of this person nearly butchering me to death, or the bone-chilling sight of my own blood splattered everywhere." Nonetheless authorities prepared to release Jackson in 1989 after he had served only seven years of his twelve-year sentence, with five years off for "good behavior." This was despite the fact that he continued to write a stream of threatening letters to Miss Saldana from prison including one in which he regretted using a knife because "a gun would have given me a better chance of reunion with you in heaven." The deputy district attorney who had prosecuted the case said: "Threats are not considered grounds to keep a person in prison. You have to act on the threats" (*New York Times,* June 6, 1989). The wave of publicity led to a change of mind by authorities about releasing Jackson, giving Miss Saldana at least a temporary reprieve.

20. Interview, Don and Peggy Richardson, July 9, 1988.

21. *New York Times,* March 2, 1988.

22. In fact, the more violent the individual, the more apt the mental health system is to slough off responsibility for him on to the family. The experience of the Pisano family is typical in this respect. Fred Pisano, who strangled his mother Jean, was in a group home designed to provide "intensive-maximum" care when he assaulted a young woman counselor there. The home took him to the hospital, but the examining psychiatrist immediately released him on the grounds he was "oriented and lucid." The group home refused to take him back, and the Pisanos were summoned to come and get him. Charles Pisano complained to the county. "It is beyond my comprehension [that] so-called professional staff . . . didn't think they were equipped to handle the situation, but thought the family was" (*Philadelphia Inquirer,* September 11, 1989).

23. *Philadelphia Inquirer,* September 14, 1989.

24. Ibid. In rare instances, unable to obtain treatment for a violent member or protection from him, families have resorted to murder. For example, in Chester, North Carolina, Lothell Tate admitted shooting her brother Malcoum, while her mother waited in the car. Malcoum had threatened to kill her young daughter "because God's telling me that she's the devil." He had a long history of admissions and releases from jails and hospitals. Lothell Tate said: "We had asked and begged and pleaded for somebody to do something." Especially incensed because she continued to feel she had done the right thing, the judge sentenced her to life in prison. *The Charlotte Ledger,* February 27, 1989; *The Charlotte Observer,* May 24, 1989; May 25, 1989. In a similar situation in Philadelphia, a judge had more sympathy for the family's situation. Vincent Gillette was sentenced to five years in prison for killing his mentally ill brother Steven. He did so after learning his brother had again assaulted their mother. Vincent Gillette told police: "There comes a time when you have to do something." The family had been turned away, again and again, by hospitals, schools, police, and the mental health system in their attempts to get treatment for Steven. *Philadelphia Inquirer,* September 10, 1989.

25. *New York Times,* December 19, 1988.

26. Carol North, *Welcome Silence* (New York: Simon and Schuster, 1987), p. 253.

27. *London Times,* January 21, 1986.

28. Interview, Penny Kostritsky, December 27, 1988.

29. Quoted in Robert Restak, *The Brain* (New York: Bantam Books, 1984), p. 299.

30. Penelope Gilliatt, "Profile: Jonathan Miller," *The New Yorker,* April 17, 1989, p. 89.

31. Darold Treffert, "Don't Let 'Rights' Block Needed Protection," *USA Today,* March 5, 1987. His seminal paper "Dying with Their Rights On" was published in *Prism,* February 1974.

Chapter 14. Winging It with Pilot Programs in the Community

1. Kathleen Jones, "Why a Crisis Situation? What Has Happened?" in Katia G. Herbst, ed., *Schizophrenia* (London: Mental Health Foundation, 1986), p. 48.

2. *Leona Bachrach Speaks: Selected Speeches and Lectures,* New Directions for Mental Health Services (San Francisco: Jossey Bass, 1987), p. 83.

3. Ibid., p. 84. It is noteworthy that while new drugs are not marketed without stringent testing, a massive new set of living arrangements for the mentally ill was instituted without any testing whatever of how it would work in practice. Perhaps

influenced by the disastrous experience of deinstitutionalization, pilot studies have recently been done on proposed substitution of home and community services for nursing home admissions for the elderly: they have found that this turns out to cost money rather than save it. (Gannett Papers, Westchester, New York, October 31, 1989.)

4. Mary Ellen Walsh, *Schizophrenia: Straight Talk for Families and Friends* (New York: William Morrow, 1985), p. 132.

5. Mona Wasow, "The Need for Asylum for the Chronically Mentally Ill," *Schizophrenia Bulletin,* Vol. 12, No. 2, 1986, p. 71.

6. See for example the *New York Times* editorial of October 26, 1989, "How to House the Mentally Ill."

7. Mona Wasow, op. cit., p. 71.

8. Interview, David LeCount, April 20, 1988.

9. Terry Hammond, "When They Are Not in Hospital, Where Should They Be?" in Katia Herbst, ed., op. cit., p. 63.

10. James Schmidt, Fountain House Conference, Seattle, Wash., September 7, 1987.

11. J. H. Beard, R. Propst, and J. Malamud, "The Fountain House Model," reprinted in Loren Mosher and Lorenzo Burti, *Community Mental Health: Principles and Practice* (New York: W. W. Norton, 1989), p. 153.

12. "A Program of Psychiatric Rehabilitation," New York, Fountain House, 1987. Steven Guntli of the Fountain House staff told us that Fountain House does not know how many of its members go on to full-time employment and keep it over time. However, it has recently embarked on a five-year research study that will provide answers on this important outcome measure. Fountain House has collected figures on wages brought in by those in transitional employment programs: in 1989 such programs in 132 clubhouses around the country resulted in wages of $7,314,736. (Interview, Steven Guntli, November, 6, 1989.)

13. John Delman, "Alternatives to Hospitalization," *Advocacy Now,* September 1980.

14. George Fairweather, "Development, Evaluation and Diffusion of Rehabilitation Programs," in Leonard Stein and Mary Ann Test, eds., *Alternatives to Mental Hospital Treatment* (New York: Plenum Press, 1978), p. 298.

15. Ibid., p. 299. In devising this scheme, Fairweather was influenced by the sheltered workshops which had begun to be used for emotionally disturbed people in the 1960s in the hope of curbing relapse rates. Fairweather felt this enmeshed the individual further in his dependency on professionals and that the solution was to build a new social subsystem that would protect the individual from a hostile community, reducing visible rule-breaking behavior at the same time as the individual would achieve social status in his own community, based on his capability, not his impairment. See G. Fairweather et al., *Community Life for the Mentally Ill* (Chicago: Aldine, 1969), pp. 13–21. Fairweather operated on the same insight summed up for us by Jerome Klein at the Solomon Mental Health Center in Lowell, Massachusetts: "Your hope is not to integrate the person into the community, but into a peer community" (Interview, May 18, 1988).

16. George Fairweather, "Development, Evaluation and Diffusion," op. cit., pp. 299–300.

17. Ibid., p. 300.

18. Leonard Stein and Mary Ann Test, "A State Hospital-Initiated Community Program," in John A. Talbott, ed., *The Chronic Mentally Ill: Treatment, Programs, Systems* (New York: Human Sciences Press, 1981), p. 161.

19. Ibid., p. 164.

20. Ibid., pp. 166–70. They did not do better on competitive employment—there was no difference between the two groups in time spent in such employment. See Leonard Stein and Mary Ann Test, "The Community as the Treatment Arena in Caring for the Chronic Psychiatric Patient," In Ivan Barofsky and Richard Budson, eds., *The Chronic Psychiatric Patient in the Community* (New York: Spectrum, 1983), p. 445.

21. Burton A. Weisbrod, Mary Ann Test, and Leonard Stein, "Alternatives to Mental Hospital Treatment: Economic Benefit-Cost Analysis," *Archives of General Psychiatry,* Vol. 37, 1980, p. 403.

22. Interview, Father John McVean, June 28, 1988.

23. Ibid.

24. Ibid.

25. Myron Magnet, "The Homeless," *Fortune,* November 23, 1987, pp. 179–80.

26. Interview, Father John McVean, June 28, 1988.

27. Dincin is unusual in insisting that Thresholds evaluate carefully each program it undertakes so that efforts will not be continued merely because they sound good on paper. For example, Dincin decided that schizophrenic women could be trained to be better mothers. Many hours of classroom—and evaluation—time later, Dincin had to admit he was wrong: classes did not in fact make schizophrenic women better mothers. Interview, Jerry Dincin, April 21, 1988.

28. Jerry Dincin, "A Community Agency Model," in John Talbott, ed. *The Chronic Mentally Ill,* op. cit., p. 224.

29. Jerry Dincin, "Programs That Work! CSP Programs for Persons with Mental Illness," Workshop, NAMI Conference, Cincinnati, Ohio, July 3, 1989.

30. Jerry Dincin, "Programs That Work: Cirrus House and Thresholds," Workshop, NAMI Conference, Boulder, Colo., July 1988.

31. Ibid.

32. Jerry Dincin, "Programs That Work!" op. cit., NAMI conference, July 1989.

33. Jerry Dincin, "Programs that Work: Cirrus House and Thresholds," op. cit., NAMI conference, July 1988.

34. Ibid.

35. George Fairweather, ed., *The Fairweather Lodge: A 25-Year Perspective,* New Directions for Mental Health Services, No. 7 (San Francisco: Jossey Bass, 1980), p. 30. Failure in this area can jeopardize the continued existence of the Lodge. In 1989 we visited a lodge in Hartford, Connecticut where some months earlier one member, who had ceased taking his medication, had killed another. The others had been aware of his deterioration, but had not been able to handle the problem.

36. Susan Estroff, *Making It Crazy* (Berkeley: University of California Press, 1981), p. 82.

37. Ibid., p. 91.

38. Interview, Father John McVean, June 28, 1988.

39. Ibid.

40. Interview, Jerry Dincin, April 21, 1988.

41. Susan Estroff, op. cit., p. 122.

42. Interview, Father John McVean, June 28, 1988.

43. Jerry Dincin, "Programs That Work: Cirrus House and Thresholds," op. cit., NAMI conference, July 1988.

44. Leonard Stein and Mary Ann Test, "The Community as the Treatment Arena," op. cit., p. 450.

45. Quoted in Loren Mosher and Lorenzo Burti, *Community Mental Health: Principles and Practice* (New York: W. W. Norton, 1989), p. 344.

46. Ranjit Chacko "The Patient Volunteer," in Ranjit Chacko, ed., *The Chronic Mental Patient in a Community Context* (Washington D.C.: American Psychiatric Association, 1985), pp. 58–59.

47. Leonard Stein and Mary Ann Test, "The Community as the Treatment Center," op. cit., p. 451.

48. Fairweather has had great difficulty in disseminating the Lodge model. Despite its low cost and viability, professionals have been reluctant to accept the transformation in their role it entails. Fairweather laments that his training had led him to believe that programs of proven effectiveness would readily be adopted by mental health professionals. Says Fairweather: "It might be called the myth of the better mousetrap." George Fairweather, ed., *The Fairweather Lodge: A Twenty-Five Year Retrospective,* op. cit., p. 33.

49. Leonard Stein and Mary Ann Test, "Community Treatment of the Young Adult Patient," in Bert Pepper and H. Ryglewicz, eds., *The Young Adult Chronic Patient* (San Francisco: Jossey Bass, June 1982), pp. 59–60.

50. Interview, David LeCount, September 28, 1989. The proportion devoted to outpatient services had been an even higher 85% a year earlier and LeCount believes it will return to that proportion in 1990.

51. Beth Sproul, *Models of Community Support Services: Approaches to Helping Persons with Long-Term Mental Illness,* Boston, Center for Psychiatric Rehabilitation, August 1986, p. 31.

52. Ibid., p. 32.

53. Susan Estroff, op. cit., p. 121.

54. Beth Sproul, op. cit., p. 30.

55. George Fairweather, ed., *The Fairweather Lodge: A Twenty-Five Year Retrospective,* op. cit., pp. 72–73.

56. Beth Sproul, op. cit., p. 32. This compares very favorably with the cost of most clubhouse programs. See ibid., p. 21.

57. Sproul writes that Texas reports a range of 1.5 to 5 staff per lodge. In addition to the staff coordinator, who has proven essential to the stability of lodges, some use technical consultants for their business.

58. Jerry Dincin, "A Community Agency Model," in John Talbott, ed., *The Chronic Mentally Ill,* op. cit., p. 212.

59. *Leona Bachrach Speaks,* op. cit., p. 23. Bachrach says the "model programs tell us only that model programs work. . . . [M]odel programs are not of themselves equipped to meet all the service needs of schizophrenic patients within a service area."

60. Fairweather says only a handful of Lodges have been established in the Northeast due to bureaucratic obstacles, notably licensing requirements that make it very difficult to provide the high degree of patient autonomy necessary for the Lodge.

61. Mary Ellen Walsh, op. cit., pp. 163–64.

62. Loren Mosher and Lorenzo Burti, op. cit., p. xxiii.

63. Ibid., p. xiv.

64. Ibid., p. 129.

65. Ibid., pp. 132–33.

66. Loren Mosher, Family Therapy Network Symposium, "Schizophrenia and the Family," Washington, D.C., Spring 1988.

67. Loren Mosher and Lorenzo Burti, op. cit., p. 128.

68. Ibid.

69. *Returning the Mentally Disabled to the Community: Government Needs to Do More,* Report to the Congress of the Comptroller General of the United States, January 7, 1977, pp. 69, 72.

70. Ibid., p. 46.

71. Beth Sproul, op. cit., p. ii.

72. *Philadelphia Inquirer,* September 11, 1989.

73. Early in his term President Carter formed a commission of which his wife Rosalynn, who had taken a strong interest in improving care for the mentally ill, was honorary chairman. The April 1978 report of the President's Commission on Mental Health became the basis for the Mental Health Systems Act of 1980.

74. Henry Foley and Steven Sharfstein, *Madness and Government* (Washington, D.C.: American Psychiatric Press, 1983), p. 125.

75. Ibid., pp. 132–33.

76. Ibid., p. 134.

77. Jeanette Jerrell and Judith Larsen, "Community Mental Health Services in Transition: Who is Benefiting?" *American Journal of Orthopsychiatry,* January 1986, p. 82.

78. Ibid., p. 87.

79. Interview, Martin Cohen, April 16, 1988.

80. Ibid.

81. Ibid.

Chapter 15. Community Services Are Not Enough

1. *New York Times,* October 22, 1989.

2. Robert Drake and David Adler, "Shelter is Not Enough," in Richard Lamb, ed., *The Homeless Mentally Ill* (Washington D.C.: American Psychiatric Association, 1984), pp. 141–42.

3. Interview, Richard Adelman, April 19, 1988.

4. Interview, Darold Treffert, September 16, 1988.

5. E. Fuller Torrey, Sidney M. Wolfe, and Laurie M. Flynn, *Care of the Seriously Mentally Ill: A Rating of State Programs* (Washington, D.C.: Public Citizen Health Research Group and the National Alliance for the Mentally Ill), 1988, p. 100.

6. Much of Wisconsin falls far short of Dane County. In Peewaukee, a short drive east of Madison, June Wild, co-chair of NAMI's Mentally Ill Homeless Committee, says services are light years from those of Dane County. She described the experiences of families with the local community mental health center: "Our center director told us that we would have to move [from] the waiting room because the mentally ill would be . . . delusional and they would upset other people [coming to the center]. . . . There you are—the community mental health center, which is built with the long-term mentally ill in mind and he [the director] is telling me they don't even want to deal with them any more!" (Interview, June Wild, April 19, 1988.)

7. Interview, Richard Adelman, April 19, 1988.

8. As a result of a court decision in State *ex rel.* Watts v. Combined Community Services Board 362 N.W.2d 104 (Wisc. 1985) there are now mandatory annual reviews. (Before this, the patient or his guardian had to take the initiative to obtain a hearing to terminate or change the protective placement.) David LeCount is concerned because Wisconsin, as a result of another case, provides that competent patients can refuse medication. Presumably a patient under limited guardianship, competent because he

was on medication, could argue for his right to be taken off protective services. Says LeCount: "They'll probably have to go through the dangerousness period again. In some situations that will be extremely upsetting to the parents. We have one situation where the person has strong issue against taking medication and when he gets unstable enough, he becomes suicidal, and homicidal. Last time he just missed his heart with a knife. He now has a scar and says he knows where his heart is and will do it right next time. But as long as he's on meds we can control that. He is coming up for a review and if given his own druthers is likely to refuse medication. He's very bright and probably can explain to the court very clearly his understanding of medication. . . . The judge is going to have to weigh the fact that this person is competent at this time" (Interview, September 28, 1989).

9. Interview, Dianne Greenley, October 16, 1989.

10. Interview, Mary Hein, April 20, 1988.

11. David LeCount, "Dane County Adult Seriously Mentally Ill; Mental Health Sequential Overview," September 12, 1988. LeCount updated the figures for us as of September 28, 1989.

12. Ibid.

13. Quoted in Leonard Stein and R. J. Diamond, "A Program for Difficult-to-Treat Patients," in Leonard Stein and Mary Ann Test, eds., *The Training in Community Living Model: A Decade of Experience,* New Directions for Mental Health Services, No. 26 (San Francisco: Jossey Bass, June 1985), p. 36.

14. Interview, David LeCount, April 20, 1988.

15. Interview, Mary Hein, April 20, 1988.

16. Beatrice K. Bleicher, "Compulsory Community Care for the Mentally Ill," *Cleveland-Marshall Law Review,* Vol. 16, No. 1, January 1967, pp. 109, 114.

17. Ingo Keilitz and Terry Hall, "State Statutes Governing Involuntary Outpatient Civil Commitment," *Mental and Physical Disability Law Reporter,* Vol. 9, No. 5, September-October 1985, p. 378. For example, Rhode Island makes no specific provision for outpatient commitment, and when psychiatrist Aimée Schwartz came to Kent County Mental Health Center, she was told the law did not permit it. But when she read the law, it said a patient was not to be committed unless there was no less restrictive alternative "including court-ordered outpatient treatment." Schwartz pioneered the use of outpatient commitment in Rhode Island and has been able to bring hospital days in Kent County down from 3,000 in 1983 to 1,000 in 1989. It has survived a court challenge by Rhode Island Protection and Advocacy Service and the state plans to develop administrative guidelines for its use. Interview, Aimée Schwartz, September 1, 1989.

18. Louise Galloway, "What Families and Professionals Need to Know About Outpatient Commitment," Workshop, NAMI national conference, Cincinnati, Ohio, July 1989. Dane County has used a lower standard for limited guardianship than for civil commitment. Dianne Greenley, of Wisconsin's Protection and Advocacy agency, says while dangerousness is needed, unlike for civil commitment, an "overt act" is not required (interview, October 16, 1989).

19. Louise Galloway, op. cit.

20. Ibid.

21. Ibid.

22. Elaine Purpel, "What Families and Professionals Need to Know," ibid.

23. Susan Stefan, "Preventive Commitment: The Concept and Its Pitfalls," *Mental and Physical Disability Law Reporter,* July-August 1987, pp. 288–96. Moreover, it can only be a matter of time before activists, perhaps through the state's Protection and

Advocacy agency, make it known to patients in North Carolina that the law lacks sanctions.

24. Jeffrey Geller, "The Quandaries of Enforced Community Treatment and Unenforceable Outpatient Commitment Statutes," *The Journal of Psychiatry and Law,* Spring-Summer 1986, pp. 153, 155.

25. Darold Treffert, "The Obviously Ill Patient in Need of Treatment: A Fourth Standard for Civil Commitment," *Hospital and Community Psychiatry,* March 1985, p. 262. In Wisconsin, confusingly, Treffert's Fourth Standard is now called a Fifth Standard. This is because the Wisconsin legislature clarified the dangerousness standard, adding a "Fourth Standard." (Interview, David LeCount, December 13, 1989.)

26. Interview, Penny Kostritsky, December 27, 1988.

27. Bert Pepper and Hilary Ryglewicz, "The Young Adult Chronic Patient," in John Talbott, ed., *The Chronic Mental Patient* (New York: Grune and Stratton, 1984), p. 34.

28. Leonard Stein and Mary Ann Test, "A State Hospital-Initiated Community Program," in John Talbott, ed., *The Chronic Mentally Ill: Treatment, Programs, Systems* (New York: Human Sciences Press, 1981), p. 173.

29. Loren Mosher and Lorenzo Burti, *Community Mental Health* (New York: W. W. Norton, 1989), p. 377.

30. Ted Hutchinson, "Obstruction of Access to Care," undated.

31. Elaine Purpel, "What Families and Professionals Need to Know," op. cit.

32. Jeffrey Geller et al., *The Massachusetts Experience with Funded Deinstitutionalization: A Decade of Promises, Products and Problems under the Brewster v. Dukakis Consent Decree,* University of Massachusetts Medical School and Massachusetts Department of Mental Health, March 1989, p. 7.

33. Interview, Elizabeth Jones, May 6, 1988.

34. Robert L. Okin, "The Massachusetts Experience," in John Talbott, ed., *The Chronic Mentally Ill,* op. cit., p. 348.

35. Interview, Jeffrey Geller, March 22, 1989.

36. Ibid.

37. Jeffrey Geller et al., *The Massachusetts Experience,* op. cit., p. 17.

38. Interview, Elaine Kirsten, November 6, 1989. Geller told us he and his associates were doing a replication of the study to see if there would be more movement now that the system was "more mature." However, Geller observed that if you talk to practitioners, "what the folklore is, what it feels like to people, they'll tell you it feels like very few people move through the system and graduate." Geller believes people pretty much go from the state hospital to the level of living at which they can function, and remain there. (Interview, December 19, 1989.)

39. Jeffrey Geller et al., *The Massachusetts Experience,* op. cit., p. 2.

40. Geller told us: "I looked at a patient's chart yesterday and I came up with what I'm going to call 'community recidivism.' This man has twenty-five admissions to the crisis respite shelter in a three-year period. . . . I just wrote down the names of the forms for each admission, that is, the respite admission check list: a financial screening form, a crisis contact patient evaluation, a general health assessment, a physician contact sheet, a medical record, progress notes, rules and regulation, and a client's personal effects log. That sounds as if someone came into the state hospital; it generates the same papers. So what does that mean? That it's in a big Victorian house and it doesn't have very much professional staff and it's close to the community? That's the major difference. . . . So they've kept him out of the state hospital for seven years. But what does that mean?" Interview, March 22, 1989.

41. Jeffrey Geller et al., *The Massachusetts Experience,* op. cit., p. 2.

42. Interview, Elaine Kirsten, May 12, 1989. Marilyn Schmidt, legal counsel for the Department of Mental Health in Western Massachusetts and Jeffrey Geller argue in "Involuntary Administration of Medication in the Community—The Judicial Opportunity" that Rogers orders can be used more effectively: "if the legal process for procuring and maintaining a court order for treatment is pursued vigorously and consistently by the care provider, it can successfully function as a case management tool for the recalcitrant psychiatric patient." They note that the mere fact of a court order sometimes secures the patient's cooperation, because of the judge's stature as an authority figure. They cite a number of case histories where Rogers orders were successfully used. *Bulletin of the American Academy of Psychiatry and the Law,* in press.

43. Interview, Elaine Kirsten, May 12, 1989.

44. Jeffrey Geller, "Arson: An Unforeseen Sequela of Deinstitutionalization," *American Journal of Psychiatry,* April 1984, pp. 504–7.

45. David LeCount provided the Dane County figures which include administration costs. For costs in Western Massachusetts see Massachusetts Department of Mental Health Fiscal Year 1989 Resource Inventory.

46. Interview, Elizabeth Jones, May 6, 1988. Someone who was an actual participant in the discussions concerning the future of the hospital (who wishes to remain anonymous) remembers them differently. He says the administrative objective, never publicly stated, was to avoid making the hospital either too bad or too good. If it were good, families would want patients to go there and if it were too terrible, this would interfere with getting patients ready for discharge.

47. Interview, Ruth Stein, August 18, 1989.

48. Interview, September 18, 1989.

49. Dixon v. Weinberger, brought by the Mental Health Law Project in 1975, established the right of patients to treatment in the least restrictive alternative.

50. *Report to the Court of the Dixon Implementation Monitoring Committee on the Progress in Dixon v. Bowen and Barry,* December 14, 1987, p. 31.

51. Ibid., p. 35.

52. *Washington Post,* May 28, 1989.

53. Ibid., May 20, 1988.

54. Ibid., June 3, 1989.

55. *Counterpoint,* Burlington, Vt., Fall, 1989, p. 1.

56. Interview, Roch Thibodeau, May 19, 1988.

57. *Counterpoint,* Burlington, Vt., Spring 1988.

58. In January 1989 the VLO received a three-year award of $150,000 a year for the production of television programs and creation of an ex-patient television network. *Counterpoint,* Fall 1989, p. 10.

59. Interview, Roch Thibodeau, May 19, 1988.

60. *Counterpoint,* Fall 1989, p. 1.

61. Nancy Scheper-Hughes and Anne M. Lovell, eds., *Psychiatry Inside Out: Selected Writings of Franco Basaglia* (New York: Columbia University Press, 1987), pp. 292–94.

62. Kathleen Jones and Alison Poletti, "The Italian Transformation of the Asylum: A Commentary and Review," *International Journal of Mental Health,* Spring-Summer 1985, p. 210.

63. Quoted in Kathleen Jones and Alison Poletti, "Understanding the Italian Experience," *British Journal of Psychiatry,* April 1985, p. 342.

64. Nancy Scheper-Hughes and Anne M. Lovell, eds., op. cit., p. 97.

65. Kathleen Jones and Alison Poletti, "The Italian Transformation of the Asylum," op. cit., p. 196.

66. Interview, Kathleen Jones, October 29, 1988.

67. Kathleen Jones and Alison Poletti, "The Italian Transformation of the Asylum," op. cit., p. 205.

68. Ibid., pp. 205–6.

69. Interview, Kathleen Jones, October 29, 1988.

70. Kathleen Jones and Alison Poletti, "The 'Italian Experience' Reconsidered," *British Journal of Psychiatry,* February 1986, p. 147.

71. Kathleen Jones and Alison Poletti, "Understanding the Italian Experience," op. cit., p. 346.

72. Kathleen Jones, "Why a Crisis Situation? What Has Happened?" in Katia G. Herbst, ed., *Schizophrenia* (London: Mental Health Foundation, 1986), p. 50. See also Jones and Poletti, "The Italian Transformation of the Asylum," op. cit., pp. 196–97.

73. Interview Luigi di Marchi, October 19, 1988.

74. Kathleen Jones and Alison Poletti, "Understanding the Italian Experience," op. cit., p. 346.

75. Jerome Gardner, "Philadelphia State Hospital Community Plan: Concept Paper," mimeographed (undated), p. 2.

76. Ibid.

77. Susan Sheehan, *Is There No Place on Earth for Me?* (New York: Vintage, 1983), p. 282.

78. Ibid. Drs. Richard Carlson and Pedro Ruiz are also critical: they say there is a tendency in public psychiatry to maintain people on what they were on before with little or no effort at reevaluation. See "The Chronic Young Adult," in Ranjit Chacko, ed., *The Chronic Mental Patient in a Community Context* (Washington, D.C.: American Psychiatric Press, 1985), p. 53.

79. Interview, Louise Broderick, May 31, 1988.

80. Interview, David LeCount, April 20, 1988.

81. Interview, Hannah Schussheim, November 1, 1989.

82. Dane County's David LeCount stresses the need for safeguards. He fears that a need-for-treatment standard could be abused. "I get a number of phone calls from people where adolescents are trying to be emancipated and parents are strongly disagreeing and there's not psychosis or mental illness; there's rebellion. . . . I almost would like to have a panel of experts make that decision and not just one or two psychiatrists have that power" (interview, December 13, 1989).

83. Quoted in "Petition of California Alliance for the Mentally Ill to Supreme Court of California" (October 1989) asking that the Court of Appeal ruling in Riese v. St. Mary's not be published. In order to avoid clogging facilities, mental health administrators often release patients who refuse treatment, no matter how serious their condition. Even in the rare cases when a patient is deemed so ill that the facility goes through the necessary court procedures *and* the judge rules the patient is competent and has the right to refuse, mental health officials are likely at this point to release the patient. Says David LeCount: "We would probably just automatically release the patient, and the court—if that person remains unstable in the community—would have to make another decision if we have to do another involuntary [commitment] on the person, simply because the taking of medication is a critical issue" (interview, September 28, 1989).

84. Thomas Szasz, "Myth of the Rights of Mental Patients," NARPA conference, Portland, Oregon, October 1989.

85. *New York Times,* September 15, 1989. In New York City too, the *Times* (November 18, 1989) reported, under the heading "Doors Closing as Mood on the Homeless Sours," that more and more public institutions were adopting policies intended to keep out the homeless. Public patience had worn thin, when despite all the money and effort directed at the problem, it seemed to grow rather than abate.

Conclusion. *Forging a New Bipartisan Consensus*

1. Interview, Dr. Paul Appelbaum, May 18, 1988.

2. Mitch Snyder, Plenary Session, NAMI Conference, Cincinnati, Ohio, July 3, 1989.

3. George F. Will, "A Right to Live on the Sidewalk?" *Medicine and Behavior,* March 1988, p. 9.

4. Charles Krauthammer, "When Liberty Really Means Neglect," *Time,* December 2, 1985, p. 103.

5. Frances E. Werner, "On the Streets: Homelessness, Causes and Solutions," *Clearinghouse Review,* May 1984, p. 11.

6. Interview, Alicia Gonzalez (pseudonym), August 9, 1989.

7. Norma Wanucha, "CSP, Programs That Work!" Workshop, NAMI Conference, Cincinnati, Ohio, July 3, 1989.

8. Charles Krauthammer, "How to Save the Homeless Mentally Ill," *The New Republic,* February 8, 1988, p. 24.

9. *Washington Post,* October 22, 1988.

10. Michael S. Moore, "Some Myths About 'Mental Illness,'" *Archives of General Psychiatry,* December 1975, p. 1483.

11. Larry Churchill and Jose Siman, "Abortion and the Rhetoric of Individual Rights," *The Hastings Center Report,* February 1982, pp. 9–12. See also, for example, Robert Burt, "The Ideal of Community in the Work of the President's Commission," *Cardozo Law Review,* Vol. 6, 1984, pp. 267–85; and David Blake, "State Interests in Terminating Medical Treatment," *The Hastings Center Report,* May/June 1989, pp. 5–13.

12. John Stuart Mill, "On Liberty," in *The Philosophy of John Stuart Mill,* Marshall Cohen, ed. (New York: Modern Library, 1961), p. 197.

13. Ibid.

14. Ibid, p. 198.

15. Ibid., pp. 296–97.

16. Larry Churchill and Jose Siman, "Abortion and the Rhetoric of Individual Rights," op. cit., p. 12.

17. Robert A. Burt, "The Ideal of Community in the Work of the President's Commission," op. cit., p. 281.

18. *Philadelphia Inquirer,* September 10, 1989. They invent stories of violence despite the fact that the petition commitment warns them of the consequences of doing so: lying in these petitions amounts to perjury and carries a maximum sentence of three and one-half to seven years in prison. Some families reported that authorities in effect encouraged this, by indicating when their story was "not enough" to secure an involuntary commitment, and asking questions that suggested the types of behavior that *would* be enough. A mother in Northampton told us that after her son was discharged from the hospital, still highly psychotic, to get him back in, "we had to resort to charging him with a criminal offense, some minor thing that you had to exaggerate to have him arrested

and taken to court and get him committed for something he did solely because he was ill."

19. *New York Times,* April 26 and May 27, 1989. Judge Leonard Sands' decision in January 1990 converting begging in subways into a constitutional right (overturned by the U.S. Court of Appeals for the Second Circuit and to be appealed to the Supreme Court) is a recent example of a court decision in this area. The overturning of vagrancy laws in the 1960s paved the way for subsequent decisions making it impossible to maintain standards of behavior in public places.

20. Schloendorff v. Society of N.Y. Hospital, 211 N.Y., 125, 129, 105 N.E. 92 (1914). Cardozo continues: "and a surgeon who performs an operation without his patient's consent commits an assault, for which he is liable in damages." In the Rogers case, the attorney sought damages for his patients on the ground they had suffered from involuntary treatment, but this part of the suit was unsuccessful. The Schloendorff case involved a woman suffering from a fibroid tumor who claimed she had consented to an *examination* under ether, not removal of the tumor. However, since she was suing the *hospital,* not the doctor, the court held it was not liable for damages.

21. *Constitutional Rights of the Mentally Ill,* Hearings Before the Subcommittee on Constitutional Rights of the Committee on the Judiciary, U.S. Senate, Part I—Civil Aspects, March 28, 29, 30, 1961. (Washington: U.S. Government Printing Office, 1961), p. 42.

22. Ibid., p. 150.

23. David Blake, "State Interests in Terminating Medical Treatment," *The Hastings Center Report,* May/June 1989, p. 6.

24. Joel I. Klein, "A Legal Advocate's Perspective on the Right to Refuse Treatment," in David Rapoport and John Parry, eds., *The Right to Refuse Antipsychotic Medication,* Papers presented at the July 1985 American Bar Association Meetings (Washington, D.C.: ABA's Commission on the Mentally Disabled, 1986), pp. 81–82.

25. Ibid., p. 26.

26. As Ted Hutchinson notes, this would have the advantage of involving the family, now often excluded on the basis of confidentiality statutes, despite the fact that the family is usually the best source of information on the patient's treatment history. And the psychiatrist cannot make intelligent treatment decisions without knowledge of that treatment history.

Still another proposed solution is that offered by the American Psychiatric Association's model commitment law, which would make incompetence to make treatment decisions a requirement for civil commitment. The difficulty with this is that it would permit technically competent, but manifestly dangerous mentally ill individuals to remain at large, something that state legislatures will rightly oppose, given their responsibility to protect the public.

27. E. Fuller Torrey, *Nowhere to Go* (New York: Harper & Row, 1988), p. 205.

28. Interview, Dr. Richard Lamb, July 8, 1988.

29. Torrey notes the cost of caring for the mentally ill, in figures corrected for inflation and population increase, quadrupled between 1963 and 1985.

30. Current chaos is being compounded by the provision of the Federal Omnibus Budget Reconciliation Act of 1987 which decrees that by April 1992 all states must have completed the removal from nursing homes of persons under age sixty-five who were placed there because of mental illness. Given the absence of alternative placements, that means inevitably even more homelessness for the mentally ill.

31. *New York Times,* November 16, 1989.

32. Interview, Dr. Paul Appelbaum, May 18, 1988.

33. Interview, Dr. Ben Lambiotte, March 31, 1989.

34. *Science,* May 30, 1986, p. 1084.

35. *Philadelphia Inquirer,* September 10, 1989.

36. Interview, Joyce Brown's sisters, February 25, 1989.

37. Brown is quoted in *Dendron,* March 1988, p. 7. See also Thomas Main, "What We Know About the Homeless," *Commentary,* May 1988, p. 26.

38. Interview, Dr. Richard Lamb, July 8, 1988.

39. E. Fuller Torrey, *Nowhere to Go,* op. cit., pp. 214–15.

40. Paul Appelbaum, "Crazy in the Streets," *Commentary,* May 1987, p. 39.

41. Quoted in David Blake, "State Interests," op. cit., p. 6.

42. Charles Krauthammer, "How to Save the Homeless Mentally Ill," op. cit., p. 24.

Index

415